# The Eighteenth Missouri

# The Eighteenth Missouri

## By Leslie Anders

THE BOBBS-MERRILL COMPANY
*Indianapolis and New York*

The Bobbs-Merrill Company, Inc.
A Subsidiary of Howard W. Sams & Co., Inc.
Publishers: Indianapolis • Kansas City • New York

Designed by Quentin Fiore

# Contents

# Introduction

Devotees of the American Civil War era have surely heard enough by now of "what Grant said to Lee" and might now wish to know more of what the common soldier and his friends thought and did about the heartrending circumstances in which they found themselves after the spring of 1861. Biographies, diaries, and letter collections have been rather conventional vehicles to convey to us the ordinary American's role in the national epic. But if such works have a common weakness, it is the unwillingness of the general reader to give book-long attention to the deeds and impressions of just one nearly anonymous member of the masses who made it possible to carry on this major war.

It may seem better, therefore, to view the sixties through the eyes of regiments or similar aggregations of common soldiers. This is particularly true when the organization is made up of volunteers and represents a *community* response to the challenge of the time. Such small-unit historiography mirrors the great social and political realities of the age and tests generalizations concerning them. It also provides a new arena for reinterpreting established truths about the war by synthesizing the documentary record with the testimony of participants hitherto ignored and unknown.

Generally speaking, two kinds of regimental histories are possible. One is the "first-generation" narrative, written largely from nonofficial materials by, about, and for the participants. Then there is the "second-generation" monograph, written by the latter-day historian with full access to official as well as nonofficial sources for the interested students of times and events not personally experienced. Each genre has built-in deficiencies and virtues, but each makes its peculiar contribution to a broader and more accurate comprehension of America's most profound emotional experience.

Civil War historiography could gain much from new unit histories. The student of that conflict needs a better understanding of what went on west of the Alleghenies than he finds in the rash of monographs and general works focused on what Liddell Hart has called "the battledore and shuttlecock tournament in Virginia." A prominent magazine's centennial book supplement on the war devoted four-fifths of its space to the "tournament," and a prestigious atlas has two plates on the eastern operations to each one on the western campaigns. Regimental histories ought to provide some of the needed correctives.

Moreover, works like the present effort afford the reader a clearer view of what moved the men of the sixties from their civilian pursuits to the perils of the battlefield, what changes of mind and mood came over them, what it was like to organize and manage a typical organization of citizens-turned-soldiers, and the wide range of experiences that came to the average soldier in cantonment and campaign. These are hardly to be glimpsed from biographies of the officers.

It should also be noted that only in recent years has Missouri's role in the Civil War come to be appreciated. The works of Richard S. Brownlee, William E. Parrish, and Duane Meyer are immediately called to mind in surveying recent efforts to redress the balance. Much more remains to be done to illuminate the paradox movingly described by Governor David R. Francis at St. Louis in 1892. "We gave liberally of our blood and treasure to the side of the Confederacy," he told a Union veterans' gathering, "still we were the sixth state in furnishing troops for the preservation of the Union, although . . . we were seventh in population in the sisterhood." Such a record deserves understanding.

A history of the 18th Missouri Volunteer Infantry is a logical initial contribution to such an understanding. Since it may well be many years before kindred works appear, it is all the more important that the regiment first studied be as nearly "typical" as possible. The 18th Missouri was in the main composed of native American Jacksonian Democrats ready to become Republicans, with a leavening of German Radicals from St. Louis and Chariton County. Thus it is possible to see this unit as much more a cross-section of loyal Missourians than would be the case with troops raised entirely either in St. Louis or the rural "Anglo-Saxon" counties outstate. Finally, the regiment's experiences ranged from peace-keeping in western Missouri to anti-guerrilla operations in Tennessee and Mississippi and conventional campaigns and battles in Georgia and the Carolinas. Its quartermaster characterized the 18th Missouri as "one of the few that . . . fought its way from the Missouri River, near Fort Leavenworth, to the Capitol."

The scholar entering this field dons a Shirt of Nessus that will scourge the spirit and flesh until he sees the finished product. Few indeed will be the neatly boxed, indexed, or printed document collections that lend themselves to convenient researching. Rather, the historian will find himself constantly traveling and corresponding as he attempts to summon back to memory personalities long since gone. The historian of the regiment will rejoice to find some soldiers' descendants whose generous willingness to help will warm his heart, just as he will be appalled by the rude disinterest of others. He will be glibly promised assistance that he will never get, and offers of help will come when least expected. The regimental historian will tramp over many a battlefield and ponder official publications, local histories, monographs, biographies, family papers, census materials, cemetery inscriptions, military and pension records, muster and descriptive rolls, city directories, maps, campaign' narratives, and wagonloads of newspapers before he begins to see the regiment as a community and its biography as a distinctive chapter in his country's history.

The present writer owes unpayable debts of gratitude to many who aided him in gathering the story of the 18th Missouri. Outstanding among these was Alpha B. Shelton, superintendent of schools of Putnam County, Missouri, himself the grandson of one unforgettable soldier of the regiment and a distant cousin of several others. Mr. and Mrs. Thomas H. Pollock of Unionville kindly loaned the author a rich collection of pertinent family letters, and their enthusiastic interest meant more to this writer than they could know. Many others who provided access to helpful information will find grateful acknowledgment in the footnotes.

Mr. R. W. Benecke of Brunswick generously furnished materials concerning his father's role in the regiment. Mrs. Velma Watt of Green City, Mrs. Evelyn Sheets of Trenton, and Mrs. Genevieve Mong Garrett of Neodesha, Kansas, did extensive local research and reporting in behalf of this work. Mr. Bert Wyckoff, grandson of a company commander, was an ever-faithful source of information and advice on a wide range of topics relating to Putnam County soldiers. Giving decisive help to bring facts into focus in specific cases were Mr. James Rockwood, Unionville; Mrs. Kate Taylor, Thayer, Kansas; Mrs. Beulah Cain, Register of Deeds of Wilson County, Kansas; Jordan R. Bentley and W. A. Lintner, Probate Judges respectively of Chariton and Sullivan counties; Mrs. Frances George, Probate Clerk of Schuyler County; Mrs. Jean Burns, Probate Clerk of Putnam County; Mr. Dayne Choate, Circuit Clerk of Putnam County; Missouri's Secretary of State James C. Kirkpatrick; Mrs. Sula Johnson and Mrs. Violet Morgareidge, present and former village clerks of Caldwell, Ohio; Mrs. Grace F. Cudworth, South Egremont, Massachusetts; and Commissioner and Mrs. R. D. Buckey, Caldwell, Ohio.

Several editors of regional newspapers rendered valuable services to this project by publicizing the author's quest for information: George D. Choate, *Unionville Republican;* Robert H. Clayton, Brunswick *Brunswicker;* Mrs. T. J. Clark, Carrollton *Republican-Record;* and Mr. Robert L. McBee, *The Pleasant Hill Times.*

A special note of thanks must go to certain archivists and librarians, including Mrs. Sara D. Jackson, Army and Navy Branch of the National Archives; Dr. Richard S. Brownlee, Director, State Historical Society of Missouri; Mrs. Ernst Stadler, Missouri Historical Society, St. Louis; Mr. Russell W. Fridley, Director, Minnesota Historical Society; Dr. Meredith P. Gilpatrick, State Archivist, Ohio State Historical Society; Mrs. Lida Lisle Green, Mrs. Aloys Gilman, and Miss Rose Kaldenberger, Iowa State Department of Archives and History; Mr. C. E. Dornbusch, New York Public Library; Mr. Thomas Turinsky, Kansas State Historical Society; Mrs. Marguerite Ward, Jewett

Norris Memorial Library, Trenton, Missouri; Mrs. Ruby Haralson and Captain Clyde B. Martin of the Office of the Adjutant General of Missouri; Mrs. Curtis Jeffries, Phillips County Historical Society, Helena, Arkansas; Mr. Travis Williamson, Secretary, Panola County Historical Museum Association, Carthage, Texas; and Mr. William A. Stanton, College Librarian, Central Missouri State College.

To Mr. Gilbert Knipmeyer, former State Archivist of Missouri, who suggested the scope and need for a history of this type, the present writer hereby renders special acknowledgment. The complete manuscript was read and commented upon by two of the author's colleagues: Dr. Perry McCandless, Chairman of the Department of History at Central Missouri State College, and a specialist in Missouri political history; and Dr. Claude H. Brown, Chairman of the Division of Science and Mathematics, a knowledgeable student of the Civil War. The author, of course, must still bear the responsibility for any factual or interpretive deficiencies existing in the finished work.

Finally, heartfelt gratitude is hereby expressed to the American Council of Learned Societies, whose generous grant-in-aid facilitated the writer's acquisition of needed materials and his extensive pursuit of other information; to Dr. Warren C. Lovinger, President of Central Missouri State, and to the Board of Regents for the summer leave essential to completion of this work; and to Dr. D. W. Tieszen, Dean of Instruction, who provided every possible encouragement to proceed with the project.

To the author's wife, Mardellya, who patiently shared the joyful memories of three long years of research and writing; to Robert C. Hunt, our son-in-law, who prepared the masterful portraits of Madison Miller and John M. Garner; and to Miss Donna King, who provided the maps, special thanks are certainly due.

LESLIE ANDERS

*Warrensburg, Missouri*

# CHAPTER I

# Morgan's Rangers

BOTH THE STATE OF MISSOURI and the Federal Union were sorely embarrassed by the civil conflict that flamed forth in the spring of 1861. With a microscopic army crippled by the leadership of many loyal but drowsy old colonels as much as by the mass defection of able young Southerners, newly elected President Lincoln desperately besought the governors of loyal states to provide him Volunteer units as had been done in previous emergencies. But Claiborne Jackson, lately elected Governor of Missouri, would have none of Lincoln's "inhuman and diabolical" plans for "any such unholy crusade" to restore the seceding states to their ancient allegiance. Was Jackson the "traitor" that Congressman Francis P. Blair considered him, or was he just a "neutralist"? The question is still argued both ways, but the weight of historical opinion is that the Governor was no Unionist. "Not one man will the State of Missouri furnish," he fumed to the Administration on April 17.[1]

Jackson was so certain that Missourians would approve his defiance of Washington that he had already secured the General Assembly's approval for a state convention. Only in solemn convention could the pro-Southern people of the state convince Lincoln that they would resist coercion of their brothers then departing the Union. On February 18, the very day of Jefferson Davis' inauguration as President of the Confederacy, Missourians cast their ballots—for a *Unionist* convention. The defeated elements shouted "foul!" for years thereafter, but Secession had been beaten. The truth of the matter, ably stated by a modern historian, was that Missouri was "a slaveholding frontier state whose people were predominantly for the Union. . . ."

Meeting in Jefferson City on February 28, the Convention chose for its president former Governor Sterling Price, a "conditional" Unionist probably none too sure of his conditions at that moment. Then, to escape pressure from the Confederate-minded "Statehouse Gang" and Jefferson City crowds, the Convention adjourned to St. Louis.[2]

From early March to late July the awkward interlude continued. Jackson made no move to raise the Volunteer units, and Blair moved heaven and earth persuading Washington to ignore Jackson, to permit Brigadier General Nathaniel Lyon's Department of the West to organize Missouri troops on its own authority, and to trust Missouri's ability to "take care of ourselves . . . if authorized to raise a sufficient force within the State. . . ." Blair, the new Chairman of the House Military Affairs Committee in Washington, commuted to St. Louis all spring to hold his state within the Union. Orders to raise Missouri Volunteers went out in the spring—from Federal authorities in St. Louis. No one knows exactly when they were issued, but posterity knows they were.[3]

The political ice began to crack in mid-June. Jackson and Price held a showdown conference with Lyon and Blair in St. Louis on June 11, only to find that Lyon's terms were unconditional submission to Federal authority. Backed by new Volunteer regiments of St. Louis Germans, Lyon was in a strong position. Price, crossing the no man's land of neutralism into secession, took his governor home to Jefferson City, and Lyon prepared to march after them. On June 12 the Governor implored Missourians to flock to Price's State Guard "for the defense of their most sacred rights and dearest liberties." The next day, Jackson and Price went up to Boonville to join the heavy concentration of Guardsmen there.[4]

While Blair, wearing the uniform of a Union colonel, assumed custody of the Statehouse, Lyon marched up to Boonville, where a brief contest between his well-drilled Germans and the militiamen settled the contest for central Missouri in

Lyon's favor. The victor then proceeded southwestward in a pursuit of the fugitive state administration that would culminate in August with his own heroic death in the battle of Wilson's Creek below Springfield. Meanwhile, the Convention returned to Jefferson City.

Things happened quickly in July. Lincoln, bowing to great pressure to put a big name in command out West, on July 3 appointed John Charles Frémont, the first Republican candidate for President, as the major general commanding at St. Louis. The much-touted Path-Finder of the preceding decade proved to be more an image-projector than a fighting soldier of Lyon's stripe. The Western Department, as Washington christened the new command, included not only Missouri but also Illinois and the states and territories between the Rockies and the Mississippi. Those who already regarded Frémont as something of a poseur took grim satisfaction from rumors that it had taken Lincoln three weeks to move the Path-Finder from the comforts of New York to his awesome responsibilities in St. Louis.[5]

The Convention, meanwhile, had removed Governor Jackson by simply declaring his chair empty. In this way, the entire State Administration and General Assembly were deposed. On July 31 Virginia-born Hamilton R. Gamble, aged sixty-two, was elected Governor by the delegates to head a regime dedicated to providing Missourians "something more and better than a desire to produce injury to those who may differ with them . . ." and an end to the "war between neighbors" which was building in intensity that summer. A newly commissioned major of Missouri Volunteers, John M. Schofield, thought Gamble "much too conservative on the question of States' rights and slavery to suit the 'radical' loyalists," but conceded that he possessed the confidence of most Unionists in the state. If nothing else, Frémont's drive to raise Missouri Volunteers would have a friendly State Administration.[6]

When the War Department told Gamble on August 5 that Frémont was to raise ten regiments of Missouri Volunteer infantrymen, for three-year terms, the new governor acquiesced. He might have raised questions of prerogative in connection with recruiting and commissioning the new regiments, but he did not get around to that until autumn. Official as well as un-official Federal recruiters were then roaming the state looking for able-bodied men willing to enter the projected units.

One such recruiter was W. James Morgan, a Chariton County farmer who had until recently been a grocer at Bruns-wick. Since late in the spring he had been scouring Linn County for young men to compose a company of mounted infantrymen to be known as "The Missouri Rangers." The forty-one-year-old New Yorker had, said one reporter, "had a good deal of military experience though not in active service"; this experience had consisted of holding commissions in the comatose prewar militia of Ohio and Indiana. What Morgan lacked in realistic acquaint-ance with military affairs, he now sought to make up by his intense devotion to the Union cause. Braving the threats of Con-federate neighbors, he doggedly traveled from community to community, stirring up interest far beyond Linn County. It was some time in late July—we cannot be sure how or when, since Frémont seldom worked that way—when Department Head-quarters bestowed on Morgan the title of full colonel and authorized him to recruit an entire regiment of infantry.

At the same time, Morgan's recruiting area was extended from Linn to Chariton, Sullivan, Grundy, Carroll, Livingston, and Putnam counties. Of these, Putnam was destined to be-come the center of gravity in Morgan's recruiting drive. Like other counties nearby, Putnam was still heavily Democratic in voting habits, but unlike the others, the area was not seriously afflicted by a Secessionist faction. In 1860 over ninety per cent of the county's voters had ignored the victorious Lincoln, split-ting most of their votes between the Douglas Democrats and the Constitutional Unionists. It is true that the local representa-tive in the General Assembly was talking a lot like a rebel, but many Putnamites ascribed this to a fear of the Secessionist majority in the House. What is most certain about Putnam is that Morgan's agents would find themselves raising seven of the regiment's ten companies wholly or partly among the fear-less and brawny Kentuckians, Tennesseeans, New Englanders, and Ohio Valley natives who had settled Putnam in the past two decades.[7]

Since recruiters for both sides were working the same ter-

ritory, sporadic violence abounded. One husky farm youth from
Grundy County, Henry Harrison Sawyer, rode into Trenton on
an August day to watch a Confederate platoon drill. He doubt-
less enjoyed the show as much as anyone until two armed Confederates approached him with an invitation to join the new
outfit. A native Ohioan himself, Sawyer said his interest hardly
went that far. Heated words followed, the crowd half expecting
and half hoping that the two Rebels would shoot the Yankee lad
as a warning to other local black abolitionists. Sawyer, gauging
the situation, quickly left the scene. Soon afterward a crowd
of horsemen visited the Sawyer farm, evidently looking for him.
After they had gone, the incensed youth came down out of the
attic and rode to Laclede to sign up as a teamster for Company
C of Morgan's Rangers.[8]

Also raising troops in Morgan's area was a prominent Linn
County farmer, Isaac Vinson Pratt. A native of Weymouth,
Massachusetts, Pratt had acquired slaves by marrying into a
family of wealthy Virginians. He had visited Missouri in early
1860 to arrange for management of extensive farmlands just
purchased around Laclede, but had found conditions too unsettled for any firm business undertaking. With war clouds on
the horizon, the slave-owning New Englander found it necessary
to "decide between Hell and the Iron Works," as he phrased
it. Once decided to "go Union," he began traveling across northern Missouri recruiting young men for service to the "Old Flag"
—a novel vocation for a onetime superintendent of schools in
Norfolk, Virginia. Toward the end of July, 1861, under pressure from St. Louis, Pratt agreed to merge his force with the
Rangers, a move that brought Morgan's regiment several steps
nearer realization.[9]

Pratt seems to have extracted at least one ounce of flesh
for having to play second fiddle to Morgan. It was at his insti-
gation that Department Headquarters gave the Rangers a
numerical designation, and it was announced that the regiment
at Laclede would henceforth be known as the 18th Missouri
Volunteer Infantry. Pratt had seen to it that the outfit would
not bear Morgan's name, and even the word "Rangers" began
to fade out thenceforth from regimental correspondence.[10]

Captain Jacob L. Clark, a forty-one-year-old veteran of

the Mexican War, had been raising a company of his own in the area between Milan and Unionville, and Morgan agreed to accept Clark's fifty-eight men as his Company E on July 27, 1861. Jacob R. Ault, a carpenter from Putnam County, was Clark's first lieutenant, and Elihu Springer of Pennville was his second lieutenant. Kentucky-born Joel M. Shelton, a Unionville hardware dealer-turned-first sergeant, had a younger brother, Daniel, and a cousin, Stephen, as privates in his company. Charles Grabosch of Berlin was one of the original corporals, but in time he would rise to lieutenant. Sergeant John Malloy, Corporal James Johnson, and Private John Kerr were Irish immigrants. Other foreign-born members of Company E were Privates James and Thomas Carrie from England, and Scottish Private George Meikle. The others were almost exclusively of Ohio Valley origin.[11]

Governor Gamble handed down orders for Morgan to assemble at his Laclede headquarters on August 17 as many of the Rangers as he had thus far enlisted. Orders never come at a convenient time for everyone, of course. Leave-taking is difficult at any time, even if a man had no unharvested crops in his fields, no uncollected debts, no aged parents, no young children or expectant wife. But into camp at Laclede went those young recruits who would, those who lived, one day be members of a first-rate regiment of Federal infantry.

After company elections were completed, the captains ratified the agreement on staff positions worked out by Morgan and Pratt in a conference at Milan in early August. Pratt was elected lieutenant colonel in recognition of his role in recruiting. Alfred Williams, another recruiter and a leading farmer of Linn County, became the major. No quartermaster having been chosen, Judge Harry Lander of Brookfield got the post by appointment on September 12 and the second lieutenancy that went with it. Dr. Norman S. Hamlin, enlisted by Morgan at St. Catherine, was named regimental surgeon, with Dr. William O. Torrey of Unionville as his assistant. A Southern Methodist circuit-rider, the Reverend John M. Garner, came in from Carroll County to become the only chaplain the 18th Missouri was ever to have. "My qualifications were ignorance, impudence, and a pair of strong lungs," he was later to explain. Mainly because the huge cleric was an ex-Tennesseean, his pro-Southern acquaintances considered him a "black-hearted renegade" just about ripe for hanging. Garner, a passionate Jacksonian Democrat, hated them right back and was bold enough to help with Federal recruiting in his part of the county. Sworn in as adjutant was First Lieutenant Eugene W. Godfrey, for years the leading merchant of Quincy, Illinois, and lately commissary sergeant of the 16th Illinois Infantry, also stationed at Laclede that autumn.[12]

The first night in camp dulled much of the romance that had colored the boys' attitude toward their adventure. There were no tents, and unless a recruit had brought his own bedding, he slept on the ground. In such strange surroundings, so devoid of comfort, there was little sleep. Some had begun to doze when Private Merritt Young, regimental drummer, began pounding the drum to roll them out for reveille.

Following a breakfast of whatever parents or wives had sent to camp with the boys, Colonel Morgan ordered Young to "beat the long roll" for the first time. This was the signal for everyone to fall in line "on the double-quick." Many were the times the new soldiers would hear Young sound *that* beat! It was 9 A.M. when they lined up for their first formation and learned how far they were from being a regiment of polished soldiers.

The Colonel wore a red sash for the occasion, and from the sash was suspended a small sword in its scabbard. His cap was a small blue contrivance "above and in front of which, mounted on a little staff like a pen holder, stood a striped ball, with a smaller ball . . . depending from it," Garner wrote. Clothing may make the man today, but it made soldiers out of nobody in 1861.

"Attention, soldiers!" cried Morgan, waving his diminutive sword. "Look to the left and right—and *dress!*"

Looking around at each other, many of the new soldiers suddenly had the idea that Morgan was gently chastising them for lining up without hats, shirts, or shoes. A mad rush for clothes started, and the line dissolved.

"Adjutant!" Morgan bawled out to Lieutenant Godfrey. "Halt those men and readjust the line!"

Godfrey, with some difficulty, rounded up all the men and assured them that Morgan was not criticizing their attire. The Colonel patiently explained: "I meant, boys, that you were to get yourselves in a straight row." The row was re-formed.

"Shoulder arms!" Morgan barked absent-mindedly. Up and down the line there came the sound of slapping as each man clapped himself on the shoulders with bare palms. Almost no one at the moment had a gun of any description with him! "By God!" Morgan laughed self-consciously. "I didn't think about guns. Parade, rest!" Clearly the Colonel could have used a bit more military know-how than the militia had provided.

Sheathing his none-too-fearsome blade, the regimental commander made a brief speech:

> Attention, battalion! Your Colonel congratulates himself on being at the head of a regiment that would have done honor to Julius Caesar or Napoleon. And I want to congratulate you upon the progress you are making. In all my experience, I have not found your equal. Break ranks!

The first formation of the 18th Missouri was over, shortly after it had started. In time, they would learn to do better.[13]

A large contingent of the regiment was now given short passes to hurry home for guns—anything that would shoot. Others remained in camp to become the victims of gun-mongers. One such sharp-eyed peddler had a strange little instrument available for the modest price of $11.00. It looked somewhat like a pistol, with a fifteen-inch barrel. With a detachable stock, it could be converted into a rifle. With or without the stock, it really wasn't much of a gun. The recruits, wrote Garner, would have gone hungry for venison even "if a deer had licked one of us on the cheek. . . ." A few specimens of Hall's breech-loading rifle were sold to trusting souls in the 18th Missouri, and although they couldn't have done much damage to a Rebel skirmish line, they were more useful to drill with than the sticks used during the first days at Laclede. By November, Department Headquarters would send in muskets, older but far deadlier than the commercial models purveyed around camp.[14]

In the opinion of the Hannibal & St. Joseph stationmaster at Laclede, Morgan "bore the honor well" of being colonel of the 18th Missouri. Wrote Darius A. Cudworth: "Colonel Morgan managed some way to get rations but nothing more; no tents, camp equipage or arms." The Colonel often took time out from his recruiting journeys to bombard Frémont directly with notices of the "desperate condition" of his Missouri Rangers. On August 20, for example, he told Frémont in no uncertain terms that the Rangers were "half naked and bare footed" and in no shape to face the "hot work in Chariton and Carroll Cos." And this was far from his first or last warning.[15]

While the recruiters continued signing up Missourians all over the seven counties during August, Brigadier General John Pope's new District of North Missouri ordered Morgan to occupy not only Laclede but also Brookfield, to guard public property and patrol the Hannibal & St. Joseph Railroad in the area. "Fort Morgan"—an earthwork built by soldiers, conscripted Negroes, and Rebels for the 18th Volunteers—became a commanding feature of the Laclede landscape as Morgan strove to develop a secure base. The chaplain, unimpressed, scoffed that Fort Morgan was "perhaps sixty feet long and just a little too thick for a sweet potato ridge." During the month of August, Morgan also took a selected force of Rangers and some attached cavalry on a "scout" through Chariton and Carroll counties. Some of the horsemen, who had been enlisted by Pratt, were badly shot in a Confederate ambush, but the infantrymen experienced little else than sore feet and the thrill of demolishing several stores that Morgan believed to belong to Confederate sympathizers in the town of Brunswick.[16]

In the meantime, Chaplain Garner was preparing for his work as "the moral and religious head of the regiment. . . ." He later admitted that in 1861 he had given up any notion that "the rebellion could be prayed down. The time had come for loyal men to get off their knees and meet sword with sword and gun with gun. Nor did I imagine for a moment that, because I wore a long black coat . . . I had the right to punch men into heaven with an ecclesiastical goad." But what was Garner to do?

"After carefully looking over my field of duty," the chaplain found "men from about every protestant denomination in the state, and also a few catholics." Some he knew he could never touch, but these were more than balanced by the "moral and upright men who sanctioned the teachings of the Bible." Given this situation, Garner wrote out a simple one-paragraph charter for "The Religious Society of the 18th Missouri Infantry Volunteers" and invited officers and men to sign. Scanning the list a generation afterward, he could read the names of enlisted men such as Branford Trunnell, William Judd, Roscoe E. Torrey, and John Johnson. "Of the officers who were most helpful to me, I find Captain G. W. Wyckoff, Lieutenant Orlando B. Douglas, Major Alfred Williams, Captain Jonas Durman, and Lieutenant John R. Dayton," said Garner. As a pioneer in the Ecumenical Movement, John M. Garner could have felt himself a success, and it is clear from his writings that military life gave him spiritual horizons beyond his denomination.

At the beginning of October the 18th Missouri had guests —about thirty Kansans captured and paroled by Sterling Price at Lexington several weeks previously. The condition of these ragged and famished Unionists touched the Rangers' hearts, and everything possible was done to make them feel at home. When they were able to leave, the visitors, as Garner put it, "blessed us with thanks, kind wishes, and our first installment of graybacks (lice)." Said Garner:

> Almost any morning some of us could be seen on the sunny side of a hazel thicket in dishabille running their seams with the energy of pigs rooting in a corn field. It was, at first, not polite—rather an insult—to ask one in this fix what he was doing.[17]

On October 4 Morgan pulled the troops at Brookfield back into the main camp at Laclede, "a bleak little prairie town of, perhaps, two hundred inhabitants." Neither public sentiment nor available buildings in Brookfield could accommodate the regiment; Laclede was an improvement mainly where local sympathies were concerned. So far as Morgan knew, Laclede was to be winter quarters for the 18th Missouri, and it was more than time to be making preparations for the season. Others thought so, too. A number of the officers had made haste to rent the few available buildings to house their families. That didn't leave much for the rest of a regiment still short of tents and bedding, and feeling itself to be the most neglected Union outfit west of the Mississippi.

Not surprisingly, epidemics of winter complaints soon broke out in the regiment. Worst of these was measles, popularly considered a childhood disease but quickly becoming widespread among the grown men of Morgan's Rangers. Measles patients, as Doctor Hamlin knew well, needed to be kept warm. Left in unheated tents, they were highly likely to develop pneumonia, in that day a major killer. Before long, the funerals began. The chaplain didn't have all the dead to bury, for grief-ridden families sometimes came with team and wagon to claim the bodies of sons or husbands or fathers for burial at home.

Not even the ritual of burial was free from the hue and cry of partisanship. Morgan and Garner at first used a small country graveyard near Laclede, but before long they began hearing rumors that Confederate sympathizers were going to "make it hot" for Garner's next graveside services. After a few such rites under heavy guard, Morgan prudently directed his chaplain to bury future victims of the epidemic by moonlight.

One poor cavalry lad from Brunswick developed measles, and Hamlin tried in vain to get the boy's uncle to take him home for proper care. The uncle, however, was a wealthy Secessionist farmer who had done his best to keep the youngster out of the Yankee army. Hamlin therefore felt that he had no choice but to ship the patient to the general hospital at Quincy, Illinois. The long day's ride in an unheated box car was a hazard that had to be faced, but at Quincy there was warmth and adequate medical attention. The surgeon and the chaplain were later horrified to learn that the box car had been shunted to a siding at Quincy and forgotten by railroad crews there. The orphaned soldier, overlooked in the confusion, had died in frigid loneliness.[18]

Wednesday, November 13, was a red-letter day at Laclede, for mustering officers had approved three companies for duty. Company E had already mustered-in separately up in Sullivan County on July 27. Now Companies F, G, and I were sworn in by Lieutenant W. H. Edgerton for Department Headquarters.

Company F, an aggregation of fifty-five men headed by Captain Francis M. Bell, a Laclede physician and hotelkeeper, was raised largely in Carroll and Livingston counties. The officers were First Lieutenant Jefferson L. Harry of DeWitt and Second Lieutenant Joseph M. Pool of Laclede. Among the few foreign-born soldiers in the company were French-born First Sergeant Joseph Darwin and German-born Corporal Henry Hamig.

Company G, sixty-seven men in all at the start, had recently been put together by Major Williams and Captain Ezra S. Havens, mainly from men in the Ayersville and Wyreka communities in Putnam County. At thirty-two, former Kentuckian Havens was a fine specimen of manhood, six feet tall, with blue eyes and black hair. He was an Ayersville carpenter and a fire-eating Unionist. John Howry, a native Ohioan farming near Ayersville, was Havens' first lieutenant. Another young Ohioan from the same community, destined to become one of the most celebrated officers of the regiment, was second lieutenant James D. Coddington, a twenty-eight-year-old former carpenter. From the Wyreka neighborhood came an interesting family delegation: Private John M. Knox and his three sons James, Joseph, and John Junior. Other Wyrekans were Privates George W. and John McCloud and their father, Alexander, who had been born in Tennessee sixty-six years before, during the administration of George Washington, and who thus qualified as the oldest man ever to serve in the 18th Missouri.

Captain John P. Mikesell, a native Virginian and a store-keeper at Quincy, brought in Company I; fifty-five energetic young citizens of Linn, Sullivan, and Putnam counties. Although only thirty, Mikesell had already had a full career, including participation in the California Gold Rush, lumber-retailing in Australia, and superintending construction of Tasmania's original telegraph line! A Milan businessman, Absalom Wells, was the first lieutenant, and a scrappy clerk from St. Joseph, Richard F. (Little Dick) Fallis, was the second lieutenant. This company boasted a remarkable family group, including Corporal Absalom Garringer and Privates Isaac and Solomon Garringer—who were to be joined a year later by a fourth brother, Samuel. All these former Ohioans were now Putnam County farmers. Also enrolled, as a drummer for I

Company, was the Colonel's second son, James. The mustering officers were given to understand that Jimmy was thirteen, but the census-takers a year before had noted that he was nine. Jimmy Morgan was obviously the youngest soldier the 18th Missouri ever had.[19]

The following day Lieutenant Edgerton mustered-in four more companies. Captain Jonas Durman had the biggest contingent of all, Company A, ninety-six men drawn mainly from Linn and Sullivan. John R. Dayton of Linn County, whose destiny was to die of wounds within a year, was the first lieutenant; George H. Morgan, the Colonel's eldest son, was second lieutenant. Durman's noncommissioned officers were a remarkable lot, numbering in their ranks several future officers: Sergeant John L. Jones, a Laclede schoolmaster; Sergeants William Brantner and John A. Marine, Linn County farmers; Corporal John A. Riggen, a Sullivan County farmer; and Corporal Samuel Frankfort, then farming in Adair County.

One of the most impressive private soldiers in Company A was John Lomax, a handsome and self-educated Tennesseean. The fifty-year-old Lomax at the time of his enlistment on August 9 had been a Laclede grocer, and his store was immediately put up for sale. The buyer was John Fletcher Pershing, whose then infant son would one day command the entire U.S. Army. Pershing, who retained Lomax's son Henry as a clerk, loaded his wares into a wagon and served as sutler to the 18th Missouri when it assembled at Laclede, and continued to serve it until the departure to Platte County. By that time, John Lomax had risen to the office of Commissary Sergeant.[20]

Captain Henry P. Stults of Putnam County provided ninety-five men to make up Company B. Calvin Morris was his first lieutenant, and John H. Morgan, a blacksmith from Kentucky, was second lieutenant. One of the most unforgettable soldiers in this company was an erstwhile Scottish sailor, Thomas Pollock, then farming near St. John in the west end of Putnam and one of the founders of the Republican Party in that county. Carried as a corporal on the rolls of Company B, he actually spent his three-year hitch as the regimental wagonmaster and one of the quartermaster's most valued aides. Pollock's brilliant and burly son David, enlisting as a private, would later rise to company commander. All but a dozen men mustered in for Stults on November 14 had enlisted from points inside Putnam County.[21]

Another Putnam County farmer, Captain George W. Wyckoff, raised Company D's ninety-two men almost entirely from Putnam. The only "foreigners" were three men from Appanoose County, Iowa, which lay just across the state line. This was the most "indigenous" of the 18th Missouri's ten companies, for only Private Charles Hanel, a German, was born outside the United States. Ex-Ohioan Sylvester S. Collins, the only man then in the regiment besides Captain Clark and Lieutenant Ault who had served in the Mexican War, and who had been active since spring as a Home Guardsman, became Wyckoff's first lieutenant. The other lieutenancy went to a Unionville physician, Dr. Joseph R. Stille.[22]

The least "native" unit was sworn in on the same day as Wyckoff's. Peter R. Dolman, a onetime Ohio lawyer and lately city clerk of Brunswick, raised Company H in Chariton County and its adjoining townships. Only nine of the fifty-nine men mustered-in on November 14 had been born in North America. A Bavarian carpenter, John J. Heisel, was Dolman's first lieutenant, and an erstwhile Prussian schoolmaster, Frederick Partenheimer, was his second lieutenant. Morris Schnapp, a very popular Hungarian-German musician, was the company musician. Among Dolman's duty sergeants was a future state senator, eighteen-year-old Louis Benecke, who owed his stripes to the fact that the infantry drill in *Hardee's Tactics* was almost identical to what he had learned while a student in his native Germany.[23]

There remained to be mustered only the small forty-eight-man company raised by the Trenton merchant, William P. Sherman. James G. Allen of Linn County and the Adjutant's son, Henry W. Godfrey of Quincy, were Sherman's lieutenants. The first sergeant was Thomas McComb, whose family had recently come from Ohio to farm in Grundy County. As mustered on November 19 by Brigadier General John B. S. Todd, commanding the District of Northeast Missouri, Company C consisted of Grundy and Linn County residents. The regiment as a whole was somewhat understrength and still lacked one of the ten

companies required in current tables of organization. But Todd
could nevertheless congratulate Morgan on the creation of a
regiment. The 18th Missouri had been born, if a bit small and
premature.[24]

The muster-in had hardly been completed when Morgan
learned that Union forces in Missouri had a new commander.
On the day that Company C mustered in, Major General Henry
W. Halleck announced in St. Louis that he was the boss of the
new Department of the Missouri, successor to Frémont's Western Department, but now including Wisconsin and all of Kentucky west of the Cumberland. It appears that the longer the
"Frémont Operetta" lasted, the more disquieting had been the
rumors drifting into Washington about the ornate staff of foreign military adventurers; the studied neglect by headquarters
that had contributed to Lyon's defeat and death at Wilson's
Creek, south of Springfield, in August; creation of haphazard
units unknown to Army Regulations; and indiscriminate
appointments of officers to all kinds of ranks with bizarre pay
provisions. Such transactions naturally were widely talked of,
and authorities in Washington could hardly avoid the most uneasy of suspicions. Secretary of War Simon Cameron and Brigadier General Lorenzo Thomas, the Adjutant General of the
Army, visited St. Louis in October for a firsthand scrutiny. The
result was Frémont's deposition from his throne at Eighth and
Chouteau.[25]

Appointing Halleck to the new post in St. Louis was the
Commanding General of the United States Army, Major General
George B. McClellan. Describing Frémont's hundred days in St.
Louis as a regime of "reckless expenditure and fraud perhaps
unheard of before in the history of the world," he told Halleck
that the biggest job to be done in St. Louis was "reducing chaos
to order." Halleck, known as Old Brains to the soldiers of his
time and a "witless pedant" to one modern writer, was a pro-
digious mover of paper. He set energetically to work firing
Frémont's useless officers, consolidating his exotic units (the
Frémont Hussars, for example), straightening out his payrolls,
and restoring Missouri authorities to their rightful role in organizing Missouri Volunteers. It must have seemed a never-
ending process, for Halleck complained to General Thomas a

month later that "some one turns up every few days holding a commission or appointment from General Frémont."[26]

To Major Schofield, Lyon's chief of staff on that tragic August 10 at Wilson's Creek, went the star of a brigadier general, for Halleck on November 21 named him commander of the Missouri State Militia, with Gamble's blessing. In this position, Schofield had direct supervision over the raising of the 13,000-man force that would keep the peace in Missouri after the Volunteers went south to the battlefields. Schofield's path would cross that of the 18th Missouri many times before victory came to the cause of the Union.[27]

Halleck also found time to look after outstate operations. There was constant trouble in Platte County, north of Kansas City, where a strong concentration of pro-Southern settlers was making life miserable for the Unionist minority. At the close of November, Halleck decided to pacify the Rebels, and turned to the Rangers for aid. Morgan was given a threefold mission as his men boarded the train for Weston on December 4: suppress Confederate activities, succor the loyalists, and find enough men to make up the last company of the regiment. "As we moved in from the north," wrote Pratt, "Si Gordon the bushwhacker went out at the south, not to return." On December 9 the 18th Volunteers, ragged and freezing and mostly without uniforms, were patroling Platte County armed with old Springfield and Harper's Ferry rifled muskets to give effect to Morgan's proclamation announcing his occupation of "Weston and surrounding country. . . ."[28]

Stepping into this scene of constant shootings and burnings in the terrible "war between neighbors," Morgan had his own ideas about pacification. His reception on entering the county was enough to make even a less-excitable man furious: guerrillas burned the Platte Valley Railroad bridge at Iatan, just north of Weston, delaying the regiment's arrival for two days. Morgan appointed Major Williams his provost marshal for Platte County, and he and Williams were soon administering the oath of allegiance to hundreds of local residents suspected of disloyal sentiments.

Hearing that there were no Union flags flying in Platte City, Morgan angrily took three companies over to the county seat on December 11 and laid down the law. As D. W. Pollock reported the incident, Morgan "raised a flag on the cort house and told the citisans that if that was taken down that we would raid the town."

Morgan described some of his pacification work to Halleck on December 14, reporting that "I have arrested two . . . for stating that they did not regard the oath. I think if I have them shot and make an example I can have peace. . . ." Morgan wasn't just talking wildly to impress the General. Four days later, having in his custody three Confederate soldiers home on furlough, he unceremoniously executed two of them at the Bee Creek bridge, three miles southeast of Weston, in reprisal for the ambush killing of two Federal horsemen there on December 1. A local attorney, riding past the scene two days later, found that someone had taken a stick and written the letters "U.S." on the bridge railing in the victims' blood, the stain of which lasted for many years as a bitter reminder of the furies aroused in the sectional conflict of the sixties.[29]

If all this wasn't sufficient to convince local folk that Morgan's Rangers were dangerous men to trifle with, the occupying forces had also treated themselves to the burning of Platte City the night of December 16. Someone had taken Morgan's flag down. The Colonel and about seventy-five of his men spent the night in the doomed town, and for some strange reason, fires began breaking out just after midnight. A Platte City lawyer, W. M. Paxton, rounded up a crew of local Negroes to fight the blazes, but with only limited success. The most alarming sight to Paxton was the appearance of a fire in the cupola of the courthouse, and he ran to Morgan for help in dousing it. According to Paxton, Morgan vehemently castigated his troops for this particular piece of incendiarism. "I told you the *courthouse* was not to be burned!" he stormed at the soldiers nearest him. "Go put it out!" As Paxton remembered it, a generation later, "Colonel Morgan's talk showed plainly that it was his intention to burn the town, but not the courthouse." An irate local historian wrote that "when the sun rose the next morning, his kindly beneficent rays fell upon the ruin that an adventurer and scoundrel in shoulder straps had wrought."

Three days after the conflagration, Morgan sent Captain

Havens and Company G into the ruined town to "tighten the cinches." The grim Kentuckian immediately ordered "national flags on all houses, and every man . . . to take the oath of allegiance." Havens saw results. D. W. Pollock told the home folks a month later that "Union flagues ar a flying awl over Platt Co. and when we cum there wasn't a flague in Platt Co."[30]

In a short time, dozens of the leading men of Platte County were complaining to state authorities about the behavior of the occupying force. The rumors and reports reached such a pitch that the Provost Marshal General of the Department of the Missouri entered the scene on December 19. He had heard disturbing tales that Major Williams was collecting a five-cent fee from each Westonian getting an out-of-town pass. "You will inquire without delay," Morgan was told, "and report on same to this office."

Meanwhile, a cavalry lieutenant from Fort Leavenworth, after an undercover investigation, reported that Morgan was *also* getting a payoff of five cents from every citizen visiting Williams' office. Petitions from outraged citizens began reaching Governor Gamble in late December. Then, on January 19, Quartermaster Lander sent Halleck a copy of an order from Morgan "compelling him to furnish certain commissary stores to settle an account of fifty dollars with a Hotel Keeper, with whom Colonel M. is boarding." Naturally, Morgan was largely ignorant of these goings-on about him.

H. J. Wolf, a Platte County representative in the General Assembly, emerged as an implacable political enemy of Colonel Morgan. Later, in November of 1863, the Conservative (that is, lukewarm Unionist) legislator was to accuse Morgan of "highhanded, villainous outrages" in a speech before the House in Jefferson City. "He burned Platte City, sir!" Wolf shouted hotly. "He murdered men in Platte County—infamously and cold-bloodedly murdered them, sir, without trial or investigation of any sort, and without a shadow of authority!" Political trouble of the worst sort was brewing for the prematurely Radical colonel of the 18th Missouri.[31]

During the same period, the regiment had helped itself to the various empty sheds and houses at Weston, and for the first time the men were bedded down in passable shelter. Wagonmaster Pollock and the chaplain found board and room with a loyalist family in town and took up something of a normal life with home comforts. This gave the chaplain his opportunity to get to know Pollock, and he soon found the wagonmaster a "walking Cyclopedia" on Scottish history and geography. "The youngest old man I ever knew," was Garner's judgment of Uncle Tom Pollock.

To the chaplain, the regiment's move to Weston was a homecoming of sorts. Here "in the brick edifice of the M. E. Church South" he had been ordained and had preached some two decades before, and there were still a few members of the congregation who remembered him and were willing to join the soldiers at worship. James Matlock, longtime sexton, now enlisted for Company F, but so long as the 18th Missouri remained in Platte he continued his service to that church. "Colonel Morgan often sat with me in the pulpit," said Garner, "and although a very profane man, the interest he showed was a power in the regiment for good."

Private J. Milton Margrave of Company A took Garner into a journalistic venture with him at Weston. It was a sort of "forced-draft" business, because the environment in Platte County could hardly support a newspaper at the time. The loyalist *Western Mail* had been losing money in this Rebel territory, and the pro-Southern *Argus* could hardly carry on with Union troops streaming across its area. Margrave, a Chariton County printer by trade, took over the *Western Mail* press room, and Garner managed the editing and reporting. While it lasted, this was a good method of spreading the word back home about how the men were doing "at the front" in Weston.

The 18th Missouri kept busy scouting and skirmishing. On December 11 a party from Company B ran across some of Si Gordon's men near Platte City and, reported David Pollock, "persued them so close that . . . one lost his hat. . . ." All too frequently exchanges of taunts between local boys and the troops led to fist-fights, in the course of which J. D. Vance of Company G, a towering Virginian, invariably flattened anyone brave enough to cheer for Jeff Davis. A great deal of fun also was Company B's reconnaissance mission to Camden Point, in the eastern part of the county, in mid-January. "We was quar-

tered in a female seminary," the younger Pollock wrote a
brother. "It is as fine a house as there is in Platt Co. There is
25 roomes. . . . There is a stove in every room. We had a great
time out there. . . ."

If any optimist in Morgan's tattered horde still thought that
Missouri's Volunteers were as well cared for as the rest of the
army, the arrival of two Wisconsin regiments on January 26 soon
disabused him. One of these, Colonel Frederick Salomon's 9th
Infantry, fairly dazzled onlookers with its neat uniforms, shiny
weaponry, and impeccable discipline. Salomon, one of the many
intellectual liberals who had fled Germany after 1848, drilled
his fellow Germans in their mother tongue, and the earth seemed
to shake as that regiment went through its paces before the
stately and articulate commander mounted on his horse. Salomon finished the war as a major general of U.S. Volunteers.

Morgan's men evidently enjoyed the 9th Wisconsin's visit
in more ways than one. "Our regiment is the bragged regiment,"
D. W. Pollock exulted. "They herd of the 18th regiment away
up in Wisconsin. They say our reg is the best regiment that the
State of Missouri can afford by ned."[32]

Colonel Morgan cultivated the acquaintance of Dr. James
A. Price, a thirty-two-year-old dentist then serving as clerk of
Weston's Court of Common Pleas, and he encouraged Price to
recruit the additional company needed to bring the 18th Missouri up to regulation size. Though a Virginian by birth, Price
belonged heart and soul to Platte's hard-pressed loyal minority,
and he gladly resigned his clerkship to start raising his company under the protection of Morgan's muskets. Signing on as
his first lieutenant was Woodson S. Estes, a native Missourian
and a tinner at Camden Point. James A. Stults, nineteen-year-old
son of Company B's commander, was second lieutenant. Some
origins of the pro-Union faction in Platte may be gathered from
a glance at the original five sergeants in Price's outfit. First Sergeant Eugene O'Sullivan was a stonemason from Ireland's
County Cork, and Sergeant Michael Callery had been a currier
in County Meath. Sergeant Gebhart Kurtz was a German-born
blacksmith, while Sergeants David Sturgeon and George W.
Waite were farmers who had come west from Indiana and Virginia respectively. In all, twenty-five native Missourians enlisted

with Price, giving his company the strongest "Missouri flavor" of any in the regiment.[33]

Price's ninety-one officers and men, who did not muster until the regiment moved to St. Louis, were to form Company K on February 28, 1862, in a muster-in ceremony at Benton Barracks. Recruiting for the other companies also continued across northern Missouri, for some were short of men to start with, while disease and growing discontent robbed the regiment of further strength each passing month. As of the end of 1861, Morgan figured that his recruiters had secured nine hundred sixty-three men for the Rangers. It is interesting to note that twenty German-born men joined at Weston, fifteen signing up with Dolman's Company H.[34]

What did the men have on their minds those chilly nights at Weston? Adjutant Godfrey complained at the end of December that he had "recd no payment as yet and only one suit of clothing (and it being damaged)." Three weeks later David Pollock happily wrote his brother the news that "James Simmons is cuming up stairs to say our close has cum. . . ." Still to the point, he noted that "We have had right smart winter here lately. The snow is about six inches deep." Young Daniel Torrey of Company B implored Dave Pollock's sister Isabella to write and "let us boys know what is agoing on up there" at St. John. "I have never heard from the Saint John folks but once," Dan wrote plaintively.[35]

John Morgan of Company B was the first officer to leave the regiment. The forty-year-old St. John blacksmith had developed hepatitis, and in a few more weeks would have to be given his disability discharge. Colonel Morgan mercifully excused him on January 1 and left it up to the boys of B Company to choose a successor. They responded by electing D. W. Pollock, and Colonel Morgan immediately confirmed him as the new lieutenant.

By this time the Colonel was beginning to cast eager eyes on a wider arena of action for his regiment. He had made the acquaintance of General James H. Lane, the enigmatic leader of the Kansas Radicals and heir to the mantle of the martyred John Brown. Morgan found in the fanatical Lane a kindred spirit. In fact, on February 5, Morgan made bold to write General

McClellan for permission to take the 18th Missouri into Kansas to serve under Lane.[36]

Little though he knew, Morgan was even then teetering on the brink of disgrace and oblivion. General Schofield, high in Gamble's councils since his appointment as head of the State Militia, had developed a low opinion of Morgan's soldiering and a high degree of determination to get him out of the regiment. The replacement for Morgan, in Schofield's opinion, was Captain Madison Miller of the 1st Missouri Light Artillery. Born in Pennsylvania fifty years before, Miller had been a captain of the 2d Illinois Volunteers in the Mexican War and had been wounded at Buena Vista. Successful in both politics and business, he had been mayor of Carondelet in suburban St. Louis as well as president of the St. Louis and Iron Mountain Railroad. In 1860 he had secured a seat in the General Assembly and soon became one of the eighteen "loyal" representatives who had vainly sought to sidetrack Claib Jackson's scheme for the State Convention. Despite a new state military law offering the death penalty for recruiting troops without the governor's permission, Miller had boldly taken a hand to help Frank Blair organize the 1st Missouri Infantry. For this, Jackson had warned the representative from Carondelet: "Miller, the rope that's going to hang you has already been made."

On January 31, 1862, Captain Miller was in St. Louis preparing to load his battery on a river steamer bound for Tennessee. While visiting Halleck's office, he ran into Schofield, who seemed to have something very urgent on his mind. In a few minutes Schofield had the puzzled captain in the governor's office, where Lieutenant Governor Willard P. Hall was in charge during Gamble's lengthy absence in the East. "This is the man I was speaking about," Schofield told Hall. "If he can't manage them they had better be disbanded."

What followed was an indignant recital by Schofield and Hall of the frightful things they had been hearing from the voters and taxpayers of Platte County about the jailings, burnings, impromptu executions, extortions, and indignities attendant upon the 18th Missouri's arrival in December. "Much to my surprise," Miller was later to say, "the Governor proffered the command of this regiment to me."[37]

Confronted with this opportunity to jump from captain to colonel, the highly competent veteran of Wilson's Creek resigned his captaincy in St. Louis that very day and left for Weston with his commission in his pocket and an order from Halleck assigning him to command the 18th Missouri. On February 6 a shocked W. J. Morgan relinquished command of his embittered regiment and left for Palmyra to start a battle for his "rights" in District Headquarters and in the halls of the state government. Surveying his new outfit, Miller found it heavily stocked with "Long-haired Democrats" who were "not going to have anything to do with a black Republican from St. Louis." It was Miller's candid opinion that Morgan had done little to make genuine soldiers out of a "pretty rough set" of men. But the newcomer had not spent one dollar or taken up one hour of his time to raise this regiment, the men told each other, and so far as they were concerned this fatally limited his right to command. That their welfare in battle might be better served by a combat veteran than by an amateur like Morgan somehow never occurred to the Missourians in the momentary frenzy engendered by the sudden change of command.[38]

For two months the anguished Morgan struggled to persuade or overrule his enemies at St. Louis. "Dear Genl," he importuned Halleck on February 15, "have I no redress?" Morgan laid out his case before Halleck and Brigadier General Benjamin M. Prentiss, commanding the Army of North Missouri at Palmyra, telling how he had braved hatred and threats to raise loyal troops, how he had "sacrificed to the Rebels" his Chariton County farm and had spent nearly two thousand dollars of his own money to raise the regiment. To General Todd, then commanding the District of Northeast Missouri, he wrote on February 21 that "It was not for the money which I enlisted . . . , but to try and help save my country from ruin and disgrace."

Whom did Morgan suspect as the chief cause of his discomfiture? "The charges," he told Schofield on March 31, "were made against me by an officer who desired promotion." He elaborated this theme three days later, explaining to Halleck that the charges were instigated by "some officers in my regiment who desired promotion and envied my *position*." It seems clear, after weighing the evidence, that Morgan's accusations were aimed primarily at Pratt, who had every reason until February 6 to think himself the chief potential beneficiary of Morgan's impending downfall. Morgan named twenty-three defense witnesses on March 31, but Pratt's name was conspicuously missing.

Curiously enough, the Colonel's hopes for restoration to his command were running afoul of states' rights. The determination of state authorities, aided and abetted by Halleck and Schofield, to be rid of Morgan in order to appease conservative Unionists in western Missouri was ultimately to decide the Colonel's fate. On the other hand, General Todd warmly stood up for Morgan and secured from the Adjutant General in Washington a ringing statement that "The Governor of a State has no authority to remove an officer who has been mustered into the United States Service. If Colonel Morgan has been removed," General Thomas declared on March 10, "he should be reinstated."

Willard P. Hall then played *his* trump card: None of the officers mustered in at Laclede had as yet been commissioned by the Governor, and a commission was one thing Morgan would never get from Hall or Gamble. And without a commission, he could never draw a dime's worth of pay. Bring Morgan before an examining board to determine his competence, Hall advised Federal authorities.

Meanwhile, Halleck's plans to court-martial Morgan on charges of "conduct unbecoming" were quietly being dropped, thanks to the War Department's legalistic stand in his favor, as well as to the departure of material witnesses to southern battlefields in March. When Morgan returned from Washington to St. Louis on March 25, Schofield personally served him with a summons to appear before the board scheduled to meet April 14. This Morgan haughtily refused to do, knowing that the War Department had taken his side in the squabble and would soon offer him another command, in Arkansas. It seems clear, in retrospect, that Washington had chosen to offer Morgan a consolation prize rather than force the wobbly Provisional Government into taking him back into the 18th Missouri. Moreover, neither state nor Federal officials could forget that Miller was bringing superior military experience to the leadership of the regiment, whether legally or otherwise.

Miller was also bringing something more important than his commission. He brought orders from Halleck to move the 18th Missouri to St. Louis at the earliest possible time. Everyone now felt instinctively that the regiment was heading for a warmer climate. Private James Carrie, the young English-born school-teacher and father of two small children in Sullivan County, was by now "well satisfied that we will have to fight another year, and there will probably be more hard fighting next spring and summer than there has been yet. But come what may," he told his wife on February 3, "I trust I am prepared to offer myself a bloody sacrifice on the altar of my adopted country, if need be."[39]

Should we call it a premonition?

THE MISSISSIPPI VALLEY
1861–1865

# CHAPTER II

# The Father of Waters

COLONEL MILLER was "all hurry and bustle," determined to get the 18th Missouri packed up for the trip to St. Louis as quickly as he could. Understandably enough, Captain Price was least anxious of the company commanders to go. "My men are getting along pretty well in drilling," he wrote Miller from Camden Point. "We have six or eight men down with the measles [and] will not be able to leave here until they get better." Besides, Price had just arrested a young Secessionist implicated in the burning of the Iatan railroad bridge, and was anxious to prefer treason charges on the fellow.

The trial, however, had to be left to Department officials. The regiment was going to leave on Monday, February 18, if Miller had his way. "On the Sabbath before we moved," said Garner, "our meeting was very affecting. The text was 'This is the Last Time,' and the sermon a regular Methodist farewell. We had a very tender time of it. Citizens and soldiers took the parting hand in tears, and in the attempt to sing the good old Doxology we all broke down at the end of the first two lines. I tried to pronounce the benediction but failed and said, 'Please file out and go to your homes.' "[1]

On February 18 the train arrived, and Miller hustled his charges aboard. The boys had to camp overnight near the station in St. Joseph before taking the Hannibal & St. Joseph cars for St. Louis the following morning. There was some excitement at Breckenridge, where several cars derailed, holding the train up for several hours. Thereafter the going was smoother, and the men unloaded on the south side of the Missouri River at St. Charles on a chilly Friday evening. "We arrived hear on the 22 and was reseved with grate cheering and smiling faces and more than abundent flags," Lieutenant Pollock proudly reported to his mother back at St. John. However, he added soberly, "I don't think we stay hear very long."

Miller rode off at once to Benton Barracks, which stood just north of present-day Natural Bridge Road, and "reported to the headquarters that the regiment was in no condition to take the field. . . ." Its armament now was a Duke's mixture described by D. A. Cudworth as "Enfield, Austrian and old Springfield [muskets], loaded with buck and ball cartridges." Miller pointed out to Benton Barracks officials that Company K had not been mustered-in, and none of the other companies had ever been fully mustered for pay. There *had* been a payday at Weston, true enough, but the paymaster had run out of money! Benton Barracks told Halleck the ugly truth on March 1 that the 18th Missouri was present, 705 men strong, but "Not ready for the field." Halleck, reluctantly slowing down the timetable, told Miller three days later to "make all necessary requisitions for your command and prepare as soon as possible for the field."[2]

Department Headquarters had reserved a spacious common at the west edge of the city, and in that litter-strewn field the men camped for the night. Miller and Godfrey helped the companies bed down in tents, while the field and staff officers were left to shift for themselves. Almost destitute, since there had yet been no payday for officers, Major Williams and several others, including Lieutenant Stille of Company D and Chaplain Garner, got a room with a fireplace—but no beds. As for Miller, suburban Carondelet was his home, and it takes little imagination to surmise that he and Pratt availed themselves of the comforts there as long as the regiment was in town.

The next morning Miller marched the troops down to Benton Barracks, one of those lice-ridden and garbage-choked staging areas that would have made any regiment clamor for the relative cleanliness of the battlefield. Cookstoves were abundant, but they were either rusted out or damaged by vandalism.

Firewood was notably scarce. City water was said to be available from the several hydrants on the grounds, but those not out of order for other reasons were frozen shut. The officers noted hopefully that a seedy little boardinghouse adjoined the Barracks, and the men saw with unrestrained glee that a little saloon adjoined the boardinghouse.

While Madison Miller flitted back and forth from the Barracks to Halleck's office, the men settled down to make the most of the garrison interlude, sure to come to an early end. Lieutenant Pollock told his mother that the regiment was having to drill six hours a day. "We ar going to get sum new cloas . . . before we leave," he wrote with evident delight, "and maby sum money and new guns and equipment and then we will be redy to go [down] the river." If the days were strenuous, so were the nights: "We have got fore fidles in the company," wrote Pollock, "and we dans half the time." There was a mumps epidemic in Company B, he told the sturdy Scottish mother back home, but he had not "bin sick sins we left home."

"Soldiering," wrote the former schoolmaster Jimmy Carrie, "is a good deal like going to school, we have to put up with a good many rules, that looked hard to us at first, but of which we now see the nesessity. We had to be broke in like oxen to work. Now we begin to work pretty well." Jimmy had one problem very much on his mind that March 7. It was his birthday, "but I dare not tell any of the boys here, for they follow up the time honoured usage of giving a feller a whipping. . . . So I keep prudently silent. Anything that will make fun for them, they readily grab at, and carry it on in great spirit. . . ."

Miller was now wearing better with the boys. Garner never took to him, being partial to the abused Morgan, but Dave Pollock said on February 24 that "we like him the best kind." Jimmy Carrie was more explicit: "The soldiers are much pleased with the new colonel," he noted. "He is determined we shant be humbuged any more. He is every inch of him a man, a thorough gentleman and soldier. He don't get mad and snort around and tear up jack, like Morgan. He is as mild as you please, yet at the same time so firm and commanding that the men obey him as if by instinct."[3]

Miller was frantically making all kinds of arrangements to

shape his regiment up for combat—arrangements about which the boys heard but little. On March 1 Miller appointed Station-master Cudworth to be regimental quartermaster, fair warning to Lander, then on detached service back at Weston, that he would soon be jobless. Whatever he thought of Morgan, Miller couldn't feel warmly toward a quartermaster who would tattle on his superior.

As Cudworth took up his duties at Benton Barracks, it is hardly likely that any of the boys realized that their witty and industrious new quartermaster, born in Massachusetts in 1836, was directly descended from the Father Ralph Cudworth who had been personal chaplain to King James I and from the General James Cudworth who had commanded the Plymouth Colony Militia. "Cud" wore his pedigree with becoming non-chalance, and like his illustrious ancestors, the gritty young officer manifested pronounced moral courage and intellectual independence.

"As the Lord's anointed, I tried to reform that Yankee," Garner later said, "but he would have none of it. If I approached him on the authenticity and inspiration of the Scriptures . . . he invariably had just drawn a splendid mule, or had got his best mule kicked or he had a mule that Old Nick could not manage. He was loaded for me every time, and always got me off over the crupper."[4]

If the men of the 18th Missouri wondered what their busy colonel was up to, they found out in a short time. Not one of the officers mustered at Laclede possessed a commission from the Governor, and it was freely anticipated that Miller would see to that little detail. He would indeed! But in a manner few expected. On the morning of March 11 he called his officers together and appeared at the assembly room accompanied by Acting Sergeant Major William Schaap and a bundle of thirty-three brown envelopes.

In a rather tactless ceremony Miller presented commissions to those who would get them, but about half of the original officers discovered that they were being turned out instead! "On the 11 day of March hell was to pay in camp," Dave Pollock wrote his sister. "Tirnd out 17 officers and I was one of them. All the rest but James Stults and I went home. We told them

that we started out to fite, not for offices." The angered men of
Company B wrote up a ninety-five-name petition in Dave's behalf, and Miller then relented. "I think I will get my place
back," Pollock assured the home folks on March 13, "but if I
dont I know I will make a good privet." Miller was not the kind
of colonel to let potential leaders with such a spirit get away
from him.

The staff was decimated, as Major Williams and ex-Quartermaster Lander were denied commissions and Halleck's provost guards lurked near the Barracks to arrest Morgan if he
should appear. Doctor Torrey had to be let go because the
Department Medical Director had just flunked him on his board
exams. However, Dr. Samuel B. Houts, a thoroughly lovable
fellow just out of the 6th Missouri Volunteers, came over to be
Hamlin's assistant.

Three company commanders were handed walking papers.
Captain Bell of Company F was dismissed along with his lieutenants, Harry and Pool. Captain Sherman, whose wife and
two small children had lately died in Grundy County, also
found himself stripped of his Company C. Lieutenant Allen
was refused a commission in Sherman's old company. Ezra
Havens was out of a command, too, although Howry and Coddington did keep their places in Company G.

Other lieutenants dismissed on Miller's recommendation
were George Morgan of Company A, Cal Morris of B, and
Absalom Wells of I. Worst of all, many thought, was the removal of Lieutenant Collins—a Mexican War veteran—from
Company D. Department Headquarters on February 28 proceeded to muster-in the ninety-one men of Captain Price's Company K, but the new captain's joy was dampened by the sum-
mary exclusion of his officers, Woodson Estes and Jim Stults.

Pratt, Hamlin, and Garner emerged from the wreckage with
commissions, but some of the companies were for the moment
desperately short of officers. Miller had foreseen all that and was
making the needed arrangements. On March 12 he asked Halleck to give him four noncoms from his old artillery outfit for
commissioned service in the 18th Missouri. Having seen them
under fire at Wilson's Creek, where he had himself been cited
for gallantry, Miller thought them officer material. Their names

were William H. Cooper, Kenton F. Breeman, Edward S. Donnelly, and Oliver H. Dodge. All but one would vindicate the Colonel's faith.

Department Headquarters granted Miller's request immediately, and the four newcomers were duly commissioned. Dodge moved into Durman's Company A as second lieutenant, and Cooper took command of Sherman's C Company as a brand-new captain. Donnelly became Clark's first lieutenant in E, enabling Jake Ault to take over as captain of Havens' old Company G. Ken Breeman took up the first lieutenancy of Mikesell's Company I. Miller filled the vacancy created by Bell's removal by appointing Adjutant Godfrey to that captaincy. Simultaneously, Miller took on William A. Edgar, a young Philadelphian, as his new adjutant.

Sergeant George W. Bywater and Private Henry W. Godfrey, son of the former adjutant, accepted lieutenancies under Cooper, while First Lieutenant John B. Sharp and Second Lieutenant Elihu F. Springer secured positions in the reshuffled Company F. William H. Minter, a 36-year-old former steamboat captain with impressive political contacts at Quincy, took over as Price's first lieutenant in Company K, while the second lieutenancy in that unit went to a transplanted Vermonter, Dr. Orlando B. Douglas, lately a physician at Brunswick.

Two others profited somewhat from the shakeup. Quartermaster Sergeant John R. McEfee stepped up as second lieutenant in Company E, and Doctor Stille put on Collins' gold bars in Wyckoff's Company D. Only Captain Dolman's essentially German Company H came through the storm unshaken. Halleck promised Miller a new major to replace Williams, but the fellow commissioned never showed for duty.

Ezra Havens was only briefly unemployed. He immediately secured a captaincy in the 1st Mississippi Marine Regiment and served the next three years in that capacity.[5]

The men and some of the surviving officers of the regiment boiled with a slow rage. It was clear that Gamble, Schofield, and Hall looked upon them as the "ruffians of Platte City" or even worse. Years later Miller would reveal that Halleck had been very near to disbanding the 18th Missouri on its arrival in St. Louis. The callous dismissal of the officers came as a pro-

cedural affront to the men, for the seventeen had been duly
elected or appointed to their posts in accordance with proce-
dures followed in organizing Volunteer outfits. Nevertheless,
the men would believe to the end of their days that the officers
thrown out were just as good as their replacements and that
they had been singled out for persecution by the headquarters
officers in St. Louis because of sins chargeable to the regiment
as a whole.[6]

Miller almost had things tidied up when Halleck's Special
Orders 220, published March 11, reached him. The 18th Missouri was ordered on board the river steamer *Nebraska* to "proceed to the District of West Tennessee on Thursday morning
[March 13] to report to Maj. Gen. U. S. Grant."

This gave the men a fresh topic of conversation, just when
they could use one. Jimmy Carrie speculated that the regiment
was going "to the south part of Mo. or Arkansas, but I suppose
it don't differ much where we were agoing. If I can't be at home,
I might as well be a thousand miles off as fifty." Sergeant Ben
Guffey of Company I didn't know what to tell his wife up in
Putnam County "a bout having a crop put in for me . . . for it is
impossible for me to say when I will be at home. I may be at
home in one month and I may not be at home in three months
but I want you to have our garden put in something for I don't
want it to lay out." Nobody could match Dave Pollock's exuber-
ance, for he twice predicted at Benton Barracks that "we will
get home for the fourth of July. . . ."

Private Carrie had sent his wife and babies a tintype like-
ness of himself in a case that "cost one dollar and seventy-five
cents." The picture had set him back a half-dollar, plus the
thirty cents postage to Sullivan County. "I don't begrudge the
money at all," he assured Fanny. "I consider it worth all the
money for the children to look at when they get big enough
providing I should not get back."[7]

Ulysses S. Grant, who would be forty on April 27, had come a
long way since his last birthday. A year before, he had been
clerking in a leather-goods store in Galena, Illinois. A West
Pointer and onetime regular army captain, he had flirted with
alcoholism in the army and with failure in civil life. But with

the drums of war beating loudly in 1861, anybody who understood the basics of military organization and procedure was sure to find his stock high. It hadn't taken Grant long to come up through the Illinois Volunteers.[8]

He possessed that uncommon strategical "sixth sense" that told him, when more brilliant officers couldn't see it, where the jugular vein of the Confederacy was. It was the Mississippi, from St. Louis to New Orleans. His opportunity to exercise his judgment came quickly, for at the end of August, 1861, Frémont had sent him as a new brigadier to command the District of Southeast Missouri with headquarters at Cape Girardeau. Once at "Cape," Grant commenced a duel with the Confederate commander at Columbus, Kentucky, some fifty miles down the river.

Major General Leonidas Polk, previously Episcopal Missionary Bishop of the Southwest, was a West Pointer himself, and a star already risen high in the Confederate firmament. He was a formidable enemy, but the leather merchant from Galena was equal to the challenge. Grant sensed that the Confederates intended to create defensive bastions along the Ohio River that would bar the Yankees from using the great river arteries as avenues of advance into the Middle South. Polk wanted a bridgehead north of the Ohio, such as Cairo, Grant reasoned. Therefore, on September 4, Grant beat him to it. Perceiving that Polk might settle for Paducah, Kentucky, Grant helped himself to Paducah as well before the end of September.

Having thus checkmated the bishop in western Kentucky, Grant developed visions of bold new adventures. Now that he had uncontested use of the Ohio and the upper Mississippi, why not mobilize them to the Union's advantage? Why not mount a slashing assault up the Tennessee and Cumberland rivers, rupturing the Rebel defense line across southern Kentucky, opening up Tennessee, and driving down the Mississippi Valley to cut the Confederacy in two?

Halleck got the point, and after some hesitation, he gave Grant free rein. Subsequently, streams of new Volunteer regiments, including Miller's 18th Missouri, began flowing toward Cairo, Illinois, in February and March of 1862.

There were two obstructions facing Grant's schemes for advancing up the rivers—Fort Henry, on the Tennessee; and

Fort Donelson, on the Cumberland. Grant probably knew that the coming assault on those positions would make or break him. There might have been serious trouble of a different sort if Grant had crossed the Cumberland into central Kentucky, where Major General Don Carlos Buell was commanding Union forces in a state that, like Missouri, had finally decided that neutrality was not practicable. But potential jurisdictional conflicts between Halleck and Buell were not Grant's immediate concern.

Giving inestimable support to Grant's offensive was a fleet of river steamers under the command of Commodore Andrew Hull Foote. There were two kinds of ships in the fleet: regular transports and the "tinclads," armored fighting ships constructed at St. Louis by the master shipbuilder James B. Eads. With his amphibious forces, Grant planned to show the Rebels some fancy river-hopping, for he fully appreciated the logistical importance of America's rivers at a time when the primacy of railroads was only dimly foreseen.[9]

In February Grant struck. Bombarded by Foote's seven new "tinclads," and hemmed in by Grant's 17,000-man ground force, the garrison at Fort Henry soon retreated before the invaders. While a loud journalistic hurrah went up all over the North, the bold Yankee commander sent Foote down the Tennessee with orders to come right on back up the Cumberland and "do it again" at Donelson. The victorious infantrymen marched the eleven miles from Henry to Donelson, and at sundown, February 12, Grant invested the place with the divisions of Brigadier Generals John A. McClernand, Charles F. Smith, and Lewis Wallace. Three days later the Confederate commander, shocked by his adversary's unchivalrous demand for "Unconditional Surrender," yielded, and the river roads into West Tennessee were open.[10]

While other Union forces were threatening New Madrid, in the Missouri bootheel, and investing the Confederate fort on "Island No. 10" upstream a few miles from New Madrid, Grant and Buell moved rapidly through the shattered enemy line into Tennessee. Buell's Army of the Ohio marched into Nashville on February 24, and Grant's Army of the Tennessee slogged confidently up the muddy roads along that river. On March 5 Grant's scouts reached Savannah, Tennessee, and ten days later

Brigadier General Stephen A. Hurlbut's division reached Pittsburg Landing, which seemed a good place to mount the coming assault on Corinth, Mississippi, less than twenty miles to the southwest. By the beginning of April, Grant's main body was in camp at Pittsburg Landing.[11]

Just as the 18th Missouri was loading on the *Nebraska* back at St. Louis, Miller welcomed a rough-and-tumble first lieutenant for Captain Stults. He was Daniel R. Hudson, who happened at the time to be on sick leave in St. Louis from his post as a first sergeant in the 2d U.S. Artillery. An enlisted man in the Army since 1849, Hudson had the ability to give Company B some much-needed regular army guidance. Hudson forgot to tell his old outfit that he was taking the commission, and it was some months before the artillery canceled plans to court-martial him. By the time his former commander found his trail, he was a prisoner of war.

By noon of March 12 the regiment was aboard the *Nebraska* at the foot of Pine Street. Unfortunately, the boat was delayed. To Miller's disgust, "there came an order from some abominable quartermaster to ship on board a couple of very heavy ordnance. Unlucky things they were—lots of trouble to put them on board by main strength, but much more trouble to get them off."

By the next morning, however, all was ready, and the *Nebraska* pulled out for Cairo. The rolls at departure carried the names of 882 men, a few of whom were not aboard for various reasons. If Madison Miller had run a statistical study on his command, he would have found that only 120 of the men were native Missourians, that over 400 were natives of states touched by the Ohio River, and that about 50 had been born in states of the Confederacy, for the most part in Tennessee. Over a hundred were foreign-born, nearly three-quarters of them from Germany. The men hailed from 25 different states and 10 foreign countries.

The dilapidated old wooden vessel had all the cargo she needed, with nearly a thousand soldiers on deck and a hundred horses and mules in the hold. The officers were billeted in tiny staterooms, but the men had to sprawl out on the deck. Whereas the officers were provided poor meals for fifty cents, the com-

pany cooks spent their days and nights around the cookroom's
pitifully small grills in a vain struggle to keep the regiment
fed.[12]

Cairo, Illinois—"a frog town at the mouth of the Ohio
River," Garner called it—must not have been much of a tourist
attraction. The chaplain thought the place a "splendid site for a
city if it only had land for building purposes. As we saw it, it
resembled a heaven constructed for frogs, tadpoles, muskrats
and dipper ducks. These creatures could be seen disporting
themselves in the filthy lagoons . . . at all hours. . . ." Colonel
Miller thought even less of the place when the commander there
refused to unload the two heavy guns and insisted that the
*Nebraska* take them down the Mississippi to the Union forces
besieging Island No. 10. This was a long side trip, adding days
to the regiment's voyage to Pittsburg Landing, but Miller was
commanding only infantry, not steamboats.

The next step, therefore, was Columbus, Kentucky, where
Bishop Polk had recently sought to establish a "Rebel Gibral-
tar." The Missourians went ashore to look over the monster
chain that Polk had designed as an underwater barrier to Federal gunboats, and they beheld also the string of large torpedoes
that had been laid in the water near the chain and wired to
electric batteries on shore. Now, however, all had been fished
out of the river, and the redoubts on the bluff were in ruins.

About thirty miles farther down the Mississippi was Island
No. 10. Strongly held by a small Confederate force, this island
position was effectively blocking Federal use of the river below
that point. General Pope was commanding Federal troops in
the area now, with troops on shore above and below New
Madrid and with a gunboat fleet upstream from the island. The
*Nebraska* reached the scene of the protracted siege on March
17, anchoring about five miles from the island. A desultory
artillery duel was going on at the time, and the boys could tell
that mighty big guns were in the game. The Missourians couldn't
help wondering how things would go if a "fifty-pounder" landed
on the deck of the *Nebraska*.

The following morning Colonel Napoleon B. Buford, commanding all ground forces with the fleet, boarded the *Nebraska*
to meet Colonel Miller and brief him on the Island No. 10 oper-

ation. For all of his enthusiasm, Buford was totally unable to convince Miller and Pratt that a sick infantry regiment caged up on a river steamer could play much of a role in this campaign.

For not too surprisingly, a new wave of illness was sweeping the 18th Missouri. A dreadful epidemic of diarrhea now intensified the general misery of crowded shipboard life. Pratt blamed it all on the "change of climate and the diet," and Garner, who had practiced medicine as well as preached in Chariton and Carroll counties, held the "peculiar properties of the river water" at fault. "I don't think fifty of us escaped," the latter wrote in 1893. "The closets on the boat could not meet the demand and holes were cut from the centers of the wheel covers to the deck each way and kept in constant use, and these did not meet the demand. There could be no delay in such cases, and the guards along the decks were laid under contribution, and not unfrequently the roof. This, with the accumulations from the horses and mules on the lower deck, rendered our condition horrible while on board that boat."[13]

But there was no going ashore at this point, much as the men wanted to go. The river stage was so high that the lowlands were largely covered with the overflow. Near a levee to which the *Nebraska* was moored there was a huge log only partially awash. A few men at a time could get some relief from the intolerable stench on the boat by going out on the log. One thing led to another, and the troops were soon collecting twigs and branches to build little fires out on the log for boiling coffee. They had not tasted the brew since Benton Barracks, and here was a chance. The best they could do for coffee was to grind the beans in their camp kettles with musket breeches, creating a coarse powder fairly suitable for boiling. The end product was not so fancy as a modern drip-grind product, but it beat no coffee at all by a country mile.

While the "Lincoln gunboats" traded shots with the defenders of Island No. 10, untimely death visited the *Nebraska*. Private Benjamin Musgrove, a fifty-seven-year-old ex-Virginian in Captain Mikesell's Company I, grew so weak from his gastric affliction that he fell critically ill. Garner, forced by circumstances back into medical practice, sat up day and night to minister to him. "A sadder death I never witnessed," he reported afterwards, "but not a murmur escaped the suffering, sinking comrade's lips." Back at Shawneetown, in eastern Putnam County, the widow had nine vigorous young Musgroves to rear, nearly all of whom lived to extremely advanced ages. Eight decades would pass before inexorable death erased the memory of their father's "getting up from the supper table one evening and telling them all 'good bye.'" Catherine Humphreys Musgrove told a granddaughter that "He said he was going to join the boys in the army. That was the last we ever saw of him."

The problem now was finding a way to bury Musgrove in the soggy land, flooded as it was for miles around. Colonel Miller instructed the pilot, an open Rebel sympathizer constantly ragged by the "Missouri Yankees," to move the *Nebraska* several hundred yards back up the levee protecting the west bank of the river. There the burial squad found a small patch of flat ground sheltered by the levee and easily reached. Even this plot was distressingly waterlogged, however, and the shovel crew had to call for a bucket. After the men back on board had fashioned a rough-lumber box and laid the dead man in it, they tried to lower it into the grave. But during one short prayer by Chaplain Garner the box floated to the surface, level with the ground. "We did not attempt to bail again," the chaplain says. "Two men stepped on the box, and this pressed the water out. They stood there until mud—very soft mud—enough was piled on the box to hold it in place."

Before the end of the same day, eighteen-year-old Private John A. Blake of Company G, a farm boy from Platte County, also died. Blake was an orphan, last surviving member of his family. The boys spliced a musket box and buried young Blake in the side of the levee near Musgrove. Within a day or so after that the regiment lost sixteen-year-old Private William Pate, a Weston boy in Company H. He was buried in a wheat field a mile or so upstream from the graves of the others.[14]

The 18th Missouri gained one officer and lost two while confronting Island No. 10. Lieutenant Howry quit Company G on March 26, referring to an "accident at Brookfield" which was still giving him trouble. Lieutenant Heisel resigned from H Company two days later because of varicose veins in his "lower extremities." Howry would later serve as a cavalryman in an

Iowa regiment, and both men lived well into the next century. Miller at this same time made good his promise to restore D. W. Pollock's second lieutenancy in Company B. Pollock announced to his brother on March 25 that his shoulder straps were back on him. "The Colonel sed if I wod go a long he wod have to give me my plase back," he wrote. "So he dun so."[15]

Some of Miller's men finally had a chance to do something for the war effort. Colonel Josiah W. Bissell and his crack Engineer Regiment of the West were cutting a temporary canal across the long peninsula north of the Island. Only with such a canal could Pope get his troops downstream to points where they would be able to cut off the island garrison's avenue of escape, to the south. Running the gantlet of Confederate batteries was out of the question, whereas the expedient canal General Pope had in mind would keep the transports a good twelve miles away from Rebel artillery.

Bissell sent his engineers into the flooded forest northeast of New Madrid in small raft-parties to trim the tops and branches of trees along the proposed channel. Large rafts followed, operating underwater saws to cut off the trunks as near the ground as possible. As the work of hacking out the channel proceeded to its conclusion, Colonel Buford set some of Miller's men to work preparing for the grand opening of Pope's Canal.

The Missourians went to work on the mighty levee with picks and shovels, under orders to open a fifty-foot gap to permit the passage of transports into the new canal when all was ready downstream. Working with feverish speed, the Missourians sliced away at the landward side of the mighty embankment, leaving its water face intact to the last possible moment. By April 4, it was time to cut through, and the thin remaining wall caved in like tissue paper under the pressure of the turbulent Mississippi. A fleet of barges and transports was soon riding through a once-lovely meadow formerly protected by the levee.

But what of Blake and Musgrove? The giant washout of the levee disrupted their resting places, and their bodies were swept away to lodge in driftwood or on sandbars down the river. "We might as well have thrown them overboard at the start," Garner lamented on hearing of the grisly event.[16]

The 18th Missouri was not around to witness the opening

of the canal or the fall of Island No. 10. On March 26 the *Nebraska* got urgent orders to take its ailing cargo up to the vicinity of Savannah, Tennessee, to report for duty to General Grant as ordered two weeks previously. The night of March 26 the ship was tied up to the dock at Cairo again. The following day there was a forty-seven-mile run up the Ohio to the mouth of the Tennessee, and the vessel docked at Paducah for the night of March 27. As the creaky old transport started up the Tennessee at daybreak, Chaplain Garner was overcome by a mixture of emotions at going home to a beloved land whose behavior he so much deplored:

> On the headwaters of this beautiful river I was born, there I had toyed with the treadle of mother's little wheel as she spun the flax to make our clothes and sang the beautiful hymns of Wesley and Watts . . . ; there on the banks of the Clinch and Holston . . . I played among the squirrels, beautiful birds and sweet wild flowers, and from their limpid waters carried home to mother many a string of nice fish. . . . Then I was taught that love should be the ruling passion of the human heart, but how was it with me as I looked up that river . . . ? Instead of love there was a willingness to contribute, to the extent of my ability, to the shedding of American blood. . . . Every ripple of that water seemed freighted with reminders of the long ago.

It was late in the afternoon of March 29 when Madison Miller went ashore at Savannah and reported as directed by Halleck's headquarters. Grant wasted no time in instructing him to take the regiment some eight or nine miles farther up the river to Pittsburg Landing. Brigadier General Benjamin Prentiss, Miller learned, was waiting there to greet the 18th Missouri and five other regiments—the 61st Illinois, 12th Michigan, 21st and 25th Missouri, and the 16th Wisconsin. Prentiss was going to organize them into the 6th Infantry Division, Army of the Tennessee.[17]

Who was this General Prentiss? Some of the Missourians thought they had heard of him before, and indeed they had. Until lately this bright-eyed forty-two-year-old brigadier had been commanding the Army of North Missouri, and he had made a significant stride toward pacifying the area by inflicting a shattering defeat on a strong Rebel force near Zion Church, in the woods northeast of Columbia, on December 28, 1861. Like many another distinguished Union officer, Prentiss was originally a Virginian, with military training at a private academy. After service as a captain with the 1st Missouri Volunteers in the Mexican War, he had read law and set up a practice in Quincy, Illinois, just before the war. Like Grant, he had tendered his services to the Illinois militia and received a command almost immediately. In fact, just before being sent to Missouri in May of 1861, Prentiss had won nationwide attention by staging the war's first seizure of contraband, when his troops stopped two southbound steamers at Cairo and impounded munitions aboard them.

As the six rawest regiments in the Army of the Tennessee reached Pittsburg Landing, they were met by Generals Sherman and Prentiss. Though most of the new army was now at the Landing, Grant was still headquartered in the splendid Cherry Mansion back at Savannah. Sherman was unable to command at the Landing, for McClernand, one of his fellow division-commanders, had just been made a major general and thus had twice as many stars on his straps. Acutely aware that McClernand's rank was due far more to his role as a "War Democrat" in Illinois than to any soldierly abilities, Grant wasn't in a mood to give him command over a genuine soldier like Brigadier General William T. Sherman, and so we are told by a perplexed witness that Grant had left Sherman with "a sort of control at Pittsburg Landing."[18]

At any rate, Sherman did have charge of assigning campsites to the forces arriving at the Landing. When the 18th Missouri and its sister regiments arrived, the grounds best suited for division-size units nearer the Landing had already been given to McClernand, Hurlbut, and W. H. L. Wallace. There remained a fairly good location about a mile and a half southwest of the Landing and not far to the west of the road to Hamburg. This would put Prentiss' camp in a line between Sherman's main body, to the west, and another of his brigades, under Colonel David Stuart, to the east near the Hamburg Road along the river. It seems almost a dead certainty that no one mentioned to the newcomers that there was *nothing* between them and a major Confederate force not twenty miles away. A half-mile to the north, near Sherman's camps, one could see a little Southern Methodist log meeting-house. It was called Shiloh Chapel, and its name would be long remembered and not alone by the Methodists of the 18th Missouri.

As the regiment unloaded, some of the men were up to their old tricks. Garner later recalled, tongue in cheek, that when the steward and cook on the *Nebraska* saw that the regiment was about to go ashore, "they removed everything from the table in the cabin and locked all the staterooms, but in some way their stuff got mixed up with ours, and when we opened up at our new camp, we found knives and forks, spoons, plates, white blankets, feather pillows, and there was one cabin arm chair. We regretted this mistake, because it was discovered too late for correction, and rather than throw these nice things away, we used them until the 6th day of April when they disappeared forever."

Miller's men went into camp beside the Eastern Corinth Road and just to the north of a 300-yard-wide field on the Spain farm, a field ideal for drilling and reviews. One of the first things Miller called for was a campaign to clear all of the logs, stumps, and brush out of the camping area. The debris thus collected was placed in a pile along the north side of the drill field. Since the men were enfeebled by weeks of shipboard living and diarrhea, the work progressed more slowly than Colonel Miller had hoped. Some time was lost on Friday, April 4, when Prentiss called for a general review of the regiment and took the occasion to make one of those florid patriotic speeches for which he became in time justly famous.

Looking about them, the Missourians saw that their camp was in a dense stand of towering hickories with occasional oaks and evergreens. The campground slanted off gently eastward toward a little ravine, to the east of which the 61st Illinois would soon be pitching its tents. Several hundred yards to the north was Prentiss' headquarters, on a thickly wooded knoll overlooking a deep gulch to its east. West of Miller's camp was the right brigade of Prentiss' division, then forming.

On Friday evening there occurred the beginning of an

episode that left a lasting scar on the soul of the regiment. Dr. Hamlin, ravaged by weeks of diarrhea, appeared at Miller's tent to ask permission to turn in for treatment on a hospital boat at the Landing. Miller could have been a little more sympathetic.

"If you're scared, Hamlin, go on to the boat," the Colonel sarcastically urged him. Sick or not, scared or not, Hamlin went —and he was never to return.[19]

General Prentiss was proceeding vigorously to shape his six regiments into a division. The job at hand called first for organizing the constituent brigades. Now, as the U.S. Army long understood it, a division holds two or more brigades, and a brigade holds two or more regiments. The Civil War norm appears to have been the four-regiment brigade in the three- or four-brigade division, but Prentiss couldn't do anything like that with only six regiments. He could build one strong four-regiment brigade and wait for enough additional regiments to fill out a second brigade. The 21st and 25th Missouri, therefore, were teamed with the 12th Michigan and 16th Wisconsin to form the First Brigade, under Colonel Everett Peabody of Illinois. The 18th Missouri and 61st Illinois were made into an understrength Second Brigade, and the 18th Wisconsin was attached to it pending the expected arrival of the 16th Iowa. Colonel Miller was named commander of this brigade, which left Pratt at the helm of the 18th Missouri.[20]

During March the higher command on both sides underwent change as plans for the spring campaign in the Mississippi Valley developed. The commanding Confederate general in the West was Albert Sidney Johnston, one of the original five full generals of the Confederacy. Jefferson Davis, who could assume "a personal, and usually crippling interest, in all Confederate military affairs," justifiably said of him that "if Sidney Johnston is not a general, the Confederacy has none. . . ." With the fall of Forts Henry and Donelson, Johnston had read the handwriting on the wall, and he thereafter prepared for the inevitable showdown with Grant in southwestern Tennessee. Major General Earl Van Dorn was ordered in from Arkansas, for his crushing defeat near Pea Ridge on March 7 at the hands of Brigadier General Samuel R. Curtis had barred the road back to Missouri.

Polk was withdrawn from western Kentucky, and Major General Braxton Bragg's forces were ordered up from the Gulf Coast. The point of concentration was Corinth, where on March 29 Johnston formed his Army of the Mississippi, a force of 35,000 infantry and 5,000 cavalry by the first week of April. Bragg became his chief of staff, and General P. G. T. Beauregard his deputy.

Corinth was Grant's next objective, for it stood in the new Confederate line of defense, at the intersection of two strategic railroads, the Mobile & Ohio and the Memphis & Charleston. Capture of Corinth would break the last rail connection between the older states of the Confederacy and the trans-Mississippi West. Lincoln, bombarded by letters from Halleck about the dangers of divided command, had decided on March 11 to create the Department of the Mississippi and place all forces west of the Alleghenies under Halleck. There was madness in the method of Old Brains, for he was determined to go down to Tennessee and command the next show himself. Grant and Buell were getting too many headlines. Under instructions to avoid the battle with Johnston until Halleck got there, Grant was to sit tight at Pittsburg Landing. Then, after Buell's Army of the Ohio arrived, a hundred thousand Yankees would march irresistibly on Corinth, sunder the Rebel defenses anew, and join the reporters in singing praises unto Henry Wager Halleck.[21]

# CHAPTER III

# The Chapel in the Woods

HALLECK'S MARTIAL DAYDREAMS NOTWITHSTANDING, Sidney Johnston had plans of his own. At dawn on Friday, April 4, his Army of the Mississippi crept out of the Corinth fortifications and moved northward through the muddy countryside toward the unsuspecting Yankees camped in the Shiloh woods. Johnston hoped that the Confederates might pounce on their victims at daybreak Saturday, but the rains of recent days had turned the roads into mush and cut down his rate of advance disastrously. One could be philosophical about it all, for the same rains were also slowing up Buell's march to join Grant. The Rebels reached the edge of the woods within two miles of Grant's outer camps late Saturday, and bivouacked. After dark, Johnston called in his generals, and they agreed to mount an assault on Grant before daylight Sunday. April 6, "the Day of Shiloh," was to be the last day of life for 3,000 Americans in blue and gray.[1]

Though Grant and Sherman seem not to have suspected Sidney Johnston's plan, Prentiss became suspicious Saturday evening that something was afoot in the brush. Colonel David Moore and half his 21st Missouri Volunteers were on picket about a mile in front of Sherman and Prentiss. Around 7 P.M. Moore rode in to report a Rebel cavalry reconnaissance, and Prentiss at once decided to double his pickets as well as the inner guard. Moore, told to advance his lines another half-mile, sent a messenger out to get it done right away. By 3 A.M. the forward move was accomplished.

Meanwhile, Prentiss was becoming convinced that a reconnaissance in force ought to be made across the entire division front. Shortly after midnight 200 men of the 25th Missouri and 12th Michigan were roused from their sleep for the probe. At 4:55 A.M. Sunday this party ran across Confederate skirmishers a mile south of Peabody's line. The first shots in the Battle of Shiloh were immediately fired, and after a brief but furious exchange of volleys, an ominous silence settled down in the woods along the main Corinth Road.

As the first rays of dawn east of the river heralded a bright and beautiful Sunday, Moore found himself staring at a moving forest of Rebel bayonets extending far to the south and west. Every inch a fighter, Dave Moore sent back to camp for the rest of the 21st Missouri and in the meantime opened up on the Rebels with all he had. With the clatter of this musketry so audible to the southwest of his front, Peabody formed up by 6 A.M. and prepared to advance to Moore's support. Until some time after 5:30, Moore held the leading enemy elements in their tracks, but disaster then overtook him. He was gravely wounded, losing a leg, and the 21st Missouri fell back toward the brigade line. Peabody then moved his main body forward to a ravine southeast of the Shiloh Church and prepared to offer fresh resistance to the oncoming Confederates.

Over in the 18th Missouri's camp, the men were astir by 5 A.M., probably awakened by the sporadic shooting in the woods to the southwest. The breakfast hour was under way by 6 A.M., by which time the sounds of fighting had grown louder and louder. A few Missourians scoffed at the racket as the routine firing off of muskets by pickets being relieved, and others guessed that a reconnoitering group had run into Peabody's pickets. Pratt and Garner had a different feeling about it. After both had risen, Pratt went over to the chaplain and asked, "Parson, do you expect to give us a sermon today?"

"No, sir," Garner answered. "I expect to fight today."

"I believe that is the feeling of the entire regiment," Pratt observed.

When the storm broke, Colonel Miller and Adjutant Edgar

were breakfasting with Pratt and the regimental staff. As prepared by Roxana Johnson, wife of Private John Johnson, breakfast consisted of cold sliced beef, baked chicken, hot biscuits, butter and coffee. It was about 6:40 and streaks of sunlight were illuminating the lush woods when the nervous little party heard the thunder of hoofbeats. General Prentiss was riding in from the west to give the alarm.

"Colonel Miller," he roared, "get out your brigade! They are fighting on the right!" And in an instant he was off to Peabody's lines again.

As the dash from the mess chests began, Merritt Young sounded the Long Roll "as he never beat it before." Garner took a piece of baked chicken and rolled it up in a slice of beef. "William," he called to the adjutant, "put this in your pocket. You may be very hungry before you get another meal." As Lieutenant Edgar leaped onto his horse to go with the brigade commander, he stuffed the meatroll into his shirt pocket. He was never to taste it.

Young Lieutenant Coddington of Company G never forgot that hurried breakfast. "Just as we were done eating," he recalled thirty years afterward, ". . . Young beat the Long Roll. We both [Ault and Coddington] ran to the company and in ten minutes the regiment was in line of battle. . . . We were formed, just in the edge of timber, with an open field in our front."[2]

Pratt's line of battle, formed at seven o'clock, was shielded by the line of stumps and debris along the north edge of the Spain field. Someone jokingly told Miller that "it looked cowardly" to hide behind that rampart, but the Colonel swore in his old age that "if it was to be done again, it would be done the same way."

Unfortunately, the regiment was not permitted to stay under the cover that Miller had so fortuitously provided. Prentiss rode back over shortly after the line formed to order the brigade advanced to the south edge of the field. The 61st Illinois, in executing its part of the maneuver, had to file across the ravine to its right to come up abreast of Pratt's line. The 18th Wisconsin, meanwhile, held down the flank in heavy brush east of the field. Garner remembered how the 18th Missouri "marched out hurriedly but in good order, and stood, without seeing a Rebel, for perhaps three minutes. Everything seemed as still as death." Coddington was also to recall the terrible suspense that lasted but a few minutes.

As Miller moved his brigade forward, Peabody went on to stalk the enemy ahead of him in the woods. "Volley after volley was given and returned," wrote Colonel Francis Quinn of the 12th Michigan, "and many fell on both sides, but their [the Confederate] numbers were too heavy. . . . They were visible in line, and every hilltop in the rear was covered with them. It was manifest that they were advancing in not only one, but several lines of battle."

Major General William J. Hardee, author of the famous infantry manual, was commanding the Confederate attack on Prentiss. Brigadier General R. G. Shaver's brigade, after colliding with Peabody's advance guard, pushed on a half-mile before Peabody checked him. After half an hour of hand-to-hand fighting, Shaver's force began to fall back, and only Johnston was able to rally it for a second try. This time Peabody's line fell back to within a quarter-mile of his camp, and Miller's line, advanced to the south edge of the Spain field, pretty well conformed to this movement.

But then, at about 7:30, there erupted from the thick brush before the 18th Missouri and 61st Illinois what Garner described as "a stream of flashes, puffs of black smoke and the bang! bang! bang! of thousands of guns, all along and away beyond our line. . . ." Miller characterized the Confederate onslaught as "coming on the right . . . by an overwhelming force moving down on us by a front and flank movement. . . ."

Brigadier General Adley H. Gladden's brigade was attacking Miller's front. Maintaining a steady musket fire, Miller also opened up on Gladden with the 5th Ohio and 1st Minnesota Batteries, both in the Spain field. Gladden himself was soon mortally wounded in the devastating fire from the Yankee lines, and his regiments fell back in such disorder that Johnston rushed Brigadier General James R. Chalmers' brigade forward in support. Chalmers charged Miller's left, but the line still held. Then Hardee added Brigadier General John K. Jackson's brigade to the effort, and Prentiss shortly after 8 A.M. decided that the

pressure was too great. He now ordered Miller's entire line back
to the camp for another determined stand.

Prentiss had no choice but to pull Miller back. The nearest
elements of Peabody's brigade, west of the road, had retired
so far that some of the enemy were almost even with the line
of Miller's camps. Coddington later mentioned the "terrible
infilading fire" from the west and the tremble in Pratt's voice
as he passed along Prentiss' order to retreat to the original line
before the camps. "The 18th Mo. stopped, after getting back,"
he said, "and took shelter behind trees, opened fire, and I tell
you, what was left of the regiment played havoc with the rebs
on that open field. . . ." Miller described the scene as the enemy
emerged onto the Spain field in these words: "Masses though
they were, they were compelled to call a halt before the deadly
fire of our now thoroughly aroused men."

However, these first collisions had put a great strain on
Miller's brigade. The 61st Illinois was an undrilled outfit, and
the 18th Wisconsin had yet to receive its ammunition. Acting
Brigade Quartermaster Cudworth was furiously working on that
as the fight commenced. After retiring to the camp line, these
two regiments wavered—then fell back to create an extensive
gap to the east of Pratt's camp line. Miller never was able to get
the Illinoisans back under control, and they eventually drifted
off into other divisions. The 18th Wisconsin, on the other hand,
later rallied for a serious effort beside the 18th Missouri.

In later years Pratt spoke of "400 killed and wounded in the
first thirty minutes." This estimate for the price of the initial
shock at Shiloh is much too high, although the regiment did lose
a number of men at this first exchange of lead with the Rebels.
Lieutenant Sharp of Company F was struck in the head and
instantly killed, and Lieutenant Dayton of Company A suffered
a shattered hip and had to be abandoned in the camp area. First
Sergeant John Downey and Private James R. Simmons of Company B were also killed in action at the same time.

Pessimistic—and most justly so—over his ability to make
a stand around the camp, Pratt nevertheless gave the Rebels a
stiff fight for every inch of the regimental camp. The scramble
to evacuate was making a big job for Quartermaster Cudworth,
but various others were pitching in to help as the need grew.

There was so little time that much had to be abandoned—mess chests, groceries, and even all the fine silverware filched from the *Nebraska*. But Cud got away with most of the bedding and knapsacks, despite the understandable skittishness of his beloved mules.

Colonel Peabody rode up to inquire for Prentiss, but Garner had no idea how far or in which direction the division commander had gone. Peabody never found out, either. Already bleeding about the head, he soon met his death on the field. Ben Guffey suffered a freak wound when a bullet, which had creased his scalp and split his cap bill loose, also badly damaged three fingers of his right hand. Somewhat dazed, and rather clownish-looking with the cotton wadding of his forage cap hanging out over his forehead, Guffey joined the retreat, using his musket for a cane.

"Ben! You look badly demoralized!" Garner called out to him.

"Yes, Chaplain," the jolted sergeant answered, "but I am not whipped—only addled. And when I sober up, I'll try another pop. My forefinger and thumb are still good, and the Rebels will have to sock it to me again before I'll leave the field!" And Ben was to prove he meant it, too.

Sherman now noticed something that had occurred to Prentiss. The Rebel assault was not really head-on, but was oblique or diagonal, moving northeastward. The Confederate aim, it now came clear, was to hit the river, move down it to the Landing, and cut the Army of the Tennessee off from its only line of supply—the steamboat line on the river. With Grant's troops fleeing into western Tennessee and away from the river, when would Buell be able to make contact with them? "Never" was soon enough for Johnston.

In Coddington's words, "there were many . . . who showed the spirit of the brave" in defense of the regimental camp. Captain Price, swarthy six-foot leader of Company K, pitched furiously into the defense. His ire kindled by a bullet that had pierced his left earlobe and grazed his skull, Price seized the musket of Corporal Talman Smith, who had just been killed on the firing line, and used it the rest of the morning with such ardor that his shoulder was black and blue for many days afterward. As Garner wrote to a friend in St. Louis, if the men of the 18th Missouri "had any fault, it was the fault of being too brave." Captain Stults of B Company, with a bloody flesh wound below the knee, limped along his line roaring at his men to "Keep cool!" To cavalry patroling the road to catch stragglers, Stults shouted "If one of Company B tries to pass you, cut his damned head off!" To Stults, as to many other Missouri Yankees, this war was becoming a highly personal matter.

Chaplain Garner now found himself not only assistant to the quartermaster in this tumultuous scene but also a practicing physician once more, at least for that part of the regiment that was able to avoid being cut off with Prentiss' main body. Heading northeastward with Cudworth's wagon train and the gathering collection of wounded men, Garner came up to one regimental ambulance containing a suffering victim he knew well. It was Lieutenant Stille, whose right arm had been badly injured. Said Garner:

> Stille's right arm was bent at the elbow and the back of his hand rested against the temple, while the elbow was raised as high as it would go. A ball had passed through his armpit severing the Brachial nerve and, I thought, injuring the Brachial artery. The Brachial nerve imparts sensation to the point of the elbow and down to the end of the little finger, and if divided, that arm becomes irrecoverably paralyzed and useless. The Lieutenant was bleeding freely and was very pale—almost ex-sanguineous, and, I feared, would sink in a short time if not relieved. We got him out on the dry leaves, and I do not remember how we separated his coat sleeve from his arm—perhaps we cut it off. I had but two shirts—one on, the other in my haversack. I took the surplus one, rolled the shirt and body around a bit of old wood that I broke from the limb of a fallen tree. This homely compress I placed well up under the arm, carried the shirt sleeves over the opposite shoulder, crossed them, carried them as far down on the wounded arm as possible, drew them tight and knotted them so as to hold that arm down and get all the pressure possible on our compress. While we were doing this a Rebel cannon ball tore a large limb from a tree very near to us, which admonished us to get the Lieutenant into the ambulance

and move on, which we did and were glad when we learned afterwards that our improvised surgery had met the indication.

Garner nevertheless felt very sad over Stille's case. "I saw at a glance that the Lieutenant was maimed for life, and that his right arm would not only be useless, but that it would be in his way—a burden without any benefit."

There was no end to such pitiful scenes in those ravaged woodlands that bloody Sunday. "Oh, Chaplain, for God's sake come to me!" cried a wounded soldier in another ambulance wagon. The teamster halted, and Garner boarded. It was Private Rolla Brantner of Company A.

Brantner's was a desperate case. A musket ball had struck above and to the right of the navel, opening a hole through which a section of intestine a foot and a half long now protruded. "I feel as if my bowels were in boiling water," gasped the soldier. In attempting to massage the loop of the intestine back into the abdominal cavity, Garner found that the wound had contracted and brought on strangulation. The physician-chaplain now widened the wound with a small knife from his pocket-case. The loop was now easily pressed back into place, and the boy's relief was immediate. "Thank you, Chaplain," he sighed gratefully, "it feels so good."

Garner tamped the wound with the tail of Brantner's shirt and advised him to keep hand-pressure on it. But Garner had no illusions about the poor lad's chances. "Rolly," he urged, "put your trust in Almighty goodness through Christ, for strength and salvation." The actors in this tragic drama never met again, for Brantner shortly died in a field hospital. Private John W. Green, also wounded that morning, told Garner later that the last words he heard Rolly say were "Captain Durman, for God's sake keep Company A in line!"[3]

Grant was breakfasting at Savannah's Cherry Mansion when the sounds of the uproar at Pittsburg Landing reached his ears. He put down his coffee cup and raced to the steamboat landing outside the building. A division of Buell's army, under Brigadier General William Nelson, had reached Savannah the evening before, and Grant left word for it to move on up the east bank of the river to a point opposite Pittsburg Landing from where it could be ferried across as soon as needed. Sensing that he had a major battle on his hands, Grant stopped at Crump's Landing long enough to warn Lew Wallace to get his battle-tested 5th Division ready for the road. Wallace, for some reason, made a wrong turn on the way and did not reach the fight until dark—and he spent the rest of his life arguing about it. Grant went on up to the front, arriving probably about nine o'clock.

The Commanding General found absolute turmoil and confusion. Sherman's division was dissolving. Prentiss had held his camp line until around nine o'clock, when suddenly Sherman's left regiment bolted for the Landing, uncovering both Sherman's and Prentiss' flanks. So furious were Sherman and Grant that they had the unfortunate Ohio colonel, Jesse J. Appler, cashiered twelve days later.

As the Confederates poured into this gap, it naturally widened. The disgusted Sherman soon had to admit of his left brigade that its commander "was personally there, but his brigade was not." While McClernand's division rushed up to bolster Sherman's failing line, Hurlbut moved to reinforce Prentiss, and W. H. L. Wallace advanced in support of both Hurlbut and McClernand. Stuart's brigade of Sherman's division, running low on ammunition, was not holding too well down along the river road.[4]

"As we drew near the rear and left of Prentiss' line," Hurlbut noted, "his regiments, in broken masses, drifted through my advance, that officer making every effort to rally them." Soon, however, it became pleasantly evident that part of Prentiss' division was going to get a grip on itself and show a resolute face to the Rebels.

At nine o'clock Prentiss rode by to order Miller's brigade to abandon the camps. Both flanks were by this time turned, but the men didn't retreat promptly enough to suit Prentiss. "I must have been a little excited," Miller confessed in 1891, "as he had to reiterate his order before I could comprehend." Garner, ever the polemicist where Madison Miller was involved, retorted to this in 1893 that the 18th Missouri "must have been like the contrary hog that had to be dragged by the ears to the swill, then dragged by the tail from the swill. Came pretty near repeating the old Weston insubordination, . . . don't you think?"

Nevertheless, the 18th Missouri fell back as directed. "This second retrograde movement," Miller wrote, "was fearful upon new and untried men, and many a brave man no doubt lost control of himself." Hurlbut's line, said Coddington, met the withdrawing Missourians about 200 yards north of the camp. "We marched right through [Hurlbut's line], and then commenced reorganizing the regiment," he wrote. Miller's brigade was now sadly decimated, with the 61st Illinois entirely out of the picture and only part of the 18th Wisconsin in sight. Isaac V. Pratt no longer had anything like a full-strength regiment either. However, Miller said, "After a refreshing drink from a wayside well, we again got into line . . ." with a "new and bountiful supply of ammunition that had been cared for by our efficient Quartermaster, Cudworth, and that best of Wagonmasters, Pollock . . ." The new line was probably 400 yards north of the encampment, and it was flanked by the Ohio and Minnesota gunners on the Eastern Corinth Road due west of division headquarters.

It was Madison Miller's good luck that he had a little time to form his new line and rest his men. But Hurlbut's force "soon got the worst of it," and, said Coddington, "back they came." It was the chaplain's impression long afterwards that if the Confederates "had not paused to forage upon our . . . provisions, the sixth division would have been annihilated within the next hour. But as it was, the Rebels were evidently hungry, and while their advance was devouring our unfinished breakfast those in the rear had to pause." This, he gratefully remembered, "enabled us to lengthen the distance between them and us, and right well did we use the time thus gained."

The 18th Missouri's loss thus far was severe. Lieutenant Sharp was known to be dead, and Coddington had seen both Jim Simmons and Sergeant Downey of Company B "shot to death on the field . . ." before the camp was abandoned. Three company commanders—Clark, Godfrey, and Cooper—were seriously wounded. Lieutenant Hudson was missing, having fallen prisoner while vainly trying to evacuate Captain Cooper and several others before the Rebels could get them. That many others were killed or wounded was quite evident, but the toll would be far greater before anyone had time to make an accurate count.

Although the 18th Wisconsin was reassembling in force on his left, Miller wasn't able to hold this new line in the heart of the woods very long. Hurlbut's scattered force over to the east was having a bitter time somewhat to the south of a little pool known thereafter as the Bloody Pond, and his line was on the verge of buckling. Around ten o'clock Hurlbut did fall back, obliging Miller to do the same.

A mile or so to the north of his abandoned campsites, Prentiss found a thickly wooded ridge traversed by an abandoned sunken road, and along it he gathered available remnants of his division. Around Wyckoff's Company D and Dolman's Company H—with some 60 men between them—Colonel Pratt put together a force of nearly 200 men of the 18th Missouri. Stults and Minter rallied 40 men from B and G, while smaller contingents were gotten together from all other companies of the regiment. Captain Clark's head wound, from which he was to die three weeks later, somewhat hampered the task of rallying Company E, but a dozen of its men, led by Lieutenant Mc-Efee, made their way into the strong new position. The remainder of the 18th Wisconsin also took a stand, on Pratt's left.

Quinn's 12th Michigan and a small detachment of the 21st Missouri were all of the First Brigade that Prentiss could salvage in the confusion, the rest finding positions to the rear with McClernand and Sherman. The 61st Illinois wound up as a tactical reserve for Hurlbut, as did the 16th Wisconsin, which went to the rear for ammunition and was grabbed by Hurlbut to plug a hole in the 4th Division's line. The 25th Missouri finished the day chinking the gaps in Sherman's riddled division. Hundreds of Prentiss' men had either lost contact with their units in the turmoil along the Eastern Corinth Road, had taken wounded men to the rear in search of medical attention, or had fled in panic to the river bank below the bluff.[5]

It was about nine o'clock when Colonel Jacob T. Tindall reported to Prentiss with the news that the 23d Missouri was just getting off the boat. Did the General still have a spot for Tindall? He did indeed! The new arrivals, who turned out to be a good fighting force, were moved eventually into a hot spot on the division's left flank along the ravine called Brier Creek, south of the hill position built along the sunken road by Prentiss and Miller. Colonel James L. Geddes' 8th Iowa came up to buttress Prentiss' right flank at about the same time Tindall's regiment appeared.

In this new line of battle, Prentiss was securely lodged between W. H. L. Wallace, whose three Iowa regiments held the sunken road to the west, and Hurlbut, to the left of Tindall. The two artillery batteries were now posted along the sunken road near its intersection with the Corinth Road. Prentiss, with Geddes' Iowans witnessing, personally directed the gunners' fire "with devastating effect." The sunken road provided a handy trench in which Prentiss' forward musketeers could blaze away from prone positions well covered by the other infantrymen behind them and overlooking them from the wooded hill bastion seized upon by Prentiss during his retirement from the previous line. "Our men were ordered to lie down on the ground," Quinn reported later, "which they did, nor did they have long to wait."[6]

General Johnston saw at a glance that if he did not storm this position, he would have a wretched time pushing on down to the Landing. Calling up Brigadier General Daniel Ruggles' brigade, Johnston launched it against Prentiss soon after the 6th Division had lodged itself in the old roadbed. "Here occurred one of the noblest and most determined resistances ever offered by an inferior number to an overwhelming foe," Quinn stated in his after-action report. "On came the enemy, yelling and yelping, and for about ten minutes kept up a dreadful and incessant firing, with but little effect, for our men were flat on the ground. . . ." Miller called to the boys' minds years later how the Confederates had "advanced column after column, first rank firing, then by open column breaking ranks to the rear, loading as they marched. . . ." Most of the Rebel bullets may have been wide of their marks on this occasion, but "the groans and shrieks in the bushes" southwest of the road told Quinn that the 6th Division was having better luck with its volleys. Things soon quieted down for a while, since the enemy badly needed time to regroup and reinforce.

During the lull that followed Ruggles' repulse, Prentiss played host to General Grant. Looking over the peculiar strengths of what Johnston would soon christen the "Hornets' Nest," Grant became quite enthusiastic. Declaring emphatically that the survival of the Army of the Tennessee depended upon it, he ordered Prentiss to "maintain that position at all hazards." Grant then saluted and rode off through the trees.

Passing the word along that "General Grant says we've got to hold 'em," Ben Prentiss ordered all hands to brace for the storm. And it was not long in coming. Ten more times would Ruggles and his reinforcements try to slash, blast, and dig Prentiss out of the Hornets' Nest. A wounded soldier of the 25th Missouri, who had found himself stranded with the 18th Missouri in the sunken road, told fellow patients on a hospital boat that "the varmints made eleven charges against our line, and we driv 'em back every time." If Johnston had not become so concerned personally about the Hornets' Nest, he might have lived to a ripe age. While working with Ruggles on this problem, however, he was struck in the leg by a musket ball. An artery was severed, but the second-ranking general in Jefferson Davis' army wouldn't stop fighting because of a bloody leg. Not long after 2:30 P.M. he suddenly fell from his horse and died from loss of blood, leaving to Beauregard the awful decision of how to carry on.[7]

Wild fighting occurred on Prentiss' flanks between 2 and 4 P.M. Hurlbut's men, driven by Chalmers from a strong position in a peach orchard southeast of the Hornets' Nest, re-formed on a line facing eastward and at right angles with the front held by Prentiss since midmorning. Something of the same thing happened to Wallace on the right, for as the afternoon wore on the Confederates forced him to change fronts continually until he wound up facing west and south. The 6th Division caught its share of punishment along the Eastern Corinth Road, where Ruggles did his best to take out the troublesome Yankee artillery. Concentrating more than sixty field guns on Prentiss' positions, he was for a time able to drive the Federal gunners to cover. But the Rebels could not brave Prentiss' musket volleys to come out and seize his unmanned artillery pieces. Grant arranged for the gunboats to take a hand in the fray at this point, but they did about as much damage to friends as to enemies, knocking limbs down from the taller trees right into the midst of Union infantry. After repulsing one assault, the 6th Division raced out and wheeled the Ohio guns back in from their exposed location. Prentiss then opened an avenue through the infantry to provide a field of fire for the guns, and Ruggles soon had to face artillery fire again.

Not long after four o'clock Grant paid one last visit to Prentiss and found him "cool as if he had been expecting victory." So well had the new 6th Division stood up under the avalanche that a great historian of the conflict was able to say a generation later that the men of the Hornets' Nest had foiled Johnston's plan for seizing Pittsburg Landing. If, wrote John Fiske, "there is anyone who deserves especial commemoration as having 'saved the day,' it is Benjamin Prentiss for the glorious stand which he made. . . ."[8]

But all was about over for Prentiss. Stuart's brigade completed its retirement across Dill's Branch around three o'clock, and this jeopardized Hurlbut's left. The Confederates pouring down the river road toward the Landing so compromised Hurlbut that when the 12th Iowa, of W. H. L. Wallace's division, reached "the high ground between our position and Hurlbut's headquarters we discovered we were already surrounded. . . ." Prentiss and Wallace, looking about them, saw quite clearly that they were being isolated from the rest of the Army of the Tennessee, and that the other divisions were in the process of retiring northward to try forming a new line on the heights around the Landing.

Many were the scenes of heroism enacted at the Hornets' Nest that day, but the image of Captain Wyckoff's ferocity lived for years in Prentiss' memory. "I can see him now," the General orated at Unionville in 1890, "as he moved amid his regiment exclaiming to the boys: 'Save your fire!' 'Let them get a little closer!' 'Take good aim!'" It was about three o'clock, as Wyckoff later remembered, when he told Pratt that the troops in the Hornets' Nest would do well to get out before they were surrounded. Pratt checked the matter to Prentiss, explaining that Sherman's rout and Hurlbut's withdrawal were uncovering the flanks. Prentiss agreed with Wyckoff, but General

Grant had forbidden such a retreat from this exposed position. "As I expected," wrote Wyckoff in 1893, "Rebel infantry poured through the gap left by Hurlbut, and Rebel cavalry passed to our right over the ground that had been occupied by Sherman. They soon came upon our rear. . . ."[9]

The curtain rang down on this tragedy soon after Grant rode away from his last conference with Ben Prentiss. W. H. L. Wallace was struck down with a fatal wound about five o'clock, as his troops were cutting their way out to the north along a ravine ahead of the Confederate pincers. There was no way out for the 6th Division and four of Wallace's regiments that re- mained with them in the Hornets' Nest. "I determined," Prentiss reported later, "to assail the enemy, which had passed between me and the river, charging upon him with my entire force. I found him advancing in mass, completely encircling my com- mand, and nothing was left but to harass him and retard his progress. . . ." Finally—Madison Miller set the time at 5:26— Prentiss decided that "further resistance must result in the slaughter of every man in the command," and he therefore hoisted white flags and called for a cease-fire. Over 2,200 offi- cers and men unable to fight their way clear now became prison- ers, the surrender of Colonel Pratt and his remnant of the 18th Missouri being taken by Lieutenant Donald McKenzie of Com- pany K, 9th Mississippi Infantry.

There was necessarily much confusion and uncertainty at the surrender. Miller tried vainly to offer his sword to Bishop Polk and Major General John C. Breckenridge, but finally a passing colonel accommodated him. Sergeant Joseph M. Brown of Company F heard one prisoner shout hysterically that the Confederates were going to "shoot all the prisoners." Wide- eyed Private Charles Meier, in later years a St. Louis photogra- pher, turned to Brown and asked anxiously, "*Will* they shoot us, Sergeant?"

"No," Brown assured the youngster.

Sergeant Abraham Van Meter, also of Company F, was not so sure. The Rebels kept on firing for some time after the Mis- sourians had stacked their muskets, he said later, and some pris- oners were killed, including one man of Company F "shot by a Rebel only a few feet distant who knew full well that he was murdering a helpless prisoner." Prentiss brought the incidents to a halt by threatening to order his men "to take their guns and sell their lives as dearly as possible." The Rebels had already had enough of that.[10]

"I think my nerve was just as good the minute before I was captured as it was in the morning," wrote Coddington in 1893. "But I became a prisoner; the day's work told on me. I was like a dish rag. I thought I could not walk one hundred yards. The excitement of battle for ten hours is certainly very straining on a man, but he does not realize it until after it is all quiet."

Wyckoff never tired of relating the drama of the surrender. The fabulous Beauregard, he recalled, rode up to the now-quiet Hornets' Nest to greet his old friend of many years.

"Hello, Prentiss," the Confederate chieftain saluted. "How many more do you fellows have back at the Landing?"

"If you want to know," the captive responded, "I recommend that you go down there and count them yourself."

"I doubt if there is time left this evening," Beauregard rejoined airily. "We'll go pick them up in the morning."[11]

In the disaster that had overwhelmed his command, Prentiss consoled himself that by their sacrifices the men of the Hornets' Nest had saved Grant's army and preserved its chances for a victorious counterattack on the morrow. Prentiss afterward lauded the courageous behavior of many of his officers and men, never forgetting the picture of Madison Miller's "distinguished courage, coolness, and ability." Colonel Peabody, the other brigade commander, had of course fallen on the field, during the fight around the camp line, and a disproportionate share of the division's officers had been lost. It would be months before the extent of such losses would be known to Prentiss and his companions in misfortune, before whom a half-year of captivity was now in prospect.

While the enemy captured over 130 men of the 18th Missouri, including Colonels Miller and Pratt and most of the company commanders, they never got their hands on the colors of Company E. Private George W. A. Preston of Pennville, on his way to a hospital, was given possession of the huge color-flag of his company to take away from the battlefield for safekeeping. The flag had been made by a half-dozen patriotic ladies of Pennville while Jake Clark was raising the company. We may never know Preston's full story, but visitors to the main floor of the Capitol in Jefferson City, Missouri, may see the encased colors of Company E on permanent display.[12]

Beauregard made one attempt to break the strong Federal line on the bluff before dark, but to no avail. Foote's gunboats poured a murderous shellfire into Rebel concentrations already weakened by casualties and by the diversion of regiments to shepherd Prentiss' men to the rear. Not long after the sun went down, a line of thunderstorms blew in, and it rained the rest of the night. The Confederates withdrew to the tents abandoned by the Army of the Tennessee and got in out of the chilly downpour, while the former proprietors, now on the bluff, had no choice but to lie out in the open or huddle under trees.

In the pre-dawn hours, Buell's divisions were arriving to prepare for Monday's return engagement. Captain Daniel McCook, an adjutant in Buell's army, has left a haunting description of the situation at the Landing when morning came. A misting rain was still falling, "the fog clung to dark forests, veiling their recesses in obscurity," and a "steel-gray sky was cold, cheerless, and depressing." Around the Landing, McCook saw "confusion was worse than confounded. Rations, forage, and ammunition were tramped into the mire by an excited and surging crowd. Officers were rushing about, endeavoring to collect the stragglers of their commands and lead them into the rapidly-increasing battle. Trains were huddled together in sheltered places; ambulances, with their bleeding loads, were coming to the steamboats; sutlers, camp-followers, and even women were adding their voices to the Babel of Sound."

Such were the recollections of Ohioan Dan McCook, son-in-law of a Confederate patriarch in Platte County, Missouri. In two more years he would wear the star of a brigadier general to his grave, following a wild charge up Kennesaw Mountain that the men of the 18th Missouri would remember for a lifetime.[13]

Buttressed by the Army of the Ohio, Grant counter-attacked and finally expelled the bedraggled Confederates from the field. With a force down to 20,000 survivors of Sunday's grueling fight, Beauregard perceived Monday afternoon that he was outmanned and outgunned. Skillfully disengaging himself, the Southern commander made his departure for Corinth. The victors regained their camps that evening and bedded down for the night; not even Grant could bring himself to order them out into the rain for the pursuit that might have ruined Beauregard.

Manning F. Force, who finished the war a major general, commanded the 20th Ohio in Buell's army that second day at Shiloh. He movingly described for posterity the horrors of the field after the fighting was done. Hospital boats bearing army doctors and nurses as well as civilian volunteers crowded the river about the Landing. "There was need for all the aid that was brought," Force wrote. "Besides the thousands of wounded were other thousands of sick. The springs of surface water . . . always unwholesome, were now poisonous." Men who seemed well on April 7 might be critically ill a day later. "Hospital camps spread over the hills about the Landing, and the little town of Savannah was turned into a hospital. Fleets descended the river bearing invalids to purer air and water."

On the shoulders of Colonel Quinn, the ranking officer of the 6th Division still alive and free, there now fell the burden of reassembling and reorganizing the 18th Missouri and its sister regiments, all of whom were represented by survivors. The senior officer left in the 18th was Captain Price, but Brigadier General Thomas J. McKean, taking over the division on Thursday, deemed it best to "import" a field-grade officer, and installed Major Stephen Walsh of the 15th Michigan as temporary commander. Surveying the human cost of Sunday's fighting, Quinn and McKean found that only Price and Ault of the ten company commanders were still on duty. Miller and Pratt—the only field-grade officers in the 18th—were on their way south as guests of the Confederacy. Checking with the medics and the provost marshal, McKean ascertained that seventy-one were wounded and in hospitals or on hospital ships along the river. Others were sick in quarters, and still others were just plain missing.[14]

Among the wounded was Private Daniel Morgan Shelton of Putnam County, who in old age described his experience in these words: "Wounded in the neck during the 1st day, came to Savana, was there treated by Doctor Davis (surgeon), who furnished me a bunk to lie on, which was not to my liking. I could walk a little and went to regemental hospital where I found my cousin [Pvt. Gilbert] Lafayette Shelton suffering from wound in arm which later proved fatal. . . . Went to Cairo where a twenty days furlough was given me—thence to Quincy, Illinois, where a transfer was effected going to Laclede, Mo. where I met my father and one brother there in service. . . ."[15]

It was a very sad time for the Shelton family, as young Daniel was to learn on arriving home in Unionville. Not only was cousin Lafayette on his deathbed, but Daniel's older brother Tom, a cavalry lieutenant, had just become the first Union soldier to be buried in Putnam County. Another older brother, Sergeant Joel, was dying of typhoid in a St. Louis hospital, with only days to live. And cousin Steve Shelton, also of Company E, would lie dead of pneumonia in Tennessee the first week of July. As it was in other outfits, so they found it in the 18th Missouri—deaths from disease far outstripped the toll exacted by Confederate marksmanship.[16]

Burial parties working over the battlefield later in the week soon counted up more of the disastrous cost of Shiloh to the 18th Missouri. At least twenty officers and men were dead on the field, and twice that number would perish of their wounds in Union and Confederate hospitals before the end of the year. The men returning to the campsite Wednesday evening found Lieutenant Sharp where Sergeant Brown last saw him, "sitting against a tree, shot through the center of the forehead." Adjutant Edgar, struck behind the ear by a musket ball, died in the Hornets' Nest. "Believing that his relatives would want to remove his remains," Garner had him buried "in a grave by himself and marked it with care. This was unusual. . . . The dead there were usually put in pits or trenches. . . . All that we could do was to spread his handkerchief over his face, put his cap on, roll him from head to foot in two blankets, slip a bread box over his head and shoulders and cover him up. Pretty rough, but the best we could do."

"To me," Garner lamented, "his case was tinged with tender pathos. A promising young officer, snatched from a doting, widowed mother and the confiding, loving heart of the

girl of his choice lay before me with a rebel bullet in his brain
. . . and I confess, when I removed the photos of the mother and
that girl from the inside pocket of his vest, my deepest sensibil-
ities were stirred. . . ."

More tragedy was reported to a St. Louis address in mid-
May, when a Confederate Army surgeon notified a sorrowing
father that Captain Cooper had died on May 4 at Corinth "from
absorption of pus" growing out of an "extensive fracture of the
upper end of the femur. . . ." Before he died, the gallant young
officer had donated all the money on him—$2.50—for his fel-
low patients, "regretting that the amount was not greater."

At the edge of Spain field they found the body of Jimmy
Carrie, whose forebodings had come true. Conveying the news
to Carrie's wife was Jimmy's comrade, Private David A. Riggins,
who later married the widow and assumed guardianship of the
fatherless son and daughter. In all, one first sergeant, one duty
sergeant, and four corporals were among those who had given
their lives on that fearful Sabbath.

Lieutenant Pollock of Company B took time the following
Friday to share the grim news with the family back at St. John.
"We lost from our Company 6 killd and 8 wonded and 15 missing. The killd was George A. [Hindman], James R. Simmons,
John Downey, Simeon Maphet [Maffit?], Noah Mullenax, J. I.
Cochran. I had the boys baried as nice as possibel." Calamity of
another dimension had also hit him. "Thay broke my trunk open
and took all of my cloas. Thay took a boutt 100 dollars worth of
cloas from me but that was nothing. The 18th Regt was all
cut to peases."[17]

Two other company commanders, Jake Clark of E and
Eugene Godfrey of F, were dead of their wounds within the
month. Both were buried the last week of April, Clark in the
National Cemetery in St. Louis and Godfrey in Woodlawn
Cemetery in Quincy. Lieutenant Dayton of Company A died
at Paducah on a steamboat bearing him to St. Louis. The
men literally died all over the country in the weeks and months
following the battle. Private Joseph von Arx, who suffered a
slight wound, nevertheless died of blood poisoning at Mound
City, Illinois, on April 21. So chaotic were military communications that the army considered him a deserter until 1868. First

Sergeant Joseph Darwin, severely wounded in the side, died at the Savannah hospital the week after the battle. Besides Von Arx, twenty-two privates lost their lives from wounds. Company F's Private Teeter Masoner, from Weston, won the doleful honor of being the last of the mortally wounded to die, for he lingered on in the General Hospital at Louisville until December 15 of that year.[18]

And what of Sunday's unfortunate captives? "We were treated as brothers by the men who faced us in battle," Sergeant Thomas Cawood of G Company recalled in 1876. "But God pity us as soon as we fell into the hands of the guard. . . ." Two regiments of shotgun-toting Mississippians surrounded the heroes of the Hornets' Nest and began marching them off some six miles to the south to spend the night in a plowed field. There they stood, hardly caring to sit down in the mud, through that long rainy night. "The only sound heard that night that was pleasing," declared Van Meter, "was the distant boom of the guns of our gun boats . . . which told us that 'our flag was still there. . . .'" With a bitterness lingering into his old age, Colonel Pratt remembered that the only food provided that night was "hardtack and fat meat"—which he contemptuously declined.

At daylight on Monday the guards ordered the men out onto the muddy road to Corinth. There was a firmer path on the shoulders of the road, but the Mississippians kept their prisoners in the ankle-deep mud in the middle. Abe Van Meter noted that the road was "filled with broken down wagons, artillery, disabled horses, mules and other material usually found in the rear of an army during an engagement." He noticed, too, that the adjoining woods seemed "full of Rebels. Many of them were wounded, and many others were stragglers whose discretion had gotten the better part of their valor." Soaking wet all day, for it rained off and on through the forenoon, the long blue line of captives reached Corinth in midafternoon. There, within plain view of firm green turf, they were corralled on a plot of soggy ground where the mud ran a foot deep in places. Here the prisoners were soon surrounded by an "excited crowd of people," who seemed, according to Van Meter, "to take great delight in applying the vilest epithets to the captives."

Something interesting was evidently going on back around Pittsburg Landing. The prisoners at Corinth could hardly help noticing that little bands of Rebels were constantly coming in from the north, and in something of a hurry. Many were hatless, and some had no weapons. As Monday wore on, their numbers increased.

Beauregard rode in before sundown, and Prentiss made bold to greet him with a question whose answer the cunning Prentiss had already fathomed. "Well, General, how did you make out gathering in the stragglers this morning?" he asked politely.

"All right," Old Bory was heard to mumble. But it seemed obvious that he was not ready to discuss the matter at any great length.

That night the prisoners were loaded on a freight train bound for Memphis. Famished now, some of the men took advantage of the darkness and confusion around the station to steal a few boxes of hardtack from Beauregard's commissary before boarding the train. By no means all of the passengers got to eat, however. Sergeant Cawood's recollection was that the men in his car got nothing at all until Wednesday, the day after the train reached Memphis.

The train stood in the yards at Corinth all night, and during that time Prentiss and Miller picked up the news that General Johnston had been killed in action and that the Confederates had been driven from the battlefield Monday afternoon in considerable disarray. "The Rebels strenuously denied the report," said Van Meter, "but their countenances and their actions proved to us that it was true."

On Tuesday morning the train pulled out, and it proved to be a slow trip. The train stopped at every station, for the commandant seemed to want to display his captives to the multitudes for morale purposes. Prentiss' reputation as an orator had preceded him, and at most stations there was a widespread clamor for a "speech from the Yankee general!" Wrote Miller in his diary: "Genl P full of life and saucy enough for any of them." Van Meter told with great relish how Prentiss, appearing at the door of his car, was always "loaded and gave it to them from the shoulder. . . ."

Arriving at Memphis Tuesday evening, the prisoners un-loaded at the station and immediately took umbrage at the reception unveiled by their hosts. Local officials had engaged the services of an all-Negro marching band to lead a big parade through the main streets. "General [Prentiss] very promptly informed them," Van Meter heard, "that they would do no such thing, and instructed the prisoners not to move if a Negro band was placed at the head of the column." The Rebels finally gave up that part of the program, but nevertheless, reported Miller, "we were marched and countermarched. . . ." Finally, these Neronian festivities ended, and the prisoners were quar-tered in a line of old buildings on the waterfront. Sergeant Brown wrote later that once his detachment was inside its warehouse, "the chivalrous sons of the sunny south brought a gunboat down in front of our prison, and told us if we did not behave ourselves . . . they would blow us to kingdom come."

But the wandering of the exiles had hardly begun. They were next loaded on a train Wednesday morning and set off for Mobile, Alabama, on a six-day ride with two days' rations. "Much of the time," Cawood wrathfully observed, "the men were deprived of even water to quench our thirst." Joe Brown objected that the ". . . stock cars . . . had not been cleaned for months, and you know how sweet they were. . . ." Nor was this the fastest trip ever made by an American passenger train: the train reached Okolona, Mississippi, early on Thursday, April 10, having gone 68 miles in 21 hours. The sun had not come up Friday when it pulled in to Canton, where the boys were furnished what Van Meter termed "a reasonably fair breakfast, the first regular meal since our capture. . . ." While the men were waiting for breakfast, the irrepressible Ben Prentiss pro-posed a serenade for their Confederate friends, and a rousing rendition of "The Red, White, and Blue" was under way. The second verse was interrupted by a furious Rebel officer who peremptorily ordered an end to such tomfoolery. In response, some anonymous prisoner deep in the crowd started "The Star-Spangled Banner," and the boys were soon singing it with even more spirit than the first song.

At Mobile the men were herded into a large cotton ware-house, on the roof of which the April sun beat down mercilessly. The Yankees found themselves a great "curiosity" to the local folks, hundreds of whom came to banter with the prisoners. "The worst frowns and bad language," said Brown, "came from the women, seemingly the best class, too." By this time, the officers above the rank of lieutenant had been winnowed out and sent on to Selma, Alabama.

For the others, however, the low point in the odyssey came at Cahaba, a little way south of Birmingham, the following week. A thousand enlisted men and lieutenants were cooped up in a warehouse on the Cahaba River, so cramped for space that they could not all lie down at once. Most of them were by now suffering from diarrhea. Neither the environment nor the diet was designed to cure their ailments, for the menu each day featured a repulsive concoction described by an unappreciative Cawood as "a pint of musty, spoiled corn meal, bran, and all other imaginable filth, with a little salt beef, so poor that I never saw one single bit of grease rise to the top of the water in cooking it."

Here the men got their first experience with really brutal camp guards. Since some of the prisoners had money, local purveyors were allowed to come to the warehouse and sell vegetables, milk, and fruit. One prisoner, Brown remembered, "was in the act of handing up his canteen to have it filled with milk, when an armed Rebel shot him dead, and if he was punished in any way, I have forgotten. . . ."

On May 4 the prisoners at Cahaba were unloaded at their next prison pen, on the old fair grounds at Macon, Georgia. Although the management here seemed more concerned with prisoners' welfare than at any previous stop, Brown was soon sick in bed. Van Meter, who had been in a group sent from Mobile to Griffin, Georgia, arrived at Macon on June 17 and found Brown "lying very low with what is termed typo malarial fever. . . ."

Something else very ominous had happened before Van Meter's arrival. Command of the camp passed at the close of May to a major of the Georgia Legion, J. E. Rylander. This officer, upon taking charge, called all the inmates together for an orientation speech. He revealed that he had been a Southern Methodist preacher before the war, but that he had patriotically "laid off the cloak of religion and put on a robe of blood." There would be no pampering of prisoners, for the new commandant would not be moved by the promptings of religion in any way. That, charged Brown, was the "only promise he made and fulfilled." The boys couldn't help thinking how much Rylander and Chaplain Garner would have enjoyed each other!

"After Rylander assumed command," Brown related in 1894, "rations were cut down to a starvation point—mostly rice or rice meal, or corn meal, ground cob and all, with the silk and part of the husk. This meal we would shake in something or other most convenient, and gather silk, husk, and cob from it, boil it or bake it and eat warm or cold as hunger compelled us, and to this day I cannot eat warm rice or stay at a table it is on." Weighing 200 pounds at muster-in, Brown had shrunk to half that by the time he was liberated from Rylander's care.

Van Meter recalled a time when Rylander showed the men how disgusting he could really get. A heifer had gotten loose and wandered into the grounds one day; the prisoners immediately pounced on her, butchered her, and divided her up among themselves. The furious Rylander rushed guards into the camp, "arrested several of the participants, and tied them up by the thumbs, with only their feet touching the ground and above their heads with a board on which hung a piece of meat and underneath which was painted the words 'meat thief.'"

After a series of episodes like this, Rylander had the gall to announce that all East Tennessee Methodist preachers among the prisoners in the stockade were forbidden to preach, under pain of severe punishment. The commandant declared fatuously that *he* would be the camp chaplain, but, Brown commented ironically, "no congregation came to hear him."

By August, said Van Meter, "there was hardly a well man among the prisoners." Malaria, diarrhea, and dysentery were the most common ailments, but there were also many cases of scurvy, "it being no uncommon thing to see men in the prime of life with their feet and legs badly swollen and covered with putrifying sores, and their mouths so sore and teeth so loose as to make the eating of solid food an impossibility. . . ." On the average, he estimated, ten bodies were carted away every morning. Brown remembered attending the burial of John

Caseldine of Company F, but others of the 18th Missouri died after he fell ill. One man of the regiment "fretted himself to death, wife and children were his only thoughts, and as long as he could speak he was calling for them. Oh! what it cost to subdue that rebellion is not shown by any treasury statement. . . ."

In the fullness of time, the alumni of such prison compounds would find that tears came easily to their eyes when they sang one familiar chorus:

> *Tramp, tramp, tramp, the boys are marching!*
> *Cheer up, comrades, they will come. . . .*

The officers lodged at Selma were in time authorized by the Confederate government to elect a three-man commission to go to Washington and initiate arrangements for a general exchange of prisoners. When the officers balloted, they almost unanimously elected Colonel Miller head of the commission. While Miller and his associates were away in Washington prodding the War Department and the Attorney General, the Confederates moved the prisoners from Selma to Richmond's dank old Libby Prison. Surviving lieutenants and non-coms at Macon joined them there early in the fall. When finally exchanged at Aiken's Landing, below Richmond, the survivors of the Hornets' Nest were "poor in flesh," in Jim Coddington's words. Said he afterward: "We never tasted a drop of sure enough coffee from the day we were captured until . . . we stepped on board the 'John Warner' at Aikin's Landing. . . . I never shall forget how good that coffee tasted, but it made me drunk until I got used to it."

The fervently Methodist Prentiss was crying like a child in gratitude to God for his deliverance from the infidels. Coddington shed "some good-sized tears" himself on the occasion. At Prentiss' suggestion an impromptu prayer meeting took place on deck, with a chaplain officiating. By the time the officers reached Washington, however, they had dried their eyes and were in a mood to appreciate the witticisms of President Lincoln, who came to the railway station to see them off to St. Louis. "This is not the first time I have been visited by a delegation from the South," he quipped.

The privates taken from Cahaba to Macon were paroled in small groups during the early summer and sent back to Union lines by way of Huntsville, Alabama, and Chattanooga, Tennessee. Sergeant Mike Callery, a sly Irish fellow in Company K, furtively took off his stripes and "qualified" to go north with the others. Few of these parolees were exchanged to go back to duty before the early weeks of 1863, however.[19]

Captivity in the Civil War was no guarantee of "living to fight another day." No less than seventeen of the Shiloh prisoners soon lay in a string of graves from Corinth to Macon. None of the fifteen captured officers died, but two sergeants and three corporals shared the fate of a dozen other enlisted men of the 18th Missouri who never again saw their homes. Sergeant Benecke of Company H, among those taken at the Hornets' Nest, more than half a century later branded those "seven terrible long months" of captivity as "the saddest part of my military service." In fact, not long after his shocked parents welcomed the emaciated youth back to Brunswick, Benecke received a disability discharge, on March 4, 1863.

His older brother Robert had been left behind in Benton Barracks with an eye injury which led to his discharge. In 1897, he was a prosperous manufacturer of photographic supplies in St. Louis, and he visited the battlefield while on a vacation. He recalled for D. W. Pollock his youthful regrets over being unable to ship out on the *Nebraska* with Louis and Company H, "but now I must confess, after having seen the boys coming back from the prisons in the South, I am glad I was not of the party."

In time, public opinion across the North would become highly inflamed over tales of miserable food, brutal treatment, impure water, overcrowding, and poor medical care afforded prisoners in Confederate camps. And while it is true that the disintegration of Southern railways and an unavoidable reliance on third-rate administrators contributed much to the squalid living conditions in the camps, Union partisans much preferred to give full faith and credit to the outraged veterans as they returned to tell their stories. Typical of the itinerary of captured officers was that of Lieutenant McEfee, Company E. After being taken first to an officers' compound at Montgomery,

Alabama, he was shunted on to Macon in July. In September he was removed to Madison, Georgia, and from that point he was taken on to the "Libby Hell" in Richmond in October. After being paroled in November of 1862, he was exchanged the following February and immediately returned to his company.[20]

As a matter of fact, being paroled didn't always bring on the millennium either. Eighty paroled prisoners of four Missouri outfits found that out in November, 1862, at Portsmouth Grove, Rhode Island, following their return to Federal custody. Led by Sergeants Brown and Van Meter of the 18th Missouri, the shivering parolees put their case in a round-robin letter to Governor Gamble:

> Now after being kept in the South all summer we are . . . brought down here to try a New England winter. We are fed by contractors and poorly fed. It is in the morning a small slice of cold beef, some coffee and bread; at noon it is some rice, bread, and molasses; supper it is bread and tea. And also our clothing is too light. We are greatly in want of overcoats and stockings. Now, Your Excellency, what we ask is this, that if consistent with your duties you will try and have us removed to Saint Louis so that we may get our pay which our families are in great need of at this time. All the boys are most willing for the field again if soon exchanged, but do not want to lie inactive here.

The plea came at an opportune moment, for Gamble was even then sojourning in Washington. The Governor got on the wire in a hurry. On November 28 the Adjutant General of Missouri demanded and got the Missourians sent home to St. Louis.[21]

Meanwhile, back in Unionville a rumor had been circulating that Captain Wyckoff had been killed in action. A public meeting was held in the city late in the spring of 1862 to express the community's regrets to the Wyckoff family, and one citizen even wrote a sorrowful poem in Wyckoff's memory. It was the good Captain's pleasure to "pronounce the report false and [repudiate] all the proceedings of the meeting."[22]

# CHAPTER IV

# On to Corinth

CAPTAIN PRICE got orders from General Grant on Wednesday morning, April 9, to move the 18th Missouri back to the old campsite and reconstruct as much of it as possible. Barely 300 strong, Price's glum and silent band trudged down the road from the Landing through a depressing panorama of dead men, dead horses, and demolished wagons. A brilliant April sun shone down on a deathly silent woodland where buzzards and crows remained to share man's meditation on this latest hideous display of his inhumanity.

Since the men had not eaten much since Saturday night, they were overjoyed to learn that their energetic quartermaster had rounded up a supply of coffee beans, hard bread, and dried meat. From dozens of throats there came the natural query: "How'd you get all this?" But Cudworth and his Commissary Sergeant, John Lomax, had a ready if oracular answer: "It is our duty to furnish grub and your privilege to eat it—without discussing methods." That finally choked off impertinent questions, and by sundown supper was "on the stove."

As K Company's only available officer, Price felt that he had to give detailed attention to the outfit he had personally raised. For that reason Chaplain Garner had to dine alone at the headquarters mess with Teamster Johnson and his wife Roxana, who had reached the regiment just before the battle to serve as cook for the field and staff men. Never could the tearful Roxana have thought she would have to prepare a meal in such shocking circumstances. The cool and heavy night air was so putrid with the odor of decaying men and beasts that the boys would often marvel in later years at their ability to eat anything that night. "We were starved to it," their chaplain explains. "A hungry stomach is good sauce. . . ."

Doubling as physician and pastor, now that Hamlin was away sick and Houts was a prisoner, Garner sat up most of the night with Lieutenant Dayton. The poor fellow's thigh had been shattered by a musket ball, and he had lain in the brush unattended throughout the four days since the Rebel onslaught. The wound, though not yet much swollen, was suspiciously hot. No morphine was available to still the pain, and all the chaplain could do for Dayton was to console him spiritually and shift his thigh out into the cold rain that fell that night. Similarly, orderlies on a hospital boat were pouring buckets of river water on a hip wound suffered by First Sergeant Thomas Mc-Comb of Company C. At daybreak Cudworth located a wagon, and the men sorrowfully bade their dying officer farewell. Amputation might have saved Dayton's life, Garner always felt. But he lived only long enough for a hospital steamer to unload him at Paducah.[1]

The effect of this dreary atmosphere on the morale of the Missourians can be sensed from Ben Guffey's letter to his wife, written two weeks after the battle. Making no mention whatsoever of the recent catastrophe, he told Caroline that "before this letter reaches its destination we shall probably be . . . in front of the enemy. God above knows whether we shall meet on earth a gain, but after all what are the few short years we might have lived in the enjoyment of each others friendship here compared to that Eternity we shall spend together beyond the grave?"[2]

It fell to the lot of Garner and Private Roscoe E. Torrey, a twenty-five-year-old Putnam County farmer, to organize a make-shift hospital for the two dozen sick and wounded men still with the outfit. Hamlin had not returned from his protracted sojourn on the hospital ship. Torrey and Garner gathered up several ragged tents and enough muddy blankets to cover the ground inside them. The chaplain-surgeon, who "knew very little of operative surgery except as I had read it," held his first sick call Friday morning, and it didn't take long to discover that the "regimental hospital" was destitute of everything that army medics need—medicines, bandages, and a host of other hospital supplies. The "surgeon" and his steward then spent several hours assembling a requisition and a written description of their situation.[3]

General Grant issued orders on Thursday morning to finish burying the dead as quickly as possible. Agreed that it was high time, burial squads from the 18th Missouri hastened to the gruesome project. As far as possible, staff officers saw that each squad worked with its own. The dead were separated into regiments, wherever identification made it possible, and laid side by side in trenches four feet deep and seven feet wide. "We heard the 'Dead March' now nearly every day," a member of the 14th Wisconsin said, "and I thought that the most solemn music I ever heard." The abundant Confederate dead were grouped indiscriminately in their "little red mounds," as Garner recorded the event, "with as much speed and as little ceremony as decency and Christianity would permit."

Another sad chore performed by Garner and Cudworth was collecting all the belongings of captured officers that could be found in the shambles that had once been the camp. Two Negroes hired as servants in regimental headquarters were given the job of taking the effects of Colonels Miller and Pratt to Mrs. Miller, in Carondelet.[4]

Halleck appeared at Pittsburg Landing on Friday, April 11, and took command of everything in sight. So jealous of Grant that his judgment was rather warped, Old Brains set out to undercut and undo his rival in any way possible. Grant was relegated to second-in-command, and Halleck persistently winked while newspapermen condemned Shiloh as a disaster, and even claimed that Grant's famous coffee cup at the Cherry Mansion was full of another beverage for which Kentucky was justly famous. The two generals would soon cross swords over the condition of the 18th Missouri Volunteers.

One of the first things Grant told Halleck was that around the Landing there were several "fragments of different regiments without field officers and much broken up and demoralized." Grant explained that in the case of the 18th Missouri the 552 men "present for duty" on April 6 had dwindled inside a week to an appalling 330. Companies A, C, D, F, and H had no officers at all and were being commanded by sergeants. He had decided, Grant said, to order consolidations, transferring the men of smaller companies to the larger ones. By reducing ten companies to, say, six, Grant felt that the regiment's remaining commissioned officers would be numerous enough to go around.[5]

If we are to believe Old Brains, he blew up at this arrangement. Didn't Grant realize that the 18th Missouri and similar regiments were state outfits, that he had no power whatsoever to consolidate companies or do anything that might alter the structure of such units? On the other hand, Halleck said, Grant could "attach one [company] to another for temporary purposes. . . ." But consolidate, never! Grant was ordered, Halleck assured Gamble, to see to it personally that all such consolidations were revoked.[6]

General McKean, commanding the 6th Division, had on April 10 detailed Major Stephen Walsh of the 15th Michigan to command the Missourians. The major's new command regarded his coming with great misgivings. First, it was feared that there was now beginning another influx of strange officers, this time to take up the positions made vacant by the shattering experiences of the previous weekend. Second, the new commander proved to be a confirmed alcoholic. Taking over, the tipsy major ordered Merritt Young to beat the Long Roll, made a wild and incoherent speech, and then took off on another drinking bout after dismissing the formation. A few days later a squad from the Division Provost Marshal's office arrested Walsh and took him in for a general court-martial. Price resumed command of the dazed regiment for a few more days, and McKean bestowed on him the rank of "acting major" in honor of the event.[7]

Garner and Torrey, meanwhile, had a wretched time of it with their requisition for hospital supplies. Cudworth and Lomax were performing wonders in divesting the region of cattle and rice, and the veal and milk and grain were indeed indispensable to the morale and well-being of those in and out of the hospital. Garner fashioned a potent tonic from Virginia snakeroot and a powerful astringent from the wild madder abounding in the lower Tennessee Valley. But all this could hardly make up for the needed medicines and other materials. The requisition, to make matters worse, was returned, because the commander of the hospital ship had never heard of Garner and Torrey. "Stick to regular channels," he said, in brushing off the shocked Missouri chaplain.

"Regular channels, the devil!" snarled Torrey in his "down east" Maine accent. Garner, 211 pounds of ecclesiastical indignation, grabbed the papers, saddled his trusty Hawk, and galloped off to see U. S. Grant. This proved to be one more disappointment. The chaplain found the victor of Fort Donelson aboard the steamer *Tigress*, but Grant was sulking over the Halleck business and unwilling to waste words. "If ever I admired General Grant," the affronted Garner said later, "I admired him less after that."

Garner then went to the hospital boat for an even more painful visit. There he ran into Dr. Hamlin, whom the chaplain had already diagnosed once and for all as a sufferer from "suspended pluck and patriotism." All Garner accomplished with Hamlin was a barrage of well-rehearsed but unproductive insults, for the latter officer stoutly protested that he was in no position to do anything for the aggrieved regiment back at the camp. After turning his back contemptuously on the former regimental surgeon, Garner paid a last visit to Captain Clark. Though Jake Clark was mortally wounded, with only days to live, he was able to recognize the burly Garner and exchange a few reminiscences with him.

Leaving the hospital ship, Garner went in search of General Halleck. After walking over a mile around the Landing, he found him with a crowd of staff officers and made for him. The Commanding General was all kindness and understanding. "Go back to your command, Chaplain," directed Halleck. "Start this requisition at any headquarters you can find, asking the officer in command to forward it. Wait three days, and if you haven't heard from it, report back to me." A grateful Garner rode back to camp and sent the requisition to McKean's headquarters. The three days elapsed without action, just as Garner expected. But Halleck's adjutant, Colonel J. C. Kelton, soon saw to it that the 18th Missouri got a wagonload of old sheets, pillow-cases, and a dozen bottles of brandy. At least he tried.

Saturday, April 12, was set by Halleck as a day of thanks-giving in the Army of the Tennessee. Everyone was ordered to fall in line at noon near the Landing for a review, after which all chaplains would offer prayers before their regiments. Even high-ranking generals, sneered Garner, could "have a religious spasm, when they could order someone else to do the praying. . . ." Since there was now a widespread shortage of chaplains, those present found plenty of work to do. Garner was convinced that "the only thing . . . for which to be thankful was that we were not all butchered." Having little else to "communicate to the Almighty," he selected the shortest expression of praise in his Episcopal Prayer Book and "prayed loud enough to be heard —perhaps—five paces."

As soon as he had finished, Garner looked up to find an orderly from another regiment standing beside him. "Please come to our regiment, Chaplain," the young man urged. "Our chaplain is absent."

Muttering something about chaplains being nearly as yel-low as surgeons, the Missouri parson performed ministrations before six other regiments in the next few minutes. But then he began to grow weary of well-doing. To a seventh orderly bearing the stereotyped request, Garner brusquely expressed his "compliments to your commander, and if God will forgive me for this day's work, I will not ask Him for anything until after full moon."[8]

Besides the twenty-five wounded men who, between April 6 and September 15, 1862, had lost their fight to survive and the eighteen prisoners who perished in the South during that time, many more were snatched from the rolls of the regiment by diseases during those same weeks. Indeed, even while the regiment was at Benton Barracks making ready to ship out, six men had died at St. Louis and Quincy. This, however, was but a token payment against the toll to come. By September 15 no less than fifty-seven others died, most of them either in hospitals at St. Louis or near the front in Tennessee. A few died at their homes in Missouri, several at Quincy or Keokuk, others at Cairo, one in rural Iowa. The scanty available evidence suggests that the major killers were typhoid and pneumonia, doing their part to account for over a hundred deaths in the 18th Missouri in half a year.[9]

Great things were happening beyond the horizons of the 18th Missouri. While the battle at Shiloh was raging, forces under Pope were forcing the surrender of Island No. 10 and the consequent opening up of the Mississippi well down toward Memphis. In late April, Union land and sea forces occupied New Orleans, rendering the great river almost useless to the Confederacy. On April 28, Halleck gave the orders to his hundred thousand Yankees, reinforced by Pope's victorious troops, to march on Beauregard's entrenched positions around Corinth, in northern Mississippi.

For the advance, Halleck divided his mighty host into three major segments. The Left Wing, under Pope, had three infantry divisions and a cavalry division from the Army of the Mississippi. The Right Wing, including McKean's 6th Division and its 18th Missouri, was a force of five divisions, mostly from Grant's old Army of the Tennessee, now commanded by Major General George H. Thomas, next year's "Rock of Chickamauga." McClernand was in the rear with a two-division reserve.[10]

Despite the dilapidated condition of the 18th Missouri, it played its part well in the drive to Corinth. Still a six-company regiment (despite Halleck's alleged warnings to Grant), the men soon learned that advancing with Old Brains was a fatiguing experience. With a force twice that of Beauregard's, Halleck moved cautiously, like a gambler who stands to lose more than he can possibly win. Each day the Union infantry would advance a few hundred yards, then stop when it received orders to dig rifle-pits and throw up earthen breastworks.

It was on the eve of this campaign, on April 26, that an able young man destined to leave his mark on the story of the 18th Missouri reported to Captain Price for duty with Company K. He was First Lieutenant William Hemstreet, an upstate New Yorker lately transplanted to Chicago. At twenty-seven he had already been a teacher and a newspaperman when the war came. During the summer of 1861 he had been briefly in service as a second lieutenant and aide to General Prentiss at Cairo. However, when Halleck had him commissioned for the

18th Missouri, Hemstreet was serving as a private in the newly formed 57th Illinois. The men would quickly take to Bill Hemstreet, and history would give them no cause to complain of his having joined them.[11]

The 18th Missouri had hardly made camp at Monterey, Tennessee, on April 29, before a new crisis boiled up in the outfit. Lieutenant Colonel John McDermott of the 15th Michigan now came with orders to supersede Price in command of the Missourians. McDermott, a thirty-one-year-old Irish ship's carpenter in civil life, had been taken prisoner by Sterling Price at Lexington while serving as a company commander in the 23d Illinois. General McKean surely intended him to have only temporary command of the 18th Missouri, but again there rose the specter of an invasion by outsiders hunting for positions. After Shiloh there was a large swarm of such officers without commands, and several were already loitering around the regimental area or conducting correspondence with St. Louis. McDermott, though not a displaced officer, would have had a hard time under the best of circumstances.

The circumstances, however, were none too good in this particular case, and McDermott would have himself to blame for aggravating them. For with the unwanted intruder there came his wife Bridget and the chaplain of the 15th Michigan, Father Thomas M. Brady. "Mrs. Lieutenant Colonel" was one of those haughty and officious colonels' ladies, just the type to upset people in a touchy outfit already suspicious that the McDermotts were adventurers. Brady was not particularly offensive; he was simply a Catholic chaplain in a regiment of Protestant Yankees. The situation reeked of trouble.

To be sure, things went smoothly on the surface for a time. Garner was romantically proud of his own Irish ancestry, and for a few weeks he happily matched the three Irish-born newcomers in a wholesale exchange of "blarney, palaver, and taffy. . . ." McDermott was a delight in mealtime banter, and Bridget initially sized up Garner as "a brick of the finest dirt."[12]

Irish solidarity eventually crumbled, but not before McDermott had made a gallant stab at straightening out the regiment's tangled affairs. While in camp at Monterey, McKean asked for regimental elections to choose new occupants for some of the commissioned spaces still vacant and likely to remain vacant unless so filled. McDermott, having completed the six-company reorganization by May 4, called for the elections two days later.

The Missourians responded by closing ranks in no uncertain terms. By acclamation they offered the lieutenant colonelcy to Jake Ault, amply warning McDermott not to get any forward ideas. Price was similarly elevated, to the major's office vacant since Madison Miller had unhorsed Alfred Williams at Benton Barracks. The adjutantcy was offered to a forty-five-year-old South Carolinian in Company F, Private Octavius B. Herriott, and Cudworth's position as quartermaster was confirmed. Since Ault was currently commanding Company A, no replacement was attempted at the time of his election, but the first lieutenant's spot was awarded to First Sergeant Shelton, even then mortally ill in St. Louis. Sergeant Robert H. Gormley was chosen as the other lieutenant in Company A.

That the men had their hearts on their sleeves is evident in other selections. D. W. Pollock was named first lieutenant in Company D, and two of the officers turned out at Benton Barracks were offered places. Jim Allen was tendered the captaincy of Company C, and Joe Pool was asked to return as a first lieutenant in B. The troops dealt kindly with Hemstreet and Donnelly, voting them command of Companies D and F. Sergeant Waite of old Company K was elected captain of Company B, and Fallis was raised by acclamation to the head of E Company.

None of these promotions, however, won the Governor's approval, for the 18th Missouri was rescrambled in June. Coming events, however, cast shadows in the election of four able young enlisted men who, although denied commissions this time, would win them later. Private Joseph M. Stanley, a Sullivan Countian, was eventually to become captain of Company C, and Sergeant Thomas W. Hatfield of Wyreka would attain similar rank in B. Lieutenancies offered in 1862 to Sergeants Daniel Carr of Company D and Phil Lowry of Company I would come to them before the end of the war.[13]

Doing its duty in Colonel John M. Oliver's brigade of the 6th Division, the 18th Missouri changed camps seven times on the twenty-mile march to Corinth. Much to the disappointment of the Missourians, Halleck seemed completely unaware that the main objective under the circumstances was the destruction of Beauregard's army—which was allowed in time to grow to 50,000. If Halleck could pull off a series of chessboard maneuvers and keep flanking Beauregard, so Old Brains reasoned, Corinth would fall like a ripe peach and with a minimum of risk to the Union general. The Confederate commanders soon calculated that the southbound Yankees were under orders to force their way into Mississippi, whereupon the Southern forces took their own time drawing back toward the breastworks around Corinth. The Missourians put in a stint of picket duty ahead of the 6th Division every few days, but most of the time they were involved in Halleck's ditch-digging. No Shiloh for him!

After a month of this snail's-pace march on Corinth, rumors swept the Union lines that Old Bory was ready for a surprise move against the Yankees. McDermott ordered the shovels aside and the muskets loaded. Before long it became clear that Beauregard had no intention of challenging Halleck's bid for Corinth. Instead, his magazine went up with a frightful roar, and his outnumbered troops filed quietly southward to a new base, at Tupelo, sixty miles away.

The battle so long expected "will not be fought hear," Dave Pollock wrote his brother on May 30, the day of Corinth's fall. Wagonmaster Pollock was among the first Missourians to go in, Dave reported, and had learned that the Rebels had "burned a good part of the town" while evacuating. "I think that thay ar geten tired of the fun," the younger Pollock speculated. "If we drive them a nother time or two I think thay will get tired of it. I dont know whare thay will make the next stand. If thay dont make a stand sum plase cloas I think that we will cum back to Mo."

After all that had happened since March, the lieutenant of Company B could be pardoned a little homesickness.[14]

The 18th Missouri and its fellow Volunteers under Halleck "had been through a hard military school," Manning Force later said. "After their experience in fighting, they had practice in the slow advance to Corinth, in picket duty, and field fortification. They had learned something of the business of war and were now ready for campaign, battle, and siege." At the time, the men of the 18th Missouri could take no such constructive view of the matter. Having "emerged from the woods into a vacuum to gaze at nothing," the Missourians, in their chaplain's words, felt that this entire army "ranked well up with the biggest fools on earth. . . . That the result of this siege weakened the confidence of our army in Gen. Halleck as a field commander, goes without saying."[15]

The time had come for D. A. Cudworth to enter into an understanding with state authorities. Notwithstanding his appointment on March 1 as quartermaster, Cud still had no commission, he told the division adjutant on May 29. Attempts to untangle the matter had been made before as well as after Colonel Miller's capture, but so far nothing had come of them. "It is very embarrassing for me to perform the duties devolved upon me unless sustained by proper official papers," he bluntly declared, closing with an even blunter demand for high-level action or "a return to my civil pursuits."

McDermott, Oliver, and McKean in turn pitched into the scrap to keep him. "This is a good man," declared McKean, "and would make an excellent officer." Action came faster than even Cudworth expected, culminating on June 3 with Governor Gamble's heavy black scrawl: "Let Lieut. Cudworth be commissioned to take effect 1st March. . . ." And it was soon done.

On June 6 the regiment marched through forlorn and shabby Corinth to a new camp about a mile southwest of town on the grounds of Corona College. A fortnight later the men were ordered to a new camp in a shady grove two miles farther west, where division headquarters put everyone to work. There was picket duty for some, of course, because the nearest friendly forces were now two miles distant. But many more of the men faced a hot and strenuous summer in the woods preparing fascines and gabions for new entrenchments constituting an inner line of defenses for Corinth. The latter were wooden cribs filled with dirt and rocks stabilizing the outer walls of the new trenches, and the former were bundles of branches and poles laid on top of the gabions. About half of the 18th Missouri marched out to help with the forts, said D. W. Pollock. They put in ten-hour days, but got Saturdays off to rest.

From Lieutenant Pollock's letters it is possible to reconstruct a clear picture of conditions around Corinth that summer. May 31 was payday in the regiment, he reported. "Muny is plenty. . . . and everything dear." It took thirty-five cents to buy a dozen eggs in May, but by late July the going rate was fifty cents. By the end of July potatoes averaged two dollars a bushel, while roasting ears were fifty cents a dozen. Dried apples sold for twenty-five cents a pint, and it usually took half a dollar to get a pound of butter.

But young Pollock had other worries. His father was leaving most of the letter-writing to him, but frequently, said Dave, he couldn't get postage stamps "for love nor money." Moreover, he complained to his sister on June 13, "I have sent a leter every weak to you but dont get one in a mounth." And whenever Isabella did write, she was always telling about the weddings of girls he knew! He grumbled on June 8 that he "was sory to think that girls was all geting married. But I think I can get one down in Mississippi." Homesick or not, Dave told her that he was getting tired of the Corinth neighborhood, where timber was so thick one could hardly "see more than about 100 yards. . . ."[16]

Moving to Corinth had failed to cure the regiment's hard luck with doctors. Hamlin wouldn't come back, and the unfortunate Dr. Houts couldn't. The War Department's temporary solution was to send in a tidal wave of civilian contract surgeons, and one soon arrived for the 18th Missouri. The man who came to take charge just after the regiment camped at Corinth was a lean and seedy character with a wrinkly suit and a battered stovepipe hat. The fellow *might* have been a doctor —the Missourians never really knew. He gulped down the regiment's entire morphine supply and went into a stupor. As soon as he was sufficiently awake to understand what was happening, he was ordered off the regimental grounds by the indignant chaplain and steward.

Soon another such contract surgeon put in an appearance, but this one turned out to be less interested in medicine than in the regimental hospital's liquor supply. He was, in Garner's words, fit only to "lie round drunk and fight flies and graybacks." After a few days of this kind of high living, the newcomer pushed Roscoe and the chaplain beyond their limits, and they shut off his whisky supply for good. The infuriated doctor staggered out into the hot sun to go to Corinth for more liquor, promptly developed nausea, and reeled back into his tent. Early that afternoon he was found dead on his cot. A squad of Missourians dug the late regimental medico a deep trench in the Mississippi soil, laid him in it, placed an inverted horse trough over the corpse, and filled up the ditch. "We sent his little belongings with a kind letter to his wife," Garner related, "and that let us out so far as he was concerned."

The third time was the charm. No regiment can have such luck all the time. Dr. E. Proctor Pierce, a charming and well-dressed young surgeon from Springfield, Massachusetts, soon reached Corinth, and Garner and Torrey found it possible to receive him with open arms. The impeccable and well-recommended New Englander attended to his clinical chores, showed no disposition to the vices so common in the army at that time, and took the best wishes of a large crowd of Missourians with him when time came for him to leave in the autumn of that year.[17]

While the Missourians, in the words of Company G's report for the month of June, "engaged in cutting timber and making fascines and gabions for brest works about two miles west of Corinth and have to hawel our water about three miles," the regiment continued its long wait for the prisoners to return and the recruits to come down from St. Louis to fill out the thinning ranks. Typical of the conditions obtaining in the regiment was that of K Company, thirty of whose sixty-one men were in hospitals, prison camps, or away with other outfits. Ault's own G Company had sixty-two men on its rolls, but twenty-four were in hospitals, fifteen were down South, and four were on detached service—leaving nineteen men on hand for company chores. Company F, so depleted that it was commanded by a duty sergeant, James Kane, had an even dozen men left by the end of June.

During May and the early part of June, Colonel McDermott

was working his way ever more deeply into the bad graces of the 18th Missouri. The irritation and apprehension of the men grew steadily as the ship's carpenter came to look more and more like a permanent fixture. Finally, toward mid-June, the restiveness found reflections in one of the chaplain's sermons. Intending at first to preach a conciliatory sermon on the text, "See that ye fall not out of the way," Garner's rancor so fed on his own eloquence that he found himself issuing a "Corinth Manifesto" warning that the integrity of the 18th Missouri was at stake, that Army Regulations and the authority of the Governor of Missouri could be called into play to repel the gathering tide of job-seekers hungry for the positions emptied by death, wounds, and captivity.

Monday's breakfast at headquarters brought on a climactic passage at arms between McDermott and Garner. Enraged by Garner's apparent characterization of him as a vulture hovering over the graves of Missouri's hallowed dead, McDermott declared that the Missourians would snap to order from then on or he would "orther outh a bathery and blow ivery spalpeen of ye to hell!" "Sir!" roared Garner, "if you orther outh that bathery you better order out an adequate infantry support, for you will have to kill every man of the 18th Missouri before you finish your little job. We have had enough of this sort of thing!"

McDermott angrily turned his back on the vociferous Tennesseean and stalked away. Garner soon found out what he had gone to do, for a provost sergeant came to the chaplain's tent at 9 A.M. and formally placed him under arrest on orders from General Todd, who had lately replaced McKean. That afternoon Major Price took Garner to division headquarters to demand charges and specifications from Todd. The division commander pulled an old yellow envelope out of his pocket and handed it to Garner. "Do you recognize the handwriting?" he wanted to know.

Garner certainly did. For in the ship's carpenter's scrawl he read the penciled charge on the outside of the tattered envelope. "Arrest Chaplain J. M. Garner. He used mutinous language in a sermon last Sabbath. He advised the 18th Mo. to claim their rights under the Regulations, and more of the same sort."

Price and Garner now proceeded to tell the whole story to Todd, who soon learned many surprising things about conditions in the angry regiment whose muster-in he had supervised back at Laclede. "Go back to duty," he said finally. "A man deserves to be arrested for sending such a paper—unsigned at that—to his commanding officer." He then tore the envelope to shreds and dismissed the jubilant Missourians.

Todd had unwittingly given the signal for the 18th Missouri to launch a guerrilla war against the Michigan intruders. Garner no longer engaged them in "blarney, palaver, and taffy." He went out of his way to show studied hostility by ignoring Father Brady's masses and vespers. At mealtime he refused to wait until the Black Irish "counted grace on their rosaries." And the rebellion spread. McDermott had only to step outside his tent to bring on a shower of missiles and catcalls from unidentifiable sources. Wherever "the other chaplain" went he was harassed by derisive noises or sectarian epithets. The climax came one evening when Mrs. McDermott, emerging in all her finery, was greeted by a booming rendition of *Matthew* 6:28-29:

> *Consider the lilies of the field, how they grow;*
> *They toil not, neither do they spin:*
> *And yet I say unto you, that even Solomon*
> *In all his glory was not arrayed like one of these.*

McDermott exploded again, and frantically tried to get the name and rank of the offender. The information was widely known at the time, but it ultimately proved unavailable. Thirty years later the chaplain lifted the veil on the secret enough to say that "a young Scotchman from Putnam County" had delivered the Scriptural serenade. To old veterans, wherever they were, that statement implicated none other than D. W. Pollock.

The visiting Irish finally turned in desperation to Price and Garner. Instead of support, they received advice. To restore order in the 18th Missouri, leave! McDermott bowed to the inevitable, and on June 27 Todd approved his return to the 15th Michigan.[18]

"The men that are here are getting clamorous for home,"

Ault warned Todd in early July. "They hear of the Secesh's depradating in Missouri and I am realy afraid that iff we do not get to go back to protect our homes there will be truble here in camp. They say they can not stand to be here and hear of their famileys being abused and their property taken and destroyed by rebels." This note of uneasiness over the widespread anarchy afflicting many parts of Missouri was to be sounded over and over in coming years, but it never completely undermined the morale of the Missourians. After all, many of them, like Sergeant Lomax, took some comfort in the knowledge that their families at home could "double up" with friends for safety. Back on Lomax's farm outside Laclede, Anna Shanks Lomax and the children frequently hosted Mrs. John F. Pershing and her children, whose father was away working as a sutler with the Union forces. With Mrs. Pershing on those overnight visits was a small boy who in six decades would be accounted the greatest American soldier of his generation.[19]

Meanwhile, Halleck was coming to thank fortune that he had complained to Grant so promptly about the consolidations in the 18th Missouri. Word somehow had drifted back to Governor Gamble that the organization of the regiment was shrinking. Since the Governor had finally become quite bossy about his troops, he was beginning to tax Halleck's staff about it. Finding that the sulky Grant hadn't done a thing about unscrambling the regiment, Halleck went to work in mid-June and settled things the Governor's way: the 18th Missouri became a ten-company regiment again. Departmental Headquarters was now apparently willing to accept Price as regimental commander, for Halleck raised him to major on June 19. But Price, whose ear and skull had been grazed by a Rebel bullet on April 6, was determined by this time to go back to Weston, where Nancy Price, his third child, had arrived scarcely a month before, and where the condition of his young family seemed to demand his presence. His "unconditional and immediate resignation" went into effect on July 7, and Jake Ault commanded the regiment until Christmas.[20]

General Todd again took a personal hand in the affairs of the 18th Missouri. The records of the regiment, he told Halleck on July 5, were "in great confusion. Many of the rolls and papers lost, and others irregular and badly kept. . . . I shall give special attention to the Regiment until its records are perfected, and its reorganization on the proper basis, established."

One aspect of the situation around Corinth was entirely satisfactory to the Missourians, and this was the bill of fare. Apples and peaches abounded, and the thrifty wagonmaster wrote his wife that "I onley wish you had shair. Some times I kil a fat hog and sometimes a fat sheep. . . . So we live on the fat of the land." Roscoe Torrey, he revealed, was now "fat as a hog." D. W. Pollock wrote his sister on July 20 that Corporal Lance Beary, the most inveterate prankster of Company B, was not only fatter but "devilisher then I ever sean him." The Lieutenant was also filling out his uniform, he admitted to his brother in August: At 159 pounds, he was 30 pounds heavier than when he mustered in at Laclede.

It was a busy and eventful summer for the wagonmaster. He made trips almost weekly from Corinth up to Pittsburg Landing to meet steamboats bringing supplies and mail from St. Louis and other points downstream. And General Grant saw to it that wagonmasters and quartermasters got to foraging more and more on the countryside. Tom Pollock explained foraging to his wife in brutally simple terms: "We go in to a farmers fild and tak his corn without [leave or license]. We went in to a fild yesterday of [40 acres] and in less than one oure thare was not one stalk standing. . . ."

Danger was liberally mixed with the work. About the first of August, Pollock got into a shooting scrape while on his way to Pittsburg Landing. Riding ahead of the wagons some distance, he suddenly found himself facing an assault by three armed local civilians. Seeing that "retreat was in vain," the elderly Scot grimly took them on in unequal combat. "I dru my revolver," he explained to Mrs. Pollock, "and dismounted one of them but on the first [shot] I was dismounted myself." One Rebel pistol shot had hit his glasses case, "which I will kep for a memerey of that event." He boldly strode forward and shot his victim a second time, finishing him off, and the other two fled the scene. This was more fight than they had bargained for. Dave proudly explained to his sister Isabella: "Those rebels was let in our lines to by salt and they past for union men whare thare was eny solders and when they got away from the solders and got one man by his self thay thought thay could do as they please. But thay slip up on it," he exulted, "and one of them slip down on that trick. . . ." Strictly Calvinist Thomas Pollock was somewhat shaken at first by the experience of taking a life, and this made it difficult for him to enjoy his reign as a celebrity in the Army of the Tennessee.

Despite all the working and fighting going on around him, the wagonmaster did not forget his duties as husband and father. At the end of August, after William had come of age and joined another regiment back home, the jubilant father urged Mrs. Pollock to "stand up to the los of his compney and his help. . . ." To young Isabella he sent stern counsel to listen to Mother "in all cases" and not keep company with any young man too cowardly "to stand up for his countrey. . . ."[21]

On August 25 there occurred a calamity in D Company. Seven men, venturing beyond the regimental picket line in the woods west of Corinth, were ambushed and captured by Rebel guerrillas. Privates Thomas Brooks, John W. Logsdon, John Leech, Wilson McClure, John W. Thomas, Henry D. Valentine, and David F. Clary were taken prisoner, and the rumor spread through camp that at least six had been summarily shot. It was a typical wartime rumor. All of the men eventually were paroled and exchanged, but most of them were gone until winter.[22]

During June and July several important events set the stage for the next act of the great drama in which the Missourians were involved. The Confederates gave up Memphis on June 6, settling the fate of West Tennessee. Four days later Halleck ordered Buell to march toward Chattanooga with the Army of the Ohio to put an early end to Confederate maltreatment of the loyal Republican mountaineers of East Tennessee. More of Halleck's once-splendid army was soon scattered across the landscape to guard the Memphis & Charleston Railroad, build fortifications, or carry on scouting and picketing.

In midsummer the paths of W. James Morgan and the 18th Missouri converged again, briefly. The first week of August,

Departmental Headquarters came into possession of an extremely peculiar letter. This document, composed by Morgan at Helena, Arkansas, on July 29, had been addressed to Captain Havens, and was an open bid to Havens to jump his current commission in the Marine Brigade and come to Helena to improve his lot in Morgan's projected First Arkansas Mounted Rangers. In the letter, turned over to St. Louis authorities by Havens, Morgan also specified that if First Sergeant John L. Jones and Private Martin Cline could slip away from Company A, he would see that they bettered themselves considerably in his new regiment. Needless to say, Grant's inspector general was soon in a huddle with Jake Ault.

"This man Morgan," Ault caustically declared in a letter to Grant on August 14, "is continually interfering with this command by promising to privates and non-coms and officers. There has been four desertions within the last two weeks of which I have every reason to believe have gone to join his command." Even as Ault was writing, Grant's provost marshal was in Helena firmly explaining to Colonel Morgan that the Army just doesn't do things that way. True, Morgan was having a wretched time of it, for his Arkansas Yankees were deserting almost as fast as he could enlist them, and a leavening of dependable boys from the 18th Missouri would have given some badly needed stability. But this was the end of the road for Morgan. The remnant of his latest Ranger outfit was soon taken away from him and sent up to St. Louis to make up the 2d Arkansas Cavalry, under a different colonel. Morgan had now lost two regiments in less than a year—surely something of a record.[23]

At supper on September 13, the men of Company H were shocked by the sudden death of Private Riley Howe, a thirty-two-year-old native Ohioan lately farming in Sullivan County. A rangy and muscular fellow seemingly in top condition, he collapsed instantly. "He was looking at me," said Chaplain Garner, who had been discussing a real estate transfer with the soldier, "and, at that moment, fell backward, knocking the poles apart with his knees, and scattering the dinner and was dead by the time his shoulders hit the ground."

Dr. Pierce performed an autopsy that night—and concluded that Howe had died of heart failure. Garner, assisting him, was privately scornful of this diagnosis. "Everybody will die of heart failure," he huffed in his reminiscences. The crucial question, unsettled in the chaplain's mind, was whether death stops the heart—or the heart's cessation causes death. "There was a clot in the large vessel above the valve," Garner related, "but that may have been formed by the returning current after life was extinct, and probably did." From this it is easy for even a modern layman to measure the progress in cardiology since September 13, 1862.[24]

Major command changes occurred on both sides in June and July. General Pope was summoned to command Union forces in the East on June 26, after the President had lost faith in McClellan, and Halleck replaced him at the head of the Army of the Mississippi with a burly and magnetic veteran of the early fighting in western Virginia, Major General William S. Rosecrans. Meanwhile, behind Confederate lines, Beauregard hadn't been feeling well recently, nor had Jefferson Davis been feeling cordial toward him. In a move typical of the Confederate President, Beauregard was dismissed on June 27 and replaced by Major General Braxton Bragg, an officer of moderate competence but an old favorite of Davis. Lincoln shortly afterward hastened to match Davis' singularly poor judgment by summoning Halleck to Washington in mid-July to become General-in-Chief of the Armies of the United States.[25]

The ill winds of 1862 did blow some good, at any rate for the Union troops in West Tennessee. The departure of Halleck reopened the stairway to glory for U. S. Grant, who had spent the past three months trying to decide whether to go back to the bottle or the store in Galena—or both. What Grant had to cure now was the effect of Halleck's dispersal of the powerful army that had dug its way across the state line into Mississippi. Later historians have often wondered how quickly the western forces of the Confederacy would have been overwhelmed if Halleck had been called east two months sooner and had left Grant with an undivided force of a hundred thousand lately victorious Volunteers. But history cannot be so greatly concerned over what Grant *might* have been able to do as over what he was in fact able to do. And, for some months to come, the situation bequeathed him by Halleck was so compromised that he was able to do little beyond "holding the line."

Not the least of the problems Halleck left with Grant was the predicament of Buell's army. As he prepared to march, Buell wanted to head speedily for Chattanooga, seize it as a base for operating in the Smokies, and develop the Louisville & Nashville Railroad for his line of communications. This railway ran back through central Tennessee and northward across Kentucky, fairly safe from easy interference by the Rebels. Halleck was of a different mind. The east-to-west Memphis & Charleston line, he insisted, was far more desirable, even though it was extensively damaged and ran close to Confederate territory for a hundred miles and could be harassed at any time by Southern cavalry. While Halleck agreed that Chattanooga was strategically vital, he insisted that Buell repair the tracks of the Memphis & Charleston *as he advanced,* an order which probably tripled the time Buell had to take in reaching Chattanooga, to say nothing of the opportunity that it gave Braxton Bragg to beat him getting there.

If Halleck had been the military strategist he fancied himself, he would not have expected so fatuously that even Bragg would oblige him by waiting for the lightning of Halleck's sluggish sword to strike him at Tupelo. Far from adopting a passive attitude, the Confederate commander determined to seize the initiative and give the Yankees a run for their money. On July 21 his main body slipped out of Tupelo on freight trains bound for Mobile. Leaving Major General Earl Van Dorn to watch Grant in northern Mississippi with a Rebel force that soon exceeded 30,000, Bragg moved by rail from Mobile to Chattanooga with almost 40,000 troops. On July 29 he joined up with the small Confederate garrison at Chattanooga, beating Buell to the East Tennessee town by several weeks.

Seeing Buell's distress, Grant began tapping his own Mississippi strongholds to send help to the Army of the Ohio, which by late July had more than 40 per cent of its manpower guarding or working on the railway. But this support for Buell was nearly too little and too late. Paced by Brigadier General Edmund Kirby Smith's flanking force marching through the Appalachian foothills, Bragg plunged across Tennessee in late August in a daring march on central Kentucky. Buell, remembering

Louisville's importance to his supply lines, turned about and raced northward in a frantic attempt to head Bragg off before he could reach the Ohio River.

Bedlam broke out in Kentucky, Tennessee, and the Ohio Valley. Rebel cavalry raiders commanded by Brigadier Generals Nathan B. Forrest and John Hunt Morgan roamed the vast arena through which the contending armies were heading. Federal cavalry still didn't amount to much in this early stage of the war, and Buell had to send a division of infantry out to chase the cavalry—a task the infantry found rather frustrating. Hardly to Buell's surprise, he met Bragg standing across his path at Munfordville, Kentucky, on September 13. With Bragg now lodged between him and Louisville, would Buell dare to accept the challenge to do battle?

Buell's answer had to be a tentative "no." Too much was at stake, and the odds were not encouraging. Lincoln was now so alarmed that he was calling for 600,000 more volunteers, for conscription if necessary, and for a bold effort to hold the Ohio Valley—and the North's chance for victory. Lee's rampaging Army of Northern Virginia was now at Sharpsburg, Maryland, and the East was holding *its* breath, too. If the Confederacy's high tide had not yet come, it is clear that the Union's was in a far more distant future.

As if by a miraculous intervention of fate, the Confederate wave began to recede in September. Lee was beaten at Sharpsburg, on Antietam Creek, barely escaping a total disaster. Instead of moving on to Louisville, Bragg turned eastward toward Frankfort and linked up with Kirby Smith. This allowed Buell to make base at Louisville after all, and he quickly refitted his haggard army.

On September 30 the Army of the Ohio began its advance on Frankfort, where Bragg was engrossed in the futile charade of inaugurating a Confederate governor. Convinced by now that Kentuckians were growing cool to Rebel pageantry, and fearful that Buell's 58,000 Yankees were bringing trouble, Bragg and Smith began clearing out of Frankfort on October 4. An autumn of hard fighting lay ahead, but Cincinnati and Louisville noted with relief that all of it would probably take place far to the south.[26]

# CHAPTER V

*Corinth*

THE COMING OF SEPTEMBER, 1862, found the Missourians endlessly busy southwest of Corinth. Some of them were detailed from day to day as provost guards in town, but most were still hard at work on the crescent-shaped maze of trenches and redoubts covering the northerly approaches to Corinth. General McKean, who had lately resumed command of the 6th Division, provided horses for some of the men to go along on scouts, expeditions against roving enemy guerrillas. These forays were usually routine and casualties rare, but Sergeant William Brantner of Company A managed to become a statistic on September 1, when he was captured along the Tennessee River northeast of Corinth. Brantner, who was from Laclede, was taken to Centerville, Tennessee, and held until exchanged at Nashville late in October. At Centerville he was treated to a compulsory but memorable interview with one of the great cavalry commanders of modern history, Nathan B. Forrest.[1]

By the time Brantner returned to his outfit, the terrible Battle of Corinth had come and gone. This engagement, decisive for maintenance of the Federal foothold in northern Mississippi, came as the climax of attempts by Union and Confederate commanders to "mousetrap" each other. At the beginning of September, Sterling Price was at Tupelo with 14,000 men, including a large number of Missourians, and General Van Dorn was at Holly Springs with 8,000 Confederates. Facing them were

Rosecrans' 17,000 Federals, around Corinth, supported by Brigadier General Edward O. C. Ord's 10,000 at Bolivar, Tennessee, Hurlbut's 6,000 at Brownsville, Tennessee, and Sherman's 7,000 at Memphis. Grant was also keeping a 6,000-man reserve force concentrated around his headquarters at Jackson, Tennessee. Outnumbered two to one, Van Dorn and Price hoped somehow to spring a nasty surprise on Grant and possibly force him back to Paducah. But Grant's mousetrap had a faster spring.[2]

Early in September the Union commander completed his scheme to destroy Price and prevent his linking up with Van Dorn. Under this plan, Ord should move provocatively down on Iuka, Mississippi, some fifty miles northeast of Tupelo. Price, it was felt, would move energetically northward to counter Ord's lunge, and in so doing would come to grips with Ord around Iuka. As soon as Ord had "fixed" Price at Iuka, Rosecrans, sneaking in from the west, would fall on the surprised Confederates from the flank and rear. Hurlbut, staging out of Memphis, would work toward the Yazoo Delta country to prevent Van Dorn from coming to "Pappy" Price's rescue. After the smoke cleared at Iuka, Van Dorn would be a lonely Rebel indeed.

Even as Grant was laying this plot against the Mississippi forces of the Confederacy, Price and Van Dorn were setting up a gambit of their own. As early as the first days of August, Van Dorn had been sounding Price out on the latter's willingness to unite forces at Holly Springs. As their planning proceeded, they began thinking in terms of concentrating at Holly Springs, working northward on Pocahontas, Tennessee, to scare off Ord's forces around Bolivar, and then swinging east and south to fall suddenly on Rosecrans at Corinth.

"We are looking for a fight hear every day," Lieutenant Pollock wrote his sister on September 15 from his camp. "Let them cum. We are redy for them." The talk in camp was that about 15,000 rebels were heading for Corinth, and were only thirty miles away.[3]

Before the Rebel chieftains could get their plans in motion, the Yankees struck. On September 18, Ord made his daring march on Iuka, with strict orders to dig in and hold Price wherever they collided. Old Pap reacted predictably, and the confrontation took place six miles north of Iuka about sundown that same day. Meanwhile, back at Corinth, everything was in an uproar as Rosecrans went charging forth to close the trap. Leaving McKean with a modest garrison in Corinth, Rosecrans moved eastward on September 18. Jake Ault turned out most of his regiment—without blankets and knapsacks, for the officers thought of the sortie to Iuka as a ritual *coup de grace* to be followed by a triumphal return within a day or two.

Rosecrans bivouacked in a pine woods six miles west of Iuka the first evening out of Corinth. This put him close enough to move quickly into the morrow's fight, but far enough away, so Rosey thought, to avoid tipping Grant's hand. After an early breakfast the next morning, however, Rosecrans discovered what some Missourians already knew—that Pappy Price soldiered any hour of the day or night. Some time before 6:00 A.M., as the Yankees were starting out for Iuka, they discovered a force of skirmishers ahead in the brush along the road. To be on the safe side, Rosecrans deployed into a line of battle and ordered out a reconnaissance. Not a Rebel was found! The line of battle dissolved, and the troops hit the road again.

Price pulled the same trick twice more that morning, and Rosecrans' forces did not reach Iuka itself until noon. Grant wanted them there at 7 A.M. Worse still, Ord, who was to have charged Price as soon as Rosecrans opened fire, never heard the latter's guns when he finally did open up—thanks to a stiff northerly wind. When the 18th Missouri marched past the public square during the noon hour, it was upwind from a conflagration that had begun when someone put the torch to a line of cotton bales set up as a Rebel fortification in the square. Price no longer needed the barricade. He had fled to the south, in the direction of Ripley.

Suddenly Old Rosey had a horrifying thought. Suppose Price veers westward and outruns us to Corinth! Poor McKean wouldn't have a ghost of a chance to hold the place. "About face, counter-march, quick time!" came the cry, and the troops from Corinth took their leave of Iuka with scant ceremony. As Chaplain Garner remembered, the 18th Missouri "made the dust fly for about four miles." Then, since scouts were reporting that Price was definitely headed toward Ripley after all, Rosecrans ordered his sweating troops to halt for the night, without rations.

That evening everyone, including the Missourians, had to get out and forage. They soon learned that foraging the countryside west of Iuka was one poor way to put a banquet together, for the Confederates had stripped the local farms. Garner and Dr. Pierce rode about and finally collected four ears of fresh corn and four pods of blackeyed peas. When they got back to camp one of the boys gave them a leg from a goose "with the hair and flipper" still on it. Dining very plainly on roast goose and the vegetables—without bread, salt, or coffee—the regiment's doctors had little desire to take up foraging as a regular occupation.[4]

Upon the regiment's return to camp southwest of Corinth, it bedded down for a good night's sleep, in familiar and comfortable surroundings. The idyll soon ended, for changes were coming to high places and low. On September 24, Ault was ordered to a new camp two miles north of Corinth, along the Purdy road. He proceeded to the new campsite with Dave Pollock, Stille, and Garner—the only officers he had with him at headquarters. Cudworth was away serving temporarily as Colonel Oliver's brigade quartermaster. The regimental command post was now at its eleventh location since leaving Shiloh.

Rosecrans' staff seemed by now to have written off the 18th Missouri as a combat outfit. There were 376 men present for duty in the regiment, with only 394 names on the rolls altogether. The prisoners were simply not being exchanged at any encouraging rate, and the Adjutant General of Missouri was sending few replacements. On the same day that headquarters was evicted from Camp No. 10, Lieutenant Fallis was ordered out with Companies D, H, and I to mount a permanent guard at Sharp's Tank, a water tank on the Mobile & Ohio Railroad eight miles north of Corinth. Hemstreet took Companies F, G, and K on a similar task sixteen miles north of town, at Jones Mills.[5]

The 18th Missouri was learning, to its great dismay, that it belonged to an army rapidly becoming "half constabulary and half track-repair gang. . . ." On September 24 Grant designated Rosecrans as commander of the Third Division, Department of West Tennessee, and placed the entire Army of the Mississippi in this new jurisdiction along with Ord's troops around Bolivar. Rosecrans, headquartered at Corinth, was made responsible for guarding the Mobile & Ohio southward from Chewalla "so far as the country is occupied by our troops." The 18th Missouri remained in Oliver's brigade of McKean's 6th Division. But, strung out as it now was, the regiment found it nearly hopeless to try keeping respectable records, operating a dependable supply service, or providing adequate hospital care. Ault repeatedly sought Grant's approval to take all or part of the regiment back to Missouri temporarily to recruit itself back up to strength. As the chaplain saw it, "we sank into a state of indifference closely allied to melancholy."[6]

The laws of war governing exchanges and paroles cut two ways in September. Fallis was startled to learn that Privates Hiram Austin and John Hensel, two fellows from St. Joseph who had enlisted in Company I in late 1861, had done so as paroled prisoners. They had been captured during the Battle of the Bales at Lexington the previous September, paroled by Sterling Price, but not yet exchanged. They were now instantly removed from duty in a company which was in no shape to lose them and packed off on a riverboat for St. Louis. It was not possible to use them again until they were legally exchanged early the next year.

This disappointment in Company I was more than counterbalanced on September 26 when Dr. Houts, properly exchanged, "bobbed up in our midst," to report for duty as acting regimental surgeon. Brave and cheerful Sam Houts was given a hero's welcome by every Missourian between Jones Mills and Corinth. Little though Garner would have conceded it, Surgeon Hamlin was "sure enough" ailing. In fact, he had resigned his commission in St. Louis on July 28, "being wholly incapacitated by an illness which has been induced by exposure since in the service. . . ." The ailment was chronic diarrhea and a fever, complications from which Hamlin claimed in 1888 had led to "sciatica of the right side. . . ." Before long, Sam Houts would draw the pay of regimental surgeon, and for two years to come he would head the 18th Missouri's medical services.[7]

Meanwhile, there were ominous developments at Ripley, where Price joined Van Dorn on September 28. President Davis having given him command over Confederate enterprises in northern Mississippi, Van Dorn took charge of a force now grown to 22,000. The Rebel generals hurriedly worked out their plan of attack, and on the morning of September 29 they unveiled their surprise for Grant. Major General Mansfield Lovell's infantry moved out to the north toward Pocahontas with Price's cavalry leading the way. The rest of Van Dorn's force followed, and the Confederates were at Jonesboro, sixteen miles north of Ripley, by the night of September 30.

The next morning, as Lovell was approaching Pocahontas, Rosecrans discovered the trap and gave alarm. Oliver was told to get up to Chewalla "on the double-quick" with the 15th Michigan and the 14th and 18th Wisconsin to get "prepared for whatever they might do." Old Rosey was well served by his intuition, for the Confederate column was indeed about to turn east for its lunge past Chewalla toward Corinth. Oliver's job was to feel out the Rebels east of Pocahontas to see how determined they were to go that way. Meanwhile, the Federal divisions under Brigadier Generals David S. Stanley and Schuyler Hamilton, south of Corinth around Jacinto and Rienzi, were alerted to watch for mischief from that quarter. Brigadier General Thomas A. Davies was ordered to man the arc of new breastworks north of Corinth, with the remainder of McKean's division to reinforce him.

Lovell crossed Davis' Bridge over the Hatchie east of Pocahontas on the morning of October 2, and the entire Confederate force crossed to the east bank in the afternoon, following the bridge's repair. Lovell soon discovered that he was going to have to fight his way to Chewalla, for Oliver was now up in force with his three regiments. Oliver was of course no match for Lovell's division, and after a day of sparring the Southern force pushed into Chewalla, where it spent the night.

These events in the wooded hill country north of Corinth caught up Lieutenant Hemstreet in a tense drama at Jones Mills. The first inkling he had of the impending crisis was the fact "that railroad trains had stopped passing camp. . . ." The last time the troops saw a Mobile & Ohio freight was September 30, but they received no word of explanation for the mysterious stillness that thereafter settled over the tracks.

Well into the night of October 1 a locomotive "came snorting up from Corinth," and Hemstreet heard someone asking the guard, "Where is the commanding officer of this camp?" Emerging from his tent, Hemstreet was handed a note from General Ord: "A large force of the enemy are in your vicinity," Ord wrote. "Keep a good lookout, and fortify the best you can."

Hemstreet thought *that* really sage advice, in as much as his three companies then had one ax and one shovel among them! The messenger, however, promised to go back and hustle up some entrenching tools before morning. While waiting, the Lieutenant went back to his cot and began planning a reception for the Rebels. By morning, when he turned the men out for reveille, Bill Hemstreet knew his course of action exactly.

One work party went down the Corinth wagon road, a few hundred yards south of camp, and laid a massive barricade across it. Another began felling trees on the secondary roads approaching the camp, while a third crew with spades started digging rifle-pits along the hillside commanding the main road. If the Rebels came riding down the road to Corinth, Hemstreet's Missourians were instructed "not to fire a shot until they heard my pistol, and then to fire on the rear of the approaching column so as to hem those in the advance in. . . ." With the 18th Missouri firing behind them, the barricade in front of them, and the side roads obstructed, the visitors would be in for a hot time.

On the afternoon of October 2, a cavalry troop came up from Corinth to scout for Hemstreet, and he had no difficulty finding a place for them in his plans. He put the horsemen to patroling, with orders to beat a retreat up the hill behind his rifle-pits if they found the Confederates approaching. After the 18th Missouri "got through peppering" the Rebels, he explained, the cavalry could "sally out with their sabres."

Sure enough, the scouts came galloping back late in the night of October 2. "Silently every man of us was in his position in the rifle pits," Hemstreet later wrote. The cavalry captain came over to him and announced in a whisper: "They are coming!"

Throughout that moonlit night the men waited on the hillside above Jones Mills for the enemy. "We could hear our hearts beat and our watches tick," Hemstreet recalled. Finally, he "ran up the hill some distance and could distinctly hear the rumble of horses feet; there we waited until daylight and no enemy."

Morning came, and with it the roar of heavy guns to the south. Hemstreet later wrote, "I told the boys I thought a battle was going on at Corinth. But never a word came to our camp from any source."[8]

October 3, the fateful day of Second Corinth, opened clear and "soon grew to be hot," Rosecrans related afterward. Reinforcements had started for Chewalla at daybreak to support Oliver, and Federal forces began moving into the outer works left by Beauregard. Hamilton marched out to positions on the right of the Union line, east of the Mobile & Ohio. Davies took up a center position between the railroads, and McKean rushed up the Memphis & Charleston to hold down the left. Oliver, having fallen back to join McKean, stationed his Michigan and Wisconsin infantry along a ridge some two or three miles from the center of town.

As the morning wore on, the 18th Missouri's staff—still camped two miles north of Corinth with Companies A, B, C, and E—was beginning to get a little anxious. Just a mile to the west was Cane Creek, where that morning Oliver gave the Rebels a furious reception in full view of Ault's camp. The Missourians saw Oliver's men wreck the bridge as they were forced back, and then watched helplessly as the Confederates repaired the structure and began crossing to the south bank. Some of the Missourians were ready to pull out without waiting for orders, but Ault refused to countenance departure until directed to do so. Chaplain Garner never quite got over Jake Ault's book-soldiering at Corinth. Ault, he scoffed, was not a man of "very great fighting proclivities," and he said flatly in 1894 that "the wrong man was in command."

Just when the men were convinced that Rosecrans had forgotten the 18th Missouri, Lieutenant Cudworth suddenly appeared with the word that McKean wanted the Missourians to join him right away over on the left. Ault's problem now was to get away without inviting enemy pursuit or artillery interference. As the men lined up, they expected to "be plugged in the back," as Garner put it. They left several tents standing to conceal their departure, but the chaplain, once astride faithful old Hawk, felt himself "as tall as a shitepoke perched on the top twig of a high cottonwood in the Missouri bottom. . . ."

The men marched a short distance before they came to a slope which took them out of sight of the enemy. They soon found their tongues again and several became very talkative. "Dang their white livers!" crowed Roscoe Torrey. "They knew better than to shoot, and if they had tackled us we would have turned them into crow bait in a jiffy. Whoopee! We are Missourians—we are!"[9]

The battle seemed to be mounting in fury as noon approached. The attackers' main force, between the railroads now, was pressing grimly on toward Corinth, and hot fighting was in progress on the wings. During the noon hour Rosecrans decided to stage a series of phased retirements designed to bring the Rebels face to face with the stronger interior fortifications and the deadly artillery redoubts covering them. Battery Robinet overlooked the Memphis & Charleston a few hundred yards northwest of town. South of the Memphis & Charleston and covering the west side of town were Batteries Williams and Phillips.

While the enemy deployed before the outer works, Ault's four-company detachment tramped into Corinth, made a right turn, and passed to the west of Battery Robinet to join McKean out along the Memphis & Charleston. Around three o'clock the Missourians reported to Oliver along a ridge position protected by artillery on the crest and rifle-pits manned by the 18th Wisconsin. Commanders up and down the ridge constantly shouted at the men to "keep your heads down!" But "Uncle Bill" Smith of Company B, a forty-five-year-old South Carolinian who had enlisted in the 18th Missouri from Putnam County, just had to see. Warned continually, he kept raising up his head to peer at the Johnnies. And then, it happened. A musket ball struck him in the mouth and shattered the upper part of his spinal column. Uncle Bill was raised to his knees by the projectile's force and thrown over on his back. Thereafter he was still, and an orphan girl back home was left to mourn a too-daring father.[10]

Not all wounds led to such sad results. Dan Shelton of

Company E, on duty at headquarters, was hit by a musket ball in the left shoulder and thought himself shot through the chest cavity. Upon closer examination, Dr. Houts was happily able to assure him that the ball was partially spent when it hit, had not even pierced the skin, and would leave the young man with nothing worse than a bruise.[11]

By sundown the withdrawal to the "inner line" was complete, but there was no cessation of firing. And in the midst of it all, with Battery Robinet blazing away behind them, stood the four companies of the 18th Missouri. Jake Ault's men caught in that witches' cauldron were never quite able to forget the "zip! zip! ping! ping! of the balls that struck the earth or trees," nor could they erase from memory the sickening "thud! thud! pom! pom! when they struck our comrades." Confederate light artillery had come in close enough to punish the Union line with grape and canister. Thirty years later, Chaplain Garner told a G. A. R. audience in Springfield, Missouri, that "for a time during the Battle of Corinth, a greater coward than I never disgraced an army. Being in direct and short range of Battery Robinet, I shook like a twig in a rifle, and for a time lost my stirrups and clenched my horse with my knees till I had time to think; then I was ashamed . . . and glad that the darkness concealed me from my comrades."[12]

Around 4 P.M. Rosecrans noticed that Van Dorn was shifting position. Severely punished by the batteries of the inner works, the attacker was obviously preparing to go around the guns next time. His line was extending across the Purdy road to the east, lookouts reported, and Rosecrans immediately decided that a new artillery redoubt should be erected there if time permitted. His chief engineer hurriedly rounded up about 1,500 men from the crowds of displaced Negroes in town and hired them to go to work with picks and shovels on what became Battery Powell. The former slaves worked all night on the new fortification, and by 3 A.M. enough artillery had been wheeled into the redoubt to make Van Dorn's next move a perilous gamble. One admiring witness, Sergeant Lomax, told his son after the battle that "I attribute much of our success at Corinth to the labours of the Black Men. . . ."[13]

Van Dorn decided after dark to wait until Saturday morning

before going in for the kill. It is quite certain that he had a more cheerful view of the morrow's prospects than circumstances could justify. "We have driven the enemy from every position," he had crowed over the telegraph wires to Richmond that evening. "The enemy are huddled together about the town; some are on the extreme left, trying to hold their position." Prisoners, five of whom Lomax himself apprehended at the close of the second day's fighting, told their captors that the general impression among the Confederates at nightfall October 3 was that they were probably going to "march into Corinth . . . without opposition." All of the hustle-and-bustle connected with Rosecrans' preparations to *hold* Corinth was misinterpreted by the Confederate leadership as preparations to evacuate.[14]

A supremely confident Earl Van Dorn thus bedded his troops down for the night in a great semicircle in the low, rolling ridges north and west of Corinth. The area was covered by oaks, hickories, and considerable underbrush, but there were occasional clearings left by Confederates who had wintered at Corinth in 1861-62 and had gotten their fuel from the densely wooded countryside. In the attacking force there was a large body of Confederate Missourians, doing their part to give the battle a strong Missouri flavor. Besides a St. Louis artillery battery, there were two regiments of cavalry and five of infantry from the state. Ex-Governor Price was there commanding the center of Van Dorn's line. And Brigadier General John S. Bowen's brigade, over on the Confederate right facing College Hill, contained the 1st Missouri Infantry, under Colonel Francis M. Cockrell, afterward privileged to represent Missouri in the U.S. Senate for thirty years.

Meanwhile, inside Union lines, General Rosecrans was boldly readying his army for the decisive struggle with Van Dorn. Hurlbut and Ord were rumored to be on the way in to take the pressure off, but no definite word came during the day or the anxious night hours that followed. After dark, Rosecrans called in the division commanders for a council of war, and it was not long before the dispositions for the coming day's battle were arranged. Stanley was ordered now to hold that part of the line centered on Battery Robinet, while Davies extended across the Purdy road to rest his right wing under the new "Negro battery." Brigadier General Charles S. Hamilton would guard the right flank of the army and hold part of his division in reserve. McKean's division, most shaken up bearing the brunt of Friday's fighting, was to dig in on College Hill, a few hundred yards across Elam Creek to the southwest of town. The 18th Missouri was represented on College Hill by its headquarters detachment and little else.

It was after 3 A.M. when Rosey lay down for a little sleep, and little indeed was he to get. In fact, very few in the Union ranks were really trying for a night's rest. Around 3:30 or so Cudworth offered to make coffee while things were quiet, "as we might not have an opportunity later on." Soon afterward the Missourians began lighting small fires—though Rosecrans had strictly forbidden it—and putting their kettles on to boil. They never finished their brew.

About 4:30 A.M. the Confederate artillery suddenly opened fire, irrevocably shattering the pre-dawn calm. That opening gun must have made an indelible impression on those who heard it. A Southern author, narrating the battle a generation later, distinctly recaptured in print his memory of that sharp flash separating the still of night from the carnage of the coming day. One of Tom Pollock's trusty teamsters, Henry Sawyer of Grundy County, had the recollection of the blast very much on his mind when interviewed by a Trenton reporter more than seventy-three years afterward.

Forgetting the coffee, Ault's party took to its heels. One six-pounder tore the drummer boy of a neighboring regiment to pieces and went on to kill a team of mules and cripple a sutler. The earth fairly shook for over an hour between College Hill and the Tishomingo Hotel. Taking refuge at the latter place, Houts and Garner rushed up the stairs just as a cannon ball smashed through the west side of the hotel, streaked down the long hall, crashed out the east window, and landed in a government warehouse next door.[15]

Van Dorn's plans for the day included an assault before 7 A.M. by Brigadier General Louis Hébert's division, across the cleared ground and against the trenches protecting Batteries Powell and Robinet. The discovery of Rosecrans' Negro battery in the early morning light, together with Robinet's devastating responses, must have shaken the Rebel general considerably. We do not know what effect it had on Hébert, but when time came for him to charge he was hunting for a doctor and begging Van Dorn to relieve him of command. Brigadier General Martin E. Green was finally hustled in to replace Hébert, but he was completely cold on the situation and unable to mount the attack for another two hours.

After Green's attack started, Brigadier General Dabney H. Maury moved against Battery Robinet in a frantic attempt to silence the guns in this strongest position of the defending line. By 10 A.M. the combined weight of Maury and Green was against Davies and Stanley, and the fate of Corinth was squarely on the line of battle. The 18th Missouri was not even pretending to function as a regiment that day; its men were fed into the line by squads wherever McKean needed firepower. Ault, Garner, Houts, and Cudworth spent the day as useless bystanders.

Between 10 and 11 A.M. an ominous situation developed. Fighting was so close in on both Robinet and Powell that they were several times neutralized. Then, a little after eleven, as hand-to-hand fighting on the parapets of Robinet was in progress, Green overran Battery Powell and drove its gunners away. The Rebel breakthrough was at hand.

The attackers streamed down the hill into Corinth, no longer annoyed by the two batteries. They rushed down the streets, passing Rosecrans' headquarters and battling their way house by house to the steps of the Tishomingo. The loss of life was heavy well into the noon hour, and rumors swept College Hill that most of the Union artillery and wagons had been lost. Rosecrans wasn't expecting to be whipped, however. There was one fresh brigade in the west part of town, and the General flung it against the Confederates, who had been badly scattered.

The tide was surely turning during that noon-hour confrontation in the streets of Corinth. The Rebels, falling back to the north, discovered that the Yankees had restored their control of Battery Robinet and were pouring terrific enfilading fire into the retreating mass. Battery Powell soon went into business again, too, showering shells into the midst of enemy soldiers trying to seize it. Missouri's very logical Colonel Cockrell was of the opinion by 1 P.M. that Corinth "was no place for us. . . ."

During the noon hour Bowen's brigade of Missourians and Mississippians made an attempt to "feel out" McKean on College Hill, but Bowen soon drew such a withering blast from Batteries Phillips and Williams that he pulled his regiments back into the woods west of Robinet to "await orders."

Some time before 2 P.M. the orders came—to retreat! The desperate Battle of Second Corinth was over.[16]

The beaten Confederates spent the night at Chewalla unmolested by Rosecrans. At Jackson, General Grant may have been jubilant over Rosecrans' success in beating off the Rebels, but he could not understand Van Dorn's clean getaway. Rosey, however, knew the condition of his army, and his only orders for Saturday evening were to cook five days' rations, get some sleep, and prepare for an early breakfast on Sunday.

Ault's headquarters crew had hardly finished breakfast that morning of October 5 when a familiar figure came riding up on a mule. "Great God—it's Hemstreet!" someone yelled, as if the leader at Jones Mills had risen from a grave. The whole staff, said Hemstreet, "thought, of course, all the outposts were gobbled up. All of Vandorn's army had passed between us and Corinth to the assault and had retreated back again without our seeing one of them."

On that morning Brigadier General James B. McPherson led two brigades up the Chewalla road in search of Van Dorn. One brigade, under Colonel Oliver, was made up of the 18th Missouri as well as the 21st Missouri and the 16th and 17th Wisconsin. Later in the day a second expedition went up a parallel road, but it got tangled up with McPherson's column at an intersection. By the time it reached Chewalla, the "pursuing force" was ready for bivouac. And Van Dorn had been gone all day.

Despite his head start, Van Dorn was having his anxieties. That morning Maury's startled division found Ord at the other end of Davis' Bridge, and after a sharp encounter Maury lost his foothold on the west bank. This was grave news indeed to Van Dorn. Ord then tried to cross over and pursue Maury eastward from the bridge, only to be wounded and repulsed. Hurlbut, taking command at the Hatchie, nailed down the Davis'

Bridge crossing, and the Confederates, caught between Hurl-but's line and Rosecrans' approaching pursuit force, were near panic. Late in the afternoon of October 5, Van Dorn found an unguarded crossing of the Hatchie six miles south of the Davis crossing, and by sundown the Rebels had made good their escape after all. On October 8 the anguished Grant called off the search for the vanished men in gray.

The following day Wagonmaster Pollock found a chance to write home about the latest excitement. He would have written sooner, he said, "but I did not know whair David was. I herd from him last night, 50 miles aheaid pursuing the eneme." Uncle Tom could not estimate the dead he had seen, for "thay lay all over. In one plais I counted 20 that lay tuching others and I heard of 30 in another. . . ."[17]

Nearly a thousand men died at Corinth on those two October days. About 4,500 were wounded, 2,500 captured—mostly Confederates in the latter category. Among the 401 Union dead Garner counted "Uncle Bill" Smith of Company B; Private William Martin of C, a sixteen-year-old lad from Platte County who had joined up at Benton Barracks; and Private George T. Crump, of E Company, a Sullivan County farmer from near Pennville. Besides Dan Shelton, four others were wounded. The most serious case was that of Private Charles H. McCully, a Pennville boy in Company E, whose wound resulted from a musket ball's "entering immediately over the outer side of the left elbow joint. . . ." Houts extracted the ball from about the middle of the forearm but was unable to prevent "complete ankylosis" of the elbow. McCully was discharged for the disability at Jefferson Barracks two months later. Private James Lewis of Company B, though reported by Wagonmaster Pollock as "killed," soon returned to duty after minor wounds healed. Private Francis M. Young, another of Pennville's "originals" in Jake Clark's Company E, and Private John Brison of C Company, a Grundy County farmer in his middle thirties, were also among the wounded.[18]

Even if Chaplain Garner thought Captain Ault the wrong man to command the 18th Missouri, higher commanders at Corinth spoke well of him after the battle. Colonel Oliver included Ault in grateful acknowledgment of the "prompt obedience to all orders" shown by regimental commanders engaged in the pursuit of Van Dorn, and General McKean singled him out for his "good conduct on the field" as well as "previous industry in perfecting the discipline" of the regiment.[19]

On the day that the pursuit of Van Dorn ended, there came the electrifying news that Buell had fought it out with Braxton Bragg at Perryville, Kentucky—and was driving Bragg back into Middle Tennessee. The Ohio Valley was safe at last, but Bragg's Army of Tennessee was still intact. Northern newsmen and politicians were howling for Bragg's blood, but Buell, instead of pushing directly after the Rebels, moved on to the Louisville & Nashville line and headed for Nashville. The net effect was to stir up a new chorus chanting for his scalp, and it was not long before President Lincoln was noticeably wavering in the face of anti-Buell opinion. Buell had the "slows," his detractors complained. Give the Army of the Ohio to a leader with enough vitality to take it places, they insisted. Then, too, Secretary Stanton didn't rate Buell enough of a Republican Radical, and Old Brains disliked any officer who could stay in the headlines. On October 30 Buell's delighted enemies learned that Lincoln had deposed him four days earlier and handed the Army of the Ohio to Rosecrans.

General Grant now disbanded Rosecrans' Army of the Mississippi and announced that all troops in the former Third Division of the Department of West Tennessee were henceforth to be known as the District of Corinth. The combative Rosecrans, now widely regarded as a coming man on the national scene, left behind a farewell message to his troops, congratulating them upon the victorious outcome of the fighting at Corinth, which had decided the "possession of West Tennessee, and perhaps the fate of operations in Kentucky."

The troops wished Rosecrans well as he left for Nashville, for, as Brigadier General James A. Garfield said afterward, they had learned "to love every bone in his body." Ben Guffey probably voiced the sentiments of the 18th Missouri when he spoke of Rosecrans as "almost a Washington for he has been seen on his knees praying in secret and he told his men not to fear the bullets but put their trust in God and this kind of advice is very strange from an officer for they generally cuss and such."[20]

# CHAPTER VI

# Convalescence at Chewalla

U. S. GRANT now turned his thoughts to a new adversary and a new objective. Command of the Confederates in Mississippi had passed to Lieutenant General John C. Pemberton, as a disgusted Jeff Davis relegated Van Dorn to "chief of cavalry" under Pemberton. The great prize held by Pemberton, as far as Grant was concerned, was the key Mississippi River bastion of Vicksburg. To take the city and clear the mighty river to the Gulf became Grant's major obsession in the second winter of the war. Eight months to the day after the victory at Corinth, Union flags would fly in Vicksburg. But before that day came, the Union commander would experience a progression of frustrations, local successes, and finally a drawn-out siege of the city itself.[1]

Rosecrans took over the Army of the Ohio, redesignated the XIV Corps, on October 30, 1862. Thirty miles to the southeast of Nashville, around Murfreesboro, lay Bragg's force, covering the city's northwesterly approaches with strong lines on both sides of sluggish little Stone's River. The expectation in Washington was that Rosecrans would soon move on Bragg's works to fight the decisive battle for Middle Tennessee. The General was sure of one thing, though: he ought not to move on Murfreesboro until the railway was repaired and his army fully equipped for the coming campaign. Throughout November and much of December, the Federals tried to repair the Louisville & Nashville line north of Nashville faster than Bragg's cavalry raiders could wreck it. Rosey's cavalry was no match for Forrest and Morgan, however, and in time Rosecrans would "take arms against a sea of troubles" rather than wait for peace and quiet to come to his rear areas.[2]

For two months after the Battle of Corinth, the colors of the 18th Missouri flew at Jake Ault's tent on College Hill. The six companies on the railway north of town remained there, but in mid-October Companies A, B, C, and E moved up to Chewalla, just across the Tennessee line about twelve miles north of Corinth. Chewalla was a station on the Memphis & Charleston, but since the road was out of order there seemed little for the Missourians to do beyond outpost duty in this heavily wooded landscape.

Most of the 18th Missouri was facing its first Deep South winter. One night in late October there was nearly an inch of snow, and Lieutenant Pollock was grateful to learn from local folk that "it is as much snow as ever fawls at one time. . . ." It was gone in less than a day, and Indian summer returned by the beginning of November. The trees remained green, and not until November 19 did the Lieutenant notice any leaves falling. He had forgotten all about the October snowfall when he wrote his sister a week before Christmas that there had not been "any snow down hear yet." Some nights there had been freezing, but David had "not seen any ice this winter yet a half inch thick."[3]

During those autumn months Captain Ault moved heaven and earth to get his troops back to Missouri. In fact, late in October he went to St. Louis to put on pressure in person. Governor Gamble, much impressed, asked Grant on October 29 to send the regiment home to recruit and reorganize, and Ault returned to camp early in November with the good news that the men could go back as soon as the Department of the Missouri could send down another regiment to take their place. Hopes soon dimmed, for Dave Pollock told his sister on November 14 with great exasperation: "I will tell you something about gowing back to Missouri. We have been gowing back for the past four months but hant got thare yett. . . ." All that now remained, he understood, was for Ault to see Grant, but since the latter had gone off with the troops advancing on Vicksburg, seeing him was easier imagined than done. Pollock gave up on

November 19, wearily conceding that "the horse is dead now." On December 11 Grant's reply went out to the Governor. Retention of the 18th Missouri at Chewalla and on the railroad he described as a "dire necessity."[4]

On November 11 the District of Corinth passed under the command of Brigadier General Grenville M. Dodge, a thirty-two-year-old officer with whom the 18th Missouri was to be deeply involved for most of the following two years. An engineer in private life, the Massachusetts-born Dodge had attended Norwich Military Academy. After locating at Council Bluffs, Iowa, in the 1850's, he had become prominent as a founder of the Baldwin & Dodge Bank there and as a surveyor of potential railway routes west of the Missouri River. With the coming of the war, he had organized and commanded the 4th Iowa Infantry, and at the Battle of Pea Ridge he had won a brigadier's star for his work in saving the day for General Curtis. He now came to Corinth fresh from a successful tour of duty in central Kentucky, where he had overcome not only the roads and railways but also the Rebel guerrillas. Similar work awaited him at Corinth.[5]

The captives of Shiloh were still missing, and it appeared that they would be many more months in securing their freedom to serve again. General Curtis, who had taken over the newly constituted Department of the Missouri, decided to do something about the officer shortage in the 18th Missouri in mid-October. Why not, he reasoned, send back to the regiment the officers who had been relieved at Benton Barracks in March?

This would certainly be a politic gesture, and before the end of October most of the "old officers" were back with their jubilant friends and neighbors. Captain Sherman reappeared as head of Company C, and Company F welcomed back Captain Bell. Lieutenant Allen came back with Sherman, and Lieutenants Harry and Pool were restored to Bell's Company. Lieutenant Estes took command of Company K, and Lieutenant Douglas joined him in November, following a lengthy recuperation from his hip wound, first in the hospital at Cincinnati and then with the provost guards there. Others rejoining their companies after seven months of exile were Lieutenants Morgan of A and Morris of B.[6]

Several officers thought they had better move to secure their positions early in December. Addressing Governor Gamble directly, Bell reminded him that "I am one of the officers relieved from duty by Col. Madison Miller in March last, and now having been put on duty, I am entitled to a commission, never having received any." Lieutenant Pool's case, wrote Bell, "is the same as my own." Ault, aware that the regiment still had no field-grade officers, decided to make a strenuous bid for the majorship. He appealed to General Dodge on December 5 for promotion to the vacancy. Colonel Moses M. Bane, commanding the Third Brigade, to which the 18th Missouri was now assigned, gave his blessing the same day. Dodge forwarded the recommendation, with his own approval, to Gamble at St. Louis.[7]

Ault and Bell should have saved their ink. The status of the regiment's officers had already become the subject of a furious high-level quarrel. Colonel Miller, although on parole and working mainly on the question of prisoner-exchanges, was in St. Louis that fall and winter—and quite ready to counsel the Governor, the State Adjutant General, and Department Headquarters on the subject of who should and should not hold commissions in his regiment. Curtis' wholesale return of the exiles was a red flag to Miller, and it underscored the nagging fact that the 18th Missouri had "two sets of officers"—the legitimacy of each set being a matter of much controversy.

"I hope your Excellency will try and arrange the affair of the 18th Regiment so that one of the sets of officers can be mustered out," the Adjutant General of Missouri wrote Gamble on the occasion of the Governor's departure for Washington in November to attend to militia matters with Secretary Stanton. If "this unfortunate complication" was not soon settled, this officer said, it would "be the source of more annoyance to these Head Quarters, than a little. . . ." Two days later the same officer notified Grant that he regarded the entire slate of appointments made at Benton Barracks "in accordance with a roster furnished by Colonel Miller by order of Act. Gov. Hall" as "void and of no effect." Colonel B. L. E. Bonneville, Commissary of Musters for the Department of the Missouri, had lately notified the Governor that his only instructions had been to muster the "original officers of the Regiment."

To say the least, it was a legal mess of the first magnitude, and the longer politicians and soldiers tampered with it the worse it became. Gamble and Stanton sat down together on November 24, and the upshot was the Secretary's suggestion that the Governor simply wipe the slate clean, start over again, and commission a brand-new set of officers. This "simple" solution still had the germs of complication in it, but at least the War Department and the State of Missouri would be working together on the problem henceforth.

Well-intentioned though the governor and the secretary were, there soon occurred an ugly complication. The organization of the ten-company line regiment of 1862 called for thirty-eight commissioned officers. As of December 1, 1862, the 18th Missouri was in need of commissions for twenty-two more to bring it up to strength. State authorities, however, instead of commissioning just enough to fill up the known vacancies, commissioned thirty-two more on December 4! Far too many men now held commissions or appointments. Obviously, someone was going to have to give when all this became evident to startled officials in Corinth.[8]

Although many of the officers thus commissioned on Gamble's new initiative were still on parole and could not yet go south, a few could take their places at once. Some of them were in their new jobs even before December. Dr. Houts was commissioned regimental surgeon on December 4, but he had been serving as such since his return in September. First Sergeant Abijah M. Everest, a twenty-three-year-old St. Louis carpenter, became Company E's new second lieutenant.

But the biggest news of all came on December 25, when Ault found himself playing host to a new regimental commander and a new adjutant. Lieutenant Colonel Charles S. Sheldon appeared with First Lieutenant Edwin J. Conway, fresh from St. Louis. Sheldon revealed that more new officers were on the way, including Colonel Miller's only son, Morton Elwood, who was slated to take over in Company E, the late Captain Clark's original outfit.

Sheldon also explained that a vigorous recruiting program was getting under way. Henry Pagin, a physician lately practicing in Putnam County, had been commissioned a first lieutenant, assigned to Company C but detailed to head a recruiting office in St. Louis. Serving with Pagin was a new second lieutenant, Rollin B. Gray, a cousin of the Adjutant General of the Enrolled Missouri Militia and a veteran of a year's experience in New York's State Militia.

When Sheldon reached Corinth with the news that the state authorities had recommissioned *all* the captive officers as well as a spate of new ones, it would have been good military management to call in the mustering officers immediately and weed out the surplus personnel. That is what ultimately happened, but for the time being, all mustering officers were south of Holly Springs with General Grant. The first offensive against Vicksburg was nearly three weeks old; moreover, as Sheldon described things, "Van Dorn was between us [and] Grant, tearing up things generally."[9]

By this time the holidays were upon the Missourians, and their pockets were about empty. The last payday had been August 31, and nobody had had any word as to when the back pay would be produced. With mild sarcasm, David Pollock told his sister on December 18 that "We ar gowing to have a tenn cent spree on Christmas if we can rase the munney." Isabella heard no more from her brother for nearly a month. Then came the news that Dave's Christmas party, such as it was, had come a day late. "My self and six or seven others went out and had a vary nice party for the South" in a spacious farm home three miles from Chewalla. The Missourians "dansed until daylight" with a dozen "rebel girls," he reported. On the way back to camp the morning of December 27, however, the Lieutenant "stept on a peas of iron and run it in my foot." For some time the foot was so swollen that he couldn't get his boot on, but by mid-January the injured foot was almost back to normal.[10]

Sheldon's arrival was the final proof that Colonel Pratt no longer had a job in the regiment. It is difficult to believe that Pratt's heart was really set on staying, for he won election as Secretary of the Senate of Missouri on December 29 and thereafter made it very plain to military officials in St. Louis that he wanted to give full attention to General Assembly business. The Missourians thus had to take a long hard look at the blond-bearded young man sent down to command them until Miller's return. A twenty-three-year-old native of Morristown, New Jersey, Sheldon had been a regular army enlisted man in the Mounted Rifles for two years prior to the war. In 1861 he had entered the Missouri State Militia and moved rapidly up the ranks. He was a cited veteran of Boonville and Wilson's Creek, and had commanded a battery of the 1st Missouri Light Artillery at Shiloh and Corinth. The handsome young colonel now came directly to the 18th Missouri from the position of an assistant adjutant general of the Missouri State Militia under Schofield. Few men of the 18th Missouri ever knew that the Colonel's real name was Charles Sheldon *Sargeant*. Sheldon maintained later that he had reversed his name "to prevent discharge at the instance of his family. . . ."[11]

After visiting his scattered troops, Sheldon concluded that they were "men strong of limb, and equally strong of heart, self-reliant and bold. Such troops, when fully disciplined, make perfect soldiers; for surprises affect them little, and panics—not at all." Somewhat guardedly, D. W. Pollock wrote his sister that the 18th Missouri had gotten "a new Lieut. Colonel for a Christmas gift. He is a very nice man but the Boys would have been beter pleased to have got Lieut Col Prat back again." Thus he invoked the unvarying rule, in effect since Weston: "Better one of our own than the best of strangers." To the men of the regiment, Sheldon's good feeling was in time to become mutual. In his old age Joe Brown remembered the boy colonel as "a soldier in every respect. . . . He always said, 'Come boys, let us do,' and it was done."[12]

Shortly after arriving in Corinth, Sheldon went to Dodge and arranged to move the regimental headquarters from College Hill out to Chewalla. Here the command post would be in closer touch with all the companies. Sheldon found Companies A, B, C, and E camped in tents in a flat open field just to the north of the railroad station, the only house in the little clearing. Captain Sherman had been commanding Post Chewalla, but Sheldon assumed that post himself at the end of December. None of the Missourians thought this much of a place to camp. "Chewalla," said Garner, "was a name without a place. The land was a white, postoaky, crawfishy flat." Sheldon studied the hills overlooking the camp and easily surmised the unpleasant situation that would result if the Rebels appeared there in the near future.

Convinced that the camp was "wrongly located for either defense or observation," Sheldon galloped back to Corinth and persuaded Dodge that it should be moved to higher ground at once. A half-mile or so to the south of the Chewalla station was a long east-west ridge, covered with hickories and large white oaks, and dotted with worn out cotton patches. Along the ridge ran a road from Corinth to Pocahontas. On that ridge, and at the intersection of the wagon road to Kossuth, Mississippi, Sheldon proposed to build a permanent post for his men.

By mid-January a new Post Chewalla was taking shape, a twenty-one-acre clearing surrounded by a split-log stockade ten feet high. An inner fort—including a palisade and a guardhouse—was also built. Each of the four companies put up a log barracks for itself. By February the railroad station itself had been moved up into the camp as "Colonel's Quarters." Visiting generals invariably pronounced Camp Sheldon the finest in the District of Corinth.

"This work diverted our mind from the horrors of war," Garner wrote in 1894, "and revived memories of the past when many of us started life in cabins no better than these." Each such barrack-cabin consisted of log walls, with a clapboard roof laid on rib-poles and held in place with weight-poles. Some of the men chinked up cracks in the walls and roof with mud and sticks, while others built chimneys with mud bricks and jambs. Anticipating the time when the other six companies might come in off the railroad, the men at Chewalla built barracks to accommodate the entire regiment.

An old road entered from the southeast corner and passed through the fort to its northwest corner, and it was at these points that gates were built. With a realistic eye to the future, Sheldon fenced off a little burying-ground outside the northwest gate.

The men of the 18th Missouri soon began to "feel very much at home," as Garner expressed it,

And this change . . . showed the wisdom and care of
our young commander, and inspired the regiment with a
feeling of self-respect that men long out of doors, as we had
been, had, in a measure, permitted to lapse into careless
indifference. Our arms were soon polished to brightness,
our hair trimmed, our shoes blacked and clothes brushed,
and we actually appeared at "Dress Parade" in white
gloves. The moral effect . . . was wonderful. We felt like
men.

There appears to have been another welcome dimension to
the security provided by Post Chewalla: Immunity from the
prying and poking of Grant's inspector-general. Although
agents from this office swarmed over the other posts from
Memphis to Corinth, there survive none of their reports, if any
were ever made, on the doings at Chewalla. Then, as today, the
neighborhood lay far back in the brush and away from well-
traveled thoroughfares.

The new post was situated on the north edge of country
heavily wooded with oak and hickory, through which innumer-
able streams ran. Thick canebrakes were much in evidence
along various of the creeks, most of which were tributary to the
Tuscumbia as it wound westward toward its confluence with
the Hatchie, just above Pocahontas. In the rain-drenched forests
of the Tennessee-Mississippi border there were now very few
bridges still standing, thanks to Van Dorn's horsemen or the
regional guerrilla bands.

Scouting became a major function of the 18th Missouri—
and would be as long as it stayed at Chewalla. And foraging
was also to be an important activity. By the beginning of January one scouting party after another was passing the Tuscumbia looking for Rebels and unprotected foodstuffs. The woods
south of the Tuscumbia looked like a promised land for foragers.
Axmen of the regiment soon put a bridge over the river south
of the fort, and Wagonmaster Pollock made ready to bring in the
bounty of this rebellious land.

However, all was not gold that glittered, as the scouts
soon found. The woods were swarming with Rebel guerrillas,
particularly Colonel W. C. Falkner's Mississippi Partisan Rangers, whose scouts were looking for vigorous recruits—and care-

less Yankees. There were also Captain T. W. Ham's battalion, as well as roving bands under Jim Morphis, Solomon Street, and several more obscure figures. The largesse of the countryside was there, all right, but the Missourians would have to use much circumspection as they went about their harvesting.

Until January of 1863 the Missourians had pestered the local farmers very little. True, Lieutenant Pollock as early as October had developed a three-man squad "that I call jay-hockers," a team that always managed to "fetch what they go after" to enrich the diet of Company B. The jayhockers were used only as a last resort, let it be said, and they were sent out only after Mississippi farm folk had refused to make a peaceful exchange of their produce and poultry for Yankee currency.

But in late December, things began to change. Thanks to Forrest's rampages, the District of Corinth went on half-rations, officially at least. However, the men ate better on half-rations than before, reported Dave Pollock to his brother. Of course, it was a little hard on the farmers' hogs and corn. Tongue in cheek, he told his sister in January that "the Citizens grumbels at the way we butcher for them." Chaplain Garner put it another way. His fine saddle horse Hawk, raised by Major Williams, had originally been a "pious horse," Garner insisted. But, during one of the chaplain's visits with Fallis at Sharp's Tank, Hawk lapsed into "wrong ways." Said Garner: "He could often be seen coming to camp with a bag of sweet potatoes or turnips, and occasionally a dead hog or a string of chickens on his back, without being able to tell where he got them." However, once the stuff was in camp, Garner conceded, "it was thought unwise to let it spoil."[13]

The terrible specter of Bedford Forrest haunted West Tennessee in the last weeks of December. Thanks to his widespread destruction of railway and telegraph lines, Union forces in Mississippi were completely out of touch with the North until New Year's Eve. One of Forrest's parties in mid-December even swept past Lieutenant Fallis' stockade at Sharp's Tank to burn railway tracks within six miles of Corinth.

With thirty men under his command at the time, Fallis could only watch helplessly as the raiders ripped up fence rails, heaped them on the tracks, and set them afire. A courier rode to Corinth through the woods west of the Mobile & Ohio, but he was unable to get a relief force out in time to catch the intruders. As the Rebels made ready to leave, they sent an officer to the stockade to arrange Fallis' surrender.

Little Dick wasn't having any of that. "I have three hundred brave Missourians with me," he lectured the emissary. "If you want us come and take us—if you can." Fearful that they wouldn't have time to subdue so large a gang of Missourians, the Confederates disappeared northward into the woods.

Chaplain Garner, visiting Sharp's Tank at the time, saw the whole exchange. And he couldn't resist chiding Fallis for his little tactical lie. "I have preached to you, prayed for you in tears," Garner scolded him, tongue in cheek. "And, this day, you are the biggest little liar I ever saw on the stand. You know you don't have three hundred men."

"Well," Fallis impishly explained, "each man in Company I counts as ten."[14]

Sheldon, a peacetime "horse soldier," got Dodge's consent to mount Companies A, B, C, and E for scouting work along the Cypress, Hatchie, and Tuscumbia. Foraging parties under Cudworth now fanned out in all directions to confiscate horses. Sheldon was not impressed by the initial results of the roundup, though, for in his opinion "such an array of broken-winded, sore-backed, one-eyed and stiff-jointed horses had never been seen in the service before. . . ." Relying on his Missourians' native appreciation for horseflesh, Sheldon kept sending them back for more until the four companies could be reasonably well mounted.

By early January the scouting forays of the 18th Missouri were increasingly effective and frequent. About forty of the enlisted prisoners of Shiloh returned during January to lend their numbers to the regiment's resurgent strength. A company of Union cavalry raised in northern Mississippi joined the men to show them how to get at the guerrillas hidden in the forested landscape around Chewalla. "They knew every hog path," Sheldon gratefully remembered thirty years afterward.

One of the thorniest problems faced by the mounted Missourians was that of the bushwhacker, the cowardly rifleman who lurked in the trees along roads to pick off Federal horsemen. Sheldon, however, soon came up with an answer to this problem. Picked men of the regiment, wearing mixed uniforms and carrying sawed-off shotguns, were sent ahead through suspected localities to warn the natives that "The Yankees are coming!" It worked. Invariably the bushwhackers would unmask themselves by emerging from the woods or houses to question their "comrades" about the oncoming Yankees. Of course, the Missourians promptly took such trusting souls into custody on the spot. "You'uns don't fight fair," one crestfallen bushwhacker pouted. "You'uns look like we'uns."[15]

Commissary Sergeant Lomax left Chewalla in mid-December to start raising a company of "Alabama Cavalry" among local youths. Department Headquarters promised him a captaincy in the projected 1st Alabama if he raised the troop. "I think I shall succeed in a short time," Lomax wrote his son, "though loyal men here are scarce." Lomax was counting on the widespread discouragement that he sensed in the disloyal population. As he left, Lomax petitioned Sheldon to relieve him of his sergeantcy effective New Year's Day, 1863.

Lomax's recruiting drive met with a serious, though temporary, disaster in January. Having developed what must have been a severe respiratory ailment while living in the clammy flats near the railroad, he made arrangements to recuperate under the care of a family living a quarter-mile northeast of the station. Lomax understood that his hosts were loyalists, but they celebrated his recovery on January 29 by calling in a squad of Rebel guerrillas to take him prisoner. This did not leave Sheldon without a commissary sergeant, however, for he had already given the job to Quartermaster Sergeant Rummell and called up Corporal William Kuemmel, a twenty-year-old German watchmaker in Company H, to take over as Quartermaster Sergeant. Five months of captivity now faced Lomax.[16]

During these winter months at Chewalla, Sheldon put the men through the only intensive training program they had ever known. "The regiment attended strictly to company and battalion drill," Sheldon wrote of the experience, "and became so proficient in all military duties as to fully merit the praises given it, when reviewed by several prominent officers who came out

from Corinth. . . ." Of course, many grumbled that the training
schedule was severe and unnecessary, but Sheldon reminded
D. W. Pollock in 1890 that there was a strict connection between
the Chewalla regimen and the "high character of efficiency and
courage" shown later by the men in central Tennessee and
northern Georgia.[17]

Events in eastern Tennessee and northern Mississippi in
late December and early January both frustrated and encouraged Federal hopes. On December 26 Rosecrans moved against
Bragg's positions around Murfreesboro, and three days later
opened the Battle of Stone's River on the northwest approaches
to the city. This bloody struggle ended in a draw on January 3,
1863, but Rosey held the field. Bragg pulled back some thirty
miles, taking up new lines covering Tullahoma. Thereafter,
the opposing commanders sought to harass each other by cavalry forays against rear areas.

Grant's move on Vicksburg ground to a halt on December
20, when Van Dorn wrecked the new Union supply depot at
Holly Springs. With a sigh of disgust, Grant pulled back to lines
around Grand Junction, Tennessee, during the last days of
December. Thanks to Forrest's inconsiderate tampering with
telegraph lines, discussed earlier in this chapter, Grant was
unable to get any word of outside developments from December 19 until near the end of the month. And when he did get
wire communications restored, he learned that Sherman had
assaulted Vicksburg from the north on December 29, and had
been beaten off by Rebel gunners manning the bluffs. The
Department commander now reasoned that he should pool
forces with Sherman, perhaps at Memphis, and go forth from
there to slay the Vicksburg dragon. To that end, the combined
forces of Grant and Sherman began shipping down the Mississippi from Memphis in February to strike again at stubborn
Vicksburg from the west, or opposite, side of the river.

Meanwhile, life continued to be increasingly hazardous
around Chewalla, especially for Missourians on picket duty in
the woods around the Post. On January 13 two men of Company
C, Corporal Vincent C. Bruce and Private James T. Riley, fell
into the hands of Falkner's lurking partisans. Three weeks later,
on the Tuscumbia, the same fate befell Corporal Charles Gra-

bosch and Privates Dan Shelton, Dave Riggins, and Joe Thompson, all of Company E. After shifting around from Columbus to Jackson and other prison stockades, they wound up at Libby prison in Richmond late in the summer before making it back to the company in September. None came back to the outfit any fonder of the Johnnies, it should be said.

Indeed, February of 1863 was a kind of emotional watershed for the Missourians. Events in the guerrilla war were rousing them to anger, for the first time. One senses this in David Pollock's letters, into which an air of malevolence now crept whenever he mentioned Confederates. On February 19, 1863, he wrote his brother that "the dammed guerrillas will slip around and pick [off] our pickets every once in a while. Thay have taking some 15 or 17 men from this Regt in the past six weeks." One outrage had occurred early in February, when Privates Andrew Morgan and David Harding of Company B fell into Rebel hands. The two, however, were back in camp on parole in less than a week.

Then, on February 10, Companies B and C flushed a covey of Rebels from a camp three miles out of Chewalla. This was a band of partisans under a mysterious Captain Smith which had infested the Tuscumbia canebrakes for weeks. Pollock pointed out that "the dammed devels was con sealed behind some rocks and as our boys went a long the road they fired on them and killed one. . . . " The Missourians fired back, he said, and the guerrillas "then runn like dam coards and throad thare gunnes and over coats as thay went." Colonel Sheldon, however, crowed in a dispatch to General Dodge that his men had "Chased the enemy for three miles, but they beat us running." The 18th Missouri winged at least two of the guerrillas, Pollock was certain. Private William Hammel of Company C, a thirty-eight-year-old German cigarmaker who had enlisted the previous November and collected a hundred-dollar bounty as a substitute, was the Missourian who lost his life in this fray.[18]

An entirely different type of peril also manifested itself during the Chewalla days. Word came from General Dodge one late-winter day that a notorious guerrilla leader had managed to smuggle a barrel of sugar and a sack of coffee into his home on the Tuscumbia below the Post. Dodge's orders: "Get the goods."

Sheldon, anxious to get the guerrilla as well as his goods, rode out of Post Chewalla at once with Adjutant Conway and a foraging party. When they reached the commodious woodland estate they found the owner "away on business," but the sugar and coffee were there, just as Dodge's informant had said. The lady of the house and two teen-age daughters were at home.

Icily informing the women of his purpose, Sheldon, in his own words, "confiscated the family ox cart, and loading up the sugar and coffee, we were about to depart, amid the weeping and pleading of the mother and one of the girls. The other was of a different stamp. Her black eyes snapped and her frame fairly trembled with passion as she said, 'Mother, I'm ashamed of you to cry and beg of a Yankee! I'd die before I'd do it!' "

Lieutenant Conway, in whose warm Irish heart the flame of chivalry was easily kindled, hastened over to Sheldon and asked permission to share some of the loot with the victims. Sheldon agreed, and Conway fetched up two waterbuckets and filled them with sugar and coffee beans. Gallantly the adjutant marched up the steep flight of steps to the front porch, accompanied by an orderly bearing the peace offerings to the Confederate ladies.

Before the mother could brush the tears from her eyes to thank Conway, the black-eyed girl lunged onto the porch from the front door. "We won't have your nasty old sugar!" the Rebel vixen screamed at Conway, giving him a shove that caught him unawares. Down the steps tumbled the adjutant, the orderly, the sugar, and the coffee. The colonel and his foragers laughed uproariously at Conway's discomfiture, but the laughter stopped as the girl followed Conway down the steps with a butcher knife!

As Sheldon recreated it in his memoirs, it was a historic moment, "the only time, during my connection with the regiment, that I ever knew any portion of it to retreat from the foe with or without orders. . . ."

Although Madison Miller did not return to the regiment until February 24, 1863, his coming cast a long shadow. On January 20 the Department of the Tennessee released the "old officers" from the service. For the second time in a year "Miller's Ax" fell on Captains Sherman and Bell, as well as Lieutenants Morgan, Morris, Pool, Harry, Estes, and Allen. Dave Pollock observed testily on February 2 that "Lieut. Morris left for home to day. He has been musterd out of service and Colonel Miller is sending sum mor of the Saint Louis stock. . . ." Colonel Pratt and Lieutenant Douglas, of Company K, were also discharged, the latter to become surgeon of the 2d U.S. Cavalry. Allen proved to be the only exile who couldn't get the old outfit out of his system. On March 17, 1864, he would return to Company C, as a private. Later, during the siege of Atlanta, they would make Jim Allen a corporal, and in that rank he would finish the war with his old comrades of 1861.

In the reorganization, a few officers won promotions. To replace the twice-banished Sherman and Bell, Lieutenant Donnelly of Company E stepped into the captaincy of Company C, and Lieutenant Minter moved up from K to the captaincy of F. Coddington transferred from Company G to the first lieutenancy in F Company, and McEfee likewise improved his lot by moving from E to I. Fred Partenheimer remained in H Company as the new first lieutenant, but it took Captain Dolman nearly a year to locate a second lieutenant who would come and muster after being appointed. Another new officer in the regiment was K Company's Second Lieutenant William M. Edgar, lately a miller in Columbia, Illinois, who was destined to rise rapidly in the next three years.[19]

Along with the second exile of the old officers, the regiment experienced a wave of resignations. Three of the original captains departed in as many months. On February 5 Captain Mikesell, during a bout with pneumonia and lumbago, decided not to return to the regiment, and Lieutenant McEfee took charge of Company I. On March 6 Captain Durman, recuperating from kidney trouble at home in Laclede, resigned, and Lieutenant Dan Hudson of B Company later received the captaincy of Company A. Jacob Ault, giving "the death of my wife" as his official reason, finally made good on frequent threats to quit, and on April 14 Bill Hemstreet took command of Company G. Lieutenant Dodge also resigned at the same time, but with much less ceremony. Company A had not seen him since Shiloh, although he had been recommissioned in December along with Captain Durman and the other prisoners.

However, on April 28, 1863, the Adjutant General of Missouri received an irate letter from a citizen on South Seventh Street in St. Louis, who claimed to have found Dodge's wallet, containing his commission and a letter of resignation, at the scene of a house burglary. Dodge was soon dropped from the rolls, and it took Captain Hudson a long time to get a replacement.[20]

Nearly all the prisoners of Shiloh were back by the end of February. Colonel Miller led a delegation of returning officers up to Chewalla on February 24, and the men turned out to welcome him, Wyckoff, Dolman, Stults, Breeman, Henry Godfrey, Hudson, and Partenheimer. Four days later a newcomer, young Captain Elwood Miller, arrived to take command of Company E. He had lately resigned as a second lieutenant in the 1st Missouri Light Artillery, a source for several other officers in the 18th Missouri over the past year. Down to an effective strength of only 347 at the end of December, the 18th Missouri boasted 482 men on duty at the close of February.[21]

The uncertainty of the mail service bedeviled the boys at Chewalla all winter. The widespread destructiveness of Forrest's raid in December shut off the mail entirely for three weeks. So undependable was the service that Lieutenant Pollock in February sent a letter home with a discharged soldier, William Viers, who had been wounded at Shiloh. He also sent $134 from his latest payday with Viers, for a friend was a more trustworthy conveyance than the mail. Yet, when the system was operating normally, it seldom took more than ten days for a letter mailed in northern Missouri to be delivered at Chewalla. A remark by Ben Guffey in April of 1863 suggests that the mail was getting through in better shape by then. Ben had missed out in the latest mail call, but "nearly all the Putnam Boys got letters."[22]

Colonel Miller had returned to find his regiment busily training and scouting under Sheldon's effective direction. While drills and lectures went on in the Post, mounted scouting parties ranged far and wide along the Hatchie, Tuscumbia, and Cypress. It seemed that the more Grant was preoccupied with Vicksburg, the more rambunctious the guerrillas became north of Corinth. And the 18th Missouri was in the middle of a region seething with partisan activities. Indeed, Grenville Dodge's District of Corinth was proving to be "the most exposed force" in XVI Corps, General Hurlbut wrote Grant early that spring. Captain Ham's irregular band was prowling along the Hatchie, and the Missourians traded shots with him day after day in February and March.[23]

In order to round out Sheldon's program of drill and in-doctrination, Miller prevailed on General Dodge to relieve Companies D, F, G, H, I, and K from guarding the M & O water tanks and bridges and permit all six companies to rejoin the regiment at Chewalla. Dodge consenting, they were pulled off the railroad between March 6 and 10. Scouting went on as usual for the four mounted companies, since guerrilla activity wasn't letting up. On March 9 Sheldon called on Captains Don-nelly and Miller to bring their companies on a reconnaissace toward Kossuth. They made their swing without incident, and checked back in at the Post on March 11. But a week later, south of the Tuscumbia, the same men under Sheldon ran into the combined forces of Falkner and Ham. A lot of lead was fired in this wild encounter—"a bout five hundred shots" was Dave Pollock's estimate. Sheldon's column chased the fleeing Rebels some thirteen miles to the southwest before they scattered in the woods. The Missourians' only casualty was Private John T. German, of Company C, captured during the fracas. Captain Miller had better luck yet along the Cypress at the end of March. He brought back five horses that a guerrilla unit had abandoned in its haste to elude him.[24]

It was about this time that a civilian from St. Louis appeared at Chewalla with an unusual request. He was John Edgar, brother of the late adjutant, on his way to Pittsburg Landing to get William's remains for final burial in St. Louis. His hope was that Colonel Miller would order out a detachment to help him, but Miller explained that the guerrillas were "con-testing every inch of the ground" between Chewalla and Shiloh. The Colonel just couldn't think that emptying one grave justified his risking the filling of several new ones.

Edgar, thrown upon his own resources, hired a notorious bushwhacker by the name of Gullet to take a team and wagon and accompany him to the battlefield. If there was "honor among bushwhackers," as young Edgar hoped, Gullet could get him through safely. But how were they to find William's grave?

Garner was "it." He was the only officer who knew where to look—or could be spared to go. Madison Miller was willing to permit the chaplain to leave, but not to *order* him. Agreeing to go "at my own risk and on my own responsibility," Garner won from Gullet a promise of safe-conduct. It was one of the hazards of his profession, Garner figured, "and I went. The little mules, an old lumber wagon, with a coffin box and spade and three men made the outfit and procession through a vast region that had been swept by advancing and retreating armies. . . ."

Garner asked of their guide one special favor, that he drive past the old campsite in the woods by the Spain field. "My heart melted when we paused at the little red mounds near our color line, under which rested five or six of the 18th Missouri," Garner later wrote. "Mr. Edgar plied me with questions to my great annoyance. I wanted to commune with the Past in silence."

That night they stayed with a large farm family, the only one still living at the site of the battle. The farmhouse was a small log hut with no bedding for guests, and as a result the night was "principally passed in conversation." Day finally broke, and after breakfasting on rancid bacon, cornbread, and well water, the party was off to do its sad work. His crew rather short-handed, Edgar hired the farmer to come along, "against the protest of his wife, who was very superstitious in such matters. . . ."

In the summer of 1894 Garner composed a detailed description of the exhumation. It is difficult to find modern biologists or physiologists who agree with the clinical details of his story, but inasmuch as Garner was a "man of the cloth" and made his story a matter of public record, it seems best for the historian to leave his words to stand unparaphrased as a literary monument to the emotionalism of our Civil War generation:

>The earth was wet and sticky, which made the red clay very heavy. The grave was four feet in depth, and, at a short distance from the top, the water filled each opening made with the spade before another batch could be taken out. By working the ends alternately, we got on for a time, but before we were half down, the water and the dirt became so mixed that we had to resort to bailing. This we

did with an old tin coffee pot, with the bottom partly un-soldered, which we found where our hospital stood. The condition and smallness of this vessel rendered our progress tedious and tiresome. It was truly a sloppy affair out of which we came with our clothes much soiled. Finally we reached the corpse, and by bailing and scraping, removed all the water and mud we could. Then we pulled the top of the box off and unfolded the blankets from his face. This revealed the head floating in water, nearly clear, which had, by some means, been confined within the box. His hair floated like a halo, in the water, and was changed from black to flaxen color and was tight in the scalp. The mustache, same color, was firmly set in his lip. After removing all the water we could, I raised the little handkerchief that I placed on that face nearly a year before. At this stage of the proceeding, John Edgar, who was peering into the grave with intense interest, exclaimed, "That's William!" and sank to the earth, weeping. It was a horrifying spectacle to present to a man who had parted with his brother, full of health and hope, so recently.

We expected to find the remains decomposed and offensive, but such was not the case. William looked as nat-ural as when he took his place in the line of battle—only his face was whiter. Anyone who knew him in life would have readily recognized him in his bed of slush. The whole man was there, except the least bit at the tip of his nose. I think his brain had passed out through the track of the ball that killed him, for I noticed that his head floated as would an empty body.

The next step was to raise the body to the surface. We were afraid to disturb the blankets, for we thought the body would fall to pieces. One trace chain from Gullet's harness was run under him at the shoulders and another at the knees, and there was work for all of us. The water in his clothes and that in the blankets with the mud attached, made the mass very heavy. It was all that we could do to raise him. The chains were hard on our hands. I was a very strong man, and never exerted my strength more than at that moment. Finally we got that horrible looking mess to the surface, when we opened the blankets and waited a spell for the water to drain. . . . His clothes were not soiled but seemed of a deeper hue than when we buried him. His shoes were clean and sound, but his spurs quite rusty. When we removed the blankets there was no unpleasant odor, the flesh was tough—seemed to have turned to fiber and every joint was supple.

The loyal mother had sent a large Federal flag for a winding sheet, but in his condition we could not use it. It was clear that an undertaker would have to be consulted before final interment. So when he drained off, we put him in the coffin and loaded him into the wagon, and started for Purdy, reaching there late in the evening. Lodged that night with an artillery squad, and next day left Edgar. . . .[25]

On the brighter side of things, the Missourians at Chewalla made ready to greet their second spring in Dixie. Since every company planned a garden to supplement its rations, Colonel Miller ordered a twenty-dollar shipment of garden seeds from St. Louis. At headquarters, Garner wrote, "we had a nice line of vegetables, and we enjoyed them very much." The chaplain made himself a little garden, dividing it into eight parts. The center represented Eleanor Hayes Garner, "who, in the innocence and purity of girlhood, left an affluent home and loving parents to follow the fortunes of . . . a penniless itinerant Methodist preacher" in the 1840's. The other parts of the garden symbolized the seven Garner children, then at home with their mother back at Laclede. The entire camp, Ben Guffey wrote to Caroline on April 18, "is covered with nice shade trees which is a great accommodation for the weather is getting hot and the timber is nice and green but it is nothing to compare with the nice green prairie in old Missouri which I long to see. . . ."[26]

The late spring months brought exciting developments in the big picture of the war. Grant's main forces, boring their way down the west bank of the Mississippi, crossed to the east side of the river on April 30. McClernand, commanding the leading corps, clashed with the Confederate defenders at Port Gibson the next day and put them to rout. On May 3 Grand Gulf was yielded to the hard-driving Yankees, and it seemed only a matter of days before they should enter Jackson and Vicksburg.

During the first week of May the Army of the Potomac, now under Major General (Fighting Joe) Hooker, came to grips with Lee's Army of Northern Virginia in the woods around Chancellorsville. Washington and Richmond alike held their

breath at the onset of the titanic struggle so crucial to them both.
By May 3 it was evident that Hooker had suffered a major
reverse, despite the almost miraculous escape of his outflanked
and outmaneuvered army. Though the Rebels won the day, they
had suffered an irreparable moral disaster in the fatal wounding of their near-legendary Stonewall Jackson.

As the eastern armies regrouped for their next moves,
Grant's forward elements under McPherson tramped into Jackson and hoisted the "Old Flag" over the capitol of Jeff Davis'
home state. Just as Napoleon had boldly thrust himself between
the Austrians and Sardinians in 1796, so now Grant had inter-
posed his expedition between Pemberton's Vicksburg garrison
and General Joseph E. Johnston's growing force east of Jackson.
Would Grant have the Corsican's luck?

Apparently so. Pemberton, advancing cautiously, ran into
the Federals at Champion's Hill on May 16 and suffered a sharp
repulse. He withdrew a few miles, only to be routed again on
the Big Black River the following day. Thereafter, Pemberton
had but one desire—to be back in the trenches and redans of
Vicksburg. On May 18 the vital city on the Mississippi was completely invested by the Union forces.

The month of May also brought a change of command at
St. Louis, where General Curtis' radical policy and iron hand
had brought him to a parting of the ways with Governor
Gamble. President Lincoln, after much soul-searching, relieved
Curtis on May 24 and gave the Department of the Missouri to
Schofield, the only available general well known to Missourians
and acceptable to the Governor.[27]

CHAPTER VII

# The Summer the Tide Turned

JIM CODDINGTON was officer of the guard on May 1, 1863, an
eventful day in the developing guerrilla campaign around
Chewalla. It had been standard procedure for the officer of the
guard to lead a mounted detail on a rapid scout around the Post
each morning, and Coddington was under orders to move out as
soon as guard mount was completed on this particular Friday.

With a picked force of eight mounted musketeers, Coddington rode out to the west. After cantering along some four
miles, the party came to a farmhouse, standing at the foot of a
high hill. The Missourians galloped up the road leading over
the hill—only to run into an ambush. "Uncle Jim" Morphis and
eighteen bushwhackers were hiding along both sides of the
road behind logs. Someone shouted "Whoa!" to the oncoming
boys in blue, and a volley of bullets ripped into their midst with
no other warning. Private George E. Pickett of Company E, a
Sullivan County farm boy not yet twenty, toppled from his
horse, slain instantly. John Brison of Company C, the same who
had been wounded at Corinth, now fell against Coddington with
four bullets in his head, his blood and brains splattering over
the lieutenant's tunic and hat. Two others were wounded seriously, and the four riders in the rear beat a retreat to Chewalla,
said Coddington, "as quickly as horse flesh could cover the
distance."

"I was riding a young four-year-old horse," Coddington

wrote, "but could not manage him, and he jumped right in among the rebels, and they grabbed him by the bits. . . ." His revolver blazing, Coddington sprang from the saddle and bent two of the bushwhackers' shotguns to the ground as he came down. Bud Morphis, brother of Uncle Jim, crumpled in mortal agony as his comrades disarmed the ferocious Yankee lieutenant.

Ben Guffey viewed this catastrophe as "the Colonel's fault for not sending out more men for he knew the demons was thick in the brush. . . ." The deaths of Brison and Pickett were much lamented, he told his wife on May 5. "They faught nobly at Shilow and Corinth. Then was murdered by the demons of Tennessee." The half-dozen Rebels in Colonel Miller's guardhouse faced a harrowing time, Ben hinted ominously, if Coddington failed to make it safely back, "for the Lieut. is well thout of by all the boys and officers."

Houts, Garner, and Torrey went out with a heavily armed guard to reclaim the casualties. "We found them under a burning sun," Garner recorded, "weltering in their blood, just as they fell, with green flies buzzing about them. . . ." Brison and Pickett lay "stiff in death, hurled into eternity without a moment's warning." The two wounded men were there, one with severe gunshot wounds in his head, the other "horribly mangled" in the chest and arms. Since little could be done for the dead or wounded in the blazing sun, they were loaded in the ambulance to return to the Post.

The recovery party made it back to the northwest gate at 1:00 P.M. Guffey recalled that Colonel Miller "went to the ambulance and looked at them and the tears rolled down his face in grait drops. . . ." Miller now bitterly resolved to visit grim retribution on all suspected Rebels within his reach. Scouting parties would start out immediately, he announced, and they would go with orders to destroy the house of every suspected Rebel sympathizer in the region.

"Boys," he told the first demolition party, "most of you can't write, and when you have to sign your name they ask you to make your mark. That's what I am asking you to do now—make your mark, and *make it big!*" Given the circumstances, they couldn't mistake his meaning.

It was Platte City all over again. The Missourians rode

far and wide, putting the torch to farmhouses that *might* have
harbored Rebel guerrillas. Lieutenant Pollock told his sister on
May 4 that his men had seen few Rebels on their latest foray,
"but we found plenty of thare houses and plenty of them went
in to ashes. We burnt more houses on the trip than I have seen
burnt be four in the Army." The practice was to give the victim
ten minutes to get his "plunder" out of the house. After ten
minutes, the Missourians would ruthlessly "stick the match" to
the house and its contents. "I have heard nothing today," Guffey
said on May 5, "but the boys mawking the women begging the
men not to burn their houses." Admitting that all this might
look vicious from a distance, he insisted that "it seems hard to
have innosent men murdered." Dave Pollock figured by May 14
that the people around Chewalla had learned a lesson that "will
do them for a while." As he told the folks at home, it simply
wouldn't do to "lay be hind logs and fire on the old *18th* Mo. She
has been out in the field to long for that."

The two wounded men, meanwhile, were taken to cots
under a big oak tree, and a bizarre drama ensued, as related by
Garner:

> One poor man had five lead balls in one side of his head.
> The balls were slightly scattered and had broken the outer
> table of the skull, and were bedded in the spongy septum
> between the two tables of that part of the head, producing
> complete paralysis. The poor fellow could not move nor
> speak. His eyes were closed, and aside from a little warmth,
> a very sluggish feeble pulse, and slow heavy breathing,
> there was no evidence of life.
> The first thing was to get the balls out of our com-
> rade's head. . . . First we removed the hair from the
> wounded side of his head; then made a cross cut through
> the scalp, over the center of the wound and down to the
> skull. This gave us four pointed flaps which we dissected
> —or skinned, back out of the way.

Dr. Houts then turned to his mallet and chisel, the use of which
would open room around the embedded pellets to make way for
the forceps or gouge to extract them. The mallet was a small
thing about the size of a baby's rattle, and scarcely heavier.

Houts put his chisel in place and swung with the mallet. Missing his chisel entirely, he whacked a knuckle instead.

"Damn the man that made such a thing as that!" Houts barked, flinging the mallet to the ground and raising the knuckle to his mouth. "It wouldn't crack a hazel nut." Garner was tempted to laugh, but he didn't dare, under the grave circumstances at the cot.

Houts drew his pocket knife, finally, and slashed down a hickory sapling. He whittled out a section of it, flattened one side, and made himself a mallet he could trust. And, competent surgeon that Sam Houts was, he soon finished the operation.

"This was done under a tree," Garner reminds us, "on a cot without tick or pillow, nor did we use chloroform." The patient "neither flinched nor groaned. I sat by him about an hour and kept my eyes right on his face and my finger on his pulse. . . ." In a little while the soldier opened his eyes, raised his hand to his head, and asked, "Where's Coddington and the boys?" Then he went on to tell Garner "where and how it all occurred."

Meanwhile the bushwhackers had scurried across the Tuscumbia with their prisoner. After reaching the west bank on horseback, Coddington removed his hat and tunic and scrubbed away the ghastly reminders of Brison's death. Looking up at the two men guarding him, he was amazed to discover that he knew them. Wash Cox and Josh Owens, supposed Union men living not far from Chewalla, had been frequent visitors at the Post and beneficiaries of the regiment's generosity. "Not ten days before they murdered my boys," Coddington subsequently wrote, "[we] had chipped in and bought them a barrel of flour. . . ." Such was war—guerrilla style—on the Mississippi border in 1863.

His grisly cleaning chore done, Coddington and the party galloped off to a hiding place "fifty miles away," he guessed. He never knew where they took him, but he did recall afterward that "they kept me in a creek bottom for four days where mosquitoes almost butchered me." There he was interviewed by a young man named Ooten who had a proposition to offer.

"You have my father in your camp in irons," Ooten told Coddington. "Now, sir, if you can secure his release, we will let you go." Would Coddington write Colonel Miller a note?

He would indeed! And within the hour young Ooten was off with the letter on a wild night's ride to his mother's home, closer to the Post. Mrs. Ooten saddled up and appeared at Post Chewalla the next morning, and the question of Coddington's liberation was soon on Madison Miller's desk.

The Colonel easily decided that the cause of the Federal Union would be well served by trading the elderly Ooten for the young and vigorous Coddington. Miller wrote a terse note to Morphis agreeing to the trade and throwing in two other impounded Rebels for good measure. Big Hill, west of Chewalla on the Memphis & Charleston, was appointed as the place of exchange, and the time was set for sundown Friday, May 8. The exchange went off smoothly, and the happy Missourians had their lieutenant back, after a little more than a week's captivity. The Rebels never got their hands on Coddington again; twice was enough.

The chaplain branded the deal as disgraceful. He darkly hinted that Miller was fearful of Dodge's wrath and was anxious to cover up the Coddington affair. "Why this night prowling and these negotiations under rebel petticoats," he later asked, "if the decks were clear and we were leading the right kind of life? Had we got into a snare out of which we were willing to get with all possible haste and with the least possible publicity? . . . Talk about that 'host of untrained, undisciplined men —men who recognized no authority, no control save their own free will'! That was at Weston—this was at Chewalla, under the guiding hand of a military expert especially appointed to round us up or pitch us out in disgrace. Scat!"

The following Monday there came news from Pocahontas that Lieutenant Colonel Jesse J. Phillips' 9th Illinois Mounted Infantry had captured two men believed to have been in the gang that bushwhacked Coddington's patrol. The lieutenant quickly put two and two together. Cox and Owens! Sure that they had been left behind to attend the dying younger Morphis, Coddington felt that the captives had to be those two.

"Colonel," he pleaded, "let me take a squad and go to Pocahontas."

"What for?" asked Miller, puzzled at first.

"For the reason that I believe those two fellows . . . are

none other than Wash Cox and Josh Owens, the men whom our boys fed; and they in turn, murdered the same boys who befriended them."

"Well, Lieutenant, suppose it is them," Miller countered. "What would *you* do with them?"

"If it is them," Coddington growled, "and I get them away from Phillips, I'm going to blow their brains out and throw them into the Hatchie."

"All right," the Colonel chuckled. "Take fifteen men and go get 'em."

Within an hour Coddington was off for Pocahontas with Sergeant Joe Stanley and a squad of men from Company C. When they reported in to Pocahontas, Coddington asked to see the men in the stockade. Sure enough, there were Cox and Owens. After hearing the indignant visitor's story, Phillips said with brutal simplicity: "All right, take 'em and hang 'em."

Denied horses for the occasion, Owens and Cox "walked or rather ran" ahead of the scowling troop of Missourians. Stanley and Coddington, each having chosen his victim, could hardly wait to get to the place of execution.

Anticipation, as it had in so many other cases, outran realization. After several miles, Coddington, deep in his own troubled thoughts, felt a hand on his shoulder. It was Joe Stanley.

"Lieutenant," he said quietly and a bit apologetically, "I can't go through with killing that fellow."

"You know, Stanley," the lieutenant responded, "it's the same way here."

"But wouldn't I love to meet those birds in battle!" breathed Stanley.

"You bet," Coddington answered him.

Owens and Cox thus escaped Jim Coddington's vengeance. So far as he ever knew, the two ingrates lived to a ripe and little-deserved old age. Department Headquarters soon took them away to Nashville, and nothing more was ever heard of them at Chewalla.[1]

The men of the 18th Missouri had many other things to talk about during those humid spring days. Lieutenant Conway resigned as adjutant on April 23, preferring to become a second lieutenant in the 4th U.S. Cavalry rather than hold a first lieutenancy in the 18th Missouri. Henry Godfrey of Company C stepped up to replace Conway. Then, an Ayersville boy in Company G deserted on May 8 and was promptly killed trying to rob a civilian near Chewalla. Two other fellows deserted and joined the guerrillas about the same time. Then Private Thomas M. Wiley, a farm boy from Carroll County, wound up a prisoner of war while on picket duty on May 25. There were few dull moments.[2]

General Dodge's concern over the Memphis & Charleston led him to disperse the 18th Missouri a bit during May. Wyck-off's Company D was ordered out to guard the Cypress Creek bridge some ten miles west of Chewalla on May 17, and Stults was told to station Company B ten days later at the Tuscumbia crossing of that railway.

Early June brought more changes in the regiment. On June 2 Joe Stille resigned the first lieutenancy of Company D. Hampered by the deformed arm which would never regain its old usefulness, he chose to go home to Unionville to practice medicine during the few short years remaining to him. Bill Edgar, later to don his gold bars in Company D, replaced Stille, just as the last of the Shiloh captives were arriving from St. Louis. Among them was Joe Brown, who stepped into the first sergeantcy of Company F as a result of an act of chivalry he never forgot. Jim Kane, since recovering from his wounds at Shiloh, had been serving as first sergeant in succession to the late Joseph Darwin. Mindful that Brown had been his senior and would have been first sergeant but for his captivity, Kane generously "resigned his position as 1st sergeant and asked that the place be given to me . . . and I shall always honor him and love him as a true and genuine comrade. . . ." Captain Minter readily consented to the switch. Abe Van Meter was another returnee, and he could easily have had a noncombatant job as hospital steward. But his long captivity in the squalor of Confederate prison pens had infected him with a strange fascination for firearms.[3]

John Lomax was also repatriated, mainly through the efforts of the Masonic Order of which he was a member, the first week of June. Now he could take up his captaincy and go back to recruiting for Colonel George E. Spencer's 1st Alabama Cavalry. Anna Lomax, back in Laclede, sorrowfully notified him of the recent death of their fourteenth and youngest child, Leonidas, who had been born during that bleak December when his father's regiment was shivering at Weston. Daughter Bettie, seventeen, angered by the privations visited upon her father, wished furiously that she "had hold of some of those rebels, I would like to learn them a lesson." Though the men of the 18th Missouri would rarely see Lomax from there on, they were relieved to know that the gallant ex-Tennesseean was safely back in friendly surroundings.[4]

Meanwhile, the counter-guerrilla war raged on in the woods and canebrakes around Chewalla. Confederate depradations throughout the District of Corinth may have seemed sporadic to the Missourians, but the Rebels had an organization of sorts. Ruggles, commanding the First District of the Department of Mississippi and Louisiana under Pemberton, had overall command of partisan operations in Grant's rear areas. General Chalmers, whom the 18th Missouri had also met at Shiloh, had direct charge of the roving bands under Falkner, Ham, and the others in the Chewalla-Corinth region. By the beginning of June, Ruggles had his headquarters at Okolona, sixty-five miles south of Corinth, and was planning trouble that would directly involve many of the troops at Chewalla.[5]

As Grant's siege lines tightened around Vicksburg in early June, it became a matter of urgency that Hurlbut's forces do everything possible to keep Confederates in North Mississippi from helping Joe Johnston lift the siege. To Grant it looked like a close race between his ability to starve Pemberton out and Johnston's struggle to put together a force capable of breaking the Union grip on Vicksburg. To the troops in Dodge's district, this meant that the counter-insurgency operation in northern Mississippi would have to intensify as summer drew nearer.

It was on June 17 that Dodge got word that Ruggles was concentrating Falkner's partisan horsemen at Ripley, about thirty miles southwest of Corinth, to stab directly at Post Chewalla, destroy it, and lay waste the Mobile & Ohio toward

Corinth. Chalmers was to strike simultaneously at the Memphis & Charleston north of the state line and west of Pocahontas.

Grenville Dodge wound up a pair of counter-punches and flung them both at once. Powerful Union forces from LaGrange, Tennessee, swarmed southward toward the Coldwater River, a few miles into Mississippi, where Chalmers was holding bridges and fords to the northwest of Holly Springs. Colonel Phillips, at Pocahontas, received orders the evening of June 17 to march vigorously on Ripley to forestall Ruggles and Falkner there. His 9th Illinois, supported by a battalion of the 5th Ohio Cavalry and part of Battery I of the 1st Missouri Artillery from Corinth, made up most of Phillips' force.

At the time Phillips was getting his marching orders, Dodge was flashing word to Miller to get a mounted battalion on the way to Ripley to back up Phillips. To Madison Miller that meant turning out Sheldon and 180 stalwart horsemen, and by 5:30 that evening the column was out of the northwest gate and thundering down the road to Kossuth. "As luck would have it," Sheldon later said, "we met [Falkner's Partisans] about midnight, in a big swamp, dark as a pocket, and the rain pouring in torrents." Rather than risk "shooting our own men," Sheldon called a halt until daylight. When June 18 dawned, his scouts discovered that Falkner had retreated southward.

It was close to four of that afternoon when Sheldon joined Phillips a couple of miles east of Ripley. The Colonel, who had ridden into the town shortly before noon, was greatly agitated by reports that a large body of Rebels had passed northward along the Hatchie going toward Pocahontas and Chewalla *the day before!* He had just sent a telegraphic warning to Pocahontas that "this rebel force is moving toward you," but he included the comforting assurance that when the 18th Missouri joined him " I can whip them." If the Rebels were between him and Pocahontas, Phillips reasoned, it was high time he got on their tails.

With a combined force of less than 600, Phillips decided to move on toward the Hatchie, about ten miles east of Ripley. Shortly after 4:00 P.M. the column started, but it got no farther than the Tippah County Poor Farm, seven miles out of Ripley.

Scouts riding in from the river reported that some 200 or 300 Rebels had galloped up the Hatchie on their way south in mid-afternoon, after reconnoitering the Pocahontas area. This was Falkner's force, which, as Sheldon saw it, "had wisely concluded to get back to their own lines. . . ."

Nervous as a tomcat, Colonel Phillips bivouacked his command near the Poor Farm and ordered out the Ohio Cavalry to see where the Rebels were headed. If he could find that out, perhaps he could determine where Ruggles was concentrated.

About 2:00 A.M. on June 19, the Ohioans returned to report that the enemy riders were bearing directly on New Albany, twenty miles south of Ripley. That was all Phillips needed to know, and by 3:30 A.M. his troops were on the road back to Ripley in a dash for New Albany. The Rebels tried to make a firm stand just north of that place about noon, but the hail of lead from Phillips' oncoming troopers scattered them. A second pitched battle took place a mile south of the town, and again the defenders took to the woods and disappeared.

Ruggles' main body was down by Pontotoc, fifteen miles beyond New Albany, as Phillips found out late that evening when a strong enemy concentration stopped the Federal skirmishers a couple of miles short of Pontotoc. Scouts figured that Ruggles had three cavalry regiments and two artillery batteries, Sheldon heard, "so we thought we didn't want to go any further south just then. . . ."

After feeding his men half of their last ration, for they had lost their pack-mules during the swamp affair with Falkner the first night out, Sheldon moved out with the rest of Phillips' command along a side road leading westward from Pontotoc. Fearful now that Ruggles could overpower him at daybreak, Phillips hoped to elude the Confederate grasp by gaining the Tallahatchie at Rocky Ford, far to the northwest, and heading for the safety of the Tennessee border. "We marched all night," Sheldon remembered, "with the enemy marching on a parallel road, and so near that we could hear their men talking."

By breakfast time the Federals learned that they had pulled ahead of the enemy, and that relieved a bit of the anxiety. Moving onto the main Rocky Ford road, ahead of Ruggles, Phillips ordered full speed forward. Soon after, however, the 18th Mis-

souri, leading the way, entered the swamp-ridden Mud Creek
Bottom and ran right into trouble. A number of creeks inter-
sected the swamp, and their bridges had long since been
thoughtfully removed by the Rebels. Work-details from the 9th
Illinois managed to get timber bridges over several of the
streams.

And then the storm broke. Sheldon discovered enemy forces
ahead in the swamp, ready to contest the next creek-crossing.
Then came a savage assault on the 5th Ohio—Phillips' *rear*
guard! Soon after that, scouts reported that Confederate cavalry
had just been seen heading to the north of the swamp with the
evident intention of intercepting any Yankees who might try
to break out in that direction.

Phillips knew he was in a bind. Sheldon, familiar with the
needs of artillerymen, was doing a splendid job of guarding
the 1st Missouri as it withdrew to the first bridge the infantry
had built; but these reports of horsemen below the swamp suggested that Sheldon had better be doing even more. A messenger was sent in haste to get the 18th Missouri on the double-
quick to an intersection three miles north of the Mud Creek
crossings to prepare the way for a general breakout of Phillips'
forces. "Sheldon moved with all but two companies of his
command," Phillips told Dodge a week later, "and sent me
information that he had accomplished his object."

After two more hours of wild fighting, the Federals made
good their escape. Phillips had to burn four of his wagons, an
ambulance, a disabled caisson, and all its ammunition—but he
slipped through Ruggles' fingers. "I drew my skirmishers across
Mud Creek," his report says, "and held this point some time;
took a position with my artillery on high ground, 1,200 yards
therefrom. . . . I here waited for them to renew the attack; but
with the exception of artillery firing, nothing was done."

So ended the New Albany and Mud Creek skirmishes.
Crossing the Tallahatchie at Rocky Ford, Phillips headed for
Ripley, by way of Salem, and camped nine miles west of Ripley
that night. Winding up "one of the hardest and hungriest scouts
we ever made," Sheldon brought his force home safely to the
northwest gate on June 22. Phillips' expedition had lost ten
killed and twenty wounded, but not one of Sheldon's men was

so much as scratched. In his report, Sheldon pointed with pride
to the "general good behavior" of the 18th Missouri "under
circumstances of peculiar hardship, they having been almost
entirely destitute of rations, and without opportunity to procure
an adequate supply. . . ." For his part, Phillips was high in
praise of Sheldon, "whose services were invaluable to me. . . ."[6]

Meanwhile in the East, Robert E. Lee's army began leaving the
Rappahannock on June 3 for a swift drive to the Maryland line.
The Confederate high command was resolved to invade the
North to convince it that a negotiated peace was preferable to
a continued war of attrition. Hooker, braying reproaches at the
alarmed authorities in Washington for inadequately supporting
him, pulled out of the Fredericksburg area to chase madly into
central Maryland in an effort to hold Lee back from Pennsylvania's verdant hills. Lincoln and Halleck, increasingly fearful
of Hooker's ability to head off the Rebel general, dropped
Fighting Joe on June 28 and gave the Army of the Potomac to
a lanky Army Engineer, Major General George Gordon Meade.
    Rosecrans sallied forth again in eastern Tennessee, on June
24. His drive against Bragg soon became a marvel of maneuvering, as his rapid flank thrusts and feinting jiggled the Confederates out of first one line and then another. Within little
more than a week Bragg was flushed out of Tullahoma and
the entire region where he had camped since Stone's River.

The latter days of June brought a welcome procession of visitors
to Chewalla. Since May a number of the officers and men had
been planning to have their wives and children come to see
at firsthand the comforts of Camp Sheldon, as many of the
men still called it. On May 9 Tom Pollock had written his wife
in St. John to invite her to visit him and Dave at the Post. He
was sending money in a separate package, the wagonmaster
said, and Isabella Wilson Pollock's orders were to "Go to St.
Louis and buy all necessary clothing," and "unless you can
come in splendid style, do not come."
    Uncle Tom became more insistent in another letter dated
June 1. Plan on staying the summer, he urged. Above all, he
cautioned her, "dont . . . burden yourself with other ladis that

wants to come here. . . ." He had an important social mission for her, to "cal on Col. Morgan in St. Louis and stop with his famley a day or two," in their home at 309 Franklin. Finally, on June 28, the jubilant Scot learned that his wife, whom he had not seen in nearly two years, was really on the way.[7]

Mrs. Houts also came down from St. Louis, "and her presence in camp was like sunshine upon chilled plants," the chaplain said. Margaret Fletcher Miller brought her little daughter from Carondelet to visit the Colonel and Elwood, and the boys of the regiment, the chaplain wrote, somewhat sentimentally, "were delighted to see a pure woman from north of Mason and Dixon's line. . . ."

A note of tragedy marred the festivities when Private John Rigler, a teamster of Company D, drowned in a flash flood west of Chewalla. Wyckoff was guarding the Cypress Creek bridge of the Memphis & Charleston, and men of his company regularly traveled to the Post. On June 25 Rigler rode out for Chewalla on a mule. There had been heavy rain most of the night, and some flooding had occurred in "dry hollows" along the trail. Rigler apparently misjudged the extent of the flooding and lost his hold on his mount. At any rate, the bedraggled mule made it to higher ground without the twenty-year-old farmer from Appanoose County, Iowa. When the water drained from the hollow the men found Rigler's body, his hand firmly grasping the roots of a fallen tree.

With all the women and children in camp by the beginning of July, it was decided to get up an old-time Missouri barbecue and greet the Fourth in proper style. Even a few local "Rebels too old for the army" were invited to share the repast and commemoration of the common holiday. Mrs. Houts sang two patriotic songs, Lieutenant Hemstreet gave a reading of the Declaration of Independence, and Colonel Miller did his impromptu best to deliver some Fourth of July oratory. As the sun set that day, the Missourians felt that they had "done the best we could under the circumstances."

But before anyone could go to bed that night, General Dodge flashed to Chewalla the electrifying news that Vicksburg had surrendered and Meade had captured Richmond. "This set us wild," Garner reminisced a generation later. "Such cheering and tossing of hats!" The next day the men learned that the report of Richmond's fall was untrue, but balanced against it was the news that Meade had thrown Lee for a loss at Gettysburg, and that Old Rosey had cornered Bragg in Chattanooga and had him in the biggest cramp of his life. One could begin to sense that the tides were slowly turning in the Union's favor.[8]

As conditions had grown more comfortable at Chewalla that spring, it occurred to many of the Missourians, according to Colonel Sheldon, "that along with the guerrillas and forage, and other good and bad things, there were also *girls* in that country, and that the most of them knew how to dance. . . ." Alas! Post Chewalla yet boasted no dance hall, nor had it a building that could even make do for one.

Obviously the men were going to have to build themselves a dance hall. The biggest foreseeable hitch was getting flooring lumber. Logs and slabs wouldn't do. As it happened, some of the men had seen an army sawmill at work down by Corinth turning out just the grade of lumber needed. With that choice flooring, the regiment would have it made, for the wealth of carpentering talent available would see to it that the roof and walls went up in a hurry, with local timber.

Even so, General Dodge might be another problem. The officers pushing the project knew very well that Dodge wasn't likely to approve requisitions for dance hall lumber unless more strictly military needs had first been satisfied. Was there a way perhaps to circumvent the General? Someone remembered that Dodge was very solicitous about his soldiers' spiritual welfare. It was conceivable that he might approve a post chapel. And would not a "chapel-type" building be easily converted into a dance hall?

Some regimental conniver thought the way to handle things was for Garner to send Dodge a requisition for flooring for a chapel. The plotters reasoned that Garner's approval of the requisition would cool off any suspicions plaguing Dodge. But what if the chaplain himself became suspicious? After all, John M. Garner was hardly the sort to give aid and comfort to such a blatant manifestation of Sin.

It was clear that someone would have to con the chaplain.

Neither Garner nor Sheldon ever named names, but it seems obvious that Cudworth got the onerous task of cozening Garner into signing the requisition—"a little 'heathen Chinee' business," as Sheldon described it. Cud was close enough to Garner to get away with it, and nobody doubted that he had the nerve.

And so the flooring lumber came, at the beginning of June, and the "chapel-builders" went furiously to work with it. It is probable that Garner first smelled a mouse when he saw that the chapel was to have a movable pulpit that "wasn't any too large for the Parson. . . ." Great indeed was his shock when his suspicions were confirmed by the none-too-churchly musical instruments being taken into the structure—violins, base viols, drums, and the like. But it was soon too late, and the regiment now had a dual-purpose chapel. It was big enough, said Dave Pollock happily, for four sets to dance at a time.

The social season started with a bang on Friday night, June 12. Chaplain Garner, livid with indignation, protested to Colonel Miller as soon as he saw the local girls gathering at headquarters that evening. Someone tried to explain to Garner that the dance was "dedicatory," and that come Sunday morning he could "be as religious as I pleased" in the chapel. "At the appointed hour," Garner later wrote with devastating irony, "the dedicatory services commenced. Horse hairs and cat guts crossed each other at a lively rate and the air was soon vocal with the sound of 'Old dolly kick-it-up, jaybird soup and polecat hash,' and many other tastefully selected pieces. . . ."

But others were less vindictive. Dave Pollock astounded all onlookers by appearing with a girl on each arm. They were sisters, his father admiringly wrote the following Monday, and "they were the bels of the baul. . . ." Dave himself was more explicit later to his brother. "We have had three nice partys at Chewalla," he reported, "first the officers had one and then the non commissioned officers, and then the privates. At the first party thare was 40 ladys and at the other tow thare was 54 ladys. So you can see that the Yankees is geting purty popular among the ladys of the South."

"I know they came home after the war," Miller told an amused Unionville crowd in 1890, "and put on long faces and talked about the fearful hardships they had down south and what infernally strict officers they had . . . and all that sort of thing. . . . I think if they had told the truth . . . they would have told you that they had as good times in Dixie as they ever had in their lives. . . . I ought not to tell their wives how much they 'suffered,' when they would go fifteen or twenty miles to get a wagon load of Dixie girls."[9]

But there was a catch to it all. These were, after all, Secesh girls, with fathers, brothers, and even husbands in the Confederate service. And the Dixie girls must have told their concealed kinfolk plenty after each "grand kick about," as Garner scornfully called the dances. In this atmosphere of relaxing vigilance, trouble was sooner or later bound to occur. And one mid-July night, it did.

The men thought they would "put on a little style," says Sheldon, and they decided to take some girls home that night in an ambulance wagon. Several enlisted men volunteered as escorts to see the ladies safely through the guerrilla-infested countryside. The gallant gesture backfired spectacularly, for the procession ran into a Rebel ambush. Several men of the regiment were captured, along with the team and wagon, and the partisans heaved the Dixie girls into the mud, finery and all.

Within a few hours some of the damage was undone by Phillips' 9th Illinois, who recaptured the ambulance and liberated the sheepish captives. Phillips' superior, Colonel August Mersy, unwilling to stop at this good deed for the day, promptly shared the glorious news with General Dodge. Not very neighborly, Sheldon always thought. The Illinoisans were probably just plain jealous, he surmised, because they weren't hitting it off with the local beauties as famously as the swashbuckling lotharios of the 18th Missouri.

Realizing at last the use to which the "chapel lumber" had been put, Dodge sternly forbade any more dances at Chewalla. It was a natural reaction. But Colonel Miller at once led a delegation of officers to Corinth to remind the General that the Secretary of War had but lately instructed Federal troops to "cultivate friendly relations with the inhabitants of the captured territory. . . ." The General had to admit that the dances were certainly friendly affairs, and he drew in his horns after tartly directing Miller to "allow no ambulances, officers, and men to go outside the lines to bring in ladies to dances." If, he said, "the ladies desire to go to dances, they must furnish their own conveyances, at least not expose government property to the risk of capture, as we have furnished the enemy enough all ready."

Garner was bitterly critical of Miller's role in the affair. The Colonel, he said, "ought to know, did know, that to grant the freedom of our camp to the mothers, wives, daughters, and sisters of men then in arms against us, was pernicious and could but be productive of mischief. . . ." To Miller's credit, however, it must be said that he now made haste to "tighten the cinch and apply the strap." Chewalla's Provost Marshal Peter Dolman now banned from the Post all civilians without permits signed by Madison Miller. Men of the 18th Missouri could leave the Post only in formation or with a pass. Officers going out were required to sign in and out like coeds in college dormitories. And Captain Dolman gave the screw yet another turn: the midnight bed-check and roll-call. True, a few boys might be able to run the guards after dark and go out for a spree, but they would have a wretched time giving Dolman a satisfactory explanation the morning after a nocturnal inspection in the company barracks.[10]

The shifting fortunes of war had the natural effect of demoralizing Confederate guerrillas and inspiring the Federal counter-insurgency operations. Throughout the summer following the capitulation of Vicksburg, the story in northern Mississippi was one of mounting Yankee aggressiveness. Dodge boasted of his growing triumphs in a letter to Hurlbut on July 19, telling how "Lt. Col. Sheldon, Eighteenth Missouri, surprised another camp and captured . . . 1 captain and 1 lieutenant, together with their outfits." Captain Miller's Company E suffered the loss of six men captured on July 24 while on picket duty near the Post. The men lost were Sergeants William Watt and John Loe, Corporals Benjamin A. D. Shaffer and Richard M. Guffey, and Privates Zebulon Scott and William E. Houston. Four of these—Watt, Loe, Guffey, and Houston—died in captivity, Watt at Richmond, the others at Andersonville, Georgia. Company C, under Hemstreet, patroled the Mobile & Ohio to Corinth on July 27 and scouted the Tuscumbia southeast of Chewalla on August 2. Donnelly's Company C fought a sharp action with Rebel marauders near Ripley the following day, with the aid of a few 1st Alabama men. Dolman took Company H on a four-day scout (August 12-15) all around the Post, just after a squad led by Lieutenant Fallis stumbled into an ambush seven miles out of the Post on August 10. Private Johnathan Valentine, a Putnam County farmer, got a bullet through the arm, but it did not disable him for long.[11]

If Dodge was exasperated over the dance hall incident at Chewalla, he was also tired of civilian complaints over the Missourians' behavior. By late August his staff was wondering how determined the Missourians really were to cultivate friendly relations in the area. One farmer complained directly to Corinth on August 31 that a week previously a dozen men from Chewalla had made off with five of his geese and one cow. An appeal to Miller had been brushed off, said the farmer, but the Colonel had done him the same way in mid-July, after several Missourians had "killed one steer and one yearling calf" on the complainant's farm. Further investigation of this complaint brought forth testimony from an elderly widow near Chewalla that Miller's boys had "robbed her of nearly everything she possessed. . . ." Miller was now called on to give Dodge a strict accounting for "these transactions," but this was apparently never done.[12]

Rosecrans attacked Chattanooga in mid-August. So interdependent were the developments on the various fronts that Rosey's daring thrust eventually caused the 18th Missouri to lose its home at Chewalla. It all came about because Rosey's Army of the Cumberland fell into such a predicament that reinforcements were urgently needed at Chattanooga as September went on. In time the 18th Missouri found itself in the tide of manpower flowing to the rescue.

Closing in on Bragg, Rosecrans divided his army into three fast-moving columns engaged in a massive flank movement to the south of Chattanooga. Perceiving the net that Rosecrans was casting for him, the Rebel commander took alarm on September 8. Abandoning the city, he began retreating toward Lafayette, Georgia, to elude the fatal embrace. The Federals hurried on, confident that he was in demoralized flight. The truth was that Bragg was even then recoiling to strike against them at the first opportunity, and therein lay a deadly peril for the increasingly over-confident Yankees.

Reinforced by Lieutenant General James Longstreet's veteran divisions from Virginia, Bragg sailed into Rosecrans' overextended forces along Chickamauga Creek, south of Chattanooga, on September 19. Longstreet, mounting a massive counterattack, suddenly discovered a big hole in the Union line caused by an ambiguous operational order, and his fast-moving Rebels made short work of Rosecrans' entire right wing. Had it not been for George H. Thomas' gallant stand on Snodgrass Hill, the Army of the Cumberland would almost certainly have been overwhelmed. Rosecrans' decimated army now retired into Chattanooga. Bragg, following him up slowly, took up positions on Lookout Mountain and Missionary Ridge from which he could gaze straight down on the Federal forces. With the Tennessee River and the Memphis & Charleston Railroad interdicted by the Confederates, and with only a rough road leading over the hills to his rear, Rosecrans was in a trap. Bragg had effectively turned the tables. Panic reigned in Washington.

Little suspecting the repercussions that Chickamauga and Chattanooga were to have, the 18th Missouri greeted September as just another month. The regiment's strength was nearly 700 now. With the arrival of Dr. Frank F. Randolph of Norwalk, Ohio, in July, the regiment boasted two full-time doctors for the first time since Hamlin had boarded the *City of Memphis*.

September brought a new commander for the 2d Division, Left Wing, XVI Corps, in which the 18th Missouri was now serving. Brigadier General Thomas W. Sweeny, a native Irishman forty-three years old, took command, and Dodge, leaving for Memphis, began preparing to assume command of the Left Wing. Sweeny had lost his right arm in the Mexican War, but he was a West Pointer and had chosen to stay in the regular army in the 1850's despite his handicap. St. Louisans could remember him as a captain in the 2d U.S. Infantry at the Arsenal in the spring of 1861, and many of them recalled how he had told a Confederate acquaintance that before he would see the Arsenal surrendered to Claiborne Jackson he would personally "blow it to hell first, and you know I am the man to do it." After recovering from wounds at Wilson's Creek, he had resumed his career, as colonel of the 52d Illinois Infantry, at whose head he served with conspicuous gallantry at Fort Donelson and Shiloh. The boys of the 18th Missouri never had occasion to doubt that "Bull Dog" Sweeny was a combat soldier after their taste.[13]

Toward the middle of August Colonel Miller made a strenuous attempt to bring the commissioned complement of the regiment back to regulation strength. He proposed to make three captains, placing Cudworth in command of Company E; Hudson, Company A; and Hemstreet, Company G. It was also recommended to make McEfee the regimental quartermaster and bestow other first lieutenancies on Pollock, Edgar, and Everest. Several sergeants merited second lieutenant's rank, Miller suggested: Thomas W. Hatfield, Joe Stanley, Henry Runnels, Jeff Rummell, John Kuechler, and John L. Jones.

So far, so good. But official eyebrows were to rise considerably at two other recommendations much nearer the Colonel's heart. For the major's commission, vacant since the days of James A. Price, he now proposed his son Elwood, the junior captain in the regiment! For first lieutenant in Company A, he offered the name of Elwood's cousin, C. C. Fletcher.

A bundle of commissions reached Chewalla about September 15, but Elwood's commission was not among them. In fact, Gamble, and his new Adjutant General, John B. Gray, disapproved everything but captaincies for Hudson and Hemstreet, first lieutenancies for Pollock, Edgar, and Fletcher. For reasons best known to himself, Fletcher refused his commission in the 18th Missouri. When the smoke cleared, Miller saw that he still had the same number of officers in spite of all his efforts. And Elwood's rejection had caused a permanent chill to settle over the Colonel's relations with the Governor.[14]

The guerrilla war went on as usual around Chewalla, judging from the number of Missourians captured by Rebel bands. Company C lost six men, E lost five, G lost three, and A lost two —just in the month of September. Quartermaster Sergeant Kuemmel made the seventeenth by getting caught on a foraging expedition. Captivity was now an increasingly serious matter, for the easy paroles and exchanges of 1861 and 1862 were almost things of the past. For a variety of reasons, men falling into enemy hands now could look forward to Macon or Libby for the duration. Soon there would be Andersonville, where five of the Missourians captured in September died during 1864. They were Private Henry Kunst, a St. Louis German serving as teamster in Company C; Corporal Leopold Volk, also a native German enlisted in Company C from St. Louis; Private James G. Dixon of Company C, a Platte County farmer; Private Thomas Lindsay of Company A, a farm youth from Saline County; and Private Johnson J. Watson, twenty, a Linn County farmer. Occasionally, though, a few exchanges came through, but only a few. Early in October there returned three men captured in February, Corporal Grabosch and Privates Shelton and Thompson.[15]

Of course, staying with the regiment was no unconditional guarantee of a ripe old age, either. During the latter part of August and most of September an epidemic of bloody dysentery ravaged Post Chewalla, and before it ran its course several funerals had resulted. Private Johnson Downen, a Kiddville boy, was the first to go, on August 19. "I went for our dear Chaplain," Private John W. Green long remembered, "but when [we] got to [Downen's] cot he was too weak to talk." Garner knelt by the cot and spoke to the young soldier, but he had died. Company G was hardest hit. Ben Varner of Wyreka died on September 3 at the Post, and Jeremiah Donovan, a St. Louis Irishman who had been in uniform only two months, died in a Memphis hospital on September 19.

Perhaps saddest of all was the case of another boy in G Company, Private Augustus Vance of Wyreka, who also died in September. Vance was only twenty, but he was a good soldier and popular around the Post. His older brother, J. D., was also in his company. "It was customary," Garner recalled, "for the burying squad to stand in line and salute the corpse with 'present arms!' as it started to the grave. The entire fraction of the company to which young Vance belonged stood in line to honor their dead comrade, and it was deeply touching to see J. D. Vance present his gun to his dead brother. There were few dry eyes . . . that morning."[16]

Up at the War Department, Secretary Stanton was frantically working to extricate Rosecrans from his trap at Chatta-nooga. On September 22 he directed Grant to get Sherman on the road east with the XV Corps and anything that Hurlbut could spare from XVI Corps. On the night of September 23 an urgent conference at the War Department, with the President in attendance, decided to detach the XI and XII Corps from Meade and send them west in the most ambitious railroad troop-movement yet attempted in the war. Would all these rescuers make it to Chattanooga in time? Abraham Lincoln, for one, was openly dubious.[17]

# CHAPTER VIII

# *Middle Tennessee*

"Uncle Billy" Sherman, concentrating four divisions at Memphis in the last days of September, made ready to move eastward. It looked like a long trip at the time, for Halleck had directed him to move on Chattanooga along the line of the Memphis & Charleston, repairing it as he advanced. Old Brains hadn't learned much in 1862.

Guerrillas now tried to hamstring Sherman's relief march by disruptive activities in the Memphis-Corinth area. Brigadier General Eugene A. Carr, temporarily commanding the Left Wing of XVI Corps, complained on October 3 that he no longer had enough troops for anti-guerrilla, sentinel, and railroad-repair work. He decided to move the 18th Missouri. "Guerrillas burned small trestle and cut wire between here and Chewalla last night," Carr wrote Hurlbut. " I shall replace Miller's regiment at Chewalla by the Seventh Illinois [Infantry] and see if they can do better."[1]

The Missourians took a last look at their celebrated fort and began loading their wagons. They pulled out "without the loss of many tears or many expressions of regret," Garner observed after the passage of thirty years. But time did embellish the memory of Chewalla, for in his old age the chaplain wondered nostalgically if even yet "the jerking song of the whippoor-will rings out on the still night air, katydids saw and chatter, and occasionally the sweet melody of a mockingbird comes floating on the breeze to be answered by another mock-ingbird still further away." But 1863 had no time for the sentimentality of 1894. The regiment moved on Sunday, October 4, to the camp of the 7th Illinois at Corinth, "befouled with debris and alive with gray backs. . . ." By way of contrast, the Illinoisans were elated at the "fine quarters and fine grounds" of old Camp Sheldon. They enjoyed Chewalla's split-log luxury for only three weeks, however.[2]

The move to Corinth cost Company K its first sergeant. Eugene O'Sullivan lost control of his mount, and it ran into a tree with him. His right leg was caught between the animal and the tree, and O'Sullivan's hip and kneecap were simultaneously fractured. Houts sent him back to Memphis, and he was never able to return. Lieutenant Edgar, who had lately transferred in to release Jim Coddington for duty in Company F, called in Sergeant Mike Callery as first sergeant in K Company.[3]

The Missourians had hardly unloaded when the word came that Chalmers was on the prowl again. On October 6 he crossed the Coldwater in force, heading north to raid the Memphis & Charleston and creating great alarm in Sweeny's division. After several skirmishes with the 9th Illinois and other mounted units, Chalmers assaulted the railway town of Collierville, Tennessee, on October 11. But for the chance arrival of Sherman and his infantry escort, on their way by train to Corinth, Chalmers might have won the day at Collierville.

In the confusion of the battle a rumor went forth that Sherman had fallen prisoner. Federal authorities panicked at Memphis, but Tom Sweeny, at LaGrange, decided to do something more than wring his hands. The dauntless Irish brigadier ordered the entire 2d Division to drop everything else and come on the dead run to rescue Sherman. On Sunday, October 11, a message was flashed to Corinth for Madison Miller to entrain the 18th Missouri immediately for LaGrange.

Miller's men arrived at LaGrange the next day, but the emergency was over. Not only was Sherman safe and sound, but Chalmers was retreating toward Oxford, Mississippi. After holding the Missourians at LaGrange the rest of the week, Sweeny ordered them back to Corinth on Saturday—on foot. The 18th Missouri returned to Corinth Monday evening, October 19, after a crippling sixty-five-mile hike.[4]

The men arrived in poor spirits, more than ready for the squabble that erupted on Tuesday. Opening his mail from St. Louis, Madison Miller beheld a major's commission—not alas for Elwood, but for William M. Winter. Allowing for peculiarities of the Governor's longhand, the angered Miller perceived that the commission was for Captain Minter of Company F. "But why Minter?" he asked, smarting at the way Gamble had blackballed Elwood. Others were wondering, too. Supported by a dozen officers, Sheldon stiffly protested Minter's appointment on October 20 "on the ground of his utter incompetency . . . and that it would be unsatisfactory to the entire command. . . ." Signing with him were Cudworth, D. W. Pollock, Everest, Pagin, Coddington, and Adjutant Godfrey. Six company commanders also signed: Hudson (A), Stults (B), Donnelly (C), Elwood Miller (E), Hemstreet (G), and Edgar (K). Wyckoff, Dolman, and Fallis did not join in the demurrer, nor did the commander of Company F, Minter himself.

Three days later Miller conveyed these objections to Gamble with some of his own. Minter, said he, "is a resident of Illinois. He has never brought a man or expended a dollar in recruiting for the regiment. . . ." Had Miller possibly forgotten that this was precisely what the men had held against *him* at Weston in 1862? True, the Colonel now conceded, Minter had received his original commission "at my request," but Miller had changed his opinion of an officer "possessing neither the respect of his fellow officers or the confidence or good will of his men." "And," chafed Miller, "if you will not appoint those that I endorse and recommend I most respectfully request that you will not thrust upon me in opposition to my own wishes as well as three fourths of the regimental officers those who are distasteful to the command. . . ." Since the commission bore the name of no officer in the regiment, however, Miller was returning it to Gamble "with a reliant opinion of your desire to do what is right in the premises."

Gamble's response was to issue a commission to Minter with corrected spelling—a personal insult that Madison Miller would never forget. The Colonel would have been even more emotional about it if he had known how Minter came by his oak leaves. On October 1, two lawyer-friends of the Captain in Quincy, whom "someone" had tipped off about the vacancy in the 18th Missouri, had appealed to Illinois' former U.S. Senator Orville H. Browning to use his influence with Gamble to seek Minter's promotion. "I fully concur in this recommendation," Browning had written the Governor, who just as promptly ordered General Gray to "Let the promotion be made." One notes with more than passing interest that the very conservative Browning had three years earlier managed the campaign of Edward Bates to take the Republican presidential nomination away from Lincoln. Since Bates was Gamble's brother-in-law, Browning must surely have felt that the Governor of Missouri would acknowledge his political indebtedness. Too, one is tempted to speculate on the use Miller might have made of this political bombshell, could he have known how Gamble had trafficked with "foreign influences" to fill the major's position.[5]

This was also a busy week for Sherman, headquartered at Iuka. On October 16 Halleck had conveyed to Grant the President's decision to give him supreme command of all Federal forces west of the Alleghenies—the Military Division of the Mississippi. Three days later Sherman publicly succeeded Grant at the helm of the Army of the Tennessee, while, also by Grant's choice, Thomas replaced Rosecrans in command at Chattanooga.

Sherman now directed Hurlbut to get a picked force of 8,000 men of XVI Corps ready to back up the XV Corps move on Chattanooga. What this meant was that Dodge, who had taken command of Hurlbut's Left Wing on October 15, would command Sherman's rear guard. To the 18th Missouri these developments portended a rapid move to central Tennessee, for Miller's regiment was one of those singled out by Sherman to make up Dodge's expedition.[6]

The 18th Missouri departed Corinth on October 28, a day after Grant's courier reached Iuka with orders for Sherman to drop all work on the Memphis & Charleston and hurry overland to Chattanooga. The predicament of Thomas was too precarious for a leisurely approach by relief forces. So far as Miller's Missourians were concerned, it was time to go. The men were sick and tired of looking at the destruction and desolation that they had visited upon the countryside since spring.

Now it was time to say farewell to the only women still with the regiment—Isabella Pollock and Roxana Johnson. Uncle Billy had ordered "all women, white or black," out of the camps of the Army of the Tennessee. Mrs. Pollock had originally intended to go home to St. John as soon as the regiment was ordered out of Corinth. Roxana, however, had been with the staff since Pittsburg Landing. She had done the cooking, washing, and ironing for the officers at headquarters, and they were going to miss her indeed.[7]

As Colonel Bane's Brigade of Sweeny's division tramped the eighteen miles from Corinth to Burnsville on October 28, its regiments included not only the 18th Missouri but also the 7th, 50th, 57th, 113th, and 120th Illinois and the 39th Iowa. The Missourians were the last to leave Corinth, enjoying the dubious privilege of bringing up Sherman's rear on the way to Middle Tennessee. "There was not a soldier behind us," shuddered Garner.

But there *were* Confederate horsemen. Brigadier General Philip D. Roddey was nearby night and day, with a brigade of Joe Wheeler's Cavalry. The 18th Missouri, being half mounted, was the logical "goat" outfit to guard the rear and trade volleys with the gray-clad marauders. It was Sherman's hope that his Federal riders, front or rear, could keep Roddey and his colleagues too busy to think about more depradations along Thomas' fragile supply line.

Miller's regiment, once camped at Burnsville in company with the 50th Illinois, was stuck with a nine-day layover. The Tennessee was turbulent and rising, and the divisions up ahead were having a difficult time crossing at Eastport. Sherman's purpose in crossing here was to make use of the river as soon as possible as a protection for his right flank against Confederate cavalry operating in northwestern Alabama. With the Tennessee on the rise during the late fall rains, it is easy to see why Sherman thought of it as a protection against the Rebels.[8]

While at Burnsville, the men had their first taste of absentee balloting. Several states were holding elections, and the experts were sure that the Administration's chances of victory in 1864 were heavily dependent on a good showing in 1863. One issue that had been fought out was whether the soldiers ought to

vote. Why, asked Radical Republicans especially, should Cop-
perhead Democrats, skulking at home, be allowed to vote,
whereas loyal men under arms should be denied the same
privilege? In Missouri, as elsewhere, this point of view had so
prevailed that the General Assembly, shorn of its Copperheads,
had voted on June 12, 1862, to legalize soldier voting. The
current election centered about a hot contest between slates
of radical and conservative candidates for the Missouri Supreme
Court. The Democratic and Republican Parties in the state had,
as such, dissolved for the duration. The Confederate segment of
the Democracy had either gone South or been disfranchised,
leaving state politics a battlefield on which Loyalist Democrats
and Conservative Republicans friendly to Gamble contended
against the growing forces of the radical abolitionists determined to prosecute the war with crusading fury and revolution-
ize the legal and social status of the Southern Negro.

"No one ever questioned the loyalty of our democratic
soldiers," Garner recollected. "Perhaps some of the dear comrades have lived to learn that true American democracy expired
when Andrew Jackson died. . . . It is needless to say that but few,
if any, democratic votes were polled in the 18th Mo. . . . Our
regiment was composed of men who had been tried in the fire of
persecution." The poll books and other records of voting in
the regiment must have been lost in the Missouri Capitol fire
of 1911, for they are to be found neither in the National Archives
nor in Jefferson City, and it is almost impossible to corroborate
or discount Garner's suggestion of a Radical landslide in the
18th Missouri. The press reported that St. Louisans in Company H had voted 9-0 for the Radical candidate in their
judicial district, and this at least tends to support Garner's
generalization.

In the elections of November 3, 1863, the Conservative
judges won a slight majority statewide. But the Radical-minded
boys of the 18th Missouri had a consolation prize. Isaac Pratt,
plunging into a special election, won himself a seat in the State
Senate. Although losing every county in his district but one to
the Conservative candidate, he nevertheless floated into Jefferson City on a tidal wave of votes piled up for him by the 18th
Missouri's home folks in Putnam County.[9]

Friday, November 6, was a busy day. With the main body of Sherman's army crossing the Tennessee, the time had come for Dodge's regiments to depart from Burnsville. The morning's march was along the line of the Memphis & Charleston to Iuka. The latter place hadn't changed greatly since the Missourians' hasty visit and departure fourteen months before, and the day's plans called for marching straight through town. The wagons and the main part of the 18th Missouri had already taken the direct road for Eastport, on the river some eight miles northeast of Iuka, when a local citizen notified Sheldon that there was a hoard of sugar, coffee, and salt hidden in the railroad station.

Unwilling to leave the stuff for the Rebels, and unable to take it with him, Sheldon auctioned off the precious commodities in small lots. "In a few minutes it was all gone," Sheldon says, "and the citizens probably had their first taste, for a long time, of 'sure enough' coffee. It was a great luxury to them, as they mostly used an imitation article, made of parched rye, and sometimes of sweet potatoes sliced thin, and roasted to a crisp."

Sheldon's small force then cantered nonchalantly out of town before noon—and right into a skirmish. Some of Roddey's men, not having bothered to check for the presence of Union troops in Iuka, had supposed that the main body of Miller's command east of Iuka was in reality the tail of Sherman's columns. A hundred Rebels, under Major Whiting, closed in on the "rear" of Miller's force. It is easy to imagine Whiting's shock when he suddenly found Sheldon's hard-riding Missourians bearing down on *his* troopers and "peppering them with Uncle Sam's lead," as Garner phrased it. The startled Rebels broke for the woods south of the railroad, and Sheldon proceeded to chase them far enough to make sure they kept going. "They didn't stand on ceremony," he reported.

As the noise subsided, it was found that Private Isaac F. Shipley of Company C had been shot in the right foot. It seemed a severe wound, the ball having entered near the little toe and passed through the foot to emerge near the base of the big toe. While the ever-present Houts dressed Shipley's foot by the side of the road and made him ready to go back to Paducah,

Colonel Bane was forming the brigade in line of battle. Then, when Sheldon rode in to report on Whiting's departure, Moses Bane decided it was time to relax and have a meal.[10]

"Uncle Billy Sherman was dreadfully in earnest," Garner recalled in later years. "We were no longer a peace commission—as at Chewalla." So, before Madison Miller ordered the troops to fall in again to resume the march to Eastport, he decided to give the local residents a little civics lesson. Major Whiting had cleanly escaped, but there was the old gentleman whose large frame house stood nearest the scene of Whiting's ill-fated attack on what he thought was Dodge's rear. Maybe—just maybe—that old fellow knew something he wasn't telling.

Mercy, no! The lord of the manor, by his own account, was a staunch Union man. He solemnly denied having known that Rebel riders were anywhere around that day. But, unfortunately for his story, one of his slaves was a young man who had decided to leave and had no reason to conceal his master's secrets.

"Cunnel," he told Miller, "a whole bunch o' armed horsemen camped down yonduh las' night, and dar's wheah they horses was dis mo'nin' afo' they done started shootin' at y'all."

"That so?" Miller quizzed him.

"Yassuh," the youth went on, "y'all jus' go down behind the house 'n' see if'n it ain't so."

Soon afterward a scouting party rode back to report that it was evident that someone's cavalry had spent the night down in the thicket.

"Well, well," Madison Miller chuckled, staring balefully at the apprehensive gentleman. "My friend, you have ten minutes to get your plunder out of that house."

The disconsolate "Union man" put his family and obedient slaves to work rapidly removing valuables, and true to his promise, Miller ordered the torch applied to the dwelling at the expiration of ten minutes. Bidding his host a cold-hearted farewell, Miller turned away on this November afternoon and rode off to join his regiment on the road to Eastport.

He had hardly ridden beyond sight of the burning mansion before one of Dodge's aides came galloping with orders for him to make Eastport before halting. With the evening sun setting, the Missourians hastened on up the winding road. While passing Sanders Hollow, they met a second courier bearing orders to bivouac right there. Eastport was only three miles away, but Madison Miller did what the General ordered and at 10:00 P.M. halted his command for the night without food or water. Quiet was settling over the Missourians when another orderly rode in with directions to move them into Eastport immediately! This was clearly a preview of the "hurry up and wait" game so familiar to their grandsons in later wars.

Chaplain Garner well remembered that "our patience was exhausted and some of us used rather ugly words to express our indignation. By the time we got to Eastport, sleepy and in bad humor, day was dawning."[11]

This was the day that Dodge intended to put his task force across the rampaging Tennessee. And while waiting, the 18th Missouri did its best to get some sleep during those daylight hours in bivouac. The XVI Corps, along with Company C of the 18th, had nearly all crossed by 3:00 P.M., when Colonel Miller turned out the rest of his sullen outfit to go down to the landing. There the men loaded themselves and their equipage on a ferry boat and an old river steamer for a rough ride to the Alabama shore.

Another night march was before them, as Miller's men assembled their wagons and horses on the far bank Saturday evening. As Dodge described it, the route of march would run through Gravelly Springs to the Ball's Factory Ford on Shoal Creek and pass within seven or eight miles of Florence. "The corps train and ambulance train will be heavily guarded in rear and front," he directed, "and at least two companies of infantry will be put in at intervals of each twenty wagons." During most of Saturday, Donnelly's Company C had acted as escort to Dodge, but late that afternoon it was sent to accompany Colonel John W. Fuller's Ohio Brigade in the advance of XVI Corps. The rest of the regiment, after a laborious overnight hike, camped Sunday evening with Bane's brigade at Little Cypress Creek, eighteen miles beyond the Tennessee.[12]

The march east from Corinth was a troublesome one. Half the regiment had been mounted since the early days at Chewalla, and now those without horses found themselves unprepared for the arduous march to central Tennessee. Most of the men had new shoes and loaded knapsacks, a poor combination for a forced march. Garner, having sold his worthy Hawk during those palmy days at Chewalla, was also in distress. Cudworth rescued the chaplain from his predicament and presented him with a sorrel and some rigging that was "shabby, but the very best he had. . . ." Even so, the chaplain found his use of the new horse rather limited. Colonel Miller instructed him to stay back with the "tenderfoot brigade," those boys who might appreciate a ride now and then to rest their aching feet. "It amounted to some relief to take as many knapsacks as I could get about me to carry them for the tired boys," said Garner, "and I remember, with pleasure, that many a time I gave a horse to a comrade with blistered feet and took his place in the moving column."

A mile or so short of Little Cypress Creek, disaster overtook the chaplain's transportation. The poor old sorrel, carrying a tenderfoot, got too close to the brink of a deep ravine. The shelf caved in, the horse slipped over the edge, and the rider fell flat on his back on the road. Down in the ravine it was evident that the animal had not been appreciably injured, but he was in a poor situation. A few hundred feet below the cave-in the ravine was blocked by a bramble of thorn-leaved holly extending for many acres. The poor brute could neither be taken out nor could he climb out. And there was no time to cut brush. The sorrel had to be left to his fate, and Garner was a foot soldier again.

Reaching the bivouac around 11:00 P.M., Garner reported directly to Miller, whose headquarters consisted of a "pine bush, under which the Colonel was trying to rest, while a dim fire burned against an old stump near by."

"Colonel, I beg to report that I am present for duty."

"Did all the tenderfeet get in with you?" Miller asked.

"Yes, sir, all except my horse, bridle, and saddle," Garner responded. "They fell into a ravine and we could not get them out."

"Hell you say!"

"No," huffed Garner, "not that exactly. But I am in great

perplexity about my situation. On foot and no possible chance to purchase an outfit. I feel deeply concerned for the morrow."

"Well, Parson," yawned Miller, "you won't need any horse tonight. You'll find a piece of beef out there on the grass. Our boys killed a calf and brought me a leg, and I think you can do on what's left till breakfast."

The morose cleric hunted up the delicacy, and not exactly to his surprise he found it a shank, trimmed rather closely, with some hide and the hoof still on it. Wiping off pine needles as best he could, Garner salvaged a few strips of the meat, which had been boiled without salt. That banquet over, he crawled under the Colonel's bush and went to sleep.

The morrow was happier than the Parson had expected. When the regiment assembled to move out, Private Lawrence Hoover of Company E brought over a splendid sorrel, fairly well rigged, and handed its reins to Garner. Hoover was then serving as cook, orderly, and hostler at headquarters. The grateful chaplain was to sing his praises for forty years.

After an early breakfast Monday, November 9, the regiment was off for three days of sustained marching. At sundown the men made camp on a plantation eighteen miles away from the previous night's camp on the Little Cypress. About noon, on Tuesday, the Missourians passed several fresh graves and saw a few dead horses and mules. This was proof enough that the Rebels hadn't given up pestering the advancing Yankees. Crossing the line into Tennessee in midafternoon, the column entered a narrow valley with high bluffs on both sides. If the Rebels had any stunts left, everyone felt, they would soon reveal them. Word came back that raiders had captured an ambulance, together with its driver and team. Miller's outfit, however, went on down the valley without a scratch, although some of the men later swore that Rebel sharpshooters on the bluffs had used the regiment's line of march for target practice.

In late afternoon the 18th Missouri entered the watershed of Richland Creek, a small stream winding through a lovely green valley. Dodge's entire force by this time was so peevish over raiders and skirmishes that the little valley was soon ablaze with house-fires. Garner remembered that "there was little respect shown the property of citizens along our route. Many buildings, with their contents, were reduced to ashes, and at night all the fencing within reach was used for fuel. . . ."[13]

It was about noon on Thursday morning when the column passed through Lawrenceburg. To Dodge's surprise there was a big cotton-textile plant running full blast here, still turning out Confederate Gray fabrics. Of course, just as the Yankees started to light their matches, there appeared the inevitable local "Union man" who happened to own the factory and was overjoyed to see his comrades-in-blue coming to liberate the downtrodden loyalist folk in Lawrenceburg. With a sigh, Grenville Dodge ordered the troops to forget their bonfire, and Bane's brigade moved on east to camp that evening at Pulaski.

And what was to be the Missourians' reward for this energetic march to the relief of Chattanooga? Another accursed railroad job! Sheldon, whose blood was up at the prospect of fulltime combat duty, was now beside himself. But there stood General Dodge with a letter from Grant, and the Conqueror of Vicksburg was ordering the XVI Corps detachment to camp along the 102-mile Nashville & Decatur line and put it back into operation as a second railroad supplying Chattanooga. Fuller, taking up work on the southern reaches of the line toward Decatur, Alabama, persuaded Dodge to leave Donnelly's men with the Ohio Brigade a little longer. Miller, meanwhile, was setting up his headquarters at Lynnville on Friday morning, November 13, and his companies were posting themselves along the line from Pulaski north to the Duck River. Companies A, D, E, G, I, and K were at Culleoka. Dolman took Company H to Gracey's Trestle, about ten miles north of Buford Station, to replace a company of the 57th Illinois. Stults camped B Company on the Duck River, taking over railroad guarding north of Culleoka. Minter, still a "prospective major" whom Miller just couldn't seem to arrange to have mustered in, lodged Company F at Lynnville.

On November 16 Dodge completed his comprehensive plan for rehabilitating the railroad, and Sherman gave it his immediate blessing. Many years later, Sheldon was able to tell himself that it made sense to put the XVI Corps on railroad work in November of 1863. Of course, neither Grant nor anyone else then thought of Dodge as the future "father of the Union Pacific." Sheldon could later admit that the job he did under Dodge in Tennessee was "inglorious, but very necessary. . . ."

Sheldon regarded the railway as "by all odds the most crooked road I ever saw." Its general course in the 18th Missouri's area was down the valley of Richland Creek. "I once asked a citizen why it was so made," said Sheldon, "and he explained that it had been built on a contract which allowed a higher price for curves than straight track! This was probably intended originally as a joke, but it had got to be sober reality. A good turnpike ran parallel from Nashville to Decatur, never more than a few miles away. The country was much more fertile than North Mississippi, and entirely lacked the interminable swamps and canebrakes that furnished shelter to our bushwhacking friends of the latter state."[14]

On November 19 Colonel Miller got orders to move some seven or eight miles north to Culleoka. Dodge, visiting Lynnville, had called Bane's attention to the fact that the troops there were "not near a bridge," and he suggested that they move to Culleoka unless they were badly needed where they were. Those who thought this move would be another piece of drudgery soon learned their error. There was a high railroad bridge just south of Culleoka, one of those towering timber-trestles so familiar in Civil War scenery. A party of Confederates was getting ready to burn the trestle just as the 18th Missouri clattered into town, but it only took one whiff of Federal gunpowder to convince the arsonists to take their matches elsewhere.

The men soon met Dr. Jonathan Hunt, the unforgettable elderly and one-eyed medic in this little town of perhaps one hundred citizens. What they remembered longest, though, was the window-display in the doctor's office. There, to the anger and amazement of the Missouri Yankees, stood a large jar filled with alcohol—and a pair of preserved Negro infants "as nude as when they were born, with all the appendages of uterine life attached to them," as Garner put it.

This, to the more radical among the Missourians, was clear proof of the moral debasement to be expected where one race was master and another chattel. Had those infants been white, Garner stormed, Hunt would never have dared display them in his front window. "Those little colored children were not considered entitled to more respect than two dead pigs or two dead puppies," he wrote. What better illustration could there be of "the gross, hardening influence of human slavery?"

Colonel Miller agreed with the gathering crowd of indignant soldiers. He crossly informed the doctor that his entire house was being taken over for a regimental headquarters. Where the doctor should go, with his "repulsive nuisance," couldn't interest Miller less. Within the hour the headquarters crew had moved happily into the best residence in Culleoka.

The radicalism of officers like Miller and Garner was beginning to show. And it was being aggravated by repeated incidents of this type. For another example, a few days after the move to Culleoka there appeared a Southern Methodist circuit-rider, known to the Missourians as Brother Ormand. The old cleric had in-laws in town, and having "starved out" in the back-country, Ormand had come in for a visit. He was an ungainly man, as Garner remembered, "made after the style of an old-time fire tongs; long legs, short thighs, slender body, a small ball at the top, denominated a head, on which bristled a topknot of flaxen, stubby hair, with flattened pedal extremities."

Brother Ormand, upon learning that the Yankee chaplain was also a Southern Methodist, set out to cultivate the Missouri parson, but only succeeded in arousing his suspicions. At least, for his part, Garner later maintained that the chumminess was one-sided. And one chilly afternoon in November provided him an opportunity to prove his ideological trustworthiness.

Ormand, it seemed, was constantly after Garner to join him for a walk in the country to a favorite spot of his, a brick church about a mile and a half out of Culleoka. There were several lovely country houses on the way, he pointed out, and the cemetery would prove most interesting.

Highly suspicious, Garner went to Miller to ask his permission. "May I have a squad of ten men to take along?" the chaplain asked. "I'm positive this fellow has a squad of Rebel friends out there waiting on us."

"Yes, damn his soul," snorted Miller. "Take the whole regiment if you want to."

Garner didn't take that many men, but the dozen who volunteered to go were anxious for some excitement and came along as cheerfully as if they were off for a turkey shoot. "I suppose I suspected Brother Ormand wrongfully," Garner admitted afterward, "for we were not disturbed."

What was disturbing was the visit to the graveyard, where Ormand led his guest rapidly through the "aristocratic division" to the Negro quarter at the back of the lot. Pausing at a grave enclosed with rails, Ormand pointed to a soapstone, "little larger than the bone with which Samson slew the Philistines," as Garner described it. On the little stone was the epitaph: "In memory of Lotta who faithfully served George Roberts and his descendants 95 years."

Turning to the chaplain, Ormand asked passionately, "What do you think now, of the south abusing the poor nigger? I wish every abolitionist in the country could see this grave and read the inscription!"

At this, Garner exploded. "Sir! I think this rail pen and bit of soapstone a devilish poor compensation for ninety-five years of hard service—and that after the poor old woman is too dead to know anything about it!" And, before the amused soldiery standing around, Garner concluded: "Ormand, this is an insult under the guise of friendship. For this these men would more than like to put ten cartridges through your pelt. Just step back and leave us return at our leisure."

With that, Ormand, deeply shocked, stepped back to let his former chum stalk out with his blue-coated friends.[15]

For a few short days in late November, the goings-on at Culleoka were dwarfed by events at Chattanooga. Grant's time to strike and reverse September's verdict had come. Bragg, thinking that the Union forces would need another month to get ready for the return match, had sent Longstreet off to Knoxville on November 3 to accomplish the ruin of Ambrose Burnside's garrison there. Once Burnside's force was dispersed or captured, Longstreet would come back to help hold Grant along the upper Tennessee.

Bragg's gratuitous weakening of his forces presented Grant with the opportunity he wanted. Hooker was at hand with his two-corps detachment, and Sherman reported at Chattanooga on November 15 that he had four divisions rapidly closing up to Bridgeport, Alabama, just west of Lookout Mountain.

Grant's plans now matured rapidly. Hooker was to lay siege to Lookout Mountain, while Sherman sneaked through the hills west and north of the city to strike Bragg's right wing on the north end of Missionary Ridge. With this going on, Thomas would bring the Army of the Cumberland up to hit the Confederate center on the Ridge south of Sherman's thrust.

It took Grant little more than forty-eight hours to break Bragg's hold on Chattanooga. Thomas nibbled away at enemy positions in the middle of the Ridge on the afternoon of November 23, while Sherman and Hooker made their moves under cover of darkness. By midmorning the next day Hooker had driven the Confederates off Lookout Mountain and was hustling them toward Chickamauga. Late that afternoon Sherman assaulted the north end of Missionary Ridge. He expelled the Rebels from the high hill overlooking the Tennessee & Georgia Railroad, but he was unable to get across the railroad cut that night to strike at Bragg's center and flank.

Late Tuesday evening, November 24, Grant readied his decisive stroke. Sherman and Hooker he directed to advance, whatever the cost, at dawn. As soon as Hooker reached the south end of the Ridge, Thomas was to launch his army against the middle of it. However, the best-laid plans often fail. Sherman was stopped again, and the flooding Chickamauga Creek held up Hooker. But four divisions of Thomas' army nevertheless charged up the Ridge—and then down its eastern slopes.

Bragg was ruined. By a miracle of luck, speed, and maneuvering he was able to take 40,000 survivors away from the scene of his disaster for a sorrowful retreat into northwestern Georgia. On December 2 he bade farewell to the Confederate Army of Tennessee at its winter quarters in Dalton, Georgia, and left to become military adviser to Confederate President Davis. Longstreet, unable to get back in time to help him, turned east to rejoin Lee in northern Virginia. As for the victorious Federals, they were content to rest on their arms around Chattanooga until spring. Tennessee, at last, was virtually cleared of Rebels.

The 18th Missouri, meanwhile, was, in Sheldon's words, "constantly on the move, and made numerous visits to Lawrenceburg, Brown's Ferry, and other points." On November 22, as the battle at Chattanooga was about to open, a force of mounted Rebels struck northward to raid the area west of Pulaski. "Get Sheldon out after them," was Dodge's terse order to Bane. Sheldon, taking Minter's Company F and Dolman's Company H, charged out of Lynnville immediately, and although his men did get off a few shots at the elusive enemy near Lawrenceburg, little damage was done. "No casualties," the company muster rolls laconically comment.

This was rather typical of other reconnaissances made by parties of the 18th Missouri. "Spent majority of time scouting and capturing many prisoners," Dan Shelton summarized. During the last weeks of 1863 there were few towns in Giles, Marshall, and Maury counties that did not see at least one hard-riding column of Colonel Miller's Missourians. On November 30 Companies A, D, F, G, I, and K went on a six-day scout of the region from Lawrenceburg down to the vicinity of Florence, Alabama. The expedition was strengthened by detachments from the 50th and 57th Illinois and 39th Iowa. On this foray Miller gathered in two dozen prisoners, Edgar's K Company snaring five in one raid on a camp. On December 11 selected detachments from the same companies made the same journey, under Sheldon, but without the spectacular results of earlier reconnaissances. Working closely with the Missourians was Colonel Dick Rowett's 7th Illinois.[16]

The New Jersey-born Sheldon now came face to face with "King Cotton." Cut off since 1861 from Southern cotton sources, the North desperately needed the commodity. Although the Confederate government strictly forbade traffic in cotton with the Yankees, many planters and speculators saw a chance to make a killing, since Union troops were moving across the area. The Nashville pike was often crowded with wagons loaded with bales and headed northward. "On one occasion," Sheldon "came down to the mussel shoals of the Tennessee, and found the river full of floating cotton, which was thus being slipped through the lines." To the dashing young Missouri colonel, it was sheer madness for Davis to prohibit such trade, for it was a sure way to improve the sagging finances of the Confederacy.

If the Confederate President failed to see his main chance, enterprising Federals saw theirs. One party, probably Illinoisans, stationed itself at a lonely spot on the turnpike and began charging a toll of a dollar per bale, which the traffickers gladly paid, being assured vaguely that the proceedings were under "orders of the commanding general." Good fishing lures more fishermen, as a rule, and a second such toll station went into business. This led to remarks and inquiries, Sheldon heard, and before long General Dodge's provost marshal, and then his judge advocate, had entered the case.

Quartermaster Cudworth found his work no easier or safer in central Tennessee than it had been at Chewalla. On November 16, Grenville Dodge had ordered Miller to stage a horse-requisitioning campaign that would enable him to mount the whole regiment, and this meant that Cudworth had to venture into the hostile farmlands. "This involved him in great risk," Garner wrote, "for as at Chewalla, so it was around Culleoka. The country was infested with squads of Rebels. . . ." Making things especially difficult for Cud was the fact that the Rebels had culled the region carefully during the past two years. The citizens considered him "the most relentless horse thief who ever infested the region," Garner said admiringly of his intrepid young friend.

Neither Sheldon nor Miller much admired the plugs that Cudworth dredged up across a two-county area. The quartermaster, undismayed by their remarks, explained that "It's my rule to take every horse that has four feet and a head. . . ." Besides, he wasn't yet through.

Some time in early December, Garner witnessed a spine-chilling scene that etched itself permanently on his memory. Some of the Missourians had quartered themselves in stock-sheds on a ridge just west of Culleoka. Since the weather was quite chilly, the men usually kept a large bonfire going with fence rails, dead limbs, and other fuel. One evening a young

Negress, being lightly dressed, drew too near the fire. Before she realized it, her dress was aflame. Naturally the frightened girl began to run with the speed that extreme terror can generate, and it took a mighty effort by the Missourians nearby to catch her in a vain attempt to save her life.

By the time they ran her down, her clothing was almost entirely burned away. "Where she was not crisped, she was blistered," the shocked chaplain found. "Part of her hair was burned to the scalp, her eyes were parched and she had pulled at her burning clothes until her fingernails were scorched. . . ." None of the men huddled about the miserable creature could ever forget that horrible odor of scorched human hair and skin. Shrouded in a blanket, she was placed in one of the sheds. The poor girl "shuddered and moaned till about midnight," wrote the chaplain, "when her untutored spirit took its flight. . . ."

There was little sleep on the ridge that night. Instead, there followed a lively theological debate between those who viewed God as a terrible and vengeful Judge and those who were equally sure that no loving God could suffer one of His creatures to endure the pangs of fire forever. The consensus reached by these amateur theologians was that "there was a mistake in the popular theology of the time," Garner said. "And I am frank to say that that trying scene produced a radical change in my own theological ideas."[17]

Corporal Grabosch was involved in a similarly horrifying situation in mid-December. Some mules were missing from the regimental pasture at Culleoka one morning, and Captain Miller ordered Grabosch out with a squad to search for them. Stopping at a farmhouse near Mooresville to make inquiries, Grabosch was met at the door by a housewife with no information but with a pile of woolen socks that she had knitted for sale to soldiers. Private John Halmark, slightly tipsy, tried on a pair, and then walked out without paying for them. Grabosch, after rejoining the squad out on the road, "told Halmark he would report him upon his return to camp."

Furious at the Corporal, Halmark became unmanageable. He jumped from his horse close to Mooresville and stalked into a house in search of more liquor. By this time Grabosch was angry himself, and he ordered two of the men to go in after

Halmark, rescue the terrified family, and bring out the intruder. They had to drag Halmark out, kicking and screaming, and Grabosch crisply pronounced him under arrest.

As the squad remounted, the enraged prisoner, calling Grabosch every name he could think of, suddenly leveled his Springfield at the Corporal and fired. To the great horror of the others, the charge struck Grabosch in the right cheek, and tore a gaping hole in his left cheek as it passed through.

While some of the men subdued Halmark, the others carried the stunned and bleeding Grabosch indoors. The lady of the house and her daughters prepared a bedroom and undertook to minister to him. Even so, it appeared for a time that the critically injured youth would strangle in his own blood. Everyone was sure that Grabosch would soon be laid beneath the soil of Tennessee, "but he was too much pluck for that," his chaplain proudly declared.

Grabosch was sufficiently recovered by Christmas that the men could bring him to Houts back at Culleoka. The redoubtable St. Louis doctor had his work cut out for him. The caliber .58 ball had done its worst. The lower jaw bone had been splintered on the right side. All the teeth on that side were gone, and some of those on the left as well. The lock of the jaw under the ear, Houts noted, was something of a problem. He decided to disjoint it, which was a ticklish proposition because of the proximity of important blood vessels. What, then, was he to do?

Houts made a long incision extending from the chin along the jaw and almost to the ear. The busy scalpel went farther, dissecting the flesh back to a line with the teeth and uncovering the joint. Using his surgical saw, Houts trimmed the chin bone. He then disarticulated the lock of the jaw, and after that it was time to sew Grabosch back up and hope for the best.

The Corporal's face was scarred on both sides, his speech impaired, and it was going to prove impossible to fit him with the ordinary dentures of the time. But just as grass and flowers in time cover the man-made scars on the earth's face, so Charles Grabosch's heavy new black beard, reaching from ear to ear, soon hid his disfigurement. In time, Chaplain Garner said, "his face was quite presentable, and he returned to duty the same patriot he had been from the first." For some unknown reason, Captain Miller never came to preferring charges against Halmark.[18]

Tragedy came in other forms, too. The general hospital at Memphis sent word that Private Asbury Burnside, of Company F, a thirty-eight-year-old farmer from DeWitt, Missouri, had died on December 5. Private John Neighbours, who had mustered with Company D in 1861, died at Mound City, Illinois, on December 8. His younger brother, Bill, had been captured by enemy raiders at Newburgh, Indiana, while a hospital patient in the summer of 1862, but he had since been exchanged and returned to duty. Originally Virginians, the boys had come to Putnam County as children. On December 13, death struck in Company K, when Private John Hackett, an Irish-born peacetime laborer, fell into the Duck River and drowned. He had been working on the railroad bridge with a detail from the regiment under the supervision of Sherman's chief engineer. Hackett, who enlisted in St. Louis, had been in the service not quite a year.[19]

Shortly after Christmas, Dodge ordered the 18th Missouri to Pulaski, where it could be on hand for the hard skirmishing expected in the Athens-Decatur region of northern Alabama. With Colonel Bane going on leave, along with thousands of other soldiers in Sherman's forces, Miller took command of the Third Brigade for the next month, and Sheldon was in command of the 18th Missouri when it started on the road to Pulaski.

The men rode out of Culleoka, where it hadn't been too bad after all, on January 22, 1864. Their thirty-mile trip to Pulaski took several days because of the roughness of the roads during the chilly forenoons and their muddiness after midday thaws.

It was on the second day that Garner and Hoover, serving as steward and cook for the headquarters mess, decided to improve the cuisine by adding some locally grown chickens if possible. At one large house they detached themselves from the procession and went in to see about the chicken situation. The occupants of the house, it turned out, were a snippish matron and her Negro maid. As it was almost noon, the women were busily fixing their meal.

Noting several fat hens in the yard, Garner politely suggested to the landlady that he would be pleased to purchase one or two for the headquarters mess. But the old woman was not of a mind to accommodate him. "Don't think for a minute," she stated flatly, "that I would furnish any supplies for this set of Yankees down here stealing our niggers and murdering our men."

Garner winked at Hoover and started for the back door. "I've just got to get at least one chicken," he mumbled. Determined that he would not, the Rebel amazon stamped briskly after him. Meanwhile, the Negress, taking up her mistress' defense, was showering poor Hoover with all manner of reproaches, even as she stirred a large iron stew-kettle full of chicken and dumplings.

"I vould like to haf a drink," Hoover suggested. The maid, to keep him from going out back to help the huge officer steal Missy's chickens, offered to get the water herself if Hoover would just kindly stand where he was. This was seemingly agreeable to him, and the hoodwinked maid soon found out why. When she returned with the dipper, Hoover was gone. And so, for that matter, was the kettle! He had unhooked the boiling pot, bounded out the front door, and loaded it in the back of a passing wagon.

"Good God, Missus!" the maid bawled out the back door. "You stan' dar and fuss at dat white man and now yo' chicken done gone, pot and all!" Then, suddenly appreciating the comedy of it, she broke out laughing. Chaplain Garner said a smiling goodbye to the flabbergasted woman and rode off to join Hoover.

A mile or so down the road, the regiment halted for dinner. Before the amazed headquarters staff, Lawrence Hoover uncovered his prize, a fat hen, dressed with dumplings and seasoned with butter. Colonel Sheldon gazed into the kettle a minute, looked at Garner, then at Hoover. "Well, Chaplain," he said, "I'll be dammed if this looks much like Christianity as I understand it." Nonetheless, Sheldon ate his share of the proceeds.

The boys in Company G were being entertained by the rise and fall of the regiment's only phrenologist, Private James W. Chenoweth. This thirty-two-year-old carpenter from Marengo, Iowa, was an odd one in the eyes of his fellows. He was attracting a lot of attention and had been since the regiment's arrival in Culleoka, for he had struck it rich practicing phrenology on the large crowd of Negroes that constantly followed the regiment. Many of them regarded him with superstitious awe, for they were sure that he had the power to feel the bumps on their heads, analyze their characters and tell their fortunes. Many of them parted with small change for the service that this strange Yankee soldier could perform.

One boy named Sam, about fifteen, wanted the "professor" to check his cranium, but Sam was totally without funds to pay the expense of Chenoweth's ministrations. Chenoweth made a deal with the boy, whereby in exchange for a reading Sam would carry his knapsack and blanket to Pulaski.

It was agreed, and the phrenologist's fingers were soon searching out the bumps on Sam's skull. "This gentleman," Chenoweth finally announced with solemnity, "has a very large acquisitiveness. With a fair chance and a long life he will die as rich as Croesus and go to his grave in a gold casket."

Sam was puzzled. "Whut do dat word 'quisiness' mean?"

"It means," the professor explained, "the love of money and the ability to get it."

As the regiment moved out for that last day's march, Chenoweth did his best to make himself completely repulsive to the men by twitting them about having to tote their own burdens. "Why didn't you boys study Fowler and Wells like I did?" he crowed, pointing to the boy walking alongside his horse with the knapsack and blankets. "Maybe you'da had a nigger, too."

Around noon the tables dramatically turned on the triumphant professor. During some confusion, Sam bolted into the woods, and poor Chenoweth soon discovered he was bereft of his boy, his blankets, the knapsack, and an entire extra uniform, to say nothing of his canteen. Now it was the turn of his comrades to tease him back.

"Hey, Chenoweth!" they kept taunting him. "Where's yer nigger?" Or, as one sassy fellow demanded, "Why didn't ya

study negro-ology before you ventured out into the world?"
Chenoweth was evidently past his heyday in the 18th Missouri.[20]

Sheldon was able to assemble all the regiment except Company
C in a tent-and-shack camp near Pulaski. Donnelly and the
forty-six available men in his company still were with Fuller
at Prospect, below Pulaski. The main body of Dodge's command
was now concentrated around Pulaski, and that left the newcomers very slim pickings for housing.

Not that it mattered much, for as Sheldon recalled in 1891,
"we . . . spent much time scouting, and watching the various
fords and ferries. . . ." Roddey's men were on the prowl everywhere along the Tennessee River. Phillips' 9th Illinois and
Colonel George E. Spencer's 1st Alabama had their hands full
around Athens, and when Sheldon's men reached Pulaski they
found out why Dodge had pulled them out of Culleoka. On
Saturday, January 23, Dodge assured Phillips that the 18th
Missouri would be on its way to his support at Athens early
Monday morning.[21]

While directing the 18th Missouri's scouting expeditions in
the neighborhood of Florence, Sheldon had an experience
that brought back some pungent memories of the Chewalla
days. Developing a hunger for buttermilk, and assured that the
area produced plenty of it, the young officer stopped at one of
the "more pretentious houses," on a prosperous-looking farm.

Sheldon was met at the door by a smiling black-eyed girl
who startled him by her strangely familiar manner. "Good
morning, Colonel Sheldon," she said. And that did shake him,
"for I had never been in that locality before," Sheldon later
wrote.

"Perhaps," she suggested to the puzzled visitor, "you'd like
to get that sugar and coffee now?"

It was the black-eyed lass who had chased Lieutenant
Conway down those porch steps with a butcher knife back in
Mississippi! "And now," Sheldon said in his recollections, "here
she stood, as smiling as a May morning, with a faraway
malicious twinkle in her black eyes." Remembering that first
skirmish with this young virago back in that clearing near

PETER MADISON MILLER
*(1811-1896)*
Colonel    1862-1864

*"He is as mild as you please, yet at the same time is so firm and commanding that the men obey him as if by instinct."*

JOHNATHAN M. YATES
*(1842-1929)*
Sergeant    Company D

*An unlucky leg wound cost him his chance to enjoy a "Blue and Gray" swimming party in the deep Chattahoochee River.*

JAMES A. PRICE *(1829-1916)*
Major, 18th Missouri, 1862

*A practicing dentist, this tall Virginian became a fighting patriot.*

DAVID WILSON POLLOCK
*(1841-1910)*
Captain   Company B, 18th Mo.

*Eldest son of a Scottish sailor, he went on from a meritorious performance as a company commander to become a banker, merchant, and cattle-buyer.*

CHARLES S. SARGEANT
*(1839-1900)*
(alias Charles S. Sheldon)
Colonel   1864-1865

*"He always said, 'Come, boys,*
*let us do,' and it was done."*

MAJ. GEN. GRENVILLE MELLEN
DODGE *(1831-1916)*

*He felt obliged to tear into the*
*affairs of the 18th Missouri with*
*all the finesse of a Mafia*
*trigger-man.*

JOSEPH GROSS *(1843-1929)*

*A native of Baden who settled in*
*Chariton County, he rose in four*
*years from private to first*
*sergeant of Company H.*

Capt. Darius A.
Cudworth (*1836-1924*)
Regimental Quarter-
master, 1862-1865

*Scion of a distinguished
house in Old and New
England, "Cud" bore his
pedigree with becoming
nonchalance and proved
the equal of those rugged
westerners with whom
he cast his lot.*

The Reverend John M. Garner
Chaplain    1861-1864

*"My qualifications . . . were
ignorance, impudence, and a pair of
strong lungs."*

WILLIAM CARL PILATZ
*(1835-1914)*

*After four years in Company H, this immigrant German stood faithful guard over the graves of his comrades, a one-man memorial society for whom the memory of "the Boys" never grew dim.*

*Below:*
LT. VINCENT C. BRUCE
*(standing)*
CPL. QUINCY R. BRUCE
*(seated)*

*Members of a loyalist farm family, these Ohio-born brothers served bravely and well in Company C.*

LAWRENCE HOOVER
(1831-1913)

*An erstwhile German tailor came out of his adopted country's Folk Epic the prototype of the modern American "go-getter."*

DANIEL MORGAN SHELTON
(1840-1907)
Private   Company E   1861-1864

*Within three years this fighting Kentuckian had been wounded twice and captured once.*

BENJAMIN GUFFEY
(1840-1924)

*The sturdy Kentuckian and future physician showed every quality of a fearless soldier in his four-year rise from private to second lieutenant in Company I.*

HENRY RUNNELS
(1839-1918)

*One of the wounded
sergeants at Shiloh, this
courageous Iowan rose in
time to become captain
of Company E.*

BRIG. GEN. JOHN WALLACE
FULLER (1827-1891)

*"He never asked anyone to go
where he was not willing to go
himself."*

Library of Congress

Louis Benecke (1843-1919)

*Military training in the Blanken-burg* Gymnasium *made him a "natural" for a sergeantcy in Company H and started his rise to postwar eminence as a Missouri state senator and department commander of the Grand Army.*

Maj. Gen. Joseph Anthony Mower (1827-1870)

*"He was especially fond of the 18th Missouri, and . . . when he had any . . . river crossings to force, he never failed to remember them."*

Brady Collection, National Archives

Chewalla, Sheldon had no desire to "force the 18th Missouri to retreat again." He meekly paid the Rebel miss what she asked for the buttermilk, and led his scouting party off the premises with a minimum of ceremony.

The male of the Confederate species certainly seemed the less deadly that cold and bitter January. Roddey stayed out of Sheldon's way in the Florence area. Twelve men of Company D had a short and noisy clash with a party of mounted Rebels near Blue Water, on January 25, but when the regiment re-assembled two days later at Pulaski, Wyckoff's twelve troopers were still the only ones who had actually drawn a bead on the enemy.[22]

For some time now, General Dodge had been hearing disturbing tales about the Missourians' behavior. Almost daily he received reports of smokehouses raided, stock stolen, farm-ers beaten and robbed, houses burglarized. Colonel Henry R. Mizner, commanding at Columbia, Tennessee, caustically in-formed Dodge on February 5, 1864, that the Missourians had recently robbed a one-armed boy of his pony and had even stolen two slaves from a plantation "after you had written Col-onel Miller severely on the subject."

Dodge's provost guards, however, had been making some spectacular headway in solving the recent crimes. On January 25 they pounced on the 18th Missouri at Pulaski and arrested five men. Four were in Elwood Miller's E Company, but the accused ringleader was one of the most renowned veterans of Company G. The crime that had tripped them up was the beat-ing and robbery of an elderly farm couple, Sam and Martha Davis, in Maury County on January 9. During the attempt to rob the Davises, which netted only fifty dollars—in Confederate currency at that—Mrs. Davis, while pleading for her husband's life, was pistol-whipped and suffered a skull fracture. Davis recognized at least one of the soldiers and several of the civilian accomplices with the night-riding party.

While the charges were being prepared, Dodge notified Grant on February 4 that he had carried out a "thorough in-vestigation and found a gang existed in the 18th Missouri which was connected with a gang of citizens, ten of which I have in irons, and every one of which I will hang if convicted."[23]

THE SOUTHEASTERN THEATER
1863–1865

# CHAPTER IX

# *"Three Cheers and a Tiger!"*

WHILE THE WINTER was passing without major operations anywhere, great anxiety was gripping the War Department. Plans
for the 1864 campaigns in Virginia and Georgia were in prepara-
tion, but it seemed entirely possible that the manpower needed
might not be on hand. The enlistments of a hundred thousand
battle-hardened volunteers who had joined up in 1861 would
soon be expiring. The Lincoln Administration did not feel
sufficiently in control of its citizens or of its Congress to extend
servicemen's terms for the duration. Secretary Stanton was
understandably agitated at the prospect of losing the hard
core of the Federal armies just as the decisive year was dawning.

One solution that seemed worth a try was a program of
incentives to induce the "1861 boys" to sign up for the duration.
In December, 1863, the veteran proposition was published to
the troops, and the drive was soon under way in each regiment
to get three-fourths of the men on the roster to re-enlist. And
what if enough signed? The Government would give each man
a bounty of $400. He would be categorized as a veteran vol-
unteer on company rolls and would wear a little chevron on the
lower part of his left tunic sleeve emblematic of his new status.
The regiment would get a month's furlough. Also, it would be
redesignated a Veteran Volunteer outfit by the Adjutant General, its name accordingly changed.

For Secretary Stanton the crucial question was whether or

not the incentives would work. And many who witnessed the discussions in the Army of the Tennessee's frost-bitten camps had their doubts. "Can it be possible," asked one soldier-diarist, "that the men will contract to prolong this life of privation and arduous duties?" Some would not, it turned out, but 136,000 men throughout the nation did catch the "veteran fever."[1]

With Miller commanding the brigade, it was left to Sheldon to "veteranize" the 18th Missouri. There was no great urgency about it, Sheldon found, since the regiment, being mounted, was among those to be held in the combat zone until unmounted troops had completed their furloughs, in February. From Sheldon's point of view, it was well that he had a little time. He reported stiff resistance, for which it is altogether likely that he was purposefully responsible. "I find it impossible to reorganize the regiment as Infantry," he complained to Brigadier General John B. Gray, Missouri's Adjutant General, on February 2, 1864. The reason Sheldon gave was that some of the men had enlisted with Morgan as cavalrymen and were still miffed because they had been kept as infantrymen. Over 300 were willing to stay in uniform if they could become cavalrymen, though.

Behind all this one sees Sheldon the eternal Horse Soldier! He brought pressure on General Gray: "I have made application to the Sec. of War to have the Regiment changed to Cavalry. . . ." He cajoled: "The Regiment is now mounted and the change to Cavalry will be but in name." And then he unmasked his real motive: "I very much prefer Cavalry myself," he told Gray. If the 18th Missouri remains infantry, Sheldon wanted to know, "what will be the probability of my getting authority to raise a regiment of Cavalry?"

Nothing came of this attempt to convert the 18th Missouri into a cavalry outfit, for the War Department vetoed the plan on February 24. In spite of the great disappointment this presumably caused, all but about a hundred men of the regiment finally re-enlisted as veterans—after months of urging. The men at the front, Sheldon later wrote, felt that 1864 would see the Rebellion's mortal wounding if not its outright extermination, for they realized better than the civilians in the North "how entirely the fighting strength of the South was already in the ranks. . . ." The men who signed on as veterans were consequently of a mind to "see the thing out."[2]

While the 18th Missouri shadow-boxed with Confederate horsemen and reacted to infantry scares during those vexatious weeks of January and early February, important developments affecting the regiment's future came one upon another. The recruiting officer in St. Louis, Lieutenant Gray, was dismissed from the Army "by direction of the President" on January 23, 1864. It seems that the Provost Guards, detaining Gray after raiding a burlesque show in December, had misunderstood what the Lieutenant said his name was, and the whole thing was blown up into a punitive proceeding by General Schofield. A week later, Schofield himself was gone from St. Louis, off to Sherman's Army for a field command, and Rosecrans was installed in his place as commander of the Department of the Missouri. On January 31 there came the shocking news of Governor Gamble's death from pneumonia, and the swearing in of Lieutenant Governor Hall as the state's second Provisional Governor.[3]

General Dodge was intervening in the affairs of the 18th Missouri with a crafty but deadly intent. In the early part of February the courts-martial of the "18th Missouri Gang" were in progress. Four received terms in the Nashville Military Prison, but the accused leader was sentenced on February 10 "to be shot to death at such time and place as the Commanding General may direct. . . ."

Grenville Dodge couldn't wait. "I respectfully request authority to carry sentence into effect," he urged in a telegram to Grant on February 17. "It is a just verdict. . . . He is a very bad man." Grant, however, wired back a tart reminder that the U.S. Army was seldom in such a hurry to shoot a prisoner. The War Department, he explained to non-West Pointer Dodge, required exhaustive reviews of all such cases before execution of sentences. And this spared the leader an appearance before a firing-squad. His sentence was soon reviewed and reduced to a term in the Nashville prison "for the duration."

To most men in the regiment, the members of the gang were actually martyred men, victimized by tremulous politicians and political generals for doing what plenty of other fellows were doing. This was war—and civil wars are the bitterest kind—and the 18th Missouri was in enemy territory. That this was the men's first and lasting judgment is clear enough today, for the convicted men were always honored and welcome participants in the regiment's postwar reunions.

Meanwhile, Dodge's purge was widening. On February 10 his provost marshal placed Elwood Miller under arrest! The charges, preferred by the Corps Judge Advocate, were two: false muster and illegal sale of United States property. Three days later Dodge moved menacingly against Madison Miller himself, demanding that he produce at Corps Headquarters two shotguns taken from a mill by Hemstreet's scouts in December. "You will also report in writing," Miller was told, "why this property was not returned and turned over to the proper Staff Department, in accordance with orders from the War Department, Department of the Tennessee, and these Head Quarters."

Dodge was declaring war on the Miller family, apparently. The men of the regiment never learned exactly what the trouble was. Sheldon did not allude to it in his memoirs, nor did Miller. "Our Colonel was in trouble," Garner remembered in the spring of 1895, "and this caused some excitement and much talk in the regiment. What the trouble was and how it was finally settled, I never knew. . . ." Yet, curiously enough, in 1894 the chaplain had seen fit to say that from the Chewalla days onward "we were under strict surveillance which culminated in our reorganization and change of commanders at Pulaski. . . ."

Madison Miller was ready to go anyhow. Accumulating grievances with Dodge's staff and with state authorities had taken from him all desire to serve beyond his three years. As early as January 10 there had been rumors at the War Department that he would resign. On February 10, the day of Elwood's arrest, he wrote a letter of resignation, giving "neuralgia in chest and right arm" as his official reason. He delayed sending in his letter, however, until Dodge threatened in writing to arrest him on March 8. The resignation was made official the next week.

The Colonel evidently held off resigning in the hope that he somehow might be able to protect his son. But there seemed no way to help Elwood at the moment. Dodge called the shots at the Pulaski Courthouse, and he demanded the start of the trial on February 22. The court gave Elwood's counsel one day to prepare, and the hearing began in earnest on February 23.

Worst of all, perhaps, for Elwood was his admission in open court that he was guilty on the charge of false muster! Sure, he said, he had a ruptured man in Company E, Pat Pepper, who was unfit for mounted service, so he had hired a local civilian, John Rowell, to impersonate Pepper on scouting duty and at formations.

What, the prosecutor demanded, did Captain Miller do about having *two* Pat Peppers around, especially at formations and musters? Elwood explained that he had simply told Pepper to leave the company area. Advising a soldier to desert! The more Elwood said, the deeper he fell into Grenville Dodge's snare.

There occurred more accusations over the alleged illegal sale of Government property. A local civilian, about to start a penitentiary term for his consulting services for the 18th Missouri Gang, testified that he had swapped a saddle-horse with Company E for a mule that he had later sold in Columbia. Regarding the trade as illegal in the first place, the prosecutor angrily emphasized this sale of "a Government mule" with Captain Miller's foreknowledge. Among the others testifying against Miller on the mule business were Sergeant Charles Rau, regimental bugler, and Private Solomon Childers. The civilian witness maintained stoutly that Colonel Miller, Elwood, and Lieutenant Everest were all familiar with the deal, but he conceded that Captain Miller might not have known he was going to sell the mule.

On February 29 the anguished Colonel saw his only son declared guilty and cashiered from the service. It was a dark hour for the proud Millers of Carondelet. Grenville Dodge's impressive trumps were now on the table, but the Millers had yet to play their best cards.[4]

It meanwhile had devolved upon Sheldon to take the veteran volunteers of the regiment home to Missouri. Orders to go were published at Pulaski on February 19, and the vacationing Missourians were off two days later by train for Nashville. "Bound for home," Teamster Sawyer joyously noted in the little pocket diary he had just begun. On February 22 the boys went aboard the steamboat *Imperial* at the Nashville wharves for a happy but unexciting three-day trip to St. Louis. Lieutenant Partenheimer remained behind with the detachment of enlisted men who, like him, had successfully resisted veteran fever.

Sheldon and his men had some cause for sorrow even at departing the battlefields of Tennessee. They were giving up their precious saddle-horses with no prospect of ever seeing them again. Dodge having so ordered, there was nothing for Cudworth to do but turn over to the quartermaster "Six hundred fine horses, that never cost the government a dollar," as Sheldon afterward lamented.[5]

Dawn was just breaking over the St. Louis water front when the *Imperial* docked at the foot of Green Street on Sunday, February 25. Greeted by a representative of General Gray, Sheldon handed that official a letter notifying Gray that "sixteen officers and four hundred enlisted men of the 18th Mo. Inf. Vols." had re-enlisted as veteran volunteers and were now awaiting furloughs and pay. The City Post Band began to play as the men filed on to the dock, and an honor guard from the 7th Missouri Volunteers presented arms.

A Veteran Reception Committee, appointed by Mayor Chauncey I. Filley and composed of prominent St. Louis men and women, was on hand to lead Sheldon's men to Turner's Hall, at 10th and Walnut. Here the 18th Missouri encountered a schedule of festivities the like of which they had never seen and would never again see. It began at the anteroom, where, as one local reporter said, the veterans had "the dust washed from their throats with copious draughts of lager beer."

Before the men could take *too much*, however, they were led on into the great hall for an address by Mayor Filley. "The Eighteenth Missouri are well known," His Honor intoned, "and so are their deeds on many fields of battle. Most of you are from interior counties of the State, and most of these counties are good ones. You have done well, but the noblest thing you have done is to re-enlist and come home."

After the applause subsided, General Gray went to the platform to make a few remarks that culminated in a rousing "Three Cheers for the Eighteenth!" Following this, Sheldon was on his feet to propose three cheers for the Reception Committee and the State of Missouri. One of the men in the regiment followed this to call for three cheers for Sheldon himself, "and the men responded at the top of their voices," a reporter said.

At noon Brigadier General Clinton B. Fisk, commanding the District of St. Louis, played host to the veterans at a banquet far surpassing anything they had been able to get from foraging in Tennessee and Mississippi. In ceremonies concluding the affair, Fisk presented to Sheldon a beautiful silk banner displaying the state coat of arms.

"Your deeds are treasured up in the heart and memory of Missouri's loyal sons and daughters, and are written on the brightest pages of our national history," declaimed Fisk. "Colonel Sheldon, I have the honor of placing in your hands this banner. Bear it with you, brave men, to the field of conflict. We know it will never be dishonored."

Of his response, Colonel Sheldon in later years could "remember but little," except that he had promised that the flag would never be dishonored and had proposed "three cheers and a tiger" for the patriotic ladies who had made it. Had Sheldon kept a clipping from the February 26 issue of *The Missouri Democrat,* he would have found his brief speech there preserved:

> General. In the name of the officers and men of the 18th Missouri Volunteers, I accept this flag, and return to you and the Committee whom you represent the thanks of the regiment for the beautiful gift, and we promise you that wherever we go this banner shall be borne with honor. I believe that in all the bloody fields where Missouri regiments have fought they have demeaned themselves with bravery—no stain of dishonor rests upon any Missouri regiment. On behalf of the 18th, I thank you for the generous reception we have received today, and promise you that when we return to the field the flag which you have given us shall wave to the glory of the cause.[6]

That afternoon the regiment marched over to Benton Barracks, from which it had departed just two years previously for those tragic adventures down the river. The memories of the sorely tried veterans were heavily laden with images of those who did not make it back to enjoy that triumphal homecoming—

Captain Jake Clark, Riley Howe, John Rigler, Adjutant Bill Edgar, Uncle Bill Smith, Jim Simmons, Lieutenant Dayton, Ben Musgrove, and how many others?

Before furloughs could be arranged, however, clothing and equipment accounts had to be brought up to date. There would be precious little time in April. The depleted ranks of officers had to be filled, and a spate of promotions at the beginning of March accomplished a little. Coddington, Fallis, and Edgar received captain's bars in Companies F, I, and K. Five new first lieutenants were drawn at the same time from enlisted ranks. Sergeant John L. Jones, a Linn County schoolmaster who had been first sergeant of Company A for two years, now became Dan Hudson's first lieutenant. A similar position in Company D went to the handsome, swarthy Sergeant Rhoderick R. Rockwood, like most of Wyckoff's men a Putnam Countian. Jim Coddington's new first lieutenant was one of the "Shiloh captives," Joe Brown. Sergeant Charles W. Mansfield, an Ayersville farm boy from Putnam, put on gold bars in Hemstreet's Company G. Making the jump to commissioned ranks also was another prisoner of Shiloh, Mike Callery, sworn in as Edgar's new first lieutenant.

New noncoms graced three companies that first week of March. Sergeant John A. Marine, a Linn Countian, took over Lieutenant Jones' old first sergeantcy in Company A, and John A. Riggen of Sullivan County received Marine's sergeantcy. Sergeant Tom Cawood, still another of the prisoners of Shiloh, stepped up to first sergeant in Company G, and Corporal Robert Ewing, a Ray County farmer who had joined at Platte City, became a sergeant. Corporal's stripes in Hemstreet's outfit went to James Knox, George W. Snyder, and John Wagle. Captain Edgar made six men in K Company similarly happy, awarding the first sergeantcy to Gebhart Kurtz; a sergeantcy to Private Charles Manda, a young German from St. John; and corporal's ratings to Privates David W. Reisch, Archibald D. Abel, Zachariah Douglas, and Daniel John.[7]

On March 8 the paper work was done, and the men could go. Sheldon and Cudworth left for Massachusetts, and the other officers departed for furloughs, mostly in Missouri and adjoining states. Those leaving for homes in Missouri soon found that the war had dealt harshly with the countryside. Said Garner: "Lawns had not grown, and the weeds and bushes had encroached upon our fields. Women could not cultivate a very broad acreage, and where there were several children in a family to feed and clothe, the mother could not hire labor out of the small amount earned by her husband.... Houses and fences were out of repair, and the general outlook was not hopeful. And many of us, on that account, would have been more contented without our ... furlough."[8]

Many of the men returning to Putnam County were, as Jacob Ault had warned division headquarters two years before, seething with indignation at stories of "Secesh depradations" back in Missouri. Men left at home, faced with constant guerrilla attacks and rumors of such, had been waging sporadic vigilante violence since 1861, and there had been at least seven killings of suspected Rebel sympathizers in the past two years in Putnam County alone. Dave Pollock, writing his brother less than a year before the veteran furlough, had declared with great feeling that "The dam rebels at home is what prolongs this war and you have plenty of them about St. John. I wish the old 18th could get back in that part of the country. . . ."

Now the troops *were* home, and the repercussions were not long in coming. On March 21, a Monday, the spring term of the Circuit Court opened in Unionville, in a courtroom crowded with boisterous and tipsy veterans of the 18th Missouri. Two secessionist lawyers from Milan were going to be on hand to argue cases, the indignant soldiers had learned. They wanted to be there to see if this was really going to happen. But the target of their heckling, it developed, was not the visiting Rebel barristers but the Reverend J. L. Woods, a Southern Methodist pastor of confessed Rebel leanings. Egged on by the circuit judge as well as the local Methodist preacher, the returned heroes of Shiloh and Corinth constantly badgered Woods with hateful partisan remarks. Mr. Woods, reluctant to banter with the veterans on so dangerous a subject, explained that he was in town temporarily on court business, that he would be off for Oregon in a day or two and thus out of their sight and hearing.

The soldiers, however, grew passionately determined to

harry the offending parson out of town immediately. It being clear that nothing less would appease the inflamed veterans, Woods saddled up and rode away at 1:00 P.M. To hasten him on his way, some of the men started firing their Springfields in the air and toward him. One ball struck Mr. Woods in the back and inflicted a fatal stomach wound. He died before daybreak Tuesday, evidently the eighth "Rebel" to die under similar circumstances in Putnam County.

The news spread, magnifying the events in Unionville. Brigadier General Odon Guitar, commanding the District of North Missouri, telegraphed Rosecrans from Macon to report "serious trouble in Putnam County, occasioned by men of the Eighteenth Missouri Infantry recently returned on furlough." In fact, Guitar was certain by Saturday that at least four copperheads had lost their lives and that scores of others were "fleeing the county in every direction." Concluded Guitar, "these men have inaugurated a reign of blood and terror in Putnam and Sullivan Counties. I have ordered fifty men to Putnam to quell the disturbances. . . ."

While Rosecrans commended Guitar's prompt and vigilant reaction to the shooting affray of March 21, it appears that very little more came of the terror in Putnam County. The Circuit Court proceedings for the day give no hint of any disturbance affecting the dignity of the court, nor do the dockets of subsequent terms of the court reveal any cases stemming from the violence of March 21. Present-day natives of the county generally discount the published tales of the March terror of 1864, and contemporary newspaper accounts from the period seem not to have survived.

Things were no better out in Platte County. Lieutenant Callery, on leave in neighboring Buchanan County, was outraged to see the public peace of both counties guarded by militia regiments made up partly of former and suspected Confederates. He expressed in heated terms to General Fisk his indignation at seeing "those same reptiles on whose hands still smoke the blood of our murdered brothers domineering over our sons and aged fathers in a most shameful manner, supplied with arms by the United States." Fisk, lately transferred to St. Joseph, was implored to rectify this "great wrong" without delay.[9]

The furlough passed all too quickly, and the soldiers of the 18th made their way back to Benton Barracks, "nearly all promptly on time," as Colonel Sheldon said. Particularly thrilling to the youthful Colonel was his discovery that they were bringing with them enough recruits to fill the regiment up to regulation strength, approximately a thousand for a Volunteer Infantry outfit. Now Army regulations would permit an early muster of enough officers, more than a dozen still needed. All that remained was to swear in the recruits.

Sheldon's optimism was soon destroyed by military red tape. By the time the Army doctors at the Barracks finished their examinations, Sheldon's horde of recruits had dwindled to a paltry hundred. Too many of the lads were simply unable to convince the suspicious medics that they were really eighteen years old. And that, Sheldon ruefully conceded, "cut us down a little below the minimum." This fussiness over physical standards, says the Colonel, was one of the Federal Government's two most serious mistakes in its conduct of the war. The other stupidity was "the policy of organizing new regiments instead of filling up the old and tried ones. . . . If all the veteran regiments at the front had been kept full to the maximum, and well officered, it would not have required much over one-half the troops that were finally needed to put down the rebellion."[10]

The officer situation was to get worse before it improved. On April 15, the day before the regiment left for Nashville on the steamboat *Prairie Rose,* the 18th Missouri lost the only chaplain it had ever had or ever would have. Apparently, during his sojourn at Laclede this time, Garner had reflected on "some of my past experiences with the disrespect with which—as Chaplain—I had been overwhelmed by just two or three of our officers with whom my official position forced me [into] painfully close association. . . ." Fearing that the discord would grow, Garner decided to unburden his feelings directly to General Rosecrans. On the morning of April 14, with his baggage already on board, the chaplain got his appointment with Rosey and laid bare his old rancors over the Chewalla dance hall and other real and fancied slights. The Reverend Doctor declared himself unwilling to continue "drawing pay from the Government for a position which, by force of circumstances, has become only nominal."

"Now, General," Garner concluded at length, "please advise me what to do."

"I would tender my resignation at once," the Victor of Corinth responded, promising to "have the answer here before your regiment can get off tomorrow."

And, writes Garner, "he did. On the 15th of April at 10 A.M. I received an honorable discharge, unshipped my baggage and . . . on the 16th landed at home a free man, with the consciousness that I had tried faithfully to make myself useful in every possible way."

The men would miss "dear, good Dr. John M. Garner," as James A. Price described him in 1892. The fiery circuit-rider had done his best for the Cause, and in the postwar reunions of his old regiment he was certain always to be a revered figure.[11]

This last visit home had been "burdened with tenderest pathos" for the boys, their chaplain noted. And events in and around the Barracks quickly showed how taut the regimental nerves had become. On April 12 a militia lieutenant with a provost guard came to arrest two men from Company A, Private James A. Arnold of Weston and Private Adam Livingston of Carroll County.

The visitors got a hot reception. Arnold and Livingston rushed into their quarters, the former to get his Springfield and the latter a revolver. "No officer of the damned Militia is going to arrest any of us in the Eighteenth!" Arnold screamed at the startled lieutenant, all the while drawing a bead on him. Livingston stood by scowling at the intruders, his weapon at the ready. "You haven't got a thing to say around here!" Arnold yelled.

The guard corporal protested that this was no way to act in front of a lieutenant. "I don't care if he is an officer or a private," Arnold raved on, tossing in several "family names" well understood by the crowd of his comrades gathering in the barracks.

"I'll shoot the first one that touches a man of the Eighteenth," Livingston growled.

It was just at this point that the company commander, Captain Hudson, appeared on the scene with the Officer of the Day, a militia lieutenant, to see what the row was about. The commander of the guard rushed over with his demand that Arnold and Livingston be placed under arrest immediately.

"Nothing doing!" Hudson roared, quickly getting into the spirit of the occasion. And, noting that the provost officer had no insignia, Hudson promptly demanded to see his shoulder straps "and then I will recognize you as an officer."

The nonplused militiaman tried to assure Dan Hudson that he was indeed a first lieutenant, but that got him nowhere. "I won't take orders from a *lieutenant* nohow!" said Hudson.

At this point in the fuss the Officer of the Day made bold to order the enraged captain of Company A to arrest the two offending soldiers, against whom authorities in Platte and Carroll counties were apparently lodging a complaint of "capital crimes." Seeing that the O. D. was just another lieutenant, Hudson walked away with a scornful glance over his shoulder while the highly partisan throng cheered wildly.

The next day all three offenders were arrested anyhow and held for trial. They thus missed the boat for Nashville. Dan Hudson was convicted in late April of "conduct prejudicial to good order and military discipline" and sentenced to a reprimand from Sheldon. General Rosecrans, reviewing the case, regretted the necessity of "reprimanding an officer whose good service has heretofore entitled him to praise instead of censure." Livingston was soon acquitted and sent south, but things went harder with Arnold. He got thirty days at hard labor, wearing a ball and chain, and did not make it back to the regiment until midsummer.[12]

Just before sundown on Friday, April 15, the 18th Missouri marched 500 strong aboard the *Prairie Rose*. At daybreak the mighty steamer left the dock and headed southward. Those who remembered that other departure from St. Louis, in 1862, were understandably depressed this time. In the words of their chaplain, "Henceforth death would lurk along the path of every soldier in Sherman's army, and many must, of necessity, sleep under the pines of the south."

Not all members of the regiment made it to the boat on time. About twenty of them were absent without leave when the *Prairie Rose* pulled out, and six more (including Hudson, Arnold, and Livingston) were residing in St. Louis jails. Lieutenant Jones would lead Company A until Hudson squared things with the local police and traveled down to Tennessee—in May. Others who were missing when the boat left for Nashville were Captain Hemstreet, in the hospital at St. Louis, and Sergeant William P. Mansfield, brother of the new lieutenant in Company G, who had died at his Wyreka home during the furlough.[13]

In 1891 Sheldon described the voyage down to Nashville as "an uneventful journey." It is probable that the years had erased from his memory the jolt that shook the *Prairie Rose* when she hit the sandbar fifteen miles above Cairo on Sunday afternoon. An extensive leak set in through the jagged rift in the ship's hull, and it was only stopped by piling mattresses over the affected area. On Monday evening, April 18, the vessel limped into Cairo, where a futile attempt was made to repair the damage. Port authorities finally decided on Tuesday afternoon to offer Sheldon the services of the *Sunshine*. The latter boat had better luck, delivering the Missourians safely to Nashville the following Friday.[14]

While his regiment bedded down at the Soldiers Home in Nashville, Sheldon applied to the transportation office for a train to haul the Missourians to Pulaski. The officials were terribly sorry. General Sherman's standing order was that no regiment would ride the rails until further notice. Sick and disabled soldiers could ride, when necessary or possible, but the Nashville & Decatur line was currently burdened to capacity taking supplies to the front for the impending Big Push into Georgia. The Missourians would, therefore, please march down the pike to Pulaski.

That was bad luck, indeed. "The march would have been a matter of but little consequence," says Sheldon, "had we been properly supplied with camp fixtures, but as it was, occasioned some discomfort. We had a good turnpike to march on, but I noticed after about one day's trial the boys carefully avoided the 'pike,' and took the dirt road to the side, mud and all. While a turnpike is first-class road for [wagon] trains, nothing can be harder on the feet of a marching column. . . ."[15]

Meanwhile, the Miller family had opened a counterattack to reverse the court-martial verdict of February 29 at Pulaski. Spearheading the assault was Colonel Thomas C. Fletcher, commander of the 31st Missouri Infantry as well as Elwood's maternal uncle. On April 15, 1864, Fletcher put the case in the hands of his Congressman and fellow Radical, Henry T. Blow of St. Louis. All he asked of Blow, said Fletcher, was that he examine the evidence and seek an order from Secretary Stanton "permitting Capt. Miller to resign or mitigating the sentence . . . to an honorable discharge. . . ."

The Pulaski trial, as Fletcher viewed it, had been a railroad job. There was bad feeling between Elwood and Major Minter, Fletcher explained, omitting to say that the fact that Minter was a major was at the heart of the matter. Minter had a brother-in-law on the XVI Corps staff, and Fletcher hinted that here was the means by which Dodge's mind had been poisoned against "this gallant young man."

"Young Miller was arrested, confined to his tent, and forbidden any intercourse with any officer or other person," his uncle went on; "his regiment re-enlisted as veterans and went home on furlough. He was left at Pulaski . . . among strangers, a mere boy without any knowledge of his rights as an accused, without witnesses." Elwood's confession on the false-muster charge actually proved his essential innocence, Fletcher insisted. Hiring the substitute for Pepper was "natural to a young and ardent man . . . over anxious to have a large company for duty." The Government, argued Fletcher, "was not defrauded as it had the services of the man, the intent of wrong was wholly wanting in the entire action. . . ."

On April 23 Blow carried the case to Edwin M. Stanton, taking pleasure in "endorsing all that Col. Fletcher has said of Capt. Miller. . . ." Brigadier General Joseph Holt, Judge Advocate General of the Army, filed the matter in a basket for routine handling, but Elwood's case was not destined to gather any dust. A month after Holt got the papers, the Radicals of Missouri nominated Colonel Fletcher for governor. Soon it dawned on the War Department that Radical Candidate Fletcher was the Administration's standard-bearer in the forthcoming fall elections in Missouri. Neither Lincoln nor Stanton had the slightest desire to embarrass their gubernatorial candidate by letting his nephew's case hang fire any longer. Early in July Stanton ordered Holt to stage a special review of the case. The Millers and the Fletchers had begun to fight.[16]

On Sunday morning, April 24, the 18th Missouri started down the pike for its march to Pulaski. At midmorning they passed through Franklin, which in a few months would behold a carnage unrivaled in the West since Shiloh. The boys camped at Lynnville on Tuesday evening and marched into Pulaski in a driving rain the following morning. The whole exhausted outfit, said Teamster Sawyer, "laid by" that afternoon.

At Dodge's headquarters Colonel Sheldon was given an extensive briefing on what lay ahead. General Grant had gone east in March to become the "Lieutenant General Commanding" the armies of the United States, and General Sherman now commanded everything west of the Appalachians. The 18th Missouri, Dodge revealed, would move on down to Decatur, Alabama, where Partenheimer's "non-vet" detachment was waiting. At Decatur Sheldon would report to Brigadier General James C. Veatch, commanding the 4th Division of XVI Corps, for assignment to a brigade under Veatch.

Before heading out for Decatur on Thursday morning, some of the men went out to visit the nearby grave of Alexander McClelland of Company I. The poor first sergeant, a St. Joseph man, had not been able to make the trip home. He had died in the general hospital at Pulaski on March 14, at the age of thirty-four. Captain Fallis gave his job to Sergeant Joel Richardson.[17]

It was a beautiful Saturday afternoon, April 30, when the 18th Missouri reached Decatur Junction, on the north bank of the Tennessee opposite Decatur. Here they were greeted by Partenheimer's troops, and the ranks of the regiment now swelled to 666 men present for duty, with 120 more still on the rolls. At Decatur Junction, Sheldon met his new superior, Brigadier General John Wallace Fuller, commander of Veatch's First Brigade.

"The Brigade," Sheldon now learned, "was composed of the 27th and 39th Ohio, 64th Illinois, and 18th Missouri. The first two regiments had formed part of the old 'Ohio Brigade,' which had distinguished itself in many a hard fought battle, and particularly in the defense of Battery Robinet. . . . So we knew at the outset what was expected of us."

Late that afternoon, Fuller waved the Missourians across the river on the pontoon bridge laid by Dodge's engineers. Once in Decatur, the companies fell to the task of sorting and preparing teams, wagons, and field paraphernalia for the morrow's march eastward. And Dodge's staff completed briefing Sheldon and the other colonels on the Campaign of 1864, about to begin. During the weeks since Grant's arrival in Washington, he and President Lincoln had developed the Union's first comprehensive strategic scheme. Meade's Army of the Potomac was to take on Lee's Army of Northern Virginia, while outlying expeditions in the Valley and at Fort Monroe would nibble away at railway communications in Lee's rear areas. Sherman—with a hundred thousand men in the Armies of the Tennessee, Cumberland, and Ohio—would move against wily old Joe Johnston, now commanding Bragg's former Army of Tennessee, and seek to destroy that army and as much of Georgia's storehouse of supplies as possible. The curtain was all set to rise the first week of May.[18]

With a bouncy step the men of the 18th Missouri marched out of Decatur early Sunday morning, May 1, "with our flags proudly floating to the soft southern breeze." The moment for which Charles Sheldon had lived was now at hand, and in all the years to come he would cherish his memory of that exhilaration and "feeling of confidence, that we would do our full duty. . . ." Now he knew that "Stirring times were before us . . . and lessons of discipline and self-reliance begun at Chewalla, were to be put fully to the test. The deadly 'sharpshooter' took the place of the wily 'bushwhacker,' and the roar of artillery and the clash of lines of battle, and quarter strategy of long flanking marches, replaced the partisan warfare we had been so long experiencing."[19]

# CHAPTER X

# From Resaca to Kennesaw

SHERMAN WOULD NOT WAIT for the 18th Missouri to march the hundred miles from Decatur to Dodge's command post on the Chickamauga battleground. At noon on May 4, Sheldon's troops climbed aboard a special train sent out to meet them at Woodville, Alabama, and the Colonel had to leave Cudworth and Wagonmaster Pollock to bring their wagons through as best they could. At three o'clock the next morning the train pulled in to Chattanooga, and from then on the Missourians were back on their feet again.

Just before noon on Friday, May 6, Sheldon reported to Dodge at Lee and Gordon's Mill, on Chickamauga Creek. "All the preparations indicated a rapid march, and perhaps a desperate engagement," the young Colonel found. Sherman was cutting every regiment down to one wagon and ten pack-mules. Service with Fuller's brigade was obviously going to be strenuous. The Missourians took fullest advantage of this stop at Lee and Gordon's to "do some laundry" in the Chickamauga; this activity consisted mostly "in swimming or wading around with their clothes on for a few minutes, and then standing in the sun until dry," as Sheldon remembered it.

The 18th Missouri was going to the front without three of its veteran captains. Wyckoff had been left in the hospital at Decatur, Stults at Chattanooga. This placed Company B back in the hands of husky young D. W. Pollock, and Company D in charge of its new Lieutenant Rockwood, already proved an able and gallant leader. Captain Fallis had been sick at Pulaski since April 29, and Lieutenant McEfee, not too well himself, was running Company I for Little Dick.[1]

Along the Chickamauga, the Army of the Tennessee, Sherman's right wing, was forming. Commanded by Major General James Birdseye McPherson, a handsome young titan barely thirty-six, the Army consisted at the moment only of Dodge's XVI Corps and Major General John A. Logan's XV Corps. Frank Blair's XVII Corps was still away on its veteran furlough and not due back for another month. On paper, at least, McPherson was 25,000 strong. Schofield's Army of the Ohio, over on the left north of Dalton, Georgia, had only 17,000. Thomas' Army of the Cumberland, the center force facing Dalton from the northwest, had 45,000 men at the start. Sherman's entire army group must have contained some 90,000 troops as action commenced, whereas Joe Johnston's Army of Tennessee was lucky to have 60,000 men near enough to Dalton for use when Old Joe might need them. Bishop Polk, however, was hastening up from southern Alabama with 14,000.

General Sherman was going to try a sneaky maneuver on Joe Johnston, a hard fellow to catch napping. The Rebels were concentrated about Dalton, in the upper Connasauga basin. Sherman reasoned that the long and wooded Rocky Face Ridge, running southward from Dalton to the western approaches to Resaca, could conceal a rapid flank march toward Johnston's rear long enough for a strategic surprise. There were several gaps in the Ridge, including the Buzzard Roost Gap, northwest of Dalton, through which ran the Western & Atlantic railway connecting Chattanooga with Atlanta. Farther south was Mill Gap, and a few miles below that was Dug (or Babb's) Gap. Johnston had his forces watching these places—but not farther down at Snake Creek Gap, which opened just west of Resaca at the lower end of the Connasauga watershed.

Sherman wanted Schofield and Thomas to put pressure on Johnston, to "threaten Dalton in front, but not to attack its defenses until further orders. . . ." Meanwhile, McPherson's army would march speedily far to the south, along the west side of Taylor's Ridge, then cross that ridge through Ship's Gap.

The Army of the Tennessee would then pass rapidly eastward through Villanow, making for the head of Snake Creek Gap, down which it would charge against Johnston's presumably unprotected rear at Resaca. If McPherson could break the Western & Atlantic at Resaca, the Confederates would have to let go around Dalton and retreat in wild haste over rutted old wagon trails leading eastward to safety beyond the Connasauga. Schofield and Thomas would spring like tigers on the rear of the fleeing Rebels. Much of Johnston's heavy artillery and all railway rolling stock trapped north of the line-break would be lost. If Sherman had any luck at all, Jeff Davis might start his 1864 campaign by losing his major army in the lower South.[2]

The drive on Atlanta began Saturday morning, May 7. The Army of the Cumberland at once chased the Rebels off Tunnel Hill, above Dalton, permitting Sherman to scale the heights for a firsthand look at the valley spreading out southward before him. With Sweeny's division leading the way, and Veatch right behind Sweeny, the Army of the Tennessee rose from the banks of the Chickamauga shortly after 6 A.M. to begin its race down "the road to Villanow, by way of Ship's Gap." Logan's corps fell in behind Dodge's two divisions.

After camping four miles north of Ship's Gap, Dodge's men started for the Gap at daybreak Sunday. Clearing it by late morning, McPherson was at Villanow by early afternoon. In a hurried note written there, he told Sherman he would be in Snake Creek Gap by sundown. But Mac was getting worried, expressing great concern over the whereabouts of Brigadier General Kenner Garrard's cavalry division, reconnoitering in the area of Rome, Georgia. "Unless he comes up soon, I am a little apprehensive about the safety of our trains," McPherson wrote. And well he might have been, with his wagons strung out along the road back to Taylor's Ridge.

Little though Sheldon or his troops realized, Joe Johnston was becoming uneasy over Wheeler's reports of a column of Yankee infantry scurrying along Taylor's Ridge toward the Confederate rear. Although Johnston still thought on May 8 that Sherman meant to stage a decisive battle around Dalton, he nevertheless ordered redoubled vigilance at *all* gaps in Rocky Face Ridge. As one result, Brigadier General James Cantey's small division of Bishop Polk's corps, arriving in Resaca fresh from the Gulf Coast on May 7, received orders to stay there, dig in, and hold on, come what may. This did not yet plug up Snake Creek Gap, but the "cork" was close.[3]

On Sunday night the men of the XVI Corps slept along a six-mile stretch of the winding wagon trail that led southward down densely wooded Snake Creek Gap. Back at the entrance of the Gap, McPherson was busy making ready for the next day's climax to Sherman's trick on Johnston. Calling in General Dodge at 8 o'clock, Mac told him to get Veatch out ahead of the army at 5 o'clock Monday morning for "a bold and rapid movement on the enemy's lines of communication." Sweeny's division would fall in to the right of Veatch to advance on Resaca itself, while Veatch would begin wrecking the Western & Atlantic north of town.

It was a busy evening to the north, where Thomas and Schofield were raising a frightful racket. Brigadier General John W. Geary's division of Hooker's XX Corps assaulted Dug Gap late Sunday afternoon, and in the brisk fighting which followed, the Federals lost "probably from 200 to 300 killed and wounded," as Thomas reported. Geary, now convinced that fighting on Sunday was a bad practice and would get no better results if he resumed it, had retired beyond artillery range of the Gap for the night. Major General John M. Palmer's IV Corps, in Thomas' army also, was finding Confederate resistance increasingly stiffer at the north end of Rocky Face Ridge.[4]

Some time after 4 A.M. Monday, Sheldon got his Missourians out of the woods and into line along the road. Veatch's orders were to make the rations go as far as possible, and the troops pretty well skipped breakfast. Soon the word came to start moving, and the 4th Division began filing through the 2d Division bivouac area toward the mouth of the Gap, with the 9th Illinois, still mounted, leading the way and followed closely by the 39th Iowa from Sweeny's division. Ahead of Sheldon's boys now was the kind of war in which massed columns of infantry would clash in broad daylight in open country, with artillery singing bass to the musket's tenor. If the 18th Missouri *was* the first-rate regiment that Sheldon thought it was, he would soon know.

Before long there was a clatter of carbine fire up front, as the 9th Illinois ran into Rebel cavalry near the mouth of the Gap. Wounded in this opening volley was an old friend of the 18th Missouri. Colonel Phillips, with whom the men had had several memorable experiences around Chewalla and Pocahontas, was severely wounded in his left leg and had to be carried to the rear. Brigadier General Judson Kilpatrick reported the scrape to Sherman north of Villanow at 8:30 A.M. and expressed the fear that an entire brigade of Rebel horse was now hovering on McPherson's right and rear.

This would hardly have surprised Henry Sawyer, back with the division wagons near the head of the Gap four miles east of Villanow. Early that morning he had scribbled apprehensively in his little diary: "the rebs is near."[5]

Just before Veatch's division reached the Rome crossroads, between the Gap and Resaca, McPherson directed Dodge to push Sweeny into the line on Veatch's right and prepare for an advance on Resaca itself. The two divisions of XVI Corps "advanced steadily," as Dodge later reported, "meeting with considerable resistance and skirmishing heavily. . . ." Then, about a mile from town, Sweeny discovered Cantey's infantry dug in on Bald Hill as well as the low ridge running north from the Rome road. Leaving Veatch to guard the corps left and rear, Dodge charged and carried Bald Hill with Sweeny's force. And there he paused.

Dodge immediately reported to McPherson his position and that of the enemy and his strength. McPherson soon galloped up and instructed Dodge "to send a few mounted men up the Dalton road to reconnoiter the country and find an approach to the railroad in that direction." One company of the 9th Illinois, eighteen men in all, cantered off toward Tilton.

It was almost 4 P.M. when McPherson committed Veatch's division to an assault on the railroad above Resaca. Mac was in a frightful turmoil, apparently, complaining to those around him that most of the roads were "running the wrong way."

"He had no accurate knowledge of the topography or of the roads by which he could turn the position," wrote an officer in Schofield's army. "Neither could he tell to what extent Johnston had already detached portions of his command to resist him." Indeed, McPherson during the noon hour had sent Sherman a complaint that dense woods in the area prevented his getting signals from Hooker's force up Rocky Face Ridge, the force which would have best observed Rebel reinforcements on the way from Dalton. Worse yet, McPherson had heard from that morning's prisoners that Wheeler was on his way over the ridge north of the Gap to join with two other columns coming up from the south in a converging movement to bottle up McPherson from the north end of Snake Creek Gap. Hopeful that his army had "been a little too quick for them," McPherson nevertheless felt that Logan should be sure that the two infantry brigades covering the train were kept on their toes.[6]

Getting set to move against the railway, Veatch formed Fuller's brigade on his left in a "column of companies" with Colonel John W. Sprague's Second Brigade on the right in similar order. The Rebels spied them crossing the west fork of Camp Creek—and cut loose with shot and shell. A major of the 39th Ohio long remembered that open field between the forks of Camp Creek, "within some 300 or 400 yards of the railroad under a fire of case-shot and shells. . . ."

In his memoirs, Sheldon told how his men "came under the fire of the enemy's artillery," discovering that "parade tactics might be all right in theory, and all wrong in practice." For the bursting shells took a shocking toll in Fuller's compact ranks. Private John W. Shaddon of Company E, a twenty-eight-year-old farmer from Putnam County's Wyreka community, was instantly killed by a shell burst that wounded two boys in A Company, Private Franklin Green from Sullivan County, and Private Joseph D. Hamilton of Linn County. The fragment that struck Green "broke the upper part of his cheek bone," Houts found, "laying open [the right] side of his face to the temple. . . ." Hamilton's most extensive injury was in the right thigh, although a "lacerated flesh wound of the right leg" was to cause him more trouble in the long run. Hamilton quit the service when his three years were up that autumn, but Green had a year in army hospitals ahead of him. Houts sent them both back to a field hospital beyond the Gap, while Cudworth bade a respectful farewell to Shaddon's remains at the soldier's cemetery on the Chickamauga.

Just as Fuller was ready to cross the east fork of the creek, Dodge ordered Sprague's brigade swung over toward Sweeny. The enemy was pressing Sweeny along that ridge a mile or so west and northwest of Resaca, and Logan was not yet up to help him. Dodge, riding with Fuller all afternoon, now instructed him to charge the infernal Rebel battery that had made so much trouble for the Federals north of town. It was no use. About five o'clock, apparently, Dodge withdrew the order, as McPherson was pressing him to bring Fuller back to cover Sprague's left more closely. Fuller had a ticklish job withdrawing across the open field, regiment by regiment, to the safety of the timber west of the creek. But he had his brigade west of the creek before the sun disappeared beyond the Gap.

Cantey's furious defense had put a new face on things, and McPherson's mind was changing about a "bold move" on the railroad and town. "Just as our skirmishers had about reached the railroad," Sheldon summarized, "we were halted, and much to our disgust, faced about, and soon returned to our positions in Snake Creek Gap."[7]

Unaware of this turn of events, Sherman was bombarding Halleck with jubilant announcements that "McPherson has destroyed Resaca." Many miles distant, the General was convinced he had "Joe Johnston in the palm of my fist." The following day, though, his tune changed, thanks to a report from McPherson's headquarters west of the Gap. McPherson defended his unaggressive behavior on the grounds that the Rebels had "a half dozen good roads" from the north available for a counterattack and that Dodge's corps was out of rations. The 9th Illinois, down to half strength after long months of hard use, was not strong enough to handle all reconnaissances, and Garrard's cavalrymen were at LaFayette, fifteen miles west— too exhausted to come in before Tuesday. With Garrard, Mac said, he could have wrecked the railroad.

The sun was up Tuesday before Sherman received this shocking information. Though masking his fury in his published memoirs, Sherman was openly infuriated over the failure at Resaca. And since that day there has been a constant drumfire from his admirers convinced that only McPherson's "timidity" spoiled the General's scheme for wrecking the Rebel Army of Tennessee. Sheldon, who faithfully followed Sherman's viewpoints in his own recollections at the turn of the 1890's, declared that McPherson appeared "to have somewhat lost his head here. . . ." Yet Sheldon provides a key to understanding the timid behavior of the aggressive McPherson. News of Geary's repulse at Dug Gap, in addition to other reports of Union setbacks and Rebel counterthrusts, unquestionably affected McPherson's judgment, Sheldon says. There is no doubt that the presence of Confederate cavalry in the rugged wilderness southwest of Snake Creek Gap restrained McPherson from committing his strength against Resaca as Sherman had wanted.

"McPherson," wrote Sherman in the 1870's, "had in hand twenty-three thousand of the best men of the army, and could have walked into Resaca (then held by only a small brigade). . . ." This line has been followed by his sympathizers for a century. But Joe Johnston gave the lie to this reasoning in the same decade, at least to observers willing to hear the other side of the story. Cantey had a division—not a brigade—holding Resaca, said Johnston, and McPherson, "a skillful engineer as well as able general, thought it 'too strong to be carried by assault by the Army of the Tennessee.'" Resaca, Johnston further declared in 1878, could certainly have been held by Cantey long enough for the Confederates to move in reinforcements to overwhelm McPherson's small army. As Old Joe phrased it, "opportunities for armies to fight detachments half their strength are rarely offered." It is possible, some historians have estimated, that Cantey had at Resaca less than the 4,000 men Johnston claimed for him on that May 9, but a modern historian observed that whatever the Rebels had on the ridge was more than McPherson had been led to expect.

A distinguished relative of the General put it this way in 1906: "Some say that McPherson failed Sherman at Resaca, but the better judgment of military critics is that he saved his army from slaughter and defeat." But Sherman was to tell him on May 12, 1864: "Well, Mac, you have missed the great opportunity of your life!"[8]

Before daybreak May 10, Veatch had his division out of the Gap again for a reconnaissance-in-force toward Cantey's ridge line. It was impossible to see Resaca from Federal positions covering Snake Creek Gap, but the Missourians could hear the coming and going of freight trains that suggested substantial enemy reinforcements. Polk was arriving in force. Until after dark there was sporadic musket-fire between the skirmish lines, but that died down in the rainstorm that swept over Resaca during the night.

It was about 11 o'clock that Tuesday night when Dodge called his outposts back into the Gap. This order was particularly welcome to the 18th Missouri, for the men had had little sleep since Sunday night. And they made the most of the opportunity, stretching themselves out for slumber as profound as the sodden ground and dripping pines and hickories would allow.

Fuller roused Sheldon's troops the next morning to work on fortifications guarding the mouth of the Gap, while McPherson's army lay huddled around it "watching the enemy retreating across our front (but making no attack)," as Sheldon put it. Crafty old Joe Johnston was disengaging along the upper Connasauga to concentrate around Resaca. Sherman, meanwhile, had decided that he might beat Johnston to the punch by slipping his entire army group through Snake Creek Gap in the hope that even yet there might be time to cut off the Rebels and visit confusion on them as they sought to escape below Resaca.[9]

The race was on, with Sherman frantically moving his armies around the bow of a strategic arc while Johnston moved his smaller force straight down its chord—with a railroad to speed him southward. On May 11 Polk was in Resaca with most of his corps, preparing to guard Johnston's escape route. By sundown, Resaca was garrisoned by three small infantry divisions and as many cavalry brigades. The next morning Sherman came galloping down the Gap for his first look at things. He was appalled by the difficulties facing his troops between the Gap and Resaca. Johnston "had all the advantages of natural position, of artificial forts and roads, and of concentrated action." The Federals, Sherman complained in his memoirs, "were compelled to grope . . . through forests, across mountains, with a large army, necessarily more or less dispersed." One cannot avoid inquiring of McPherson's detractors why these considerations, so impressive to Sherman on May 12, should not have been equally so to McPherson earlier.

At 5 P.M. on May 12, Fuller got orders to move his brigade out of its works in the Gap to take up a line south of the Gap on the right of XVI Corps. Troops from Hooker moved into the vacated works. Sheldon's men now found themselves on Dodge's extreme right, forming a line of battle after dark on the very bank of the Oostanaula River within a half-mile of Rebel-held Bald Hill.

During that night the bulk of Sherman's armies made it down the Gap, and when morning came the Johnnies could see what was coming. McPherson's army was on the Union right, Thomas in the center, and Schofield on the left facing the north tip of Cantey's ridge. But Johnston was now concentrated before them, moving Polk out to face McPherson, with Hardee manning most of the ridge, and Lieutenant General John Bell Hood guarding the Rebel right along the railroad north of Resaca. It was Friday, May 13.

That morning the Northern soldiers began a cautious approach to Old Joe's lines. Most of the bloodshed occurred along the ridge, where the Army of the Cumberland mixed it with Hardee all day long. That evening Veatch regained Bald Hill, and the 14th Ohio Battery was now able to train its guns on the town. Veatch ordered Sheldon to dig the 18th Missouri in along that hillside to defend the battery against any mischief that General Polk might be tempted to try.

"The fight is still a going on," noted Teamster Sawyer, as the battle raged on into Saturday. Schofield and Thomas proceeded to close in on Resaca from the northwest, but the strenuous Rebel defense was holding them to a snail's pace. The XVI Corps was doing no better at the south end of the line, but the Ohio gunners were at least able to lob an occasional shell toward Resaca.

As the fighting rose in fury Sunday morning, Sherman came to the conclusion that there must be an easier way to get Johnston out of Resaca. Garrard's cavalry having been ordered out to demonstrate along the Oostanaula toward Rome the day before, Uncle Billy now put his Pioneer Brigade to work on a pair of floating bridges over the Oostanaula at Lay's Ferry, near Calhoun. Protecting the work were two of Sweeny's regiments who had crossed the river on Saturday to set up a bridgehead on the Calhoun side. The first pontoon bridge was ready Sunday noon. This would have been enough to make Johnston exceedingly nervous about his rear areas again, but then there came to him the news that Garrard had also breached the river line several miles beyond Calhoun. Soon after dark that bloody Sunday, during which day McPherson and Thomas had carried the ridge west of Resaca, Johnston decided that the sooner he crossed the Oostanaula the better off he was going to be. The Ohio Battery was already hammering his vital bridge.

Back in the Gap with the wagons, Henry Sawyer wrote hurriedly in his little diary early Monday afternoon: "We ar a moveing. The rebs has left." The Army of the Cumberland, furiously repairing the fire-damage done the railroad bridge by Polk's rear guard, was crossing the river at Resaca, while Schofield was going across upstream. Meanwhile, the Army of the Tennessee was swarming over the Oostanaula on the Lay's Ferry pontoons. The 18th Missouri crossed on Monday morning and went into line of battle behind light works with the rest of XVI Corps on the northern approaches to Calhoun. When the Rebels abandoned Calhoun later that day, Sherman was able to boast that he had compelled Old Joe to retreat twenty miles in five days.[10]

Wagonmaster Pollock and Teamster Sawyer now conducted the regimental wagon train across the Oostanaula in midafternoon on Monday, May 16, and for a while Sheldon's transport would be with him more regularly than had lately been the case. It wasn't much of a train, for Sherman had cut everybody down to the barest minimum. This insufficiency was bad enough, Sheldon grumbled, but it seemed to him that the train "was never . . . on hand when wanted, if there was any danger." This was an understandable impression, even if the imputation in the Colonel's remark was entirely out of place when made a generation afterward. It is impossible to believe that Sheldon meant to be derogatory, for Pollock and Sawyer had to wait wherever McPherson and Dodge told them to stay.

It was no deficiency in courage on their part if the wagons of the whole army were north of Snake Creek Gap while the rifle companies were at the south end of it.

The enlisted men were finding their newly issued pup tents, made by joining "shelter-halves" together, pleasingly comfortable, Sheldon noted. Mess arrangements were also handled on the cooperative "buddy" system. "A tin cup answered to boil the coffee," he wrote, "while half a canteen made a very good frying pan for the 'hard tack' soaked in water until soft, and fried with fat side meat (commonly called 'sow belly') which made our 'square meal' when we had time enough to attend to it." Once in a while supplies of evaporated milk, dried vegetables, and sausage came up from the commissaries, but Sherman found that "somehow the men preferred the simpler and more familiar forms of food. . . ."[11]

The Confederate retreat, slow and defiant, continued during the following day, Wednesday. Adairsville, eight miles below Calhoun, was apparently Johnston's next stop, for Rebel resistance seemed to grow as the Federals advanced that rainy afternoon. Constant skirmishing went on as the three Union armies inched southward from Calhoun. In one savage encounter, involving Ed Donnelly's Company C of the 18th Missouri, Private Conrad Fischer was wounded. Fischer, living at Parkville when Colonel Morgan brought the regiment to Platte County, was one of the fifteen young Germans who had responded to Morgan's recruiting drive by signing up at Weston.[12]

In a council of war at Adairsville Wednesday evening, Johnston proposed a little trick on Sherman. Roads leading down toward Cassville formed two sides of a strategic triangle, Old Joe explained. The railway and a wagon road ran slightly southwest toward Kingston, while another road pointed in a southeasterly direction at Cassville. The Kingston-Cassville road formed the base of the triangle. Sherman, Old Joe reasoned, would certainly divide his forces on the two roads as he moved south from Adairsville, seeking to keep both roads covered. And there would come Johnston's chance: Concentrated at Cassville, with the railroad at his disposal for mass movement of troops, he would unleash an overwhelming attack on the weaker of the two Federal wings coming down from Adairsville. Should Sherman fall into the trap, some eight or nine miles of winding and brushy wagon roads would separate the relief force from the one under attack. On Thursday Johnston set up his command post at Cassville and made ready to fight.

The Confederate trap, set to go off on May 19, never snapped. Just after Johnston told his troops to "turn and march to meet" Sherman's oncoming columns, Hood began to see things in the wilderness to his northeast. There was some Union cavalry there, true, but no force so large as the vast legions conjured up in Hood's inflamed imagination. Unable to convince Hood or Polk that such fears were exaggerated, Johnston decided to abandon the Cassville position. That night his forces crossed the Etowah River south of Cartersville.

When the sun rose on Friday morning, May 20, Sheldon's men were snoring in their little tents along the west edge of Kingston, surrounded by similarly quiet tent cities of the XVI Corps. McPherson's outer lines were protecting Kingston to the south and east. Thomas was dug in around Cassville, while Schofield was holding Cartersville and patroling the upper Etowah.

The 18th Missouri spent three warm days in bivouac at Kingston. "The sun is a baring down," observed diarist Sawyer. And Sherman made it plain that he was planning more excitement, for the orders now came down for Dodge to collect "twenty days' short rations for men and animals. . . ." The pause at Kingston was put to good use otherwise, for the men not only drew new clothing but also got a big shipment of mail as soon as the railroad opened.

"Most of the boys had numerous correspondents (generally the fair sex)," says Sheldon, "and much of their leisure time was spent in answering letters. No one who has not been through it can tell the good those bright encouraging letters did for our army. They were as bracing as a tonic, and I always thought the boys did far better marching after receiving mail from home."

One feature about the mail from Missouri long puzzled New Jerseyite Sheldon: "The most astonishing thing . . . was the number of 'cousins' some of them seemed to have—you would have thought everybody was 'kin' in Missouri!"[13]

Sherman, meanwhile, was taking a squint at Johnston's new line across the Etowah. Southeast of Cartersville the railroad ran through a deep saddle in the hills along the river. Having examined this Allatoona Pass while a young lieutenant some twenty years before, Sherman wasn't about to tackle it today, with Johnston lurking there. Knowing how hard it would be to blast a way through the Pass, Sherman "resolved not to attempt it, but to turn the position, by moving from Kingston to Marietta *via* Dallas. . . ."

May 23 was the day for the armies to emerge from their lines along the Etowah, and just after daybreak 80,000 Yankees moved forward over the broad river. Schofield, crossing to the southwest of Cartersville, headed south toward positions on the lower Pumpkinvine Creek due north of Dallas. Thomas, in the center, passed the Etowah south of Kingston to march on Dallas by way of Euharlee and Burnt Hickory. McPherson's army, on the right, swung far to the west of Thomas to hit the Dallas road at Van Wert, from which place the troops would march rapidly eastward.

Throughout these marches across northwestern Georgia, there were few incidents with local civilians. There were two reasons for this. First, the area was sparsely settled, having been Cherokee territory closed to whites until the preceding generation. Second, plantation families had gone with Johnston's army, or else into the woods to hide. David P. Conyngham, a young reporter for a New York paper, noticed that "Old men and women, decrepit Negroes, and squalling picaninnies, were the only persons at home."

Leaving camp two miles west of Kingston at four o'clock on the afternoon of May 23, Sheldon's Missourians joined the XVI Corps in "three days and two nights' tedious marching" toward the upper reaches of Pumpkinvine Creek southwest of Dallas. The 18th Missouri was plunging with McPherson's other regiments into a landscape "very obscure, mostly in a state of nature, densely wooded, and with few roads," wrote Sherman. After going into camp at two o'clock the next morning, Sheldon had his regiment back on the road by 7 A.M., May 24. The troops were privileged to knock off for a two-hour supper break at 4 P.M. that day, but Dodge thereafter kept them steadily on the march until 1:30 A.M. on May 25, when they fell into a deep sleep in bivouac at Blandsville, just north of Van Wert.[14]

Meanwhile, repair of telegraph lines from Dalton down to Kingston was enabling Sherman's armies to get news from Virginia. There, during these opening weeks of the campaign, it did not seem that Grant was doing half so well as Sherman. During the period May 5–7, the Army of the Potomac had struck into the Wilderness along the Rappahannock to dig Lee out. But the Rebel general, having taken the full force of Grant's onset, now delivered some telling counter-blows. Checked with frightful losses, Grant recoiled, but instead of heading back north he started moving southeastward around Lee's right and toward the banks of the North Anna. On the way south, the two armies collided at Spotsylvania Court House and blasted away at each other for nine days. After running up a casualty list twice Lee's, Grant slipped off again, toward the North Anna, on May 19. But before the Federals could cross that river, Lee managed to entrench his forces on the south bank facing Grant's approach. So matters stood with Grant as Sherman's armies set forth into the forested hills south of the Etowah.

Having marched "mostly by night over rough roads through a mountainous country . . . the rain often pouring down in torrents," Veatch's division struck the main road to Dallas at Van Wert at 9 A.M. on Wednesday, May 25. There was a brief halt here, while Dr. Randolph loaded Lieutenant McEfee onto an ambulance and saw him off for Nashville. Since McEfee would shortly resign, the men were not to see him again. Abijah Everest, of Company C, became the third man to command I Company within a month.

Now McPherson began to close in toward Sherman's center in a swift all-day march from Van Wert to Dallas—roughly eighteen miles. Rain set in on the wilderness again, and that could hardly help the marching columns. But they pressed onward through the day, Logan's corps in the lead. The 9th Illinois went on as the advance guard of XVI Corps, while the 1st Alabama watched the flanks. Sweeny's 2d Division marched in the advance of XVI Corps, and Veatch brought up the rear. Some time around midnight the weary men of the 18th Missouri pitched their little tents on the west bank of Pumpkinvine Creek, a few miles southwest of Dallas. McPherson's headquarters was across the creek at Pumpkinvine Church, near Logan's camps.[15]

McPherson, conferring with Dodge and Logan, came to the view that "we will have a heavy battle near Dallas tomorrow." That very afternoon, as the Army of the Tennessee closed up to Pumpkinvine Creek from the west, Hooker's XX Corps had fallen into a ferocious exchange of volleys some four miles northeast of Dallas on the Allatoona road. The fighting had been particularly heavy around a little Methodist chapel called New Hope Church.

Joe Johnston clearly understood Sherman's tactics. The Confederates were crowding in on Dallas from the east and northeast. This meant a fight, McPherson correctly surmised, and he forthwith instructed Logan to advance his corps to Dallas "at an early hour in the morning in light fighting order." Two roads ran from the Pumpkinvine crossing into Dallas, and Logan would go in on the more southerly of the two. Dodge's orders were to start for the crossing at 3 A.M. in order to form promptly on Logan's left and move on Dallas along the more direct road from Van Wert. The wagons were to keep west of the Creek until McPherson called for them.

As that rainy Thursday came on, McPherson gave the order to advance, and his army reached forward to claim the city. A Rebel skirmish line unmasked itself along the way, but the muskets of the 18th Missouri and its sister regiments soon discouraged enemy hopes of saving Dallas from its Northern visitors. Within a couple of hours the Army of the Tennessee had taken possession, with the aid of Jeff C. Davis' division of XIV Corps.

Beyond Dallas, commanding roads to Allatoona and Marietta, was a range of high hills thoroughly infested by Rebel infantry and artillery. Neither McPherson nor Sherman was quite ready to charge the Confederates up there, and all Dodge and Logan could do for the moment was bivouac east and south of town in full view of enemy sharpshooters.[16]

At seven o'clock on the morning of May 27, Hardee's corps opened up with artillery on Logan and Dodge. Back with the wagons, having moved forward into Dallas the night before, Henry Sawyer recorded that "the Bols fell on us." Sheldon formed up the 18th Missouri on Dodge's left and "moved up in line of battle to the foot of the mountain . . . and built a line of works under fire from sharpshooters." This was a costly day, for the Rebel marksmen fatally wounded one of Ken Breeman's men of Company E, Private John A. Tharp. A small-town Illinoisan, Tharp had left his home at Clarksville in March of 1863 to enlist at St. Louis. He was only twenty. Cudworth saw him off to an early grave in the red soil of Georgia.[17]

Sherman looked things over during the day and decided to readjust his lines. The XV Corps was strung out along the Marietta road for some distance out of Dallas, while Dodge was holding a semicircular position around the south and east edges of the town. Sweeny was entrenched south of Dallas, while Fuller was serving as "corps center" with Davis' borrowed division standing on Dodge's left and commanding the Allatoona road, northward from Fuller's works. Between Davis and the Federal positions around New Hope Church was a three-mile gap, and Sherman was beginning to suspect that Johnston might notice it before the Federals could cover it. "I concluded to draw McPherson from Dallas to Hooker's right," says Sherman, "and gave orders accordingly. . . ."

Mac found it easier to order than to execute his shift down the Pumpkinvine Creek watershed to New Hope. For on the afternoon of May 28 the Rebels, massing under cover of timber, launched a determined attack against Logan and Dodge's right. This had the understandable effect of delaying McPherson's march, but Logan and Sweeny made a bloody evening of it for Hardee along the Marietta road. Against the works of the 18th Missouri east of Dallas, "only a demonstration was attempted," which Sheldon described as "easily held in check by the skirmish line."

Fuller sent up the 27th Ohio at daybreak the next day to relieve the 18th Missouri, and the latter regiment retired to rest in a secondary line of works. Two days later, however, with the corps still pinned down, the Missourians went back up to the skirmish line. On this day Company I's bugler, Private George R. Robinson, a twenty-year-old Iowan, lost his life, picked off by a sharpshooter.[18]

By this time, McPherson was managing to extricate his

army from Dallas and close it up on Thomas. Veatch's lot was to cover the leftward shift, and the 18th Missouri brought up the rear of McPherson's move. Aided by the withdrawal of Confederates from Dallas to reinforce Johnston's right, the departure of the Missourians began on June 1. That morning they crossed the Pumpkinvine northwest of town and moved down the creek some four or five miles to Owen's Mill, where they commenced a line of trenches to occupy for the night.

Fighting was slowly dying down, as Sherman and Johnston desperately sought to outmaneuver each other by a general northward displacement of forces. Before long, the Rebel commander saw that he had better be picking out a new line for himself, for it was starting to look as if Sherman were doing it for him. Union horsemen took over the Allatoona Pass and station on June 1, and three days afterward, in a heavy downpour, the Confederates vanished into the wooded hills east of New Hope Church. The railway town of Acworth, four miles southeast of the Pass, was also abandoned as Johnston withdrew to a new line.

The men of XVI Corps must have been developing a world of self-confidence by this time, for Dodge was inspired to write his brother while at Dallas that "The morale of our army can't be beat, and I feel certain of victory every time we put them in."[19]

Sherman's immediate reaction to Johnston's departure was to switch the Army of the Tennessee to his left flank "at and in front of Acworth," with Thomas holding down the center two miles to the south and Schofield guarding the right somewhat farther south of Thomas. This movement went off without a hitch, for the Confederates were nowhere to be seen, and on Sunday morning, June 5, the 18th Missouri camped near the west edge of Acworth. The wagons and pack-mules came in after dark.

Sheldon's Missourians spent a memorable five days in bivouac here. The telegraph wires were crackling with news of a horrible blood-letting at Cold Harbor, Virginia, and Grant's subsequent drive to cross the James below Petersburg. The wires also brought Sheldon the sad news that Dan Torrey had died the previous week at Decatur from the effects of "flux and chills." This was a shock to everyone in Company B, as well as to his older brother Roscoe, for young Dan was one of the original "boys from Saint John." The Pollocks and Lance Beary would join with Roscoe to face in sadness a future without him. Captain Stults rejoined B Company from a sick leave just in time to share in the first impact of the company's grief.

News now came over the wire that Lincoln had been renominated at the National Union (Republican) Convention under way in Baltimore. The gritty military governor of Tennessee, Andrew Johnson, went on the ticket as the President's running mate. Although in after-years the men of the 18th Missouri might deny it with vehemence, it is altogether likely that they were proud of the futile struggle of the Missouri delegation to derail Lincoln in favor of U.S. Grant. The Radical Republicans of Missouri, dominating state politics more and more, far excelled Governor Hall in ideological ferocity, as the fall campaign would demonstrate.

On the day of Lincoln's renomination, Frank Blair reported in at Acworth with his XVII Corps, 10,000 strong, and this more than offset the losses that Sherman had experienced in a month of rugged campaigning.[20]

With rail service restored nearly to Acworth, Sherman's armies moved forward on Friday, June 10, to feel out Johnston for the next round. This was no parade-ground exercise, for each hour brought fresh report of cavalry skirmishes back along the vital railroad as far as Resaca. And Johnston's skirmishers in the brush along the roads to Marietta were making it dangerous for unwary Federals. Then, too, there were the thundershowers which had drenched the area daily for over a week. The men didn't particularly mind marching in the rain, but camping at night was miserable at such a time.

Breaking camp at Acworth at 5 P.M. on Friday, the 18th Missouri was in the line of march all night. Shortly after daybreak the division moved into the abandoned railroad village of Big Shanty, known today by the more dignified name of Kennesaw. After a hurried conference with General Dodge, Veatch sent Sprague's brigade to reconnoiter Rebel positions down the railway in the direction of Kennesaw Mountain, about four miles south of Big Shanty. Sprague found the Rebels dug in, three miles out of town. While he went to work to entrench on a line running east from Moon's Siding, Fuller began moving the First Brigade into line to the east to connect with works being prepared by XV Corps in the wilderness southeast of Big Shanty. For its part in Fuller's southward push, Sheldon's regiment "advanced south upon the railroad, forming in line of battle and erecting works upon the edge of an open field, within sight of the enemy's line, at a point known as the Peach Orchard."[21]

The Yankees had found Johnston again, holding a line ten miles long and covering the approaches to Marietta. Crowning points of the Rebel works were now Kennesaw Mountain, just above Marietta; Pine Mountain, dominating the center six miles to the northwest; and Lost Mountain, anchoring the position nine miles west of Marietta. "On each of these hills the enemy had signal-stations and fresh lines of parapets," Sherman noted. "Heavy masses of infantry could be distinctly seen with the naked eye, and it was manifest that Johnston had chosen his ground well. . . ."

Sherman proposed to invest that line in a manner calculated to exploit its weakness—too much length for the manpower holding it. "As his position . . . gave him a perfect view over our field," Sherman said, "we had to proceed with due caution." McPherson was to close in on the Kennesaw position, while Thomas faced Pine Mountain. Schofield, standing on the Sandtown road west of Thomas, was "on the general right, looking south, toward Lost Mountain."

There began a slow and painful advance toward Johnston's formidable new line, an advance which must have reminded the old hands in the 18th Missouri of Halleck's march on Corinth more than two years before. For more than a week the troops spent their days, as Sheldon said, "moving forward slowly, with heavy skirmishing, and building light works at each successive advance."

The rifle-trenches devised by the soldiers in the contending armies were pretty well standardized by this time. "We thought almost as much of our intrenching tools as we did our rations," Sheldon recalled later. Wherever possible, the boys would cut down trees and undergrowth for at least a hundred yards in front of their works. This mass of tangled tree trunks and brush was sure to break up any formation trying to march against the defending trenches. In front of the trenches parapets of excavated dirt were thrown up, often to a height of six feet above the surface of the ground. Larger tree trunks were pruned of branches and slung along the top of the parapets for head-logs that rested in notches cut in other logs, known as skids, extending backward across the trenches in an inclined plane. The spaces under the head-logs and between the skids served as handy firing-slots for a line of men with muskets. If artillery fire struck the head-log and dislodged it, the skids would keep it from crashing into the trench and injuring those waiting their turn to step up and fire.

Adept though the soldiers were at digging such works, Sherman felt that it was a shame to waste their energy in this way if it wasn't necessary. Noting the hordes of former slaves hanging around the rear of his armies, he concluded that it would be best to form some of the Negroes into "pioneer corps" of 200 men for each division, and he authorized each division commander to pay freedmen a ten-dollar monthly wage. This took advantage of recent legislation giving generals in the field authority to contract for auxiliary services. "These pioneer detachments became very useful to us during the rest of the war," Sherman said, "for they could work at night while our men slept...."

Such ingenuity did not always grace the Confederate defense of Georgia, apparently, for the sarcastic General Hood, increasingly disenchanted by Johnston's tactics, was later to complain that the Rebel soldiers were forever throwing up "temporary works . . . behind which it was never intended to fight. The men became travellers by night, and laborers by day."[22]

In the fighting south of Big Shanty, Colonel Sheldon found that "the slightest exposure brought a bullet." On the first day, three men of Company A were hit. Private James E. Phillips, an eighteen-year-old recruit who had joined up at St. Louis three months before, was killed. Private William J. Brewer, twenty-three, a farm boy from the Brookfield area, was wounded, as was Private William Tilman, a Saline Countian and one of the originals who had mustered in at Laclede. On June 16 more tragedy struck, when Private Chesley A. Wall, of Company B, was killed in action, Wall, a farmer from Monroe County, Illinois, had signed up in October of 1862, when only nineteen years old.

Major Minter was also wounded on this day by a bullet which grazed his skull two inches above the right eye, leaving an ugly puncture and a small fracture which led to his evacuation to the rear. Houts returned him to duty a few weeks later, but the wound had inflicted an injury that would cause Minter untold misery in years to come and finally drive him to suicide. His place on the staff was temporarily filled by Dolman, and Company H was turned over to Lieutenant Mansfield for the time being.[23]

Private Benjamin Sweet of the 27th Ohio left a priceless description of what it was like up on General Fuller's firing-line during this tortuous advance on Marietta. "While here," he wrote, "I came very near getting shot. A sharp-shooter killed one of our men. I always had a good eye and I got to looking for the sharp-shooter. At last I saw his arm move so I loaded carefully and laid my gun on the breast works and when his arm came up again [I] was taking aim, when a ball struck just below my chin, and filled my eyes with dust and bark."[24]

Men on the other side were also being killed and injured, as Sherman's mud-caked veterans burrowed forward in the rain-swept woodlands below Kennesaw. On June 14, one of the few clear days thus far in June, a Federal shell struck and killed the great "Bishop-General" Polk on the summit of Pine Mountain. Within hours the Union signal-station near Big Shanty intercepted the news, and the old-timers of the 18th Missouri, who had been hearing about Polk ever since they started down the River in 1862, now joined the men of both armies in bidding farewell to one of the most picturesque figures among the high-ranking Confederate officers.

The day after Polk's death, Johnston ordered Pine Mountain abandoned. On June 16 he gave up Lost Mountain to draw in his lines toward Kennesaw itself. Sherman had been right: Johnston couldn't possibly man a line such as he had presented June 10. McPherson now advanced to the north end of Kennesaw Mountain, with Hood contesting every inch of the way.

There was one more day of heavy fighting in drenching rain, and then the Rebels let go and withdrew to the mountain and the flanking positions east and southwest of it.

In that last flurry of fighting Company K lost Private Josiah Early, a Clay Countian who had signed up at Weston. He was laid to rest at Chattanooga, beneath a headstone bearing a garbled version of his name: "M. Showecy." More fortunate was Private Elkanah W. Howard of Company B, wounded in action the same day. Hit in the face, he sustained a jaw fracture. In the army less than a fortnight, he had a year yet to serve, and he would spend the duration in army hospitals.[25]

For the next day the Union generals were rearranging their new line while closing it in toward Confederate positions. Fuller's brigade, following the enemy down to the Burnt Hickory road, just west of the railroad, moved up to what Henry Sawyer called "the foot of the mountain." The line Dodge was marking out for Fuller was a north-south ridge position running south from the railroad, where it bent eastward to skirt the mountain, and adjoining trenches being dug by the XIV Corps. Like its companions, the 18th Missouri set about digging in a hurry, working in plain view of Rebels swarming on Kennesaw's summit.

Sherman's left flank, covered by Garrard's horsemen, was out along Noonday Creek east of the railway. Schofield's Army of the Ohio held down the right, southwest of the mountain on the upper reaches of Nose's Creek. Major General William W. Loring, temporarily commanding Polk's corps, held the enemy right, guarded by Wheeler's cavalry along Noonday Creek. Hood moved on June 21 from Johnston's right to the extreme left to confront Schofield. Hardee, whose lines ran southward from Little Kennesaw and across the Marietta-Lost Mountain road, held the Confederate center.

"This is the nineteenth day of rain," Sherman wrote Halleck on June 21, "and the prospect of fair weather is as far off as ever. The roads are impassable; the fields and woods become quagmires after a few wagons have crossed over. Yet we are at work all the time. . . . I am all ready to attack the moment the weather and roads will permit troops and artillery to move with anything like life."[26]

There was little action on McPherson's front the rest of that week, and the troops were occupied with refinements on their fortifications, keeping dry, or writing letters. On June 22, Hood sacrificed a thousand men in a fruitless charge on Schofield out on the Powder Springs road three miles from Marietta, and that provided something to talk about besides the massive siege U. S. Grant was conducting before Petersburg. Casualties in the 18th Missouri were rare, despite occasional artillery duels. However, Lieutenant Pollock of Company B left June 23 for medical treatment in the division hospital back of Big Shanty. On this day the weather began to clear, and the troops could sense that Sherman would soon be enlivening things.

On Sunday, June 26, the Georgia sun looked down on a battlefield gripped by an ominous silence. "Quiet on the picket line," noted Henry Sawyer as he peered at the heavily forested crests and rocky ribs of Kennesaw. At his headquarters near Big Shanty, Sherman was writing his wife back in Ohio: "My lines are ten miles long, and every change necessitates a large amount of work. Still we are now all ready and I must attack direct or turn the position. Both will be attended with loss and difficulty, but one or the other must be attempted."[27]

Monday morning, June 27, seemed a good time for Sherman to try his "direct" assault. The sun rose "in a murky blaze," as one writer has said. It was obvious that this was to be one of the hottest days of the summer, and one witness to the events of that day thought the mercury hit 110 degrees by afternoon. Somewhere around 9 A.M. the Army of the Cumberland delivered the main assault—on Hardee's lines along the south slopes—while Schofield and McPherson were limited to demonstrations.

Soon the crash of artillery and crack of muskets had mounted to a "roar as constant as Niagara," as the fighting on that bloody Monday blazed up all along the line. Ohioan McPherson must have wanted to thin out Illinoisans, for he chose for his portion of the attack the much-tried 9th Illinois, the 64th Illinois of Fuller's brigade, and the 66th Illinois from Sweeny's division. The 64th, Fuller reported later, "advanced with great gallantry, and a few bold men got close to the enemy's line of works; but the task . . . proved more than men could accomplish, and nearly 50 brave fellows fell in the attempt. They drove the enemy back to his main works near the crest, but

the steep and rocky face of the mountain was an obstacle of itself more formidable than a line of men. . . ."

By noon the attack was clearly a failure, and an elated
Johnston was saluting his men as "unsurpassed by Napoleon's
Old Guard. . . ." Sherman prudently called the whole thing off.
Inflicting barely 800 casualties on the entrenched Rebels, he
had sustained over 2,500, and had better sense than to keep up
the carnage. Particularly shocking to many of the men in Company K of the 18th Missouri was the news that Colonel Dan
McCook had suffered severe wounds leading a brigade in
Thomas' attack. The gallant young Ohioan died on July 21, five
days after the War Department made him a brigadier general.
"He had won the star he set out for," commented Whitelaw
Reid, "and a soldier's grave as well." Perhaps his widow's Secessionist relatives from Platte County would find it difficult to
mourn him very long, but his passing laid a burden of grief
on his old law partner, William T. Sherman.[28]

A grim silence fell across the ravaged countryside in the
days that followed. "Not much fiting," Henry Sawyer wrote in
his diary Tuesday morning. Sergeant Guffey of Company I
wrote his wife that "We are still laying behind our works in
front of the enemy. Our army made an attemped to charge the
Rebles works but was unsuccessful." Like Sherman, Ben Guffey
admired Johnston's defensive works: "But one thing I know is
that they have a splendid position here. And will be hard to
get out if they are disposed to stay and fight. If we had 50
thousand men to hold this position and an army of about 50
thousand more to send on to Atlanta, they would be compelled
to leave or surrender. . . . Our loss in trying to charge the Rebles
works is 2700. But we still hold a splendid position. We are
where they cannot hurt us with there rifles or artillery and our
artillery is in our rear and plays over us. The Rebles sometimes open their batteries but they can't get to shoot but few
shots until our guns silence them."[29]

Sherman was somewhat miffed in the weeks to come because "too much stress was laid on the repulse of June 27th" by
journalists and other observers. "I was forced to make this
effort and it should have succeeded," he wrote Ellen Ewing
Sherman. The attempt had to be made, to his way of thinking,
because his own soldiers as well as Johnston needed convinc-

ing that he *would* fight hand to hand as well as maneuver around to achieve his strategic objectives.

Colonel Sheldon, usually no hand to criticize his old chief, found it impossible to take Sherman's justification of the Kennesaw fiasco at its face value. "It was," he later wrote feelingly, "certainly no evidence of capacity, or even courage in an officer, to recklessly lead his command into a slaughter pen and all such desperate charges as 'Marye's Hill' and 'Bloody Angle' and 'Kenesaw' told in verse and story, as evidences of what American soldiers can do, and dare, had no appreciable effect, excepting to prolong the war."

To sum up his view, Sheldon gave his opinion that the "test of bravery in troops and ability in officers was not a large mortality list (often largely incurred in escaping from slaughter pens), but a willing and courageous performance of all orders on the part of the officers. This included cool and efficient self-reliance and an avoidance of all losses not rendered necessary by the military situation. It has been well said, that in actual war one brave living soldier is of more military value than any number of dead heroes."

The struggle for Kennesaw Mountain must have made a lasting impression on Sheldon's quartermaster. When Cudworth left for St. Louis on business the following September, he took with him a letter of introduction to General Gray in which Sheldon invited the Adjutant General to ask Cudworth about the battle. "Lt. Cudworth," Sheldon hinted, "never refuses to 'take Kenesaw.'"[30]

On Friday night, July 2, Sherman ordered McPherson's army out of its works for a rapid march around Thomas and Schofield to the right. The objective now was to rendezvous along Nickajack Creek, some four miles south of Marietta, in the expectation that the Rebels would take alarm and abandon their lines on Kennesaw. That night the 18th Missouri made it as far as the banks of the Nickajack, west of Ruff's Mills.

Johnston took one look across the landscape north of the mountain Saturday morning and saw that his hours on Kennesaw were numbered. Before daybreak the Confederate defenders pulled out for the Chattahoochee.[31]

# CHAPTER XI

# "Atlanta Is Ours . . ."

GENERAL FULLER ordered his brigade to cross Nickajack Creek shortly after daybreak on July 4. The Rebels were at first nowhere to be seen, but Dodge and Veatch were convinced that Confederate lines were just ahead. The 39th Ohio and 64th Illinois formed in line of battle on the hill east of the creek, with the other two regiments right behind them. The 18th Missouri, as Sheldon later described its position, was "in column of companies in rear of the 39th Ohio. . . ." Moving out, the forward wall of skirmishers soon met with hostile fire, but the brigade promptly chased the enemy pickets back to a line of works that Fuller hardly cared to assault without giving the matter further study.

While Fuller was probing the Rebel line, the rest of Veatch's division came up and fell to work building rifle-pits and hauling up a battery to make things hotter for the enemy later in the day. It was almost noon when General Dodge directed Veatch to crack the enemy line as soon as possible. Fuller's two Ohio regiments began a stealthy approach through heavy woods up to the brigade picket line. Dodge, however, becoming fearful that the assault was too hazardous, called the whole thing off for the moment.

Not long before sundown, Dodge reinstated his order, and the Ohioans moved up again. This time the 64th Illinois followed as flank-guard, while the 18th Missouri and Sprague's

Second Brigade moved up to cover the retreat—should the assault fail.

But the attack succeeded marvelously. Rushing a hundred yards to climb the enemy parapets, the Ohioans began shooting and bayoneting the defenders right and left. As the men of XVI Corps let out a huge cheer for their fellows up front, the panic-stricken enemy, as Fuller put it, "abandoned his entrenchments and retired. It is doubtful whether so small a force . . . ever emptied a longer line of works."

The cost to the 18th Missouri was hardly excessive. Two German immigrants suffered wounds. Lieutenant Partenheimer of Company H, even now counting the days until his enlistment expired, was shot in the right leg and taken back to Marietta. With him also went a thirty-five-year-old farmer from Company E with the pious name of John Baptiste Priester, wounded in the left hip.[1]

On the larger front below Marietta, Johnston was drawing his forces into a large bridgehead position on the north bank of the Chattahoochee covering the Western & Atlantic railway bridge south of Vining's Station. During the night of July 4 Johnston's withdrawal was complete, and from a hill at Vining's Sherman could "see the houses in Atlanta, nine miles distant, and the whole intervening valley of the Chattahoochee" and "could observe the preparations for our reception on the other side."[2]

In the cautious investment of Johnston's bridgehead that followed, McPherson's army maintained its accustomed position on Sherman's right while Schofield's troops moved toward Roswell Factory, up the river from the Rebel stronghold. Soon after dark on Thursday, July 7, the 18th Missouri slipped down the bluff on Sherman's extreme right to dig in along the river at Green's Ferry. In keeping with Sherman's plans, most of XVI Corps was held back on the bluff out of sight of the enemy. All the Missourians had at the moment to dig with were bayonets and mess gear, for the entrenching tools were back in the hills on the wagon. But the soil was sandy and easy to work.

At daybreak Friday a few Missourians peered across the Chattahoochee and beheld, a hundred yards distant, a long line of Confederate trenches bristling with troops! Without a command given or a bugle blown, the shots began to fly, and the valley soon sounded like a vast corn-popper. Before long, a Rebel bullet found its mark on the north bank, wounding Sergeant Johnathan M. Yates of Putnam County. The youthful ex-Kentuckian was shipped out to Marietta for treatment of a leg wound, but Dr. Randolph, serving in the XVI Corps hospital, soon had him back on duty.

Yates thus missed what could have been the most unforgettable swimming party of his life. Toward noon white flags began to flutter on the Rebel works, and the firing dwindled away. "Hey, Yanks," someone called presently, "what say we stop shootin' and go swimmin'?"

Well, the gently swirling Chattahoochee *did* look pleasantly cool on this July day in Georgia, the Missourians thought. Why not a truce? After a little haggling, and without any officers getting involved, the men arranged an extraordinary but indefinite truce providing fifteen minutes' notice before resumption of hostilities. And the swimming began. "I think the boys enjoyed themselves hugely," said Sheldon. "It was reported at the time that some of our men went over into the enemy's lines, and vice versa—a 'Yank' and a 'Johnnie' in a state of nature look very much alike. . . ."

Under cover of the truce, the holiday spirit went right on after dark. Henry Sawyer said seventy years later that "sure enough" coffee from Federal mess-wagons somehow found its way into Rebel hands in exchange for a supply of the juicy "chawin' terbaccer" usually on hand in Southern knapsacks. "If the guards were heard coming," the teamster recalled, the enterprising traders would quietly swim away from the large boulder used for a trading block out in midstream.[3]

This pleasant sojourn by the Chattahoochee couldn't last long. In a barrage of telegrams to Washington, punctuated by conferences with the army commanders, Sherman was making up his mind to bypass the bridgehead by "feigning on the right and crossing on the left." Schofield had found a good crossing, over toward Roswell. Once the armies had passed the Chattahoochee, Sherman was going to make an indirect approach to Atlanta, circling it to cut all its railroads. Accordingly, on Saturday, McPherson got orders to move quickly back through

Marietta and up to Roswell to prepare for a crossing in force to the south bank of the river there.

Things were quiet at Green's Ferry the afternoon that Fuller's orderly rode down to report that the brigade was about to leave. Seeing that the Missourians would have to scramble a half-mile up the hill with their backs to the enemy in broad daylight, Fuller was agreeable to Sheldon's waiting until dark to pull out for Marietta.

As the orderly saluted and rode off, Sheldon began to wonder if it would be possible to exploit the truce for a fast getaway. After a huddle with Dolman, Cudworth, and several others, he decided that it might be worth a try. A few minutes later, he gave the word, and the regiment emerged from its rifle-pits at "quick-step" and "right shoulder shift," making for the safety of the bluff.

The Rebels swarmed up to their parapets, indignantly shouting, "Notice!" and "Time!" But no shots came. "It was an anxious quarter of an hour for all of us," Sheldon recalled, "but we went out in safety, and . . . reported to General Fuller (who was already on the road) much to his astonishment."

The 18th Missouri forded the river at Roswell on Sunday evening, July 10, after a hard march of more than thirty miles from Green's Ferry. Henry Sawyer spoke of how the boys crossed on "a stone foundation, knee deep under water so swift that walking and standing were difficult." Once across, the regiment joined the rest of the corps in building an extensive lodgment on Jeff Davis' side of the river. When daylight came, the Pioneers showed up to start rebuilding the bridge recently burned down at Johnston's behest.[4]

Along with its companions, the 18th Missouri remained in camp on the hill by the Chattahoochee for a week. Just as the surgeons were beginning to fret about the rising rate of scurvy in Sherman's forces, the men found themselves near large apple orchards and ripening patches of blackberries. Railroad crews had had their hands too full bringing in ammunition, forage, and standard rations to spare any cargo space for antiscorbutic fruits and vegetables. Speaking afterward of the locally grown fruits and vegetables, Sheldon was sure his men had "made good use of them." It was about this time that the roasting-ear season started, too, and Sherman soon "heard no more of the scurvy."

In the early evening of July 14, tragedy struck in Company I. Severe thunderstorms were sweeping the valley, and at 5 P.M., according to Sawyer's notation, a bolt of lightning struck a large tree under which several Missourians were huddled, their muskets stacked. "The guns were all discharged," Sheldon wrote, "and the lightning flew in every direction, like sparks from a blacksmith's anvil." Corporal John W. Taylor was instantly killed. A Putnam County farm boy, he had been in the army since New Year's Day, 1863. Dying with him was Private John Hensel, the immigrant German who had illegally enlisted in late 1861 while holding a parole from Sterling Price following his capture at Lexington. Six others were much shaken by the blast.[5]

July 17 saw a return to feverish activity. The XVII Corps had closed up to McPherson's bridgehead, and the other armies were also passing the river. So also, as a matter of fact, were Joseph E. Johnston's outflanked Rebels north of the river. A fifteen-mile line of Yankees was all set to start its "great wheel" toward Atlanta, pivoting on Thomas' army, back near the confluence of the Chattahoochee and Peach Tree Creek. McPherson held the left, Schofield the center.

On this day General Veatch, too sick to stay in the field, bade farewell to the division and left for Marietta. The gallant Hoosier never came back to duty with his troops in Georgia. General Fuller stepped up to command the division temporarily, and his senior colonel, John Morrill of the 64th Illinois, took the brigade command.[6]

With Sherman's "great wheel" on Atlanta under way the next morning, McPherson's columns marched steadily southeastward on a line for Stone Mountain. Along the headwaters of Nancy's Creek the 18th Missouri and its companions encountered a small cavalry force. After several volleys, the Rebel equestrians made off into the brush beyond New Cross Keys. That night Fuller camped most of the 4th Division along Nancy's Creek. The next morning saw the long blue lines press ever more closely on the doomed city. The Confederates continued to fall back, and only occasional exchanges of shots marred the strange quiet. The 18th Missouri and its comrades camped the night of July 18 along the famed Peach Tree Creek.

As the troops in Fuller's command pitched their tents that Monday evening, they had a hot topic of conversation. The news was out that Johnston had been fired by Jeff Davis and replaced by Hood. Sherman and McPherson saw at a glance that this portended "fight and plenty of it," nor did either much regret the prospect. They promptly voted John Bell Hood the Confederate general most likely to wreck an army on the breastworks of a more numerous Yankee force.[7]

Tuesday, July 19, found the Federal lines moving more cautiously, since an early Rebel counterattack appeared a certainty. The Army of the Tennessee, reaching the Georgia Railroad near Stone Mountain, began ripping up ties, twisting rails, and tearing down wires. As the Army of the Cumberland began to cross Peach Tree Creek just above its mouth, Schofield entered Decatur from the north. Late in the afternoon Fuller's division, in line of battle on the south side of Decatur, came under brief artillery fire from a Rebel battery in the woods near the town. The heavy guns of the 14th Ohio soon hushed Southern protests over the Yankee occupation of Decatur.

The Union forces moved steadily toward Atlanta on the morning of July 20, Schofield north of the railroad, McPherson astride it with Logan's corps in the lead and Blair following Logan. By evening the Yankee lines were in plain view of Atlanta and only three miles out from the center of the city. One needed no strong binoculars to see that Johnston had been planning for a long and drawn-out defense of Atlanta, for it was now ringed with "strong parapets, with ditch, fraise, chevaux-de-frise, and abatis . . ." to say nothing of well-placed batteries commanding the approaches.

How much use the Rebels would now make of Johnston's fortifications was anybody's guess on this warm and humid Wednesday. During the noon hour there came to Sheldon's ears the roar of battle to the north, where Hood was charging the Army of the Cumberland on lower Peach Tree Creek. The heaviest pressure in late afternoon came on Thomas' left, separated from Schofield by a wide gap. Hardee might well have crumpled Thomas' wing had not Hood, startled by Logan's appearance just east of Atlanta, pulled some of Hardee's force out of line to check XV Corps. Thomas emerged with his army intact, but he had seen a nerve-wracking afternoon north of the "Gate City."

During the night of July 20 the 18th Missouri camped just south of the railroad behind works being constructed on McPherson's left by Blair's XVII Corps. The other three regiments bivouacked around the same wooded spot, the last fragment of XVI Corps that General Dodge could call his own. Sweeny's 2d Division had to be put into Logan's line to plug the gap between Schofield and Logan north of the railroad. With Sherman getting nervous over the safety of the trains, Sprague's regiments now had to go back to Decatur to stand guard against Wheeler's horsemen. How ironic it must afterward have seemed to General Fuller that on the eve of his greatest battle two of the division's three brigades were absent —one at Decatur, Georgia, the other at Decatur, Alabama!

That afternoon Sherman directed Fuller's remnant to move up for close support of Blair's left flank, then very much "in the air" south of the Bald Hill from which Brigadier General Mortimer D. Leggett's division could peer across Major General Benjamin F. Cheatham's works into the city itself. Fuller deployed his four regiments in two lines of battle on the south slopes of Bald Hill. The 64th Illinois stood next to the hill, the 18th Missouri to the south and near a wagon road leading back to Fuller's command post. In the second line, the 27th Ohio stood right behind the Illinoisans, with the 39th Ohio supporting Sheldon's troops.

On Friday morning, July 22, the lines drew more tightly about Atlanta on the north and northeast, with the result that Sweeny was squeezed out of Logan's line and sent to the rear at 8 A.M. Late that forenoon Dodge and Fuller rode down to the rear of Blair's left, near Bald Hill. "The enemy allowed myself and staff to approach their works on the south side of Atlanta to within easy musket range without firing a shot," Dodge reported. "When I turned about, however, to return in the direction of the old line, they opened a heavy fire of artillery and musketry on us. . . ." McPherson's engineers were staking out a line running generally eastward from Blair's flank, Dodge told Fuller, and the latter ought to expect orders to move down there to dig in some time later in the day.

Around noon, it appears, McPherson had developed another idea. He notified Dodge that Sweeny was "going into position on the left" of Blair, and that Fuller's remaining brigade might as well be put to work wrecking the railroad toward Decatur. Events overtook this directive, however.[8]

The regimental staff dined with Sheldon that noon in a little log shanty just behind the 18th Missouri's rifle-pits. All they had was coffee, hardtack, and raw onions, but it was a hot day and nobody was really hungry. The conversation drifted casually on until two sharp cracks of rifle fire were heard some distance to the south.

"What's that?" someone casually asked. And just as casually, someone else replied: "Oh, only the boys shooting hogs." But then there came a scattering of shots—unmistakable racket of a skirmish.

"No hog shooting there!" Sheldon barked, springing to his feet. "That means business." Leading the rush outside, he ordered Bugler Frederick Hackh to sound assembly, and the Missourians grabbed their Springfields.

Everybody was jumping to Sheldon's conclusion, for as far as the eye could see the preparations for battle were beginning. As the Missourians were lining up, Sheldon saw Fuller's orderlies leading the two Ohio regiments out to the wagon road which led to the east. And then the 64th Illinois filed out behind them.

The Missourians didn't piece all these events together until late that night, but the volleys to the south of Bald Hill resulted from a Rebel assault on Blair's hospital. Fuller, hosting Dodge at lunch, had also thought hog-killing was going on, but he and Dodge quickly saw that something more was afoot in that vast, trackless woodland southeast of Atlanta. Fearful that hordes of Rebels might be coming through the woods, Dodge ordered the 39th Ohio pulled back to guard the forward elements of McPherson's wagon train, then parked in a wide field north and south of Fuller's headquarters.

Sweeny's division, meanwhile, had moved into line facing

southward and covering a hill several hundred yards southeast of Fuller's tent. The Ohio Battery, on the hill, prepared for action, while Sweeny sent a reconnaissance into the woods to the south. Sweeny found the timber alive with enemy skirmishers, and Fuller immediately realized that a major attack was imminent. Without hesitating, he decided to commit all his regiments to the fight shaping up to the south along Sugar Creek.

Shortly after 12:30, one of Fuller's aides dashed up to Sheldon with orders to bring the 18th Missouri on the double-quick. Conducted down the wagon road by the aide, the Missourians came shortly to the edge of the field where the trains had been standing all morning. Bedlam had broken out, for the quartermasters and their teamsters were also apprehensive. "At this point," Quartermaster Cudworth later said, "we came near losing our train." While he was responsible for only one of the wagons, "that one was a sacred trust to me and I did not want to lose it." Asking Dodge's quartermaster for instructions, Cud drew only the reply that there was yet nothing anybody could do because the General had given no orders. The disgusted Cudworth could very well see the danger, as most of the train was to the south of the road where Fuller's men were forming in anticipation of the coming onslaught. "Follow me!" he shouted to Teamster Sawyer, and rode off northward across the road. All the other wagons followed, notwithstanding the difficulty of passing through Fuller's firing-line. And so, wrote Cudworth, "we got our train through the line, Henry Sawyer in the lead, going down the ravine in rear of the 17th and 15th Corps, where shot and shell passed over them."

With the skirmishers' rifles beating out a tattoo along the edge of the woods to the south, Fuller rode up to the head of Sheldon's oncoming column. "He said the other regiments were in line to the front, with the 64th Illinois just in the edge of the timber," Sheldon later wrote. "The 18th Missouri would be considered in reserve, and he indicated a position along a hill which we were to occupy. We had great difficulty in forming a line, as the frightened teamsters . . . broke through continually on their way to . . . the rear."[9]

On a little rise overlooking a tributary of Sugar Creek, Sheldon deployed his regiment. Directly in front, across the ravine, was the 27th Ohio, with the 39th on its left next to Sugar Creek and right under the protecting guns of the Ohio Battery. The 64th was to the west, where Fuller had stationed it at the edge of the woods southwest of division headquarters.

Sheldon's deployment was completed about 1:30, just in time. "Here they come!" an Ohio officer yelled. And, sure enough, emerging from the woods in front of Sweeny and Fuller came a heavy gray line moving northward in "quick time and perfect order." Another of Hood's dirty tricks! Instead of evacuating Atlanta, as the Union commanders were expecting, he had sent Hardee's corps southeastward the night before with orders to swing back in on Blair's dangling flank. Such an action, Hood thought, might roll up Sherman like an accordion.

The oncoming Rebels "seemed surprised to find our infantry in line of battle, prepared for action," noted McPherson's inspector-general, Lieutenant Colonel William E. Strong, who saw the whole affair. Cudworth praised Dodge's "well-planned reception." The attackers were shocked indeed, for there wasn't supposed to be anything protecting Blair's flank. "The Rebels formed three lines of battle right in front of us," said Ben Sweet. "I would judge that there lines was about 80 yards apart but marched directly in front of each. . . . We were ordered to lie down and not fire a shot until the front line was within forty steps, then we got the order, to rise and fire a solid volley. When we got the order 'fire' the very force of the volley turned men over. It looked to me as tho there was about as many men hit in the second line as in the first. When our men fired it made a perfect stampede."[10]

Meanwhile, McPherson had ridden up to witness the XVI Corps' confrontation with Hardee. What he now beheld was a drama in which Dodge was "cutting all red tape" to become "a colonel, brigadier general, and division commander all in one." The Rebels seemed, to Dan Shelton, "determined to conquer or die." Thousands more now came into view moving on the flanks of the Ohioans, who had pursued the survivors of Hardee's first assault-waves across the open field to its south edge. Dodge had no choice now but to pull the Ohioans back to their original position to face the approaching lines of Major General William H. T. Walker's Confederate division.

"The scene at this time," in Colonel Strong's words, "was grand and impressive." It seemed to him as if every one of Walker's officers were with the first line, as the colors of nearly fifty regiments waved in the gentle breeze. Hardee's artillery back in the trees was carrying on a thunderous dialogue with the Ohio Battery. If some Rebel shellbursts were felling Dodge's infantrymen, these were nothing as compared to the "iron and leaden hail" ripping great swaths out of the gray ranks. On came the Confederates, closing up their gaps but holding their fire.

Fuller, meanwhile, was beginning to fear a stampede of his two Ohio regiments. Jumping off his horse, the sturdy little brigadier raced among the retiring troops, his sword high in the air and the color-bearers of his old 27th right behind him. His former regiment did not fail him, Fuller reported to Dodge, and "with a great shout came up on either side in less time than I can write." With the 39th Ohio formed on his left, Fuller now ordered a bayonet charge.

By the time the Confederates reached the center of the field the frightful toll exacted by XVI Corps' storm of lead had begun to create uncontrollable confusion in the Rebel formations. The 64th Illinois was hitting hard on one side, and Sheldon had wheeled the 18th Missouri around far enough to pour a raking fire into the Confederate flank. Trying to rally the waverers, a Rebel general rode into their midst, swinging his hat above him. Fuller always believed it was Walker himself. "The next moment his horse went back riderless," Fuller later remembered. At this point, the Ohioans' bayonet charge took place, and it had the effect of chasing the rest of Walker's men into the woods.

McPherson and Dodge were vastly relieved and jubilant. The latter officer declared in New York after the war that "until the two forces struck and the Sixteenth Corps stood firm, I never passed more anxious moments." McPherson was heard to shout to the officers around him, "Hurrah for Dodge! He has got them!"

Concerned now about Brigadier General Giles Smith's situation out on Blair's flank, McPherson decided to go on over to XVII Corps. It was two o'clock. Strong vividly recalled in

1873 this "closing scene in McPherson's life. I see him now as I saw him that last time, straight as an arrow, a smile lighting his handsome face, and his eye full of the fire of battle. 'Join me at Giles Smith's,' he said, and stooped over and patted the neck of his favorite horse that had carried him safely through scores of engagements from Shiloh down. . . ." Gathering the reins firmly in his left hand, the army commander galloped off westward through the timber toward Bald Hill, along the road down which Fuller's brigade had come little more than an hour ago.

A few minutes later Sheldon gaped in amazement when he saw the 64th Illinois charge into the woods along that very road. Equally astonishing to him was the fact that General Fuller was going in with the Illinoisans—as were Colonel Strong and several officers from army headquarters. Then Sheldon saw the two Ohio regiments sweeping across the field toward the woods south of the wagon road.

"As I had been ordered to remain in position as first placed, and in reserve as well, I did not feel authorized to make any forward movement," Sheldon said, "though I remember, it seemed to me at the time, that I ought to have followed the brigade. As it turned out, it was extremely fortunate that I did not do so."[11]

It was near 2:15 when the 64th began streaming back from the underbrush into which it had charged for reasons still unknown to the 18th Missouri. Heavy enemy reinforcements had come up from the southeast to drive the Illinoisans out into the open field whence they had come. "They are outflanking us!" Sheldon heard somebody shout above the commotion. The Ohioans were exposed south of the road, and their one thought now was to seek safety in careful withdrawal.

At this moment, Captain Frederick Welker, commanding Sweeny's artillery, rode up with the startling news that McPherson was either dead or captured, and that Sherman had sent for Logan. Now it was clear to Sheldon why Fuller and the Illinoisans had raced into the woods. Sheldon "hardly knew what to do. General Fuller was out of reach, but it was evident that the movement of the enemy to the rear must be checked immediately."

Sheldon decided on his own to redeploy the 18th Missouri in a bold effort to bail out the hard-pressed 64th. "It could not be done without changing front, and to do this, owing to the nature of the ground, the regiment had to face about and march a short distance to the rear—a very risky movement . . . especially in the face of the enemy." Within a few minutes the Missourians had calmly lined themselves up in a new position almost at right angles with the first line of the 4th Division. Now they looked squarely into the flank of the Rebels chasing the 64th Illinois.

At a word from Sheldon, the men proceeded to hand the enemy three devastating volleys, "causing them to retire into the woods, from which they did not again emerge." Much to his horror, Sheldon now found that some of the 64th troops had mingled with the retreating enemy and thus were in danger of being cut down in continuing fire from the Missourians' weaponry. Racing down the line, he began trying to choke off further firing.

Just at this point, he felt a frightening sting in his chest. "This is my turn!" the bold young commander must have thought. Telling Dolman to take over, Sheldon galloped to the rear where Dr. Houts could "ascertain the amount of damage." Happily, it was only a spent shot, and all the Colonel had to contend with was a painful bruise.[12]

Half an hour later—probably near three o'clock—Sheldon resumed command. Fuller in the meantime had reappeared and, under Dodge's supervision, was readjusting his line. Logar, now commanding the army, was filling that 600-yard gap between Fuller and Blair, that fatal gap into which McPherson had ridden, with Colonel Hugo Wangelin's brigade of the XV Corps, consisting of the 3d, 12th, 17th, 29th, 31st, and 32d Missouri Volunteers. During that afternoon's wild fighting, Blair's exposed flank had swung around toward the rear, anchoring on Bald Hill, until it extended due eastward toward positions taken up by Wangelin and Fuller between 3:00 and 4:00 P.M. In the process, Blair's men had had to fight from both sides of their works in fending off alternating attacks by Hardee's left and by Cheatham's forces coming out from Atlanta's eastern works.[13]

As the badly beaten Hardee retired into the timbered hills

that he had come from, there spread through the Army of the Tennessee as much bad news as good. It was known by nightfall that a sorrowing General Sherman had announced the death of McPherson, "in battle, booted and spurred, as the gallant and heroic gentleman should wish." Logan, onetime Illinois Congressman, had succeeded to command of the Army, certain it was his from that day forward. The best news came from Decatur, where Sprague's troops, in a hard afternoon's fighting, had driven off Joe Wheeler's cavalry. Sprague had had to give up Decatur for a while, but he had saved the rear trains, and won a brigadier's star.[14]

Just before dark, Sheldon sought to clear up one matter with General Leggett. Some infernal artillery battery, apparently on Bald Hill, had narrowly missed the 18th Missouri several times, and had wounded a man in another regiment. Rather provoked by such reckless gunnery on the part of Leggett's men, Sheldon sent an orderly to him with a pointed request that the battery either aim higher from now on or else quit firing altogether.

Leggett's response must have been easy to memorize, for the orderly rushed back to say that the offending battery was a Rebel outfit over in Cheatham's works! "General Leggett sends his compliments, sir," the orderly reported, "and says he has been trying to stop that damned battery all day, and if Colonel Sheldon thinks he can take the works in Atlanta he would be pleased to see him do it."

"The General rather 'had it on me' that time," Sheldon conceded, "and as we had already enjoyed all the fighting we wanted for one day, I concluded we wouldn't take that battery."[15]

During the night the company commanders were busily figuring the cost of the Battle of Atlanta to the 18th Missouri. The death of McPherson was the biggest shock, for in the few months the men had known him he had become "the idol of the Army of the Tennessee," as Sheldon put it, "always kind and gentle, with ever a cheering word for all he came in contact with. . . ." Among the ranking officers wounded the same day was Colonel Morrill, whose misfortune shifted brigade command to Lieutenant Colonel Henry T. McDowell of the

39th Ohio. When Sheldon sent his morning reports to McDowell the next day, he reported that the action of July 22 had cost his Missourians one officer slightly wounded (Sheldon himself), fifteen enlisted men wounded, and nine missing. The most seriously wounded were Privates Simon Kredel (Company H), James Dawson (K), and Joseph Anderson (K). The German-born Kredel, forty-five, died shortly in the division hospital, as did Dawson, a twenty-four-year-old Buchanan County boy who was a former prisoner at Shiloh. Another of Platte County's fighting Kentuckians, Anderson had signed up with Colonel Morgan when only sixteen. Now he suffered a wound that cost him his right leg below the knee. The war was over for Joe Anderson, who went home to the bride he had claimed during his veteran furlough at Weston. Sergeant John A. Drake of Company B, hit in the head and shoulders by shell fragments, was to remain at Marietta for treatment until the following March.

There were also "silent casualties" suffered by the men on that bloodiest day since Shiloh. Lieutenant Pagin was hit in the lower right leg by a spent ball, but he never reported it until necrosis affecting the site of the wound put him on crutches in the 1870s. Back near Wyreka, in Putnam County, three-year-old Jackie Cawood lay dead that very day, and it would be at least a week before the first sergeant of Company G would learn that death had taken his son from him. Finally, Private Andrew J. Morgan of Company B, suffering a gunshot wound in the right side of his head, was rushed back to Marietta for surgery. The medics patched Morgan's head, gave him a discharge, and ordered him a pension. But they couldn't give him a full and happy life. He never recovered, and within two years died of "traumatic encephalitis" at his farm home near West Liberty, in Putnam County. They said Morgan was only wounded on July 22, but he met his death that day just the same.[16]

Fuller's men lay camped behind their works for four days after Friday's carnage. Taking its turn at picket duty on July 24, the 18th Missouri manned the brigade's works and roamed the timber to the south. This was dangerous business, and Private William A. Stockton of Company D, a Putnam County farm youth, lost his life to a Confederate sharpshooter during the anxious day. Two men of Dan Hudson's Company A, Daniel Dewitt and Benjamin F. Johns, fell prisoner after one scrap in the woods. They were promptly sent by train to the dread Andersonville prison, where a half-dozen tragic heroes of the 18th Missouri lay buried. The two captives were brought back in September and exchanged at a truce camp south of Atlanta. There was a dark side to this picture, though, for Ben Johns returned to Union lines suffering from nephritis and scurvy, and he would spend the rest of the war in a hospital at Dalton. Two more men were lost, one permanently, to artillery fragments late at night, July 26. Company F's Corporal Charles Wellington, a forty-year-old farmer from near Laclede, died of wounds a fortnight later at Marietta. Sergeant Silas W. Haynes, of D Company, whom Sheldon regarded as a "gritty soldier" well worth a commission, was hit in the back and left shoulder by shell fragments and bullets, and the surgeons had to confine him to bed at Marietta.[17]

Meanwhile, the troops had a first-rate scandal to occupy their minds. On Monday, July 25, General Sweeny's Irish was up, and it cost him command of his division and very nearly his career. If postwar orators could admire Dodge's conduct of the battle of July 22 as "a colonel, brigadier general, and division commander, all in one," Tom Sweeny could not. Old Regular Sweeny, who cherished the chain of command, was outraged by various things Dodge had done, not the least of which was his peremptory manner of bypassing Sweeny and his brigadiers to give direct operational orders to regimental commanders.

It was widely known in XVI Corps that Sweeny had never been one of Dodge's admirers, that the two had been "crosswise" ever since their days together at Corinth. Corps records abound with incidents in which Sweeny sparred with Dodge over procedural matters, for the latter, a "political general," had frequently violated Old Army usages. One long-standing cause of irritation was the attempt of Dodge's medical director, Dr. Norman Gay, to give orders to Sweeny's surgeons. The "book" said that corps staffers had to channel such operational directions through the division commander, and Sweeny won several tilts with his corps commander on technicalities of that kind.

On July 10, during the XVI Corps' march across the Chatta-hoochee, Sweeny had run afoul of Gay again by using a division ambulance for his staff officers' convenience. Gay said that couldn't be done, whereupon Bulldog flew into a rage and ordered the astonished surgeon horsewhipped by orderlies. Gay quite understandably chose not to stick around for Sweeny's brand of physiotherapy, and as he spurred his horse into a gallop he distinctly heard Sweeny threaten to "shoot me the first time he caught me alone. . . ."

It was now Dodge's turn to be enraged; on July 11 he wrote McPherson from Roswell to ask that Sweeny be relieved and court-martialed. Mac primly advised Dodge to do the dirty work himself "if he deems it for the best interests of the Service." Dismissing a general officer while facing the enemy was, declared the Army commander, "inadmissible" unless extreme provocation could be established.

The Corps commander, raised to major general the following week, bided his time. The torrid aftermath of the Battle of Atlanta, however, brought the feud to its inevitable climax. Sweeny sent Dodge several protest notes over his actions in giving orders directly to the colonels during the fighting, and Dodge rudely ignored them. Then, about midmorning on Monday, Dodge and Fuller, riding the lines with their staffs, happened in at Sweeny's command tent.

Sweeny was obviously enraged, for he sat down between Dodge and Fuller and began making remarks about how the Army had been led into a near-disaster on Friday by incompetent "political generals." Such verbal missiles were well calculated to land close to both of his visitors. Then the Bulldog tossed in a barbed remark about how his own line had been compromised by Fuller's failure to hold firm. Dodge and Fuller at last rose to the bait, protesting in one voice that Fuller had waged a stout fight. Sweeny immediately put Captain Welker on the spot to support his contention, which Welker did, but with obvious trepidation before Dodge.

Dodge declared angrily that anyone implying that Fuller had not carried out orders faithfully on July 22 was saying "that which was not so." That did it. Dodge and Sweeny rose instantly to their feet, with Bulldog barking out "*I said so!*" and following it up with several epithets clearly implying canine

ancestry in the female side of Dodge's family. The two immediately came to blows, notwithstanding that Dodge had one
more star and one more arm than the furious Irishman.

Welker and Captain J. W. Barnes, corps adjutant general,
pulled them apart and seated them again by brute force.
Sweeny, still fuming, challenged Dodge to a duel. Thereupon
Fuller, ". . . small, compactly built, with piercing black eyes . . ."
came over to talk sense to the berserk Sweeny. This led
only to a round of fisticuffs between the brigadiers, in the
course of which Fuller wrestled Sweeny to the ground and
tried to strangle him. The enraged Briton might have done it,
but Barnes and Welker brought in enough help to drag him
away before he could add murder to the morning's trouble.

The indignant Dodge then instructed Barnes to arrest
Sweeny. The latter, however, won his last technical victory by
reminding Barnes that he would need to have his sword on if
he did any arresting. Noting that Barnes was only a "damned
militia captain" anyhow, Sweeny triumphantly screamed, "You
don't know HOW to arrest an officer!" Barnes left in a hurry
to get his sword, and was soon able to assure Dodge that "the
Dog" had been muzzled.

The Irishman was hard to silence completely, however. As
Dodge rode away, Sweeny shrieked for all to hear: "Go, Mr.
Dodge of Iowa, you God-damned political general! I shall ex-
pect a *note* from you, sir!"

Dodge, as a matter of fact, did do some writing, but not to
Sweeny. He scribbled a note to Logan summarizing what had
taken place. A troubled Sherman promptly packed the offender
off to Nashville to stand trial on charges of insubordination and
"conduct unbecoming." Brigadier General John M. Corse was
sent in to replace Sweeny, as Sherman importuned Logan to
"see that no injustice is done to General Sweeny."[18]

On the heels of this controversy there came another thunderbolt from Sherman's headquarters. After pondering the
Army of the Tennessee's future a few days, Sherman had concluded that Logan's role as a political general qualified him less
for the Army command than a regular officer whose attention
might be concentrated more on Sherman's wishes and less
on the voters of postwar Illinois. On July 26 the news broke that

Major General Oliver O. Howard, late commander of IV Corps, would come in as McPherson's permanent successor.

If this angered Logan and Frank Blair—second and third in seniority after the lamented McPherson—that is understandable. But their chagrin was mild compared to Fighting Joe Hooker's tantrum. Hooker, who outranked Howard and all the other corps commanders, furiously vowed that he would have no further association with an outfit in which "rank and service are ignored." He threw in his resignation and headed north, insinuating to reporters that Union operations in Georgia were in the hands of a maniac and that the public should brace itself for a catastrophe in Georgia.

The men of the 18th Missouri took well enough to their new commander, who, at thirty-one, was even younger than McPherson. The right sleeve of his tunic was empty, due to a wound received in Virginia a couple of years back. Sheldon said of him that the deeply religious Howard "was not as affable as McPherson, but he both gained and held . . . the confidence of his army."[19]

Federal forces were hardly strong enough to encircle Atlanta, considering the strength of Hood's army inside it. A half-siege was no siege at all, particularly as long as freight trains were still supplying the defenders, and Sherman saw that he was obliged to "move to the right rapidly and boldly against the railroad below Atlanta. . . ." The Army of the Tennessee received orders July 26 to leave its works east of the city, file out behind Thomas and Schofield, and take up new positions directly west of town. Henry Sawyer knew in advance that something was afoot, for the wagons were ordered north at 6:30 P.M., whereas the infantry did not move until near midnight.

Sherman's plan called for Schofield to slip a token force over into the evacuated works to conceal the departure of the Army of the Tennessee. It didn't work. The Rebels caught on to the ruse, and initiated a fearsome artillery barrage (striking down Haynes and Wellington). With the 18th Missouri leading, the XVI Corps moved out first, with Blair and Logan peeling off in that order. General Howard, appearing at daybreak to assume the Army's command, found his new charges moving swiftly westward "from the field of their bloody triumph. . . ."

Late that afternoon, XVI Corps passed Proctor's Creek to move in on the right of XIV Corps. Howard was upstream with Corse's men, placing them in a line somewhat in advance of XIV Corps and to the northwest of the Poor House and White Hall Mansion. Fuller's division formed up between Corse and Blair's oncoming columns. Howard was still impressed forty years later with the way "each successive brigade covered the rear and then the flank of its predecessor." Blair's front curved around to the east, and Logan "hooked on" to the XVII Corps with a line that was "refused," bent back to the southwest, just in case Hood tried another flank attack. The Army of the Tennessee, said Correspondent Conyngham, on the morning of July 28 stood on a line "something in the shape of a horseshoe, with the toe to the enemy, and resting on a wooded ridge with partly open fields in front." Logan's right was near Ezra Church.[20]

During the morning of July 28 Dodge moved his line a quarter-mile eastward, with the 18th Missouri out ahead as a skirmish line. A fresh cluster of rifle-pits soon dotted the earth between the main works and the skirmishers, as the Army of the Tennessee chopped and dug all morning to make its new "home" west of Atlanta as secure as possible.

The need for security became evident at noon, when a heavy cannonade, accompanied by a storm of musket-fire, burst forth along the Lickskillet road skirting Logan's works. Hood had struck again, trying on Sherman's right what he had failed to accomplish on the left the week before. Hood's third sortie was a worse fiasco than the near-miss of July 22, but it gave Howard some tense moments. The Confederate charge slightly overlapped Logan's right flank, but Howard brought up enough reserves to save him from catastrophe. Dodge had to send his 35th New Jersey and the 64th Illinois, both toting breech-loading repeaters, to Logan's rescue. The 18th Missouri "had hot work all day," Sheldon commented, "but nothing more serious than demonstrations" occurred along the XVI Corps front. "The enemy's main line advanced no further than the edge of the woods in our front," said Sheldon, "though it remained in sight all afternoon." By dark, the onslaught against XV Corps, staged by five Rebel divisions, was spent. To cover their withdrawal, the Confederates shelled Howard's entire line, and some troops of his Army found it safer to be *in front* of their parapets than huddled in trenches behind them.[21]

"Hood will soon have no army if he continues 'butting' against our works," Sheldon wrote General Gray three days later. Indeed, Hood wasn't coming out any more. Even Jeff Davis was now dismayed at the cost of those "Lee and Jackson" methods in Sherman's presence. He now counseled the defenders of Atlanta to employ less aggressive means of checking the Yankees. "Hood had castled," said Conyngham, "and Sherman moved to checkmate him."

A month of siege warfare followed, with the armies preparing elaborate breastworks and exchanging artillery salvos. Occasionally the 18th Missouri went out on picket, but its biggest project in early August was the construction of a massive "casemate" to house Battery F, 2d U.S. Artillery. The cannoneers were just getting one of the new long-range "Rodman 4½" guns, with which Sherman expected to shell the center of Atlanta, 4,000 yards distant. Having built the casemate, complete with earth-and-log roof, Sheldon's troops were then detailed to guard it. This made them high-priority targets for Hood's guns in the "Big Fort" over at the Fair Grounds. The officers found it highly advisable to put up little huts with heavy log roofs to protect against bursts and stray fragments.

Most annoying to the Missourians was the "64-pounder" at the Fair Grounds. The lead base used to fit the rifling grooves always trailed each shell, swishing along, hacking limbs off trees and scattering them along the regiment's camping area. The worrisome gun also spoiled Adjutant Godfrey's love for bean soup. One August evening, as he was reaching for a second helping, a shell fragment knocked his plate out of his hand. At that, Godfrey was "let off easy," considering what the fragment *might* have done, but from then on the men at headquarters noticed that the Adjutant wasn't quite so interested in bean soup as formerly.[22]

The first days in the new line west of Atlanta took their toll, even if the regiment was not involved in major combat. On July 28, Private Thomas Nolan, an Irishman of twenty-four who had enlisted in Company F in the spring of 1863 at St. Louis, was seriously wounded. The former medical student died on August 21. Less severely injured was Company A's Private Reuben Pinion, thirty-six, who had joined up during the veteran furlough. As the siege wore on, the cost would rise.

The slow-down of operations gave Sheldon a chance to get back to the two-front paper war he had been waging since late spring. Two allied issues were on his mind, the question of mustering out the "1861 boys" who had not re-enlisted, and the "battle of the promotions." On the former issue, Sheldon tried in June to get the "non-vets" mustered out in August, pointing out that they had been *on duty* since August of 1861. Sherman and his mustering officers were quite agreeable to an August muster-out, but the War Department vetoed the idea on June 29, declaring that "the date of muster-in fixes the term of service, and no deviation can be authorized therefrom." The men would wait until November.

By the coming of July the regiment was feeling the effects of its officer-shortage. On the rolls were 802 names, somewhat shy of the "minimum" regiment in which new officers could be mustered to the extent that Sheldon needed. Governor Hall and General Gray were all set to make Sheldon a full colonel and act on a dozen other necessary promotions, but the inadequate strength of the regiment had them—and Federal officials—stumped. Some of the companies were down to one officer by late July; with Dr. Randolph away at the corps hospital it had been necessary to lift Lieutenant Pagin out of Company C to make use of his medical training as an assistant to Houts.

A few companies happened to be strong enough to justify commissioning the men they needed, and a few lieutenants were made in late July. First lieutenant's gold bars now went to Abijah Everest of Company I, while second lieutenancies were given to five first sergeants: Bill Brantner (A), Thomas Hatfield (B), Joe Stanley (C), Henry Runnels (E), and Joel Richardson (I). As a result of Richardson's promotion, the first sergeant's stripes in Fallis' company were sewed on Ben Guffey's tunic. These commissions, first in the regiment since March, were little more than drops in the bucket, but Sheldon pronounced them "a great lift to the 18th. . . ."

No ignoramus when it came to army regulations, Sheldon hit on a possible technical solution to the impasse at the beginning of August. "At the time Capt. Ault commanded the Regt. he ordered dropped from the rolls *all* the enlisted men who were absent from the Regiment," Sheldon reminded Gray. "Many were in hospitals, some deserters. As the act was illegal —no one except the President having the power to *drop* men from the rolls—it becomes my duty to see that they are restored . . . and then properly disposed of. . . . This will, I think, bring the regiment up to the minimum for a few days."

This encouraged Hall and Gray to start more commissions rolling. On August 15 the Governor even signed a commission making Sheldon a full colonel, a fair achievement for a young man who had been a private four short years earlier. At the same time, Minter, whose last promotion Sheldon had fought so bitterly less than a year before, now rose to lieutenant colonel, on Sheldon's recommendation. Captain Dolman was offered the major's gold oak leaves. Out in the companies, Sergeant Haynes of Company D, recuperating at Marietta, became a second lieutenant on Sheldon's special request. Tom Hatfield, second lieutenant less than a month, left Company B to take over as first lieutenant in E. Ken Breeman, who had been performing ably in Company H before they shipped him to the hospital, got the captain's bars formerly worn by Dolman.

Nevertheless, the rolls of the regiment never quite got up to the magic number 845, which would have made it legal to muster Sheldon in for his "eagles." The time came in mid-September when it seemed to Sheldon he might never make it unless fragments of disbanding regiments should be transferred to him. A number of veterans in the 23d Missouri were appealing to join, he told Howard. Finally, on September 16, Howard in effect told him to be patient and keep quiet for a while. There should, said Howard, soon be enough draftees from Missouri to do the trick. But if not, he would ask the War Department to muster Sheldon in "for gallant and meritorious conduct in the Field."

Sheldon's policy was to make promotions strictly on the basis of seniority, he always said, and many equally deserving men were obliged to wait for later recognition. Even so, very few of the men promoted in August managed to get mustered-in to their new ranks until mid-September. Sheldon, last to make it, mustered-in at Christmas. Of the promotionees, it is interesting to note that Minter, Dolman, Haynes, and Breeman had been prisoners at Shiloh, while Richardson and Runnels had been wounded there. All the others, including Sheldon, had been present on that tragic field.[23]

During those torrid August days the two armies sniped away and moved their lines inch by inch southward from Atlanta. It was a splendid rehearsal for 1914, with men burrowing into ever deeper and more complex trench-systems, thus compelling their enemies to do likewise. During the first three weeks of that month the 18th Missouri lost three men killed and six wounded. Sergeant William T. Wilson of Company B died in the corps hospital from the effects of an accidental bullet wound on August 6. A veteran of the Kentucky migration to Putnam County in his childhood, Wilson was twenty-six. On August 11, during a heavy cannonade, Private Jonathan W. Watts, also of B, was killed. Watts was a twenty-one-year-old farmer from Putnam, another of the prisoners at Shiloh. Wounded on August 13 was Private Karsten Theede, one of the German boys who had joined K Company at Weston. Dr. Randolph and the stewards at the corps hospital were unable to save him, and Theede on August 25 joined Wilson and Watts in the rapidly growing legion in the Marietta cemetery. Among the seriously wounded was the top sergeant of Company K, Gebhart Kurtz, whose right arm was mangled by a shell on August 11. Removed to Marietta for an amputation, he was later shifted northward to other hospitals. The 18th Missouri never saw him again, for he mustered-out at Jefferson City the next summer.[24]

"The continued presence of great danger seemed at times to have a tendency to make men reckless," Sheldon found. The 35th New Jersey, in Sprague's brigade, was the daredevil regiment of Dodge's corps. These former Zouaves, whenever they were on guard at night, did their infernal best to see that nobody in camp got a wink of sleep. Prowling the woods beyond the trenches, the "Zoos" would let out war whoops and blaze away with their muskets. "The boys soon got onto them," Sheldon tells us, and before long "nothing short of the confederate yell" could bring off-duty regiments back up into the breast-works.

The pesky Zouaves rigged up a dummy, put a Federal uniform on it, and occasionally stuck a part of it above the works. Invariably, this brought a Rebel sharpshooter's bullet. Jerking the dummy back into the trench, the Zoos would groan, inspiring the snipers to exult that "We got him!" Finally, though, the Jersey boys held the figure up on a pole high enough to show the other side how badly they had been tricked. It was the blue-coats' turn to crow, then.

While in the massive earthworks southwest of Atlanta, the Army indulged itself in nightly "singing duels" with all Confederates within easy earshot. Typical of the songs the Yanks led off with were "The Star-Spangled Banner," "Yankee Doodle," and "Hail Columbia." The Confederate soldiers usually responded with "Maryland, My Maryland," "The Bonnie Blue Flag," and, of course, "Dixie." Julia Ward Howe's popular new "Battle Hymn of the Republic," described by a modern Southern writer as "the most haunting and meaningful of American battle songs," probably raised the Rebel hackles a bit, appealing so little to the common heritage of the two armies. At any rate, such songfests generally wound up with "Home Sweet Home," Sheldon recalls, "and both sides heartily joined."[25]

Two high-level casualties shocked the Missourians on August 18 and 19. First of all, Dr. Houts broke the news at headquarters that Colonel Sheldon was coming down with typhoid or malaria. Houts loaded him into an ambulance and rushed him to Marietta. Fortunately, Minter was coming back on duty and would take the reins during Sheldon's absence. A day later came the report that General Dodge had fallen with what was first thought to be a mortal wound. As General Howard described it, "some sharpshooter got in a bullet that plowed his head . . . I don't think he was expected ever to do anything more." Dodge had been looking through a peep-hole in the headlogs of the 7th Iowa's trenches when the Rebel marksman creased him, knocking him senseless.

Brigadier General Thomas E. G. Ransom, who had taken over the 4th Division in early August, now stepped into Dodge's shoes, and Fuller resumed command of the division. Colonel McDowell took over the First Brigade again, a position that would have gone to Sheldon, had he been mustered as full colonel, without a case of malaria. This was not, as it happened, Sheldon's last chance at brigade command.

The summer's campaign had been hard on captains. Ken Breeman had been sent to Chattanooga on July 1 with a stubborn case of dysentery. Then, in late August, Dan Hudson, having developed kidney stones, had to be sent to the general hospital at Lookout Mountain. The traffic was not all outbound, however, for Wyckoff and Fallis returned to duty in Companies D and I during August.[26]

While the 18th Missouri continued to take part "in all the advances that were made upon the enemy's works, and performed its full share of skirmish duty," Sherman was anxiously hunting for the key to a successful climax for his Atlanta campaign. On August 19 he launched his cavalry southward from Sandtown and Decatur to cut the two railroads still operating south of the city. This stroke paid scanty dividends, Sherman found, for on August 23 freight trains resumed the use of railway tracks that Kilpatrick claimed to have destroyed two or three days earlier. Sherman, now convinced that his horsemen simply "could not or would not work hard enough to disable a railroad properly," decided to move infantry across those vital lines.

For this southward movement against Hood's last railroad, Sherman worked out a complicated maneuver. Schofield having recently moved down to Howard's right flank, the trick was for Howard now to pivot on Schofield's rear and swing south through Lickskillet toward Sandtown. This would make room for Thomas to slip around to Schofield's right and resume his regular position in the center of Sherman's line, between Howard and Schofield. To cover the movement, Sherman ordered two special projects. Major General Henry W. Slocum's corps would retire to Johnston's old fortifications around the Chattahoochee crossing to guard the railroad bridge. Second, the 18th Missouri early on Thursday, August 25, would start building a line of "refused" east-west trenches to be used by troops defending the rear of Sherman's southward march.[27]

The Missourians spent two days on this excavation project. Then Lieutenant Rockwood, having started his own diary, noted that "There seems to be more riding about of the officers than usual. Perhaps some forward movement on hand," he surmised. "Am not much decieved in apprehension." Sure enough, the 32d Wisconsin, of the long-absent Third Brigade, appeared late Friday afternoon with orders to relieve Minter's troops for the forward movement. And off they went. With Blair and Logan leading Howard's march, Ransom's corps followed. And for the moment, the 18th Missouri brought up Howard's rear.

Federal hopes that the move could get off before the Rebels found out soon dimmed. As the Army of the Tennessee began filing quietly out of its works after dark Friday, enemy artillery opened up all over their lines. Branches fell from the big trees onto Howard's chosen roads, and solid shot crumpled the smaller trees. One soldier was killed, another wounded, Howard was informed. Most of all he feared the panic that might ensue in this violent hurricane of shot and shell. But his fears, he soon acknowledged, "were rather born of previous experiences with other commands than from the knowledge of these Western veterans." There was no stampede.

After a careful two-day march involving frequent brushes with cavalry and infantry, Howard's army camped around Fairburn, on the West Point line, on Sunday evening, August 28. The 18th Missouri pitched its tents next to Owl Rock Church and got ready to help destroy the railroad on Monday. By sundown on August 29, the six-mile track from Fairburn to Red Oak was utterly useless.

Sherman had a rather simple prescription for the operation. The rails were worked loose with wrecking bars, and the ties were heaped up for burning. Rails were piled on the bonfires and then twisted until only a rolling mill could restore them. From now on, when Sherman ordered a railroad wrecked on Monday, he wouldn't hear locomotive whistles along it on Tuesday.[28]

The sun was not yet up when the 18th Missouri rose from its bivouac on Tuesday, August 30. No bugles sounded reveille anywhere in Howard's army, wrote Lieutenant Rockwood. "All was done in quietness," the men being "aroused by the Colonels orderly." This day's march was from Fairburn southeastward toward Jonesboro, on the Macon & Western line, running from East Point southward toward Macon. At 3 A.M. on Wednesday, the weary Missourians flopped down for a brief nap outside Jonesboro.

General Howard's drive for Jonesboro had encountered Rebel skirmishers constantly, and there was a noisy clash around the Flint River bridge a mile or so northwest of the town. Kilpatrick's horsemen, however, did a fair job of hustling the enemy out of the way, and by the morning of August 31 the Army of the Tennessee was across the Flint and dug in on a ridge line overlooking Jonesboro. Ransom's corps was guarding the right flank, Logan was holding down the center, and Blair was defending the left. Howard's artillery now commanded Hood's last railway, "which necessitated the enemy and not myself to take the initiative," the Yankee commander happily noted.

Toward noon that day, General Hardee, commanding Confederate troops around Jonesboro, did his best to shove Howard off Hood's last railway link with the Georgia hinterland. Adding urgency to Hardee's thrust was the fact that Thomas and Schofield were even then on the railroad, below East Point, and were ripping it up as they advanced toward a junction with Howard. Hardee made several charges, but each time Logan's men, bearing the brunt, sent them back.

The next day the 18th Missouri served as the brigade skirmish line, and as such it probed at will around the approaches to Jonesboro. The Rebels, the Missourians found, were quitting the area, apparently leaving to rejoin Hood closer to Atlanta. Late that afternoon Thomas' forces struck Hardee's vanguard above Jonesboro, and in that thunderous encounter a Confederate brigade was surrounded and captured. Sherman rode eagerly into the act, telling Thomas to hold on while Blair slipped around to the south to head off a possible attempt by Hardee to disengage and withdraw into the wilderness northeast of Jonesboro. Much to Sherman's disgust, the wily Rebel snatched his troops safely out of the Federal embrace.[29]

Hood now very clearly saw the folly of staying in Atlanta. The evacuation thus began at 5 P.M. on September 1, with the

leading forces marching rapidly through to McDonough, southeast of the city. In the early hours of Friday morning, September 2, Sherman, down at the Rough and Ready railroad station,
heard repeated explosions as the Rebel commander put the
torch to warehouses and freight cars full of ammunition and
powder. He slept no more that night. Had Slocum blundered
into a major battle? Sherman could not sleep until he knew.

By daybreak there were rumors that Hood had vanished,
and that Slocum had staged a triumphal entry into the city.
Later in the day Sherman received Slocum's confirmation of
Atlanta's capture, and the joy and relief of the victorious
Yankees knew no limit. On Saturday morning Sherman's Order
of the Day congratulated his armies on the happy outcome of
the struggle that had begun in May along the fringes of Rocky
Face Ridge. "Atlanta is ours, and fairly won," he had notified
Washington; and the men camped around the city now enjoyed
Lincoln's telegraphed "applause and thanks of the nation." On
Sunday morning the Army of the Potomac's artillery in Virginia
fired a monstrous salute to Sherman's armies—aiming every
shot at Robert E. Lee's trenches around Petersburg.

As Hood gathered his forces at Lovejoy's, the Federals began tidying up around Atlanta. For their part, Minter's Missourians had the job Friday afternoon of marching a group of
356 prisoners from Jonesboro to Rough and Ready, where
Sherman was establishing a "truce camp" to facilitate prisoner-
exchanges. That night the boys camped at East Point, in Rockwood's words, "well worn out." On Saturday morning, September 3, the regiment was detailed to guard an ordnance train
moving into Atlanta from the south. Having reached the city
by early afternoon, the men were given a four-day respite from
the marching, digging, and skirmishing of the past several
weeks.

The Missourians roamed widely through the "Gate City"
of the South, looking over the Rebel stronghold that had been
the goal of Sherman's summer-long campaign. "Entering the
city," wrote Rockwood, "one may be hold the marks of Shot and
Shell in all its forms on buildings, fences, and trees and on every
Obsticl that chanced to be in range of our lines." A good many
of the men later told Colonel Sheldon of their pilgrimages to

the Fair Grounds to see that "camp kettle gun," the 64-pounder that had spoiled Lieutenant Godfrey's appreciation of bean soup, and of the torrent of epithets that had expressed their "more emphatic than polite" sentiments concerning that hateful item of enemy ordnance.[30]

Sherman's forces were now camped in a long semicircle, protecting Atlanta, with cavalry concentrations along the Chattahoochee at both ends of the arc above and below Atlanta. Howard was headquartered at East Point, where the 18th Missouri and its companion regiments were under orders to prepare themselves for an indefinite stay. What Sheldon termed a "fine camp" was soon hacked out of the patch of pine shrubbery allotted the regiment.

At East Point "the principal Avocation . . . was drilling, appearing in dress parade and going on Genl. review from time to time," Rockwood noted. The drill and parade schedule could hardly have been very tight, for nine of the last twenty days of September were rainy, according to Teamster Sawyer's figures. Many of the company officers commissioned by the Governor in August were now mustered-in, but Sheldon was still waiting for Howard to have him mustered as full colonel.

Sheldon returned to duty on September 10, eternally grateful for Dr. Randolph's "skillfull attention," and promptly walked into one of his nastiest disciplinary problems. Captain Coddington and Lieutenant Callery had been wearing on each other's nerves lately. Their growing dislike of each other erupted on September 12 into a salvo of haymakers and uppercuts that entertained a swarm of enlisted men, but left Sheldon unamused. He clapped both officers into close confinement "for quarrelling and fighting in the presence of Enlisted Men." If he ever knew what the trouble was, Sheldon never told of it in print. Nor, apparently, did either of the principals. Callery tried to resign on September 15, but Sheldon stopped him by preferring charges of "conduct unbecoming." In time, though, the Colonel thought better of this and withdrew the charges. His solution ultimately was to talk Jim Coddington into mustering-out when his three years expired in early November, and then to release Callery to duty the day after Coddington's departure. Meanwhile, Lieutenant Joe Brown, back from the regiment's

Fifth Street recruiting station in St. Louis, took charge of Company F, and Sheldon's faithful work-horse, Abijah Everest, strode over from I to handle Company E while Mike Callery sweated out the next two months confined to his quarters.[31]

There were other ways to lose good men. Wagonmaster Pollock, nearing sixty, was physically ready to go home to St. John. During the action before Kennesaw Mountain he had been struck across the back of his shoulders by a tree limb knocked loose by an exploding shell. Complications, in addition to a persistently sore back, set in: pleurisy, lung-congestion, difficult breathing. Houts and Stults at length persuaded the courageous Pollock to call off his personal crusade against the Confederacy. Sheldon signed his discharge at East Point on September 23, and Pollock was off for Missouri. Since Sherman was holding every regiment to one wagon, compared to the two dozen formerly allowed, Sheldon appointed no replacement and thus reserved for Pollock the distinction of being the only wagonmaster the 18th Missouri ever had. As Dolman said of him in 1893, he had "done more for the Union than many a man that wore an eagle. . . ."[32]

In summarizing the regiment's operations for General Sherman, Sheldon reported that since May 1 the regiment's battle casualties had included nine killed in action, two killed by lightning, fifty wounded, and one missing. The two men captured on July 24, Dewitt and Johns, were returned to Federal lines at the truce camp on September 22. Because of battle casualties, detached service, disease, and desertions, the 666 men who had marched out of Decatur in early May had dwindled to 416 present for duty at the end of September.

The XVI Corps went out of business on September 22. Fuller's 4th Division was then redesignated the 1st Division of the XVII Corps. General Blair, anxious to get home to safeguard Missouri for the Lincoln-Johnson ticket, took off for St. Louis and left his enlarged corps under General Ransom's temporary command.[33]

By this time it was generally known in the 18th Missouri that there had been significant developments in the two controversies that were most on the troops' minds. General Howard had secured Sherman's consent to postpone indefinitely the trial of General Sweeny, which would not take place until December. Howard had also reviewed Elwood Miller's case and found the sentence unduly harsh. On August 26 he reduced it to forfeiture of three months' pay and allowances and ordered Captain Miller to "resume his sword." Instead of returning to Company E, however, the younger Miller chose to remain at St. Louis to serve for a brief time as a major on his father's staff in the Provisional Enrolled Militia during the autumn months.[34]

Back home in Missouri, a red-hot gubernatorial campaign was shaping up, featuring the Conservative (Democratic) candidate, Brigadier General Thomas Lawson Price, and the rising young Radical (Republican) Colonel Fletcher. Creating great anxiety for the 18th Missouri and a thorny public relations problem for Democrat Price was the sudden appearance of a major Confederate force in southwestern Missouri at the close of September. This was to prove the Confederacy's last stand in the state, but for some weeks it seemed on the verge of success. It was the bad luck of the Conservative candidate that the raid was commanded by Sterling Price. The candidate might remind the voters every day that he was not related to the man, but the voters at home and out in the regiments were not very clear on the point and were hardly disposed to take chances.[35]

# CHAPTER XII

# *To the Alabama Line*

IF THE MEN of the 18th Missouri were tiring of battalion drill and general reviews at East Point, they could soon thank Jeff Davis for an end to such fol-de-rol. The Confederate president was touring lower Georgia in late September, making incendiary speeches at every stop. On September 25 he inspected Hood's battered army at Palmetto and wound up his stay there by delivering a memorable oration. Sherman's Yankees would eventually have to relax their grip on Atlanta and get out of Georgia altogether, Davis shouted, "And when that day comes the fate that befell the Army of the French Empire in its retreat from Moscow will be re-enacted." The details of this bold prophecy were soon widely circulated by Southern publicists, but in none of his later writings did Davis dwell on the prediction for the benefit of posterity.

On the morrow of the Palmetto talks came Hood's daring thrust against Federal communications north of Atlanta. On September 29 over 40,000 Rebels began crossing the Chattahoochee at Phillips' Ferry, thirteen miles west of East Point. The Confederates marched rapidly northward behind a cavalry screen, through the wooded hills beyond the Chattahoochee, and by the night of October 2 they were in the Lost Mountain-Powder Springs area.[1]

This sudden move against Sherman's rear areas came at an awkward time. Thousands of the "three-year" men were now mustering-out, and some of Sherman's key generals (such as Logan and Blair) had taken off to handle political chores. Equally alarming was the report of a new raid by Forrest along the Tennessee River in Alabama, which now caused Sherman to send Thomas with part of the army back to build up the defenses of Tennessee.

"Hood is evidently across the Chattahoochee," Sherman telegraphed General Grant on October 1. If the Rebels were heading for Alabama, Sherman was now inclined to leave them to George H. Thomas, but if Hood moved instead against the Western & Atlantic, Sherman promised, "I shall attack him. . . ." Two days later it became obvious that the railroad was in danger, and Sherman prepared to make good on his promise to give battle. Detailing Slocum to guard Atlanta with XX Corps, he issued orders to the IV, XIV, XV, XVII, and XXIII Corps to rendezvous without delay at the Smyrna Camp Ground just below Marietta. Although his units were generally under-strength now, Sherman still had about 60,000 men available to pursue the marauding Rebels.

Sherman's reaction to this new emergency in northwestern Georgia came none too soon. The next day Hood struck, capturing small Union detachments at Acworth and Big Shanty, and demolishing the railway between those points. The following morning Confederate forces surrounded the major supply depot at Allatoona Pass, and Sherman realized that he had a fight on his hands. The Yankees at Allatoona, after hours of bloody fighting, managed to beat off the attackers by late afternoon. One enemy brigade consisted of Confederate Missourians under General Cockrell, Sherman learned afterward. Hood now vanished into the hills between Dallas and Rome.

By now Sherman's five corps were moving up rapidly to engage Hood. On Wednesday morning, October 5, Sheldon got his orders to march for Atlanta at daylight. Said Lieutenant Rockwood, who had again taken over Company D upon Wyckoff's return to the hospital, "the Bugle agane sounds the revilles too often heard to suit the apatite." Hitting the northward road in Howard's line of march, the Missourians briskly headed for Atlanta. At sundown they stopped near the July 22 battlefield to rest and boil coffee, but there was to be no overnight camping; Sherman wanted all hands at Smyrna, and in a hurry.

The night was cloudy, and the troops soon were marching in a driving rain. Not long before midnight the 18th Missouri crossed the Chattahoochee on the new wagon bridge. It was nearly dawn on the soggy morning of October 6 when the tired Missourians got to Smyrna. They had endured, said Rockwood, "a march of nearly 30 miles through Mud and Slop."[2]

The 18th Missouri, like many another regiment, was obliged to undertake this march seriously short of key personnel. Only four regular company commanders were with their outfits. Cudworth was still in St. Louis, pounding desks in the offices at Department headquarters. Hemstreet was away on court-martial duty at corps headquarters, and Minter had been left at East Point, where he was commanding the XVII Corps Convalescent Camp.

While Federal cavalry hunted for Hood northwest of Lost Mountain, the Army of the Tennessee lay in its camps at Smyrna for two rainy days and humid nights. Then, early Saturday morning, Fuller turned out his entire brigade and sent it up the muddy road through Marietta. The 18th Missouri reached Big Shanty at 2 P.M., and an hour later went into bivouac a mile northeast of town.

Most of Sheldon's regiment lay in camp here through October 9, but some work-parties were routed out to help the engineers rebuild the railroad between Big Shanty and Acworth. "As the 18th Missouri boys were reputed handy with their axes," Sheldon wrote, "they got their full share of that work, and spent a day or two, cutting and hauling and laying ties." In the forenoon of Monday, October 10, the brigade hit the road again, moving on to Acworth. On Wednesday evening Sheldon bivouacked his sweating warriors a few miles east of Rome, after an overnight stop at Allatoona. For most of the boys, this new martial drama seemed rather like an abbreviated version of a drama they had already staged. The campgrounds and the station-names were all too familiar.

Just as Sherman had concentrated his troops around Rome, in the expectation of chasing the Rebels into Alabama, there came the news that Hood had veered northeastward, toward the Connasauga. On October 12 he had drawn a siege-line around Resaca roughly similar to the front that Sherman had shown Johnston the previous May. But then, after trying without success to browbeat the Federal colonel at Resaca into peaceably surrendering, Hood decided to pass on to the north, wrecking the Western & Atlantic as he proceeded toward Dalton.

Sherman immediately "turned all the heads of columns for Resaca," on the night of October 12. The 18th Missouri hiked eastward to Kingston on Thursday. Then, after a few hours in bivouac, there came the order to set out by night for Adairsville, where General Fuller expected to put his troops aboard a freight train hastily making up there to move the division into Resaca.

At Adairsville, while the XVII Corps milled around and waited to board the cars, several emergency changes in command took place. General Ransom being down with typhoid, and evidently getting worse, Howard thought it best to send for Leggett as his stand-in, leaving Fuller to take charge of the 1st Division. Colonel McDowell had left to go north on recruiting duty in Ohio, so Sheldon, as senior lieutenant colonel, now stepped up to brigade command, a position he was to hold the rest of this campaign. Major Dolman took over the 18th Missouri during the reshuffle at Adairsville.[3]

As the 18th Missouri unloaded at Resaca on Friday, October 14, all signs pointed to an impending battle above the town. Word had come that the thousand-man Federal detachment at Dalton had surrendered to Hood Thursday evening. And the tracks had been ripped out by the Rebels from near Resaca all the way up to Dalton.

While his brigade was clambering down from the cars, Sheldon went into a hasty conference with Fuller. Passing on instructions from the bed-ridden Ransom, Fuller now directed Sheldon to move quickly out to reconnoiter Snake Creek Gap and determine how much resistance the enemy would likely offer to Howard's passage through the Gap. Mindful that old Federal breastworks had been left near the mouth of the Gap last May, and that the Rebels might now use them to bar the way, Fuller proposed that Sheldon take the 18th Missouri and the 39th Ohio out there to probe for resistance.

"Your boys built the works," Fuller told him. "You can locate them more easily than anyone else. We've got some of our cavalry between here and the Gap, and they can give you what other information and help you may think you want when you get out there."

"What," asked the wary young Missouri colonel, "am I specifically supposed to do once I'm in the Gap?"

"Just move forward," Fuller responded, "until you find something you cannot drive. Then come on back in and report."

"This," Sheldon reflected, was rather indefinite and "more than likely to get us into trouble. . . ." Forming up the two regiments, he started them toward the Gap. The Federal cavalry supposed to be waiting for him never showed up, and Sheldon concluded unhappily that there "had been some mistake made." This was a poor time to leave one's guard down. Halting the two regiments, he threw out a small skirmish line of Missourians. "We then again moved forward," he wrote later, "and had not gone over two hundred yards, when we were fired into by the enemy's pickets. . . ."

"I pushed forward as directed," Sheldon said in a terse note rushed back to Fuller and Ransom, "but found none of our cavalry. Ran on the enemy's vedettes near the Dalton and Rome road. Drove them out of the first line of works, and am now pushing for the gap and second line. Have not yet found a skirmish line, but think there is one, as the signs in the works indicate a strong resistance."

Since several roads led into this area, Sheldon decided to parcel out the Ohioans by companies to guard against counterattacks. He then pushed on toward the Gap with the Missourians deployed in a heavy skirmish line. As it was too dark to see, he gave all his orders through Fred Hackh's bugling.

On crept the Missouri line, for about a mile, and then it came to the foot of a little "rise in the ground." At this point, Colonel Sheldon deemed it wise to halt and check his line. "The ground had a *familiar* look," he thought, "but it was too dark to be certain." Turning to Hackh, he said simply: "Sound the 'forward' now."

At the signal, the 18th Missouri scrambled up the rise—and found itself atop the works it had built in May! "Just at that time," Sheldon afterward recalled, "pandemonium broke loose. The intrenchments were a sheet of fire, both to the right and left as far as we could see. . . . In this case our very boldness proved our salvation, for the enemy naturally supposed Sherman's whole army was right after us, ready for a night attack."

The uproar in the Gap caused great excitement back in town. Sherman was infuriated over the possibility that Sheldon had been carelessly thrown into a suicidal operation. The cavalrymen supposed to have been out around the crossroads had meanwhile cantered nonchalantly into Resaca, where Sherman stormily ordered them off to the scene of the action on the double-quick. Ransom notified Howard, then galloping furiously up from Adairsville, that at 2 A.M. "sharp firing was distinctly heard at these headquarters in the direction of the gap; it ceased about 3 A.M. I placed my command under arms, but have since sent them orders to rest. . . ."

When the firing died away, Sheldon ordered "recall" blown, and the regiment pulled back from the Rebel-infested works. "I am withdrawing my force," he wrote in a dispatch for Fuller. "My men received a fire from about 300. I think the force is a rear guard of cavalry, as signs of horse-feed were very abundant. The object of this reconnaissance being accomplished, I relieved my skirmish line, and bring off my wounded."[4]

One modern historian tells us that not a man was lost in Sherman's armies in this campaign after the Allatoona affair of October 5, but this would have occasioned great surprise to Surgeon Houts on the morning of October 15, 1864. Sam Houts certainly knew better. Rhoderick Rockwood's Company D had suffered one killed and four wounded. Private Harmon Brown, a twenty-four-year-old Kentuckian who had been farming in Putnam County before the war, was killed instantly. Brown had mustered-in at Laclede as a member of Company I, but in September of 1862 he had been given a disability discharge for chronic dysentery. However, he subsequently recovered sufficiently to return, and during the veteran furlough he had re-enlisted, this time in Company D.

Private Thomas G. Wade, thirty-one and Hoosier-born, was also seriously wounded, when a minié ball ripped open his abdomen. Under the care of his anguished half-brother, Private Alexander Collins, he clung to life barely a day, and they laid him to rest beside Brown at Marietta. In the years that Tom Wade never saw, the Grand Army of the Republic named its

Post 54 in Unionville in his honor. And a women's auxiliary of that post flourishes to the time of this writing, keeping posterity ever mindful of him.

Within days after the battle, two others died at Resaca. Private Isaac Underwood, born a Virginian, died on October 18, and Private Perry Thornton, originally from Indiana, followed him six days later. They were buried at Chattanooga. The skirmish at Snake Creek Gap had thus been costly for Putnam County. Only Private Elias Johnson, twenty, a native Missourian farming in Putnam before his enlistment, recovered from the wounds inflicted by Rebel fire that bloody night in the Gap.[5]

Sheldon was an object of much high-level attention when his weary fighters got back to the divisional bivouac well before dawn. General Sherman, nervously chomping on a cigar, brought Howard and Fuller over to call on him. The General gave Sheldon the third degree, or so it must have seemed, and was for a while unconvinced that the 18th Missouri had actually gone as far as its old entrenchments in the Gap.

"Sure you aren't mistaken on your locality?" he queried.

"Sheldon ought to know," Fuller interjected. "The 18th Missouri helped build those works."

"Very well," grunted the conqueror of Atlanta. "Sugar Valley is then clear. Howard, start your men up the Gap at daybreak."[6]

With the 1st Division of Ransom's Corps leading the way, the Army of the Tennessee moved toward Villanow on Saturday morning, October 15. The Rebels had made a mess of the Gap, obstructing it with fallen timber from one end to the other. The trees, Howard found, "were of every size, crossed and crisscrossed in our path." While the advance troops skirmished slightly with the retreating enemy, the main body, as Rockwood said, "cleared the road of logs and timber. . . ." That evening, after dark, the Army went into camp at Villanow.

Meanwhile, Wheeler's cavalry had rejoined Hood south of Lafayette. Here, around Lafayette, Hood was determined, he said later, "to select a position and deliver battle. . . ." However, after a council in which his corps commanders disapproved this idea, Hood decided to go on into Alabama. The fight had just about gone out of the ill-used Rebel Army of Tennessee, and it gladly faded away into the hills of northeastern Alabama. Sherman gave pursuit, of course, but finally called his chase to a halt on October 20, some sixty miles southwest of Resaca, at Gaylesville, Alabama. Here the Federals rested for over a week.[7]

While at Gaylesville, Sherman doggedly pestered Grant and Halleck to approve his plans to "let Hood go" and undertake a systematic devastation of central and eastern Georgia. The Washington officers continued skeptical for some time about Sherman's plan, but Hood's movement toward western Alabama, which brought him to Tuscumbia at the end of October, gave the General a strong advantage. Obviously, if Sherman turned eastward into Georgia again, Hood wasn't likely to follow him very closely, so he reasoned. And General Thomas was exuding complete confidence that his forces gathering in Tennessee were strong enough to crush Hood, Wheeler, *and* Forrest. On October 28, Sherman ordered his forces back to Georgia. Schofield's XXIII Corps and Major General D. S. Stanley's IV Corps went north to join Thomas, but the XIV, XV, and XVII Corps marched for Rome.

The 18th Missouri was ready. "Nothing of any interest" had occurred at Gaylesville, to hear Lieutenant Rockwood tell it. "The regiment lays in camp . . . until the morning of October 29 . . . and as usual takes up her old tricks for as soon as men stop traveling and marching drills dressparades inspections and reviews must be going on in dipendant of the feelings of the men and the few days in camp at this place it was practiced very strongly."

A long-feared tragedy struck on the first evening of the return march. General Ransom, sinking rapidly, was taken into a farmhouse near the road and died shortly after sundown. "He was a man of much the same disposition as McPherson," Sheldon said in postwar tribute to him, "and was much loved and respected by all his command. His headquarters were close to my tent, at Gaylesville, and his uncomplaining endurance of suffering, and cheerful serenity under severe trials, greatly endeared him to all who came near him." Sherman picked a special guard to take Ransom home to Chicago.[8]

Ransom's death introduced the 18th Missouri to Major

General Joseph Anthony Mower, regarded by Sherman as "one of the boldest and best fighting generals in the whole army." The Vermont-born Mower, a Captain of Engineers before the war, had been groomed until lately by Old Billy as the Yankee answer to Nathan B. Forrest. Now, however, with Forrest seemingly less a threat than in previous campaigns, Sherman felt that he needed the dash and vigor of this utterly fearless warrior for his new project in Georgia. Appearing at Gaylesville on October 24, he had superseded Leggett as "caretaker" of XVII Corps, but upon Ransom's death Sherman had placed him fully in command, pending Frank Blair's return from the political battlefields in Missouri. "Mower," said Sheldon, "seemed always to be 'spoiling for a fight' and invariably asked for the advance in any movement, and appeared much disappointed because he could not always get it." Bill Hemstreet, soon to know the thrills of being Mower's judge advocate, recalled in 1907 that Mower "was also a burning patriot, and war came to his thirsty soul like rain to a desert; he was absorbed and saturated by it. . . ."

While commanding the 11th Missouri, the brown-bearded Mower had distinguished himself in those early skirmishes in southeastern Missouri. At Second Corinth he had been shot in the neck, captured, and liberated from a Rebel hospital tent in a matter of hours. Recently he had led a division in the Red River campaign in Louisiana and the chase after Forrest in western Tennessee. With this man around, the 18th Missouri would know few dull moments. "He was especially fond of the 18th Missouri," Sheldon was to find, "and consequently, when he had any burning bridges to charge, or river crossings to force, he never failed to remember them."[9]

On October 30, Sheldon's troops bivouacked at Cave Springs, Georgia, preparatory to mustering for pay the next morning. Resuming the march at 7 A.M. on November 1, the regiment moved on, by way of Cedartown and Dallas, until it reached the Smyrna Camp Ground south of Marietta, on Monday, November 7.

At Smyrna, it transpired, there was much to be done, and very little time in which to do it. General Blair having rejoined, Mower stepped down to 1st Division. Fuller, returning from a short leave, bumped Sheldon out of his brigade headquarters. And this was just as well, for Sheldon had his hands full mustering-out over a hundred 1861 troops whose enlistments had expired and who had declined to become veteran volunteers. Among the best-known figures taking leave were Major Dolman; Surgeon Houts; Captains Breeman, Coddington, Stults, and Wyckoff; and Lieutenants Pagin and Partenheimer.

Wyckoff in particular saw precious little reason to stay, in view of his recent ill health and the fact that he had served "with the rank of captain since 27 July 1861. . . ." A vigorous campaign by his friends, notably State Senator Isaac V. Pratt, had failed earlier in the year to get him the lieutenant colonelcy, which had finally gone to Minter. We are sure of this much, that Sheldon hated especially to have to part with Sam Houts: "He was never, even for a day (so far as I can remember) absent from his post, and he both merited, and received, the gratitude of all." Leaving with Doctor Houts was Roscoe Torrey, hospital steward, who in three years had collected enough tragic memories to last him a lifetime.

Several reassignments became possible and necessary. Now that Coddington had left for home, on November 9, there was no harm in releasing Mike Callery from confinement to resume command of Company E. With Dolman gone, Captain Donnelly was taken into headquarters as an "acting field officer" on November 10, clear evidence that Sheldon intended to raise him to major. Henry Godfrey was away temporarily on private business, and Joe Brown had to come into headquarters and serve as Sheldon's adjutant for a while.[10]

News from Missouri was much more encouraging now. Sterling Price, finding Jefferson City strongly defended, had moved on to Boonville in early October. Pausing to survey the situation, and learning that Rosecrans and the Enrolled Militia were rapidly gathering to halt him, Price chose to head westward toward Kansas City. There, however, the Federals on October 23 inflicted a signal defeat on Old Pap at Westport, southwest of the City. The invaders retreated rapidly toward Arkansas ahead of the pursuing victors. Price left Missouri on October 30, and the last hopes of the Rebel cause in the state went with him. Within a week the voters delivered a decisive verdict for the state's Radical element. Tom Fletcher was swept into the governor's mansion by a margin of over 40,000 votes, about the same majority given Lincoln's electors. Eight of Missouri's Congressmen would be Radicals, and heavy Radical majorities were chosen to command the General Assembly and the forthcoming Constitutional Convention.[11]

On November 12, Sherman ordered destruction of the Western & Atlantic from Atlanta back to Kingston. Only a few insiders knew that this meant that Lincoln and Grant had consented to the General's forthcoming march through Georgia. The 18th Missouri participated in the destruction north of Atlanta by helping tear up "the railroad from Maryetta to Kennesaw Mountain Burning and Bending the Irons," as Rockwood reported at the time. Following this, Sheldon's men packed up on November 13 and marched the thirty miles from Smyrna down to White Hall, just south of the Gate City, where they camped at seven o'clock Sunday evening.

Lieutenant Rockwood thought he had deciphered some of the handwriting on the wall. "Anticipation of hard times ahead," he warned his diary. "We are cut off from all Communication. We have no Rear, are all front. I think the enemy will cach thunder."[12]

# CHAPTER XIII

# Marching Through Georgia

A CALCULATED CATASTROPHE overtook Atlanta on November 14, 1864. Sherman's engineers, determined to leave nothing for the Confederates to come back to, began applying the torch to shops, stores, warehouses, and mills. For a time, Federal soldiers struggled to confine the flames to these structures, but the immensity of the conflagration and the ubiquity of "volunteer firebugs" finally rendered the holocaust a general one. The flames raged on throughout the night, consuming "eleven-twelfths of the city," as a Southern writer later charged. On Tuesday morning, said a Yankee reporter, the sun rose "through the hazy cloud, like a blood-red ball of fire; and the air, for miles around, felt oppressive and intolerable. The Tyre of the South was laid in ashes, and the 'Gate City' was a thing of the past."[1]

Sherman was about to unleash a tide of 60,000 men against the paper-thin Confederate defenses of central Georgia's rich agricultural districts. Blair's XVII Corps was teamed with the XV Corps, temporarily under Major General Joseph Osterhaus, in Howard's Army of the Tennessee, south of Atlanta. Meanwhile, set to depart eastward from the city was Slocum's new Army of Georgia, the XIV and XX Corps, moving along the Georgia Railroad toward Milledgeville, in those days the state capital. Osterhaus' corps, forming Howard's right wing, had as its initial task the destruction of the Macon & Western from

Atlanta to its junction with the Central of Georgia at Macon. Protecting Howard's right flank were 5,000 cavalrymen under the ruthless and swashbuckling Judson Kilpatrick, operating under Sherman's direct orders.[2]

Announcing his order of march on Monday evening, Mower directed Fuller's brigade to escort Kilpatrick's train in the Army's rear. At the same time, he borrowed Bill Hemstreet to be judge advocate of the 1st Division, the beginning of a memorable association. "From that instant on," said Hemstreet, "my military service took a new life and inspiration, for I saw that he was a thorough soldier and gentleman." Company G was left in Lieutenant Mansfield's capable hands.[3]

The Army of the Tennessee was all hustle and bustle as the day of its departure broke. Ben Sweet remembered that "the bands played as if we were on a regular picnic." The favorite tune seemed to be "Battle Hymn of the Republic," another witness found. Brigade by brigade, Howard's brawny Westerners swung out onto the McDonough road on that November 15, and by noon the local residents of White Hall were "shut of" Yankees at last. To the southeast and the east Sherman's two armies were marching, pillaging and burning on a fifty-mile front. "You could follow the line all day by the smoke," Sweet insisted, and another Union soldier was heard to exclaim that "it looks as if 'Old Billy' has set the world on fire!"[4]

Two questions now preyed on the minds of his fighting Missourians, and Charles S. Sheldon, for one, could find no answers to either of them. "Where are we heading?" "How many Rebs are in our way?"

Sherman was playing his strategic cards close to his vest. True, in an Order of the Day, he went so far as to assure his troops that they were "an army for a special purpose, well known to the War Department and to General Grant. It is sufficient for you to know that it involves a departure from our present base, and a long and difficult march to a new one." From this, many deduced that Sherman was going to march directly up the Carolinas to fall on the rear of Lee's Army, now locked in combat with Grant's main body. This plan, or some plausible variant, was assumed by nearly every Yankee in Georgia. Sherman, however, had a different trick up his sleeve.

"I only regarded the march from Atlanta to Savannah as a 'shift of base,' . . ." Sherman wrote later, "from the interior to a point on the seacoast, from which it could achieve other results." And those results included bleeding the South's economy, demolishing the railways supplying Lee, and fatally weakening civilian and military morale throughout the Confederacy.[5]

Sherman's "oasis of loyalty planted in a desert of rebellion" was spreading through Hardee's Department of Georgia, South Carolina, and Florida. The Confederates had less than 20,000 men in the entire area, only half this number being near enough to Atlanta to contest Sherman's opening moves. Fighting Joe Wheeler's 7,000 cavalrymen and a force of 3,000 Georgia State Militiamen were concentrated around Lovejoy's Station, South of Atlanta, reflecting Hardee's suspicion that the main Yankee advance would be toward Macon. Considering the relative strength and experience of the contending forces, it is clearer to modern readers than it was to Sherman's mystified troops that the march through Georgia could hardly be a prolonged struggle.[6]

The very first day's march of the 18th Missouri suggested that such would indeed be the case. The journal of neither the regiment, brigade, division, nor corps suggests anything more eventful than fifteen miles of steady marching down the Mc-Donough road to the first night's bivouac several miles north of Stockbridge. Sherman's orders were, as Sheldon described them, "to forage liberally on the country, and to gather up all horses and cattle, and everything that could be of use to the enemy." We are assured by Sherman's aide-de-camp that foragers were especially vigilant in their quests for roosters capable of putting up ferocious fights to enliven off-duty hours during evening bivouac.[7]

Like all other regiments, the Missourians were now permitted one ambulance and one "kit-wagon." There being little space left to haul rations, each soldier started out with a three-day supply on his back. It depended on forage parties to see that the regiment was kept supplied with the pork, sweet potatoes, turnips, chickens, turkeys, and other commodities available on Georgia farms in late autumn. Sherman's quartermaster had a herd of cattle coming along in the rear with fresh beef on the hoof. Sufficient oats and corn had been loaded to provide a five-day supply for the thousands of horses and mules toiling down the roads toward Savannah. Sherman figured that within five days his mighty columns would be crossing the Ocmulgee River into the agricultural heartland of Georgia, "a country well-stocked with corn, which had been gathered and stored in cribs, seemingly for our use, by Governor Joseph Brown's militia."

As Cudworth looked back at it, this march developed into "a pleasant campaign with little fighting and plenty to eat. . . ." Most enthusiastically did Sheldon remember "those hams, cured with but little salt," as "the nicest we had ever eaten." Along the route the Federals found great shocks of fodder, bound up in bundles of juicy tops and blades, and ideal feed for Yankee horses and mules. Blair's quartermaster would commandeer a rolling mill about every other day and detain the rear guard for a few hours to help grind out enough high-grade corn meal for the entire XVII Corps.

To supply the milling operation, the troops, in Sheldon's words, "developed various ingenious methods to get the corn out of the crib. A favorite plan was to drive a wagon up close to the crib side, and raise the wagon cover on that side. Boards were then knocked off the side of the crib, and a line of men, lying on their backs, would draw their feet up and kick the corn into the wagon, filling it in less time than I can write it."

It was, Sheldon wrote, "considered almost a mortal sin to let a hog escape alive." General Leggett was still amused a quarter-century later by the intensively competitive spirit between the Georgia hogs and the Federal soldiery. "You could never get them except by shooting them," he said at Toledo in 1888. "They would outrun a soldier and outrun a horse." Leggett was probably embellishing things somewhat, but he loved to describe the test that Union soldiers devised to tell how fit a hog was to eat. After shooting the porker, the boys would punch a hole in each ear, poke a sapling through the holes, and lift the carcass off the ground. If the snout tipped the body up into the air, there was no use in bothering with the animal.

On one occasion that Sheldon recalled, Blair's aides were unusually nettled by straggling or otherwise dropping out of the line for any purpose. But as luck would have it, a fat and saucy hog had the nerve to swagger provocatively across the road in front of the 18th Missouri. Despite strict orders to stay in the line of march, several enterprising Missourians greedily pounced on the unwary victim, slit his throat, and slipped a musket-barrel through the tendons of his hind legs. The luckless four-legged Georgian "was elevated on the shoulders of four men, and two others skinned, and divided, and distributed him, while their comrades carried their guns. All this was done without stopping the march, or leaving the ranks for a moment."[8]

Major General Howell Cobb, commanding the Georgia district under Hardee, was in somewhat the predicament of the proverbial one-armed paperhanger: he was badly outnumbered, and unable to fathom the enemy's objective. Was Sherman driving for Macon? Or Augusta? Hood's demoralized survivors of the Atlanta campaign couldn't help much now, for they were far away in Alabama. The truth of the matter, which dawned on the Rebels too late, was that Milledgeville, being the political nerve-center of Georgia, was Sherman's immediate target. Certainly Cobb's perplexity was hardly alleviated by Kilpatrick's demonstration near Macon at the outset of the Federal march. The ferocity of Kilpatrick's southward drive may be gauged from the militia commander's report that, having withdrawn his men to entrenchments at Griffin on November 15, he found "Wheeler's cavalry . . . jammed back to our positions" early the next day. From there, Kilpatrick cantered on to the southeast to devastate about a mile of track west of Macon.

After a second brush with Kilpatrick, Wheeler retreated to Macon on Friday, November 18. At that place, the next day, he went into a hurried conference with Hardee and Beauregard, who was now commanding all Confederate forces in the Lower South. The outcome of this parley was that a small force would stay behind to hold Osterhaus away from Macon while the bulk of the State Militia and Wheeler's horsemen would be shifted eastward to bar Sherman from Savannah or Augusta. The attempt of the militiamen to get away proved costly, for they collided with the Yankee rear guard between Macon and Gordon on November 22, suffering disastrous losses in an exchange of lead with the battle-hardened XV Corps. The surviving militiamen were then loaded on a freight train southeast of Macon and carried to Savannah. Wheeler swam the Oconee River with his cavalrymen a week later, with Kilpatrick in hot pursuit.[9]

Meanwhile, Sheldon's Missourians continued their march with the XVII Corps. Breaking camp on Cotton Indian Creek at dawn, November 16, they tramped past Stockbridge toward McDonough, bivouacking for the night on the Walker farm, two miles north of the latter place. The next evening they camped at the edge of Jackson. On Friday they reached their first major river, the Ocmulgee, at Planter's Factory, and participated in an uncontested night crossing on the 200-foot pontoon bridge laid by Lieutenant Colonel William Tweeddale's 1st Missouri Engineers that evening. The next three days were spent in a steady thirty-mile march on Gordon, where Sheldon established his regimental headquarters Tuesday afternoon, November 22. On this day, Slocum's Army of Georgia entered Milledgeville, ten miles to the north.[10]

When they reached Gordon on a raw late-autumn day, the Missourians began work on what was to prove the most distinctive feature of Sherman's Savannah campaign: railroad-wrecking. The method of demolition was systematic and quite military. Divisions assigned to such work would deploy along the right-of-way in sectors laid out by Howard's chief engineer. As each regiment reached its sector, it stacked arms and fell to the task. Sheldon's boys were now well supplied with picks, claw bars, and light sledges taken from depots along the tracks west of Gordon. It was a simple matter to pry up the first spikes. With further prying, the rail could be lifted so that a block four inches square could be rammed underneath it and toward its middle. Strong hands gripping the rail could with almost miraculous ease work the remaining spikes out and toss the rail over the shoulder into the ditch.

Other crews from the regiment then followed up this operation to gather the ties, build little "log cabins" with them, and fill these cabins with pine knots, brush, fence rails—anything that would do for kindling. As soon as the fires were started, other work-parties coming along would hoist the rails up onto them. When the rails became red hot, the engineers would come along to give them one last treatment. Sheldon thought their tools "very simple, consisting of a broad flat hook and two or three links of strong chain, ending with a round ring. Making the hook fast to the flange, they carried the links first under, and then over the rail. A stout handspike was inserted in the open ring, and strong men, one at each end, twisted in opposite directions." Rails were pretty useless after all that.

Wednesday, November 23, saw the 18th Missouri assisting with the destruction of the "railroad and other public property at or near Gordon," as Sheldon put it. After the station was burned, the men proceeded to wreck the Central of Georgia spur from Gordon up to Milledgeville. The next day, however, the Missourians moved out toward the Oconee crossing with their division. The regiment's journal relates that "we moved down the Savannah R. R., destroying it as we went, and passed through the towns of McIntyre and Toomsboro, destroying the Depots in both places. . . ." Mower credited his division with tearing out fourteen miles of track on November 23, 24, and 25, but it is impossible to determine the exact mileage attributable to Sheldon's men.[11]

Although the Missourians were finding that "the yams and the chickens were ripe," as Sheldon said, and although the corn and the hams were plentiful in central Georgia, it was not always entirely safe to be hustling up fresh supplies of them. Several privates from Company A, out scrounging in the area south of Milledgeville on November 24, were ambushed and captured by Confederate militiamen. John W. Garrison was shot, apparently out of hand, following his capture, and Edward Winegar was later to die in a prison at Florence, South Carolina. Garrison, an ex-Kentuckian, had enlisted at St. Louis in April of 1863. The War Department's information about his fate was so garbled that he was regarded as a deserter for over fifty years. Winegar had been a soldier only eight months; he had signed up with the regiment during the veteran furlough. Private Sion Green (Lieutenant Brantner's brother-in-law), along with

Privates James D. Morgan, William Mitchel, and Francis M. Brewer, was taken off to South Carolina. By the middle of March all four had been repatriated.[12]

On November 24, the 18th Missouri left Gordon, on a road that generally traversed forested ridges. Because of the presence of the towering Georgia pitch-pines along the road, there were plenty of pine knots lying around. These highly resinous knots were detachable from the fallen trees, which have a fairly short life, and provided the troops with a bountiful supply of long-burning torches to illuminate their camps by night. What was more, Sheldon recalled, the 18th Missouri's bivouac was not only well-lighted but was "generally very musical, especially if the foragers had brought in a good supply of apple-jack or peach brandy."[13]

It was after sundown on Saturday, November 26, when the weary Missourians marched across Tweeddale's 300-foot pontoon bridge built the previous day over the Oconee. This particular Sabbath was not to be one of rest, however. Blair's orders, sent up from Sherman that morning, were to continue tearing up railroad property beyond the river. Sherman rode in to join Blair and Mower on Monday to watch the XVII Corps in action. It was on this same day that the 18th Missouri suffered its only other fatalities of the entire campaign. A dead tree blew down near the Oconee bridge, fatally injuring Privates McCoy Sell and William McRorie of Putnam County, both of whom had but recently joined Pollock's Company B. On Wednesday, November 30, Sheldon's men closed up to the Ogeechee, just east of Wadley. They were 135 miles out of Atlanta, as the crow flies.[14]

While no battle casualties had yet occurred among Sheldon's troops, they were rarely out of earshot of skirmishing. Any breeze might bring sounds of battle, as Kilpatrick and Wheeler blazed away at each other almost daily. After Milledgeville, Sherman had swung Kilpatrick over to Slocum's left to demonstrate toward Augusta. And this ruse had worked beautifully, for during the last week of November Wheeler was so busy defending Augusta that he could not contest Howard's crossing of the Ogeechee, the last major river on the road to Savannah.

Blair's men crossed the Ogeechee east of Wadley on November 30, using Tweeddale's floating bridge. The stage was now set for Sherman's final drive down the valley toward Savannah. Slocum's entire force had already passed the Ogeechee some miles upstream, and Osterhaus' XV Corps remained on the west bank to anchor the Grand Army's southward push. After the crossing, "the army moved steadily on Savannah," in Sherman's words, "the corps on parallel roads, driving the Rebel cavalry so rapidly that it could hardly be called a hindrance." Sherman's flanks were "perfectly protected by swarms of mounted 'foragers,' so that not a single wagon was lost during the whole march, and but few stragglers captured." After camping on the Ogeechee with the General as their overnight guest, the Missourians were up at dawn on Thursday, December 1, to commence wrecking the Central of Georgia tracks toward Millen. Blair's corps ruined eighteen miles of railway before halting at Millen on Friday.

The following days saw the Grand Army of the West greedily devouring the remaining mileage down to Savannah. From the time the 1st Division left Millen on the morning of December 3 until it got to Pooler Station, about ten miles from Savannah, it wrecked nearly a fifth of the sixty miles of tracks between Millen and Pooler. Typical of the Confederate resistance during this period was the effort of a small force under Major General Lafayette McLaws to hold the XVII Corps at Ogeechee Creek, fifty miles north of Savannah. On the far bank, Blair's scouts noted what Sheldon described as a "rude line of pits." With Lieutenant Colonel Dennis T. Kirby, 27th Missouri Volunteers, acting as picket officer and directing the battle, Mower formed up to face McLaws. But before the skirmish line could cross the creek, the Confederates "prudently retreated toward Savannah without a fight," according to Sherman, who witnessed the scrape. The only other evidence of Rebel opposition was an occasional "faint reverberation of a gun in our left rear," where, Sherman later said, "we knew that General Kilpatrick was skirmishing with Wheeler's cavalry. . . ."[16]

The general pattern of Sherman's advance on Savannah was now ruthlessly simple. Blair, after wrecking the railroad all the way to Ogeechee Creek, was to march swiftly down the Central of Georgia on Savannah. The XV Corps would follow the west bank of the river to the neighborhood of Eden Station, where it would cross to join the formations closing in on the city. Slocum's XIV Corps would hug the Savannah River, while his XX Corps would take the middle route down the corridor between the two great rivers. Foraging was no longer so productive as it had been back in central Georgia. Stretches of towering pines alternated with corn-fields and rice-fields. The inhabitants appeared so "hard run" that even the most rapacious Yankee foragers hesitated to clean out their cellars and cupboards.[17]

The easy advances ended abruptly on Friday, December 9, as those acquainted with Hardee knew they sooner or later would. Mower's division, leading the XVII Corps, on reaching Pooler's, found massive earthworks on the far side of a crescent-shaped cypress swamp effectively interdicting the Federals' use of the Louisville road (modern U.S. 80). Blair ordered Mower to go in after the Confederates. Detailing one brigade to hold the enemy's attention with artillery and rifle-fire, Mower sent the rest of his division into the swamp to surprise the enemy's right flank. Sheldon's men, sharing in this messy operation, "moved through the swamp, the water frequently waist deep, driving the enemy from their works. . . ." The Rebels energetically cleared out of the area, withdrawing to a ring of works guarding Savannah's landward approaches.

Not one of the water-logged Missourians was so much as grazed in this successful thrust. On the other hand, there would occur in those swamps many "silent casualties," such as the aggravation of Joe Stanley's arrested pulmonary tuberculosis. The resumption of his long-dormant affliction was to lay the commander of C Company in his grave before he reached middle age.[18]

Goateed William Hardee was a native of Savannah, and the terrain seemed to be actively conspiring with him to keep Sherman's Yankees out of his home town. On December 10 he presented Sherman with a maddening tactical puzzle: deep ditches, earthworks, swamps, and canals with only narrow strips of land between them, covered by deadly concentrations of Confederate fire-power. The defenders "even ran some guns up to our lines, on platform cars, puffed a few volleys, and then fell back," said reporter Conyngham. "Everything is a black muck," one veteran noted in his diary. The visitors could take their choice: cold water or hot lead.[19]

The cagey Sherman wasn't going to accept either of Hardee's alternatives if he could possibly avoid them. As his troops invested Savannah from the south, west, and north, Sherman came to the conclusion that an immediate all-out attack on the city had best be postponed. As at Atlanta, so here he again preferred the indirect approach. Putting Slocum to work demolishing the Charleston Railroad north of the city and wrecking the bridge over the Savannah, some fifteen miles upstream, Sherman turned his attention toward the coast south of town, where he hoped to make early contact with a Union flotilla believed to be nearby.

Attempts to rendezvous with the Navy were sure to be hazardous as long as the 250-man enemy garrison at Fort McAllister, on the south bank of the Ogeechee, continued to dominate the estuary. On December 9 Howard had sent a boatload of scouts down the river to notify the Navy of Sherman's arrival at Savannah, but not until December 13 would Sherman know the mission had succeeded. Kilpatrick, crossing the Ogeechee below the fort, galloped to St. Catherine's South to verify the fleet's presence at 10:00 A.M. on Tuesday, December 13. Meanwhile, one of Osterhaus' divisions, passing to the south bank of the river, closed up to McAllister and overwhelmed it just before sundown the same day. At least a fifth of the defending force was killed and wounded, with Union casualties twice those suffered by the Rebels.[20]

Meanwhile, the 18th Missouri Volunteers were in the thick of the skirmishing at the approaches to Savannah. The 4th Division was holding positions along the Louisville road, while Mower's troops were developing a lodgment on the south side of the Ogeechee Canal during the afternoon of December 10. "The field I occupied was found to be bordered with swamps all around except in front," Mower discovered. In front was an open field a half-mile wide, but Hardee's guns had it covered. Mower's troops worked all night to confront the Confederates at daybreak with opposing breastworks buttressed by two artillery redoubts. The firing went on into Sunday forenoon, when the 18th Missouri suffered its first battle casualty since leaving Atlanta. To German-born Private Lorenz Mohr, a St. Louisan with nearly two years' service in Company H, went the unpleasant distinction of being the only man of the regiment wounded in action throughout Sherman's march to the sea.[21]

On December 12 Blair pulled Mower out of the line and put his division in corps reserve on the Anderson plantation eight miles west of Savannah. Arriving there after dark, the 1st Division boys spent Tuesday, Wednesday, and Thursday (December 13–15) in bivouac, drying out and resting from their exertions in the swamps and bayous above Savannah. Meanwhile, Blair's other forces were reshuffled and concentrated south of town between the XIV Corps on their left and the XV Corps to their right.

If Sheldon's weary men thought their campaigning was over, Blair changed their minds on Friday, December 16. Some forty miles to the southwest was the Atlantic & Gulf Railroad's bridge over the Altamaha River. Mower's mission: Destroy the bridge, wreck twenty miles of track leading to it, and be back on the Anderson plantation in five days! Mower was flabbergasted: "This limitation would make it necessary for me to march 20 miles per day, and give me one day in which to destroy 20 miles of railroad." All attempts to persuade Blair to extend the time limit for Mower were useless. On December 17 his regiments streamed southward across the Ogeechee.[22]

On the afternoon of December 18 Mower's men bivouacked beside the doomed railroad eight miles north of the Altamaha. With only the rest of that afternoon and the next day in which to finish the job, time was precious. The 92d Illinois Mounted Infantry showed up to help, and Mower ordered the newcomers to destroy the bridge by Monday evening, December 19. The Illinoisans managed to demolish some trestle-work approaching the main structure, but the defenders had the bridge itself so well covered that there seemed to be no quick way to rout them from it. Swamp-flanked redoubts on the north side were supported by enfilading artillery on the south bank and a locomotive-mounted cannon on the bridge. By Monday afternoon, Sheldon later told General Gray, "it was found this bridge could not be reached. . . ." Bowing to the necessity of breaking camp in time to get back to Anderson's plantation by Wednesday evening, Mower gave up hopes of destroying the bridge. He assured Blair, however, that the span would thereafter be "useless to the enemy," and that his troops had demolished eighteen miles of track.[23]

Blair's desire to reassemble his troops in a hurry stemmed from his expectation that Sherman would soon order an assault on the defenses of Savannah. But the eventuality did not occur. Instead, Hardee began wrecking the navy yard and scuttling the vessels in it during the night of December 20. By Wednesday morning it was evident that the defenders had already crossed the Savannah into South Carolina, abandoning the city and "all the heavy guns, stores, cotton, railway cars, steamboats, and an immense amount of public and private property" to Sherman. This, Sheldon noted, was a "fit and glorious ending to a year of almost unceasing marching." Sherman dramatically presented President Lincoln "as a Christmas gift the city of Savannah," with over 250 heavy coastal guns (mostly spiked) and 31,000 bales of unburned cotton.[24]

The march to the sea thus came to its end, and although Sherman later modestly discounted the importance of the drive toward Savannah, it rapidly became in the public imagination the military epic it has ever since remained. "The march through Georgia is still the wonder of the campaign of 1864," one observer wrote typically the following spring, "filled as it was with strange events and startling and original movements. Undertaken with deliberation . . . it is now recognized as the boldest move of the war."[25]

During the period of December 23–27, Sheldon again commanded the brigade, while Minter commanded the regiment. And it was during this time, on Christmas Eve, that Mower marched the division from Anderson's through Savannah to a new camp in a large pine forest three miles southeast of town and near Thunderbolt Landing. The men greatly admired the stately old city, whose citizens were the friendliest Southerners they had seen east of Chewalla. Double rows of lovely trees lined the principal streets, making for the handsomest of drives and walks.

Adjoining Camp Thunderbolt was Savannah's famed old Bonaventure Cemetery. "No one could mistake its sacred character," said Sheldon. With its majestic live oaks, clad in deep green foliage, and draped with the gray Spanish moss for which the Deep South is noted, Bonaventure seemed "truly sublime in its grandeur," to quote Sherman, and a highly appropriate setting for the mausoleums of the Revolutionary patriots there interred.

Situated on one of the distributaries of the Savannah River, the Landing was a paradise for the 18th Missouri's long-frustrated sea-food lovers. It is evident from the diaries of Lieutenant Rockwood and Sergeant Perry that they nearly lived on oysters for at least a week. The favorites were what local people called "raccoon oysters," creatures with a tendency to fasten themselves together in great masses weighing several hundred pounds. It was difficult to find the openings in their hard shells, but that didn't save the oysters. "Missouri Ingenuity," said Sheldon, hit on the plan of "standing them in front of a hot fire, and when the heat caused the oyster to open his shell—out he came!" With obvious sincerity, the young colonel insisted that his whole outfit would not "have regretted it much if we had been ordered to remain here all winter. . . ."

On Thursday, December 29, the XVII Corps turned out at 6:30 A.M. for a review by General Sherman. Sheldon, having just mustered-in in his new rank, now wore his shiny eagles to their first review. Blair's troops marched into Savannah for the great occasion, stacked arms at eight o'clock, and stood at parade rest waiting for the General to appear. Then, about ten o'clock, the fearsome redhead made his appearance, gnawing on his eternal cigar. "He passed in review," Elias Perry reported to his diary, "then placed himself on the Big Street for the troops to pass in review. After passing the general we then turned to the left passed through the city and returned to camp at 3 P.M. . . ."[26]

The incoming mail brought all manner of good news to the 18th Missouri while at Camp Thunderbolt. For one thing, the national conscription law was in operation, and word from St. Louis was that a big group of draftees would soon be coming. Welcome news indeed to a regiment whose "present-for-duty" strength had lately sagged to 382! Another item that must have warmed hearts at Camp Thunderbolt was the news that General Dodge, recovered from his "Confederate leave" of August 19, had succeeded Rosecrans in command of the Department of the Missouri in early December.[27]

While gains were being made, losses were also being registered. Dan Hudson's discharge from the service for disability became official on December 27, and Sheldon prepared to hand the captaincy of Company A to that tried and hardy warrior, D. W. Pollock. On December 23 Sergeant-Major Schaap, long ill, mustered-out, and his office passed to a former schoolmaster, Sergeant Jack Riggen.[28]

The general hospital for officers at Lookout Mountain now made a strange report to Sheldon. Ken Breeman, mustered-out in November while undergoing treatment there for dysentery, had been given a ten-day leave on November 19. However, he still hadn't returned to the hospital a month later. He never would. Sheldon soon picked up a rumor that Ken Breeman had been "murdered for the money he carried on his person." However, in 1880, a former 13th U.S. Infantry enlisted man, one Nelson F. Cheeney, whose wife believed him to be Breeman, died in the State Hospital for the Insane at Mount Pleasant, Iowa. The Pension Bureau, after a handwriting comparison, soon accepted Mrs. Cheeney's claim that her late husband was in reality the missing Captain Breeman. Few men of the 18th Missouri would ever know the tragic story of their captain who had disappeared from Lookout Mountain into the gloom of his own tormented mind.[29]

Campaigning in Georgia had taken its toll of the 18th Missouri. Boasting in pre-Shiloh days a muster roll of nearly a thousand men, the unit had declined to a force of 778 by October of 1864. But of this number only 441 were present for duty the day the march-out from White Hall began. The assigned strength was virtually the same at the close of the Savannah campaign, but the actual strength was 382, attributable to the loss of the two men killed at the Oconee, the eleven hospitalized (including Private Mohr), and nearly four dozen others attached to other units temporarily or simply missing since November 15. Three companies of the regiment had experienced no casualties whatsoever. Not only did the 18th Missouri belong to the corps that had marched the farthest, but it belonged to the division that had covered the most miles, nearly 300, thanks to that headlong dash down to the Altamaha.[30]

The fighting was over in Georgia. Confederate hopes that Hood might somehow find a way to hamstring Sherman's seaward march had faded in mid-December, when Hood's valiant army was overwhelmed by an ocean of Yankees hurled by Thomas in central Tennessee. The dour Rock of Chickamauga thus became, in the words of one uniformed historian, "the only General of the war . . . to crush an army on the battlefield. . . ." Hood's remnants were afterward transported from Alabama to North Carolina to join other Confederate forces staging a series of fruitless confrontations with Sherman's irresistible columns along the roads leading up the Carolinas.

Predictions of Southern and foreign commentators that Sherman had plunged to his ruin in Georgia were now categorically discredited. If the 62,000 participants had ever had any such presentiments of doom, they were soon forgotten and replaced by memories of the "protracted Hallowe'en." As long as the men lived, said a modern writer, they "would carry the thought of these marching days and feasting nights as life's high tide." For his own part, Colonel Sheldon finished that momentous year's work by telling General Gray that "I have only to say that the regiment which I have the honor to command has borne its share of the hardships of the campaign with fortitude and without murmuring, and I am especially thankful to the officers of the regiment who, by cheerful and ready obedience to orders received, have done much to lighten a task difficult and at times seemingly almost impossible."[31]

# CHAPTER XIV

# *"Grab a Root, Colonel!"*

THE TIME had come to apply the "terrible swift sword" to South Carolina. General Sherman, writing away in his office at Savannah's Charles Green Mansion, made the final arrangements. With "sixty thousand men, forty thousand animals, and three thousand wagons and ambulances," he was going to cross the broad Savannah with Slocum and thrust into the mainland with Howard's force by way of Beaufort. "I know full well that I enjoy the unlimited confidence of the President . . . and better still of my own army," he wrote his wife on December 31.

The next morning he called in General Howard and came right to the point. Unfolding a map, he growled: "Howard, I want you to take the Army of the Tennessee and move over to Beaufort, and then up across the island, and across to the mainland, and get to Pocotaligo by the 15th of January. Can you do it?"

Howard stared at the map for a moment. "It is rather a short time," he countered warily. "How are we going to get transportation?"

"Oh, the Navy will help you," Sherman assured him, "and the Quartermaster Department is always ready."

"We'll do the best we can," was Howard's Yankee-like response.[1]

Howard handed out the orders on Monday, January 2, 1865. Blair's XVII Corps was alerted to move out at 8 A.M. Tuesday by ship for Beaufort. Since Fuller was on leave in Ohio, Sheldon would command the First Brigade in Mower's division again. General Logan was even now sailing from Washington to resume command of the XV Corps, which would follow Blair's move to the Federal base on Port Royal Island.

The *W. M. Hoyt* pulled up to Thunderbolt Landing early on Tuesday afternoon, and nine companies of the 18th Missouri filed on board. Lieutenant Mansfield and Company G stayed another day at 1st Division headquarters as Provost Guards. The *Hoyt* had not gone three miles before she ran aground. Attempts to fight the old scow clear availed the distraught skipper nothing. Finally, the Navy sent the gunboat *Harvest Moon* out to the rescue, and, said Sergeant Perry, "we got on bord and left the first boat stuck in the mud." The *Harvest Moon* being something of a speed demon, the sixty-five-mile coastal run to Beaufort was over well before daybreak on Wednesday.

Sheldon assembled the brigade on the wharf at seven o'clock that morning and marched it "through Beaufort two and one half miles, and went into camp beyond the works arranged for the defense of the town." Most of the Missourians hated to leave the water front, for breakfast had turned into another oyster banquet. When Lieutenant Everest got orders the next day to bring Company E back to the wharf to guard regimental property, it is easily conceivable that the men lined up in a hurry. But there were some consolation prizes even for the oyster-lovers repining in the island's hinterland: "sanitary stores, issued by the U.S. Sanitary Commission—something we never found elsewhere in the whole course of our service," Sheldon said later. These consisted of canned fruits, jellies, and juices for which the 18th Missouri was more than commonly grateful.[2]

General Howard's immediate objective was, of course, Pocotaligo, on the mainland some twenty-five miles northwest of Beaufort. Once in force there, the Yankees would put a clamp on the Atlantic & Charleston Railroad. Since Sherman had set January 15 for the concentration at Pocotaligo, time was getting short when the tail-end of Blair's corps put in to Beaufort on January 11. Windstorms and rain squalls were rising in such ferocity that shipping was now too hazardous to bring all of Logan's corps to Beaufort by sea. Some of the XV Corps finally had to come into South Carolina with Slocum, after crossing the Savannah forty miles inland in mid-January.

Forced to move without Logan, Howard ordered Blair forward on January 13, roughly along the route of modern-day U.S. 21. The XVII Corps bivouacked that night along the Coosaw River to wait for the engineers to put a bridge of canvas pontoons across to the enemy shore. The next morning a wretchedly difficult crossing took place, with Leggett's division leading. The pontoons had seen too much damp weather and were getting rather waterlogged. The bridge, Howard later grumbled, "had to be pieced out on the enemy's side, and frequently broke near that shore." The 18th Missouri, guarding the wagons, got across during the noon hour, and by midafternoon the XVII Corps was firmly planted on Scott's Neck, mainland South Carolina.

Some three or four miles inland, Leggett's men hit a snag. At Garden's Corner, General McLaws was holding a "well-constructed outwork having a long parapet beyond an intervening plateau." Rockwood took note of "heavy skirmishing in the front. Some artillery mixed in." Perry fixed the time as 4 P.M. General Howard cautioned Leggett to turn the position to his right, and the Rebels broke for the rear and the safety of stronger works around Pocotaligo.

That Saturday night the 18th Missouri camped in the enemy's abandoned works at Garden's Corner, while the advance forces dug in around Rose Hill, four miles short of Pocotaligo. Howard, regarded by Sherman as the general "who looks after religion in my army," dreaded the thought of having to fight on Sunday. Such an affront to the Lord was serious enough by itself, but Howard was reluctant to take on those "emplacements for twenty-four cannon, and the marsh. . . ." A costly charge on the Rebel works at Pocotaligo proved unnecessary, however, for at dawn it became apparent that they had slipped away under cover of night.

Southerners later often insinuated that McLaws was temporarily incapacitated by his Saturday night drinking, and the Confederate commander never entirely lived down the charge that he was too drunk to defend Pocotaligo. If true, this was the kind of liquor party the abstemious Howard could approve. "The 15th was Sunday," he observed, "and I was glad the enemy had left. . . ."[3]

On the march to Pocotaligo, the 18th Missouri suffered its first casualties of the Carolina Campaign. Three foragers of Company G were rounded up by enemy horsemen: Privates Lorenzo D. Smith, Newton J. Varner, and Elijah Mansfield. It is altogether probable that Lieutenant Mansfield would have been outraged at the loquaciousness displayed by his brother and the latter's comrades when Joe Wheeler called them in for a friendly chat at Steep Bottom Church, across the Salkehatchie, two days later. The men had told him, Wheeler wrote McLaws, that the Confederates were facing the whole XVII Corps, with the XV Corps coming right up behind from Beaufort. Sheldon's brigade, Wheeler learned, had four regiments and 2,000 men, and it had drawn ten days' rations before crossing the Coosaw. Talk in camp, the prisoners had said, had it that Sherman's next objective was Charleston. The verbose trio had gone somewhat beyond the "name, rank, and serial number" prescribed for their grandsons in later wars.[4]

Until near the end of January the 18th Missouri was in camp at Pocotaligo, as Howard and Blair patiently waited for fair weather and John A. Logan. Almost every day the boggy coastal flatland was deluged with sheets of midwinter rain. The temperature rarely dipped below freezing, but in the clammy environment even Yankees could appreciate a warm fire and a good supply of blankets.

Colonel Minter was earning a name as a stringent commander, for the men had no sooner camped at Pocotaligo than he signed an order breaking Sergeant Dyer J. Olin of Company A for drinking too much on the march up from Beaufort. In the same order, Minter reduced Corporal James Harding of Company B for "firing off his gun in violation of orders." At Pocotaligo he put into effect a rigid training schedule for the recruits, providing an hour of squad and company drill every morning, ninety minutes of regimental drill every afternoon. Of course, with one eye on General Howard, it was provided that Sundays were excepted. But, warned Minter, "any officer excusing the

men of his command without sufficient cause will be recommended for dishonorable dismissal. . . ."

Bill Minter nevertheless would promote a fellow, if occasion warranted. For example, he raised Corporals George D.
Earl and Pleasant C. Jarman to sergeants in Company D on
January 15, and four days later he made Philip Linscott a corporal in A Company. On January 20 he handed corporal's stripes
to four of Lieutenant Richardson's men in Company F: George
McAuley, Humphrey Perry, Edmund Weabson, and Silas
Wheeler. On January 16 he lifted two privates out of their
companies to join the Staff. Henry S. Wells came in from Company B to take over as quartermaster sergeant, and Dan Carr
of Company F took on the job of commissary sergeant.

Plans for installing D. W. Pollock in command of Company
A did not work out, however. Though Sheldon had lately asked
a captain's commission for him, Pollock elected to muster-out
at the expiration of his enlistment, computed from the time
Colonel Morgan had appointed him a second lieutenant back
at Weston. Heavy cannonading in northern Georgia during
the summer of 1864 had impaired his hearing, and Dr. Randolph
saw little hope of its improvement in the Carolina bogs. The
husky young officer, who had seen his share of the war from
the very beginning, bade farewell to the remaining "boys from
St. John" and many other admirers on January 19. They would
see him again, and would on numerous occasions be indebted
to his never-ceasing generosity.[5]

The men were also getting plenty of news from home.
Colonel Fletcher had taken office as governor on January 2,
predicting in his inaugural that "the coming spring-time will
bring the final blow, and amid the battle-cry of Freedom the
death of the Rebellion will be consummated, and blessed Peace
once more breathe its benisons over the land." Elwood Miller,
ending a tour of duty as a major of the Enrolled Militia, was
now summoned to Jefferson City as his uncle's aide-de-camp
with the rank of colonel. On January 20, Madison Miller, lately a
brigadier general of the Militia, as well as a state senator, was
appointed fund commissioner for the Pacific Railroad. Within
another month the new governor would make Senator Pratt a
brigadier in the Missouri State Militia. Never again would the

men of the 18th Missouri feel themselves so influential in state politics.

Lieutenant Brantner of Company A had equally exciting news from home. Sarah Green Brantner now wrote from their Sullivan County home that his second child and first son had been born in mid-December. Mindful of her husband's employment at the time of the baby's coming, Sarah had appropriately named the youngster Sherman.

By this time, it was well known at Pocotaligo that General Sweeny had been cleared on January 2 on all counts of Dodge's case against him. Secretary Stanton offered to send the Bulldog back to Sherman's command, but O. O. Howard primly declined to associate with a brigadier so demonstrably capable of swinging at major generals.[6]

With hardly any warning, Mower ordered everyone to pack up and be on the road north by 8 A.M. Friday, January 20. Sheldon's brigade, leading the way, ran into Rebel pickets three miles out of Pocotaligo, and things were rather noisy for two or three hours. In midmorning Sheldon wheeled the brigade to the right for a crossing of the Salkehatchie, just above the Atlanta & Charleston railroad bridge. Here the troops had a real foretaste of campaigning in South Carolina. The Salkehatchie was fordable, to be sure, but they had to splash through a half-mile of swamp to reach it, and in a steady rain to boot. The river was up, thanks to January rains, but the brigade went across and clambered over some flooded trenches temporarily given up by the Confederates, who had wisely taken off for higher ground.

At this point, Mower rode up to Sheldon's dripping brigade. "Bring 'em back, now, Sheldon," he ordered. "General Sherman isn't ready to scare the Rebs out of Charleston. All we want now are 'make-believe' demonstrations. We'll give 'em the genuine article later on." Elias Perry wearily noted that the men arrived in Pocotaligo at 8 P.M., after a twelve-hour foray.[7]

After raising a similar commotion along the Salkehatchie the following Wednesday, the brigade returned to camp at daybreak on Thursday, January 26. There it was learned that General Fuller, back from leave in Ohio, had reached Pocotaligo. Sheldon, returning to his regiment, found it absorbing a flood of recruits and draftees. A detachment of 125 men had just arrived, and 76 more were due in very soon. One big problem was finding enough Springfields to arm the new men, but "after some difficulty" Sheldon got the job done.[8]

By the end of January, as Sherman arrived at Beaufort, Slocum was across the Savannah and moving into South Carolina. Howard's army was well assembled around Pocotaligo, and the Navy was doing a first-rate job of running supplies up the river from Beaufort. The wretched weather that Sherman had expected to clear by mid-January began to improve only in the last week of that month.

On January 27 frantic preparations for the big push were under way. All surplus articles were ordered "sent to the rear or abandoned to-day." Company-grade officers had to give up their good wall tents to bivouac in pairs, using canvas stretched over poles and sticks chopped out of the woods along the route of march. This order, plus another to form "messes of not less than five," made it possible to discard wagonloads of furniture and kitchen utensils that most officers had heretofore considered indispensable.[9]

Now that the Army of the Tennessee was ready to strike into the heart of what D. A. Cudworth had sarcastically called "that sacred state," the officers and men had a good idea of what lay ahead. "True," said Correspondent Conyngham, "we had no Buzzard Roost nor Kenesaw to scale, but we had to cross wide rivers, whose sedgy, oozy banks were covered for miles with dismal swamps." Untold hours would be spent, in daylight and dark, walking and standing in ice-strewn swamps, hoping against hope that the local alligators were neutral. The boys of the 18th Missouri, like their colonel, "hoped and believed that *this* march *must* surely wind up the confederacy—and the war —and that one of the numerous streams between us and Richmond would prove to be the . . . anxiously looked for 'Last Ditch' we heard of so often!"

The Confederates, outnumbered by more than 2–1, were now commanded by a galaxy of stars, some of them banished from Jeff Davis' imperious presence over the past two or three years. The durable Hardee had three small divisions, two patroling the Salkehatchie and the other holding Charleston.

Lieutenant General Daniel Harvey Hill was in charge up at Augusta, with Wheeler's cavalry and the all-but-useless Georgia Militia operating under his jurisdiction. Hood's shattered army was even now crossing northern Georgia under Lieutenant General Alexander P. Stewart to resume a hand in the fighting. Lieutenant General Wade Hampton was hurrying down from Virginia with some cavalry to aid in the defense of his native state, and Bragg was coming back to the field with a few troops. Above them all, however, there towered the figure of Beauregard. The Rebels in South Carolina were short of many things they were going to need, but they would have rank in abundance.[10]

Blair's corps spread itself out for some six miles along the road leading north from Pocotaligo on January 30, in order to make room for the XV Corps and the army's trains coming up from Beaufort. The weather had cleared satisfactorily over the past few days, and the hour of the great march was near at hand.

If the way north was hard and perilous, Sherman's troops had this consolation: The people in their line of march were frightened to death of Sherman's terrible Yankees. Citizens of Savannah, he had learned, "regard us just as the Romans did the Goths and the parallel is not unjust." He wrote Grant on January 29 that the Rebels had scattered at Pocotaligo as soon as they found themselves facing Sherman's army. This "undue fear of our Western men" was to Sherman a potent psychological weapon, and he vowed to use it for all its worth.

The die was cast on Wednesday morning, February 1. The 9th Illinois, saddling up before daybreak, swept briskly up the road toward Broxton's Bridge. Sheldon moved the 18th Missouri out right behind them, and Fuller's entire brigade soon swung into the line. Colonel Milton Montgomery's Second Brigade followed Fuller, and Tillson's Third brought up Mower's rear.

Bitterly contesting the advance was the 3d South Carolina Cavalry, and throughout that morning carbine shots rang out sporadically among the pines on either side of the road. Before they had gone two miles, the Illinois horsemen ran up against a barricade of fallen trees. This didn't hold them up long, for the defenders were into their saddles and out of sight after the first volley. Thereafter a close pursuit was on, with Sheldon keeping skirmishers constantly in the woods watching for ambuscades.

A brisk march of eight more miles brought Mower's column to Whippy Swamp Creek—ten parts swamp to one part creek. Here the advance came to a halt, as Howard and Blair rode up to survey the mess that McLaws had made just for them: Tall pines stood the length and breadth of the watery morass, but many others were lying where the Rebels had thoughtfully felled them—on the causeway through the swamp. That road traversed seven plank bridges, but they had been burned. Elias Perry described a breastwork of "rail piles" flanking the causeway at its far end.

It was around two o'clock that afternoon when Fuller rode over with the news that Mower had selected the 18th Missouri to wade Whippy Swamp and come up on the east end of the Confederate works. The horsemen couldn't possibly go through the tangled swamp like Sheldon's infantry, Fighting Joe had decided, nor could riders give the protection needed by the pioneers "cutting away and clearing the road of this felled timber." Forming a heavy skirmish line, the Missourians plunged into the cold water and headed for the other side. They were about halfway across when the Rebels began to blaze away at them, but the defenders' aim was hardly better than their determination to stick around and fight it out. The first Missourians to scramble out of the swamp completely unnerved the small force behind the rails, and they fled without any further resistance. Whippy Swamp was now clear, and the 1st Division could move across it with no more delay.

General Howard rode up to praise "the celerity with which the front was cleared" by the 18th Missouri, Sheldon proudly noted in 1891. But Howard's autobiography published after the turn of the century vaguely referred to the Missourians only as "my skirmishers." Blair's report merely notes that the Rebels beyond Whippy Swamp "were quickly dislodged." Mower was no more generous, calling the 18th Missouri "one regiment." Be that as it may, even if the men received little public recognition for their charge, they had the satisfaction of knowing that for one heroic hour they had been the very tip of Sherman's sword, while even the Illinois riders sat uselessly in their saddles back at the edge of the swamp.[11]

Sheldon bivouacked the regiment on the Harrison plantation a quarter-mile north of the swamp that night. Tillson's brigade came over the causeway to get into position to lead the division out at dawn, February 2. Montgomery, said Mower, would now follow Tillson, and Fuller's brigade would come in the rear.

Thus to the 18th Missouri fell the dubious honor of serving as train guard. The boys found that more was involved than hovering solicitously around the teamsters. Many a mile of roadway was going to need corduroying, and whoever marched in the rear with the wagons was also going to have *that* to do. "As soon as the train struck a mud hole and stopped," Sheldon's men "pushed forward until they reached the obstruction . . . came into line, and stacking arms, proceeded to fill the road with fence rails (if they were not to be had, small trees were cut down) and over this solid . . . but rather rough causeway the trains passed in safety. . . . This took place nearly every day, and . . . the service was as heartily disliked as it was promptly executed." Whereas the autumn march to the sea was characterized by railway-destruction, Sheldon always thought the "march through the Carolinas was made forever memorable by the miles of road we built!"

Mower's troops moved at daylight Thursday, but the 18th Missouri didn't get on the road until eight o'clock. Sheldon soon heard the sounds of a skirmish up front, where Tillson had run into a pocket of resistance near Broxton's Bridge. However, after a short exchange, the enemy skipped out and left the bridge over the Salkehatchie a smoldering ruin—a typical Rebel prank. Mower then directed Tillson to leave a regiment there to watch the enemy on the east bank, while the main body of his brigade pushed on to the north.

Late in the afternoon, after a skirmish in which Lieutenant Colonel Isaac Kirby of the 9th Illinois was seriously wounded, the advance forces came to the point north of Jenny's Corners where the Pocotaligo road joined another from River's Bridge to Buford's Bridge. Mower sent Tillson and the Illinoisans a mile or so to the west up this road to guard against Wheeler's marauders and cover Logan's approach to Buford's later in the afternoon. Since Blair was to cross the Salkehatchie at River's Bridge, Mower now turned Montgomery's brigade eastward into the vast swamplands of the Salkehatchie bottoms.[12]

Mower boldly pushed Montgomery's troops down the causeway leading through the swamp, intending to force a crossing then and there if at all possible. The old mile-long plank road, which bent to the north in mid-swamp, spanned sixteen different streams, the last being the Salkehatchie itself. Overlooking the main crossing on the far bank was a rather steep bluff, on which a long string of Rebel entrenchments and gun-emplacements pretty well "commanded the situation," as Howard ruefully noted. Flushed with excitement and cursing at the top of his voice, Fighting Joe Mower ordered the 25th Wisconsin to get across the main bridge and gain the enemy works whatever the cost.

Easier shouted than accomplished! Storming down the last and fairly straight stretch of causeway, the Wisconsinites ran into an artillery barrage which killed three and wounded four in a matter of minutes. The Wisconsin boys quickly found it healthier to get off the open road. The flooring of the river bridge being gone for some odd reason, the skirmishers plunged into the woods to flush out any remaining pickets west of the river. Montgomery began moving his other regiments into the soggy woodlands to back up his forward line. The race to the river had not carried McLaws' new breastworks, but it had saved the plank-bridges over lesser streams west of the Salke-hatchie.

General Fuller reached the edge of the swamp about two o'clock and halted his three forward regiments in Montgomery's immediate rear. He was only too well aware that "the enemy's artillery was firing at the troops in front of me," and that a difficult engagement was shaping up along the river. While he was drawing up his forces near the swamp, Fuller saw Mower and learned that it was useless to expect an early passage of the Salkehatchie, and that Fighting Joe was pulling all but a skirmish line back from the swamp. Fuller's brigade, the division commander decided, was to move up in support, putting the 27th Ohio out in the bogs below the road, the 39th

Ohio and 64th Illinois into the swamp above it. In case the opportunity could be developed somewhere up front, Mower wanted Fuller and Montgomery to hold their men in readiness "to cross the river at any moment. . . ." He was still determined to leap the Salkehatchie somehow to give the Rebels the genuine article.

Not long after five o'clock the 18th Missouri halted at the intersection north of Jenny's Corners to wait for Fuller's instructions. Rockwood noted that over in the swamp "heavy Skirmishing is going on with now and then a Shell mixed in." Cudworth soon showed up to tell the company commanders that he was making a quick ration-issue, for he had it on good authority that Fuller was going to have to send the Missourians out on picket after dark.

Cud was right. There was barely time for each company to draw its quota of hardtack before Fuller's aide appeared with the word for Sheldon to push on and bivouac near the swamp. After the move, made in darkness, was completed, each company was to send back for the rest of its rations. At the new bivouac alongside the causeway, Sheldon learned that Fuller was indeed preparing to order the Missourians into the swamp to relieve the 64th Illinois and 39th Ohio. These fellows had had about all they could stand, and Fuller wanted them brought out to dry and feed. It would suit the occasion, the little brigadier said, if Sheldon maintained half the regiment on picket in the swamp and kept the rest on the road as relief parties.

It was a pretty hectic night in the clammy marshes north and west of the causeway. Elias Perry heard the "pickets firing some little through the night." Worsening matters was a heavy rain that started about midnight and lasted until dawn. Rockwood grumbled in his diary about having to stand "in water from Boot top to waist deep." Sheldon found that the planks of the main bridge were missing, but that the stringers were still in place. Several of the men then crawled across in the dark, unnoticed by the shivering Rebels in their redoubt overlooking the far bank, and in the course of this furtive probe the troops at least informally gained for the 18th Missouri the distinction of being the first of Sherman's troops to cross the Salkehatchie at River's Bridge. On this occasion, however, the Missourians were going over only to spy, not to stay. And they brought back the news that the enemy had "four guns in position, covering the causeway. . . ." Darkness must have magnified things, for it turned out at daylight that McLaws had only two pieces of artillery. Since Sheldon thought it might be a good tactic to move up some sharpshooters to keep the gunners' heads down during the daytime hours, the Missourians pitched in and soon had a comfortable little rifle-pit ready alongside the causeway about two hundred yards from the Confederate works.

Meanwhile, the generals were conferring back at Jenny's Corners, where Sherman's headquarters was now located. They all agreed that Mower should spearhead the crossing, and that particularly suited Fighting Joe. But how would 1st Division go about it? Mower's solution, rubber-stamped by the others, avoided a frontal assault along the existing road. Tillson, he proposed, should set up a diversion along the road to engage Confederate attention, while Fuller and Montgomery would go through the swamp above the road, building corduroy lanes down which their brigades could advance simultaneously. In fact, late in the afternoon Mower had already put his Pioneers to work felling trees and constructing a road toward the north end of the Rebel entrenchments.

At dawn, February 3, the action commenced anew. To the accompaniment of artillery and musketry, axmen began laying about them in the swamp. Montgomery, on the left, had the 63d Ohio and 32d Wisconsin chopping down the tall pines, while the 35th New Jersey—those irrepressible Zoos—were sent to dismantle farmhouses and barns to get planking. General Fuller ordered the 27th Ohio into the swamp to relieve Sheldon's boys at 6 A.M. The Missourians willingly "marched to the rear," as Rockwood said, "wheir they dried there Cloths and took something to Eat. . . ." The 10th Illinois sent a squad of sharpshooters to the rifle-pit the Missourians had dug during the night. To hear Blair and Mower tell it later, the Illinoisans beautifully squelched the Rebel gunners that morning, but Sheldon was later "sorry to say that the plan did not work, for at break of day, the guns silenced the sharp shooters instead by covering them with mud."

While Howard and Blair anxiously bided their time back on firmer ground, Mower waded through the swamp, raucously urging his division to superhuman efforts to cross the river. The Salkehatchie bottoms resounded to the ring of axes, the crashing of trees, and the whine of minié balls. The Third Brigade's ruckus-raising on the road did not, Mower admitted, "create the desired diversion at the right," but Tillson's skirmishers were getting bolder by the hour along the river. Just before two o'clock that afternoon an excited aide reached Mower with the news that some of Tillson's men had gained the east bank 800 yards above the old bridge by scrambling across on a fallen cypress tree.

Fighting Joe hesitated not an instant. He bawled out the orders to his aides: Tillson was to hustle all of his brigade across the river immediately. Fuller was to drop his road job and follow Tillson at the double-quick, and Montgomery would bring up Fuller's rear. The Pioneers would complete Fuller's plank road to the crossing to facilitate the passage. Fuller rushed a work-party from the 27th Ohio to the crossing to cut down the cypresses lining the stream, felling them from both banks to create slippery but sturdy bridges. "While I was chopping," said Ben Sweet, "the balls were flying all around and two men were killed so close to me that I could have touched them from where I stood. I did not stop to see if I was tired out."

In the rush across what Sheldon termed "this novel bridge," there occurred something of an organizational breakdown. When Fuller brought his own brigade over to the far edge of the swamp, he found Tillson forming there and swung into line on Tillson's left, facing the Rebel flank from the northwest. Since Mower was still west of the river and Fuller was the division's only other general officer, the doughty little Ohioan notified Colonel Tillson that "I would assume command." This was understandable, except that Fuller's first order was for Tillson to hold his position until Fuller's own brigade, temporarily under Sheldon, could form up and swing forward. The 18th Missouri, with Minter commanding, would stand just behind the interval between the two brigades.

Mower was as angry as a wet rooster for several days afterward because Fuller had taken "the responsibility of ordering

Colonel Tillson to halt . . . whereas, if Colonel Tillson had been allowed to push forward, according to my previous positive orders, the movement might well have resulted in the capture of some of the enemy's artillery and wagons, if not of more prisoners." Fuller countered testily that Mower's aide had told him to "act on my own judgment," and he implied very strongly in his own report that a forward push by Tillson alone would have squeezed the Rebels out before Fuller's regiments could swing around to block their line of retreat from the River's Bridge entrenchments.

In any case, Sheldon declared, the Rebels "were quickly put to flight. . . ." Elias Perry recalled that "now and then a stray ball would whiz through our ranks but did not do any damage in our regt. There was wounded men carried to the rear every few minutes. In a short time orders came to move forward. The Colonel gave orders to fix bayonets and moved to the front, the mud and water knee deep and fighting heavy in front. We moved on within supporting distance of the front line yelling like so many wild cats. As we got out of the swamp we came to a halt to get the lines dressed for a charge. The front lines then moved on and our line followed close. It being nerely night, the flash of the Rebbel guns was a nice seen. The Rebs gave way without a general engagement." The defenders must have been unhinged even more by the news that Giles Smith's men were now getting across the Salkehatchie below River's Bridge.[14]

While Tillson's men were linking up at dark with the 10th Illinois around the old main bridge, they also began settling down in McLaws' old breastworks for the night. Fuller's brigade had no such luck, and it consequently worked until past midnight preparing new works along the road. After all, McLaws *might* come back. And in these old and new works around River's Bridge the entire 1st Division spent the rest of that frigid night. Rockwood heard that Mower's losses were about 300, but the official reports set them at 125. Of his brigade, Fuller listed seven men (of the 27th Ohio) as wounded in action. Private Christopher C. Cash of Company D, 18th Missouri, had the misfortune to be hit by "friendly" fire.

The next morning, as Mower and his staff were making the

rounds to visit the regiments, Hemstreet saw him brush several small icicles from his cloak. Those icicles, Mower's immediate reward for "a night of exposure in wading the swamps of the Salkehatchie," would, Hemstreet told the General, "count for him in history." They counted for more than Bill Hemstreet then realized, for the General soon developed the pulmonary trouble that laid him away in Arlington only five years afterward.[15]

By Sunday, February 5, it was generally known in Blair's corps that Black Jack Logan had passed the Salkehatchie up at Buford's Bridge. Moreover, Slocum's forces were making their way across South Carolina even farther up the watershed. Looking northward, the men of the XVII Corps beheld throughout the day immense arms of smoke rising toward the heavens. The spectacle convinced Rockwood that the Palmetto State was now "paying penence for her grate Sins."

With Force's division leading, Blair moved out for Orangeburg at dawn Monday. The first day's march, through a broad belt of pine forest, was obstructed a little by cavalry and somewhat more by Rebel axmen, busily "falling timber acorst the Crossways in the swamps," as Rockwood said. At Cowpen Ford, on the Little Salkehatchie, Force's sharpshooters prepared the way for engineers to lay a 260-foot pontoon bridge over the stream. And that evening the 1st Division camped ten miles up the road from River's Bridge.

It started raining before daylight Tuesday, but the XVII Corps marched out anyway. The 3d Division took the advance and sloshed along "almost impassable roads," as Blair said, toward the little town of Midway, on the South Carolina Railroad connecting Charleston and Augusta. Since Mower's division was in the rear on this sodden Tuesday, it fell to the Missourians and their companions in misery to do the road-repairs constantly needed to keep the supplies on the way toward the front. By evening the 4th Division had reached Midway to intercept the rail line at that crucial point.

While watching his men wrecking the railroad the next day between Midway and the Edisto River, Frank Blair got fresh orders from Howard to start an immediate drive on Orangeburg, fifteen miles to the north. Mainly because crossings of both forks of the Edisto were involved, this directive was a large order. But Mower happily took the lead to see how much he could do.

At dawn Thursday, Tillson's brigade moved out for Binnaker's Bridge, on the South Edisto, and by noon the skirmishers were up to the bank, firing at concealed Rebels beyond the burned bridge. "The advantages of position were decidedly in our favor," Blair told Sherman, "a high bluff bank upon this and low flat swamp on the opposite side of the river, beyond which the enemy was entrenched." As the other brigades closed up in the early afternoon, the Pioneers and engineers approached to prepare rafts for the crossing.

Mower rode up to find Rebel marksmen and cannoneers playing havoc with the work on the rafts. Certain that there must be a safer place to stage a crossing, he questioned a few skirmishers and soon learned that they had seen, some 150 yards below the burned bridge, a wooded rise shielded from enemy view and excellent for mounting a river-crossing effort. The work crews promptly moved to the new location, floating down the rafts they had already fabricated.

While standing on the rise and contemplating the cold, deep waters of the Edisto, the division commander was moved to perpetrate a bizarre stunt which amused his rough-and-ready Westerners even as it defied their ability to explain it. A huge ex-slave came walking along the bank, and, spying Mower, stepped up closely to look at the bearded and brooding warrior commanding this dramatic scene. Without so much as a word, Mower suddenly seized the startled Negro by the shoulders and hurled him down the steep bank into the river. "He went clear under," wrote one puzzled witness, "and the General marched us back a short distance where we went into camp."[16]

Not long after dark Tillson's boys ferried enough riflemen and raft-crews across the main channel to string out and pull over a floating bridge. Once that had been done, Mower hurried Tillson, Montgomery, and Fuller, in that order, across the bridge and into the marshy approaches to the Rebel breastworks bordering the swamp. Tillson was carrying on a brisk skirmish up ahead when Fuller's leading companies jumped from the far end of the pontoons into the quagmire. Elias Perry found the water "very cold and thigh deep." So did Colonel Sheldon, whose bad luck it was "just as I neared the further shore, to fall over a cypress knee . . . and take an involuntary plunge bath, and worse than all, soaking my overcoat, which I found frozen stiff when we returned from pursuing the enemy. Nor were my lacerated feelings at all soothed by the subdued cries of 'grab a root! grab a root, Colonel!' which could be heard on all sides."

The 18th Missouri and its soaking wet colonel were now across the South Edisto, and Mower's division had hurdled a barrier "second only in importance and the difficulties to be overcome to the crossing of the Salkehatchie," as Blair said. The first thing the men thought of, once they were on firm ground at the Stevens plantation, was to build several huge bonfires to dry their sopping trousers and coat-tails. The Rebels, as usual, had dispersed and were nowhere in evidence.

It was the 18th Missouri's dubious privilege, as the rear regiment of Mower's division, to bring up the rear again on February 11, when the march to Orangeburg resumed. Giles Smith moved out ahead, skirmishing frequently with small parties of enemy horsemen doggedly barring the way. The drive on Orangeburg culminated the next day, when Force's 3d division, according to Perry, "made a charge on the rebs and made them skedad from the river. . . ." The fleeing enemy left the city and the usual heap of blazing cotton bales in Blair's hands. The XVII Corps streamed across its pontoon bridge to campsites north of Orangeburg. How the Yankees celebrated Lincoln's birthday is clear from Sergeant Perry's stark notation: "The Town Burned."[17]

While the 18th Missouri lay in camp that Sunday evening, Colonel Sheldon passed out some overdue promotions. Corporal John H. Wilson rose to sergeant in Company A, and Barney Mayfield got Wilson's old job. In Company E a sergeantcy was bestowed on Corporal John P. Clark, while corporal's ratings went to John Halmark, Henry Dannenburg, and Henry Newsom. Corporals Orange Caseldine and Samuel Fisk were the new sergeants of Company- F, and Daniel McLane got a corporal's stripes in the same outfit. Company I greeted three new corporals: Isaac N. Barnett, Daniel B. Stains, and James W. Summers. Fisk was a prisoner at Shiloh, and Caseldine had lost a brother in the pestilential Rebel prison pen at Macon, in the August following Shiloh.[18]

The drive on Columbia started Monday morning, February 13. Four days of steady northward marching, interrupted by occasional Rebel sorties, brought the XVII Corps within sight of its destination. The men of Mower's division usually bivouacked on an abandoned plantation each night of the march, thereby providing at least the officers with a few home comforts. Rockwood noted on the second day out that "Still the Clouds of Smoke go upwards." A good observer, he thought, could plot every corps' line of march by studying the patterns of smoke swirling over ravaged South Carolina. Thursday was the worst day of that week for the 18th Missouri, for, says Sergeant Perry, "the reg. was train guard. Started at 2 PM & marched slowly as the train could not go fast on account of bad roads. Just at sunset we had to cross a bad swamp which we had to wade. Traveled 8 miles, stoped for camp at 8 PM. . . ."

Forward elements of Logan and Blair drew up on Thursday to the Saluda River, across which the Yanks could gaze eastward into Columbia itself, the very cradle of Secession. This "Southern Holy of Holies"—as Sherman's aide called it—had been laid out in 1787 at the confluence of the Broad and Saluda Rivers. Conyngham thought the Confederacy had no other city "more beautifully situated, or more gorgeously embellished. . . ." Within the city stood the uncompleted but already beautiful granite capitol as well as Columbia College, "the Alma Mater of the Tazewells, the Barnwells, the Rhetts, the Hamptons. . . ." One witness found in Columbia none of the "commercial" air that pervaded Savannah. Equally impressed was Lieutenant Rockwood, who at noon on Thursday had "assended a high hill . . . had a fair view of the Grate Capital of South Carolina, the Grate Pride of Southern Shivalry."[19]

Howard's Pioneers laid pontoon bridges over the Saluda on the morning of February 17, Logan's bridge being about three miles above and Blair's directly opposite the city. Cudworth and Randolph went over on Logan's bridge and were in Columbia by 3 P.M., well before the 18th Missouri. They arrived to feel the first shock-waves of a furious argument over whether or not Logan's men or the XVII Corps had "taken" Columbia. That very morning, Blair was claiming, men of the 13th Iowa, Giles Smith's division, had paddled across in a small boat and planted their colors on the old and new capitols. Conyngham supports Blair's claim for the Iowans, but Sheldon never quite saw it that way. "For the honor and glory of the 17th Corps," said he, "I am sorry to report that they were not successful in accomplishing their laudable enterprise, as Wheeler's Cavalry had not yet left town, and 'escorted' them back to the river on the double-quick!"

The Rebels were abandoning Columbia, though, and by sundown the Army of the Tennessee had taken full possession of the area. But even as Sherman was grasping the prize, it crumbled to ashes. Widespread fires broke out after dark, and the Blue and Gray were to argue for decades over who was to blame. Sheldon's men had not seen such an inferno since Sherman's incineration of Atlanta. From the regimental camp north of town Rockwood saw around midnight that "the principle part of the City is on fier. . . ." The billowing flames, explosions, and shrieks of the citizens combined to make the night a far from restful one for the Missourians. Cudworth vindictively judged the nocturnal conflagration "just retribution to the headquarters of secession."[20]

"The morning sun of February 18th rose bright and clear over a ruined city," wrote Sherman. And not long after reveille Blair began sending work-parties into the smoldering capital to get on with the demolition of railway-equipment and track. The 18th Missouri broke open a freight car and found it filled with newly printed Confederate bonds and currency. For one heady hour several poor country boys from northern Missouri were "Confederate millionaires."

The next morning, however, the Missouri millionaires and everybody else in Fuller's brigade had to march out a few miles northwest of the city to start wrecking the South Carolina Railroad toward Winnsboro. For the 18th Missouri and 64th Illinois this proved to be a dangerous job in several ways. It was Wade Hampton's intention to slow down the destruction of the railroad if not entirely stop it, and to that end, Sheldon said, the Rebels "used some artillery on us, but finally retired." A fast-moving skirmish line of Missourians swept down off the right-of-way to capture several of the Rebels before they could saddle up for Hampton's getaway.

The days that followed saw Mower's division probing boldly up the line toward Winnsboro, about thirty miles out of Columbia. Since there were trestles to burn and rails to pry up, a good day's march took them little more than ten or fifteen miles. On February 20 the Missourians were out in front skirmishing with small hit-and-run parties of Hampton's elusive cavalry, and the day after that they were in the rear as train guards. Rockwood morosely described the day as given over to "Marching through swamps and Makeing several miles of Cordroy rode."[21]

Still working as train guards on Washington's birthday, Sheldon's troops reached Winnsboro at 1 P.M. Howard's line of march from this point bore sharply to the northeast, and the XVII Corps now left the infernal railroad work behind for some genuine field-soldiering again. Hardee had just evacuated Charleston, and Sherman calculated that the Rebel force was now on its way to Cheraw. If possible, Sherman meant to head it off by beating it to Cheraw. A rapid march in that direction now began, with the XV Corps leading the way at first. Logan got his last regiments across the Wateree River west of Liberty Hill on the afternoon of February 23, and Blair started Giles Smith's troops after them without delay.

It took about eight days to traverse the hundred miles from the Wateree to Cheraw, not on the face of it a remarkable performance for Howard's muscular Westerners. But heavy rains set in on February 24, and that slowed everyone down considerably. The crossings of the Little Lynch and Big Lynch Creeks went off smoothly, although Fuller was held up nearly a day waiting for the lumber with which to bridge Big Lynch on February 27. After a day of increasingly heavy skirmishing, Fuller's men bivouacked at four o'clock on February 28 in what is today the Sandhill State Forest. Confronting them was a strong line of entrenchments barring the road to the northeast.[22]

Despite a rickety railroad and stormy weather, Hardee managed to beat the Yankees to Cheraw after all. Blair, apprised of that fact, was in no hurry for a scrap with the men defending the place. Since Sherman's main body was at least a day behind him, he was compelled to ask Mower and his division to sit and glare at the Rebels all day long on March 1. The next day, however, Tillson's brigade was sent forth to test Hardee's left flank in the direction of Society Hill. Tillson found Hardee very much on the alert, as usual, and prudently relocated to Mower's lines before dark.

Sherman told Blair to go in for the kill at daylight Friday. Thus the drive on Cheraw began, Mower's division leading the corps, and Fuller's brigade the division, behind a skirmish line of the 27th Ohio. All Confederate positions in the first seven miles were found abandoned, and Fuller was halfway to Cheraw without firing a shot. The going soon got rougher, though. At Johnson's Creek the bridge was afire, but the brigade miraculously saved it. Just beyond the creek, wrote Perry, "We . . . found the Rebel force. We pursued them so close that we captured some of them & made them leave their tents." Hardee's force scattered before Fuller's charge, and the 27th Ohio sprinted boldly through Cheraw heading for the bridge over the Pee Dee just east of town.

Hardee had covered the bridge with pitch preparatory to incinerating it, and by the time the Ohioans reached it there was a towering blaze there. Bill Hemstreet soon raced back with the news that Mower wanted the 18th Missouri up front in a hurry. As his men scurried forward to the river, Sheldon reported to Fighting Joe and found him "somewhat out of humor" and "at first inclined to order a charge through the burning bridge, to capture the works at the other end. . . ." The commander of the 18th Missouri, doubting that it would profit the Union to barbecue his boys, made bold to object on their behalf. To Mower's everlasting credit, he let himself be persuaded that Sheldon's proposal for a pontoon-raft crossing would be safer and surer.[23]

That night the 18th Missouri camped in Cheraw, while the rest of the corps drew up and Howard's engineers made ready for the next day's crossing of the Pee Dee. Cheraw had a rather prosperous atmosphere, and it was found that the place was bulging with military supplies sent up from Charleston for safekeeping. The troops were particularly happy over the bountiful stores of coffee and blankets—and eight wagon-loads of choice aged wines. General Slocum afterward gave fervent thanks that all this high-class liquor had been discovered by subordinates of the "generous and chivalrous" Frank P. Blair, for the famous soldier-statesman saw that the wines were rationed out to all units of Sherman's armies "with the spirit of liberality and fairness characteristic of him." Sheldon said of the XVII Corps that it "safely disposed" of the portion that General Blair reserved to it.

Saturday, March 4—the day of Lincoln's second inaugural —was just dawning when Companies E and F of the 18th Missouri launched a little pontoon boat into the Pee Dee in the face of scattered musket-fire that hit nobody. As the two companies shuttled across, taking Colonel Minter over to command the forward echelon, scouts reported sighting Rebel cavalry a mile and a half to the east. At this, Minter dispatched a call to Cheraw, and Sheldon moved up the rest of the regiment to get it across as quickly as possible. The 39th Ohio also joined in the crossing. While waiting, Minter ordered Lieutenant Everest to put Company E to work on a trench system covering the bridgehead, and posted Joe Brown's Company F out in front as skirmishers.

By midafternoon a floating bridge was ready, and Mower's command was hastening across to expand Minter's lodgment on the far bank. As the reinforcements poured over from Cheraw, Mower ordered Sheldon to push his skirmish line forward. "We moved off slow," Elias Perry remembered. "The rebs did not fire but little. A few volleys from the line drove them off in all directions." Even so, General Howard deemed it best to send over a division of Logan's corps as "insurance" for Mower.

As Sheldon set up his headquarters just before dark at a point two miles beyond the bridge, the 18th Missouri went on picket. After sundown the pickets moved out another two miles, Rockwood estimated, but encountered no Rebels. The only disturbance that night was the explosion of a farmhouse full of ammunition that Hardee had chosen to detonate because he was unable to have it hauled away. The blast was in Rockwood's words a "turrible racket" and created "considerable of alarm." But after the men found out what it was, the confusion subsided.[24]

Sunday was exciting for two explosive reasons. Thanks to the carelessness of a teamster, a major part of the Confederate ammunition captured at Cheraw went up with a roar and killed several of Howard's men. Rockwood, over on the east bank of the river, saw the blast and mistakenly assumed that Sherman had ordered the old arsenal in town "blown up in Heavens." The other shock came from a newspaper item telling of Old Joe Johnston's recall to active duty, and in the Carolinas at that! Jeff Davis was evidently drinking the bitter dregs of defeat. Animosity between him and Johnston was public knowledge, and it must have galled him beyond description when Lee, whom he had just elevated to supreme command of the Confederate Armies, handed his fellow Virginian the overall command of the Carolinas. Sherman, for quite different reasons, didn't like the change any better than Jeff Davis, for he knew that Johnston's return to the field "would somehow compel me to exercise more caution than I had hitherto done."[25]

The week of March 6–11 saw the armies move confidently to Fayetteville, North Carolina. Mower's chagrin may be easily surmised, when one hears that the 1st Divison made nearly the entire seventy-mile march with the train instead of "up front." It would probably have been the lowest point in the campaign for Mower, but for the fact that most of the action occurred in the rear, where Rebel horsemen were "bothering" the wagon train, as Rockwood phrased it. The 9th Illinois, still aboard the horses they had ridden since the "old days" back at Pocahontas, had more diversion than anyone else. Galloping ahead of XVII Corps, they seldom saw an armed Confederate but had plenty of chances to burn depots, trestles, and factories. "The route was over a very swampy country," says Sheldon, "and 'corduroying' [was] our constant occupation. . . ." About noon on Wednesday, March 8, the Missourians crossed over into North Carolina. Passing this milestone seemed little to cheer about, since, as Elias Perry sadly noted, "It rained all day."[26]

After the 3d Division chased the Confederate rear guard through Fayetteville on Saturday, March 11, Sherman pulled

them back to allow XIV Corps to pass into the city. Sheldon inti-
mates that the General was mostly concerned about the pride of
Slocum's men, since it was "their turn—to take something!" At
any rate, Slocum's troops put in a rousing weekend burning public buildings and blowing up the arsenal. Just before lunch on
Sunday, a steam tug from Wilmington put in at the Cape Fear
River docks with a load of mail for Sherman's troops. The diary
of Mower's headquarters suggests that the tug went back that
evening with a load of homeward-bound letters from those
thousands of boys whose contact with the North had been
pretty uncertain since leaving Thunderbolt Landing.

Sherman, headquartered that weekend at Fayetteville,
mapped out his next moves. Orders went to Schofield, commanding the XXIII Corps at New Bern, and to Major General A.
H. Terry's X Corps, at Wilmington, to close in rapidly on Goldsboro. Sherman's four other corps would do the same in this vast
convergence on that place. Slocum would march toward Smithfield, while Howard proceeded over roads leading more directly
to Goldsboro, twenty miles down the Neuse River from
Smithfield. Sherman, once again having to read Joe Johnston's
mind, felt that the area around Bentonville, just south of the
Neuse and some twenty miles southwest of Goldsboro, was the
point where Johnston would have his "only chance to meet
the army before an easy junction with Schofield" could be
effected. Howard and Slocum, he reckoned, had better plan to
join near Bentonville before crossing the Neuse. Blair was to
hold down Sherman's right flank and move along an arc stretching eastward from Fayetteville toward Clinton and bending
northward toward Goldsboro, sixty miles from Fayetteville as
the crow flew.[27]

# CHAPTER XV

# The Last Ditch

SHELDON WROTE to Colonel Samuel P. Simpson, Governor Fletcher's new Adjutant General: "March 15th, the army started for Goldsboro, which was understood to be the objective point of the campaign." Sheldon recalled a generation later that the men were "expecting to make [Goldsboro] without opposition, as it was supposed [Johnston] would not attempt to hold any position this side of Raleigh." The advance was more equitably distributed this time, and a joyful Mower led XVII Corps down the Clinton road that first day on the march.

Fighting Joe's ecstasy was short-lived. The next day the region was drenched by one of those day-long rainstorms with which the Deep South greets the coming spring, and Frank Blair's men spent the day huddled in their tents and wagons. Worse still, from Mower's standpoint, there came the sounds of a heavy skirmish over toward Averysboro, where the XX Corps had run into Hardee's forces entrenched in the muddy neck of land between the Cape Fear and South Rivers. The bellicose Mower could easily have sympathized with the girl who was "always a bridesmaid," and he must have wondered often if the remaining combat in this dying war would pass him by completely.

On Friday and Saturday, March 17–18, there was good marching weather. But now Giles Smith's troops took the lead, with Force's 3d Division following them. That left Mower's

troops to assist the train again, and thanks to Thursday's downpour the wagons hadn't moved far before the 18th Missouri, in
Perry's words, "stoped and fixed some road so the trains could
pass." Despite delays of this kind, the troops managed to cover
about fifteen miles on each of those two days.

Some time Saturday night, in the vicinity of Troublefield's
Store, Blair called in Mower to tell him the good news that the
advance Sunday morning would be given the 1st Division.
Mower's orders were, in short, to push on to the vicinity of
Everettsville, just south of Goldsboro, as quickly as possible.
"We . . . then moved forward," said Blair, ". . . via Doctor
Faison's plantation, to Smith's Chapel, about seven miles from
Mount Olive."[1]

The sun had not risen far into the heavens on that radiant
morning when Sheldon's sensitive ears detected a distant thunder in the direction of the XIV Corps line of march, some twelve
or thirteen miles to the west. No mere clash of horsemen there!
Had the cannonading over toward Bentonville died down right
away, Sheldon's Missourians might have been able to dismiss
it as a skirmish. As it was, however, the reverberations went
right on throughout that anxious day.

At his headquarters wagon at nine o'clock that evening, a
restless General Blair greeted a breathless aide from Howard's
headquarters at Falling Creek Church, to the northwest. Sherman had found Slocum's situation grave in the extreme, and he
was directing Howard to get XVII Corps "up here with at least
two divisions disencumbered." Blair, said Howard, should be
on the road by 3 A.M. Monday. Johnston, Colonel Sheldon now
learned at corps headquarters, "had placed his whole army
numbering some 25,000 men, in such a position that [Slocum]
would be obliged to pass by the flank in front of it, for nearly
three miles." Sheldon felt in retrospect that "the Battle of Bentonville was entirely unexpected by our Generals, and was an
attempt by Johnston . . . to imitate the tactics of Napoleon, and
striking fiercely at each portion, endeavor to destroy the separated detachments, before a concentration could be effected."
The crafty Rebel had caught Sherman's columns strung out
over a wide area and had gained a sporting chance to over-

whelm the Federal left before Howard could swing over to save it.

Frank Blair hastily dictated the marching orders. Mower, he decided, should leave Montgomery to guard the army's train and start for Bentonville with his other two brigades. Smith would lead the corps, with Force following Mower in the dash to rescue Slocum. There was to be no sleep that night for the 18th Missouri, which was out on picket when the excitement started. Around midnight, Fuller summoned the troops back into the bivouac area at Smith's Chapel to enable Cudworth and Commissary Sergeant Carr to issue hardtack preparatory to shoving off right away.

Blair and Mower saw no point in waiting until 3 A.M. if they could get off sooner. And so it was at 1 A.M. that XVII Corps pulled out for the scene of the battle. After retracing its steps some five miles, said Perry, the 18th Missouri "turned to our right and marched in all twenty miles. Waded several bad swamps. Heavy fighting heard in front. . . ." At daybreak the men filed past General Sherman and General Howard at Falling Creek Church and shortly afterwards came to a halt. Logan was passing through ahead of Blair, and it took some time for XV Corps to clear the vicinity.[2]

Early that afternoon the Missourians came in sight of the action. Whereas the day before the Confederate lines had bisected the Goldsboro road and looked directly west at Slocum's approaching columns, the appearance of Howard's army from the east now caused Old Joe to pull back his left wing from the south side of the road. Now his line formed a large "V," its point resting on the road near the Cole plantation and its flanks drawn back to the edges of Mill Creek and covering Bentonville. The area chosen for the Confederates' last stand south of the Neuse consisted, Howard was sorry to say, of "so much more woodland than open ground . . . and so much marshy or spongy soil that quick maneuvering was impossible." In the bogs and the blackjack patches around Bentonville it would certainly be primarily an infantryman's fight.

While Logan was hooking his line onto the XIV Corps positions, Blair moved Giles Smith's division up to Logan's right to face the Rebels' new left-flank entrenchments. As Mower's men came up next in midafternoon, Howard borrowed the 18th Missouri to support the juncture of the XIV and XV Corps, and the Missourians got their first chance to draw a bead on the enemy at Bentonville. For about an hour the regiment crept cautiously through woodlands toward the Goldsboro road a mile or so southeast of Cole's, but took no casualties. Around 5 P.M., Blair's aides rode up to order the troops relieved, assured that Logan and Davis had made good their linkup. As a rainy night came on, Mower and Force bivouacked south of the road to rest up for the exciting day ahead.[3]

Tuesday, March 21—"the day of Bentonville" for Sheldon's Missourians—began with gloomy clouds from which a driving rain developed toward noon. Fighting Joe's blood was up, and he turned out the division early in the morning. Few doubted that events were building to a climax on this day as Sherman's mighty host moved in to grapple with Johnston amid the marshes and tall pine woods. Joe Johnston was at bay, and everyone now knew that assembled with him for the impending *Götterdämmerung* were generals of such imperishable fame as Bragg, Hampton, Wheeler, A. P. Stewart, Robert F. Hoke, Harvey Hill—and the everlasting Hardee.

General Howard, who had risen bright and early, wanted his army's line extended considerably to the right. The 1st Division, its commander in the lead, started out at 8 A.M. for the heavily timbered countryside some five miles north of the Goldsboro road and beyond Giles Smith's front. Immediately behind Mower was the 18th Missouri, leading Fuller's brigade.

On its way into the wilderness, the column met General Blair and his staff, waiting beside the trail on horseback. Blair took great pains to show Mower where to form his new line. A little road led almost due north for nearly a mile along a small swamp-flanked creek, tributary to Mill Creek, the eastwardly course of which came within a mile of the north side of Bentonville. Between the creek and road, and facing almost due west, was the line on which Blair wanted the 1st Division to dig in and get ready for action. On the importance of securing the line by adequate breastworks, few admonitions had been necessary in Fuller's brigade since Snake Creek Gap.

"I suppose, General," Mower said finally, "after I get into position, there will be no objection to my making a little reconnaissance."

"None at all," Blair answered him, apparently oblivious to the inflammatory effect such words might have on a subordinate with Fighting Joe's impulses.

Pushing on up the road, Mower saw that it curved north-westward and crossed the little creek at a "ford." Some officers present (including Sheldon) called it a bridge, and the only way to reconcile the conflicting terminology is to speculate that a "low-water" masonry bridge spanned the creek in those days. The suitability of this crossing for a Rebel counterattack inspired Mower to post a strong guard north of it to keep intruders away "at all hazards." Colonel Minter got this job, and he soon arranged to dig in and stand guard over Mower's right flank with the help of Companies A, C, G, H, and K of the 18th Missouri.

Leaving Fuller to establish his new line, Mower galloped off to the rear to bring up Tillson and connect him with the left of First Brigade. Fuller, after sending the 64th Illinois out as skirmishers, dug in just west of the road, the 18th Missouri's remaining companies (under Sheldon) on his extreme right, the 27th Ohio in brigade center, and the 39th Ohio on the left. Before them all, said Sheldon, there stretched a "wide marsh."

It must have been two o'clock that afternoon before Tillson's line was ready and the rains had slackened sufficiently to encourage General Mower to start the reconnaissance he had been aching to try all day. At any rate, seeing his chance had come, Mower gave the command to advance, and, said Sheldon, "in we went. In our front the marsh was so deep and such a tangle of vines that all the mounted officers were speedily on foot, and the intrenching tools thrown away."

So thick did the underbrush and wood become on Fuller's front that Mower was soon forced to hold up Tillson's regiments to allow Fuller time to pass the swamp and recompose his part of the division's line of battle. Some time after 2:30, while Tillson was marking time, a new frustration confronted the 1st Division. The Rebels, Elias Perry complained, were "all the time shelling from the high ground on the opposite side of the swamp." The nervous Confederates on Johnston's left were evidently catching on to Mower's act, their skirmishers having brushed a time or two with the 64th Illinois at the swamp's edge.

Not long after 3 P.M. Fuller was through the worst of the bogs and ready for the next move. Mower hurriedly sent the orders up to double-quick across the open ground that sloped toward the top of a rise to the west. Together, Tillson's and Fuller's wildly cheering lines streamed across a jagged ravine and climbed toward the crest of the hill, terrifying Rebel cavalry and driving a handful of infantry from a line of rifle-pits on the slope. The men apprehended several bedraggled prisoners and one caisson full of artillery ammunition, which the Confederate gunners had had to abandon after the Illinois skirmishers killed two of their horses.

As the skirmishers passed down the other side of the hill heading for Johnston's headquarters, Old Joe and his staff broke for it and barely made their escape. It now fell to Hardee's lot to find the troops to fend off Mower. Bentonville itself and the Rebels' last bridge over Mill Creek were in jeopardy if the Yankees' main body should come rolling on down the hill. But as it was, Mower wasn't quite ready to press his advantage, and he halted his forces on the hill and dressed the line for a second charge. It was clear to Fighting Joe that his sudden eruption into the Confederate rear had opened up all sorts of glittering possibilities, and a member of his staff went galloping back to Blair with a plea to get all of Sherman's forces onto the attack everywhere along the line, to seal Johnston's doom.

"There could have been but one result," Sheldon felt, "providing Mower could hold his position. Johnston's army must either surrender, or lose all its artillery and stores, besides many prisoners, in a disorderly scramble to cross the almost impassable creek at other points than the bridge."

"Providing Mower could hold his position." There was the rub! But now the strapping Vermonter's luck began to desert him. Tillson stunned him with a message that Third Brigade's left was not yet in sight of Giles Smith's line! That had the makings of a bad situation, Mower realized, suddenly aware that "I had obliqued to the right in moving through the swamp.

. . ." He now got hold of Tillson and Fuller and told them to face about and oblique to the left, in a southwestwardly direction, to come into contact with the XVII Corps line. While this readjustment of the line was going on, a second dilemma faced Fighting Joe. Now it was the Confederates' turn to jolt him. First came a dash by Wheeler's horsemen against and around Tillson's left; before their thrust the 10th Illinois and 25th Indiana recoiled, threatening to unhinge the Third Brigade's line in so doing. Behind Wheeler came a two-battalion line of Confederate infantry, assailing Tillson's line perpendicularly. Around 4:15 Mower, perceiving Tillson's distress, sent to Fuller for the 39th Ohio, the nearest regiment in Fuller's outfit.

J. W. Fuller was in no mood to give up the 39th Ohio at this moment, for Hampton's cavalry was now approaching First Brigade's withdrawing right flank, manned by the 18th Missouri. Mower was for a few minutes unaware of Hampton's attack on Fuller, the roar of musketry in front of Tillson drowning out the noise from the right.

Sheldon's troops, backstopped by the 27th Ohio, seemed very likely to have their hands full. "Engaged the enemy and having no support was Compell to fall Back," said Rockwood bitterly. Fuller's entire line had to retreat down the hill, the Ohioans into the jagged ravine and the Missourians to the very fringes of the swamp. Tillson, meanwhile, was having a wretched time getting his line back into shape. His 32d Wisconsin and Fuller's 39th Ohio, standing shoulder-to-shoulder and then back-to-back, proved solid pivots on which the two brigadiers could retract the lines without their shattering.

As soon as Howard realized that Mower was in trouble, he sent orders up for Blair "to support him with his whole corps if necessary, and Logan to advance and seize the skirmish rifle-pits along his front." Mower by 4:45 had decided that Tillson should dig in along the old Confederate firing-line and that Fuller should pass across his rear to fill the gap between Mower and Giles Smith. Since Mower's right was still too closely engaged for such a movement, Sheldon tried to interest him in counterattacking Hampton's cavalry as well as Colonel R. J. Henderson's small brigade of infantry, about 300 strong, trotting along behind him. The only reply Sheldon could get from Mower "was profanely expressive of his utter contempt for the 'aforesaid cavalry.'"

In truth, the commander of the 1st Division was the very picture of a caged and frustrated lion. Glaring at Hampton's "roystering, cheering, and defiant" troopers, Mower shook his fist in the air, raised himself high in his stirrups, turned to his faithful Hemstreet and yelled: "God, man, wouldn't you like to wade in there with a saber!"

By five o'clock the Confederate threats to Fuller had fairly well evaporated. Sheldon was sure in 1891 that his troops remembered Hampton's charge and how the 64th Illinois handled it. "We certainly could not avoid laughing at the peculiar antics of some of the skirmishers as they jabbed the horses with their bayonets in the flanks, while the Confederate riders were slashing at them around the great pine trees."

After Hampton's disappearance into the woods to the north, there remained Colonel Henderson's infantry. This was a brigade in name only, containing the survivors of fifteen Georgia outfits. When Sheldon heard these Rebels described in the 1880's as a brigade, he doubted that had he known this in 1865 he could have "resisted the temptation to take them in with half a regiment." To Sheldon it was supremely waggish of Hampton to insinuate in 1887 that "this little squad could defeat Mower's Division. If that division had fired one volley at them, there wouldn't have been a man left."

Following Henderson's rapid disappearance in the direction which Hampton had taken, Fuller's skirmish line moved back to the top of the hill, followed by the brigade's disorganized battle-line. Mower sent up an aide with the word that the line should halt and re-form on the hill while the division staff brought up a fresh supply of ammunition. His double line was ready for the charge on Bentonville itself by 5:30, but at that moment there came an order direct from Sherman to bring Fuller back down that hill and put him in the gap between Smith and Tillson, as earlier contemplated.

In fact, Sherman had directed Frank Blair to call off the entire advance on the Confederate works. General Howard did not know of this order, though, until he saw Blair's retirement going on and started to scold him.

"The withdrawal is by *Sherman's* order!" said the righteously indignant Blair.

Not long before dark, Tillson's brigade moved behind Fuller and took up a position on his left once more. "It is a dark night," wrote an officer in Logan's corps, "a cold March rain is falling upon the tired soldiers. The chilling winds make mournful music through the branches of the tall pines." Sporadic picket-firing kept up until 3 A.M., but the Battle of Bentonville had gone into the books. This was the last battle of the 18th Missouri, but if any of the men suspected as much on the evening of March 21, 1865, evidence of this feeling has not come to light a century later.

The regiment had of course paid a price for its starring role at Bentonville. In bivouac that night, company commanders learned that Private Henry Talkins of Rockwood's Company D, killed in the afternoon's fighting, was the regiment's only fatality. Thus to the Hoosier-born Talkins who had enlisted at nineteen back at Laclede with the other originals of Company D went the sad distinction of being the last man of the 18th Missouri to be killed in action. His brief life had been an action-packed one, for he was also a member of that long blue line of prisoners at Shiloh. Private Amaziah Bacus of Company D was also hit, but he soon returned to duty. Two others were reported by Sheldon as wounded that tumultuous day, but their injuries were apparently not sufficiently serious to become matters of medical record, and their identities are probably forever secret.

The regiment also lost four prisoners, the most indignant being Company F's commanding officer, Joe Brown. This was his "second time around," for he, too, had been caught in the Hornets' Nest by Beauregard that terrible April evening in 1862. There was one consolation now for Brown as well as for Corporal Stains of I Company and Privates Thomas S. Cook of Company F and Milton F. Clawson of B—and this was the fact that they weren't likely to be in captivity very long. They were, in fact, to be free men inside a month.

Another distinction came to Lieutenant Brown that March 21. Among the nearly 200 casualties suffered at Bentonville by XVII Corps, Sherman reported no officers missing. Joe Brown, now a very special "statistic," could have straightened the General out on that item.[4]

Wednesday morning confirmed what many Federal officers suspected: Joe Johnston's men were nowhere to be found. The 18th Missouri, along with the rest of Mower's troops, now "fell in," said Elias Perry, "and marched out and found their works all evacuated and the Rebs all across the river." After a brief search along the Neuse, the division returned to camp at noon. Some of the pursuers hated to let Johnston get away so easily, but Sherman was frankly "content to let him go."

Meanwhile, Howard's forces were burying the dead and rounding up the wounded. Slocum's army was moving on toward Goldsboro, which had fallen to Schofield on the last day of the battle. Sherman rode into Goldsboro on Thursday, March 23, gratified to think that he had "brought the army from Savannah in good order. . . ."[5]

That same day, Howard's army took up the march for Goldsboro, and by sundown Friday his forces were also beyond the Neuse. The 18th Missouri went into camp seven miles east of Goldsboro at 5 P.M. on Friday, but its hopes for an early bedtime were shattered by orders to go out foraging. "We got some corn," Perry wrote, "and started back at 9 o'clock." At that, the Missourians were abed by midnight.

For more than two weeks the regiment stayed in its camp near Goldsboro. Here an accumulation of administrative details had to be looked after, and Sheldon soon found himself a busy officer. Some two dozen recruits caught up with the regiment now and were parceled out to Companies B, D, F, and H. Dan Carr's appointment as commissary sergeant was at last made official on March 25, dating from January 1, and four noncoms were made in Company K. Meanwhile, Lieutenant Rockwood was probably voicing the feelings of many who were deeply disgruntled at all of the "drilling appearing on dress parade going in inspection passing through reviews and so forth." With intransigent irony he wrote in his diary: "The authoritys think that all men are fools. But all men know they are fools."

It was also time to say goodbye to more of the old hands. Adjutant Godfrey, "for personal reasons," handed in his resignation on March 30. Since his father's death in 1862, only he had been available to "look after the welfare of my mother and sister. . . ." In spite of this personal concern back at Quincy, Godfrey might have been willing to stay a little longer if only he had not twice been denied captain's bars "without any reason therefor other than the gratification of personalities with the appointing power." Sheldon, ignoring this barb, let him go without a fuss. Four days later Colonel Minter quit also, specifying his head wound as the cause of his desire to shed the uniform and go back to Quincy. Mike Callery, still deep in Sheldon's bad graces, left the same day, April 3. Along with the eleven commissions Sheldon had asked for on January 16, there came a captaincy in Company K for Quartermaster Cudworth, "a tardy acknowledgment of his almost invaluable services," as Sheldon said. But Cud was eligible for muster-out now, and he did muster-out on March 26. Sergeant Major Riggen, whose second lieutenancy had come, took over as quartermaster. Abijah Everest, who had lately been doing most of the adjutant's work, stayed on at headquarters.

On March 26 all of the new officers and promotionees mustered into their new ranks. Bill Edgar rose to major, and command of K Company passed to Second Lieutenant John J. Abrigg, also newly appointed. There was one other new captain in the regiment, Henry Runnels of E. Second lieutenants made at this time included Phillip C. Lowry (I), James R. Wilson (F), and Charles Manda (K).

Colonel Sheldon was plainly miffed because Governor Fletcher "should have seen fit to over rule my recommendations in certain cases." Sheldon had asked in January that the major's commission go to Captain Donnelly, a thoroughly competent officer who ranked Edgar by fifteen months. Moreover, second lieutenancies asked for Dan Carr and First Sergeant Lewis Fitzpatrick of G Company had also been turned down by the Governor. All evidence of the reasoning that prompted Fletcher and Simpson to substitute their judgments for Sheldon's, totally missing from the personal files of these officers in Washington, must be presumed to have been destroyed in the Capitol fire of 1911 in Jefferson City, Missouri. "In the cases referred to, I was actuated only by a just regard for the best interests of the service," wrote Sheldon rather testily to Colonel Simpson on

March 28, "but as my recommendations do not appear to have any weight, I shall refrain from making them in the future."

However, the young colonel was not too furious to send along a fresh list of urgently needed promotions and call Simpson's attention to the fact that Surgeon Randolph had been serving the regiment alone all winter.[6]

Sherman now resurrected the Army of the Ohio, placing in it the X and XXIII Corps and giving command to Schofield. On April 3 the Missourians were horrified to learn that the high-level shuffling was going to cost them something, too, before it was done. Fighting Joe was going to leave the division—to command XX Corps in Slocum's Army of Georgia. It was quickly realized that Mower had richly merited the advancement, for he stood high in the esteem of the Army and would probably have risen to even higher command had the war gone through 1865. Before leaving, Mower graciously bestowed on Hemstreet a testimonial letter praising the latter's "great Efficiency, Coolness, and Bravery" and certifying his readiness for promotion to major or lieutenant colonel.

Blair now gave the 1st Division to Brigadier General Manning Ferguson Force, "bumped out" of the 3d Division by the return of General Leggett, who had been hospitalized since Pocotaligo. Force, a highly articulate officer, was a Harvard Law School graduate now in his forty-first year. He had commanded the 20th Ohio under Lew Wallace at Shiloh and later distinguished himself at Vicksburg. Despite serious wounds received on Bald Hill at Atlanta on that bloody July 22, 1864, Force had recovered to command one of Leggett's brigades in the march to Savannah and one of Blair's divisions in the Carolinas.[7]

As spring came on, Robert E. Lee's tenacious defenses of Richmond and Petersburg were weakening. At the end of March, U. S. Grant's forces struck, and the Army of Northern Virginia, its morale undermined by the apparent hopelessness of the situation and its ranks thinning with desertions, retreated into the interior of Virginia. Petersburg was given up on April 2, and Jeff Davis fled Richmond within forty-eight hours. The impression was naturally growing among Sherman's men in North Carolina that the war was about over for General Lee.

This was obviously not the time to leave Joe Johnston un-occupied. And on Monday, April 10, Sherman's three armies started for Raleigh, fifty miles to the northwest, the Army of the Tennessee comprising the Right Wing of the 90,000-man host moving on the Confederacy's last state capital. The days ahead were painless to Sheldon's regiment, so far as wounds were concerned, for the Rebels were staying well out of Sherman's way. There was some wading through "Swamps and Quag-mires," Rockwood said, but the march was tactically routine.

On the evening of April 12, as the 18th Missouri was going into bivouac a few miles north of Smithfield, there came the thrilling news that some Yankees in North Carolina had known all day. Lee had surrendered on April 9, at Appomattox, Vir-ginia. "The Union men went wild with joy," Henry Sawyer re-membered long afterward, "and threw their hats in the air and shouted." The anxieties and exertions of four long years of civil war were coming to an end.

Sheldon was never sorry that Sherman's armies missed the Appomattox ceremonies. It was to him just and proper that the Army of the Potomac should take Lee's surrender. It had wres-tled so long and so bravely with Robert E. Lee! The main Union Army in the East had suffered fearful losses, Sheldon pointed out, "principally because it had been slow to appreciate and as-similate the peculiar flanking methods of the Confederates, and perhaps partly owing to the large preponderance of regular offi-cers, who had been educated in the school of European military tactics, and who had much to unlearn before they made a suc-cess of the war. In our western army we learned these lessons sooner, and we also learned the folly of assaulting earthworks held by equal numbers."[8]

Federal troops nearing Raleigh on April 13 found the Rebels clearing out and concentrating around Durham Station, over twenty miles to the northwest. During the next day, Friday, Sherman's warriors tramped in long and impressive columns through the oak-lined streets of the Tarheel capital, near which Vice-President Johnson had been born fifty-seven years earlier. That evening the 18th Missouri camped about two miles west of the city.

Sheldon had the troops ready for the road at eight o'clock

on Saturday, but before they could move out an orderly rode by to report that Joe Johnston "had surrendered or would surrender." Rockwood declared this "joyful news." Sure enough, Johnston had proposed to Sherman that the opposition commanders now initiate "needful arrangements to terminate the existing war." For the time being, this news meant that the 18th Missouri could stay in camp awhile. In the long run, anybody could dream.

On Monday, April 17, Johnston and Sherman held an exploratory conference at the Bennett farm near Durham. Unknown to his soldiers until dark, Sherman had gone to the parley with a dreadful burden on his heart. As he was about to leave Raleigh, he had been handed a telegram revealing the assassination of President Lincoln three nights earlier. A deeply shocked Johnston was the first person Sherman told. That evening, on his return to Raleigh, Sherman issued his Special Field Orders 56, announcing "with pain and sorrow" the murder of Lincoln at the very culmination of his four-year struggle to preserve the Federal Union.

Sherman later shuddered rhetorically that "one single word by me would have laid [Raleigh] in ashes, and turned its whole population houseless upon the country. . . ." His fears were groundless, however, as his troops took to heart their commander's prudent admonition that the soldiers and civilians of the Confederacy were by and large above such acts of senseless terrorism.

The next day the talks at Bennett's farm ended in a provisional truce. Sherman, confident that he was perfectly representing Administration policy, forwarded to Washington a truce memorandum providing an armistice, disbanding of Rebel armed forces, storage of weapons in the custody of "state authorities," guarantees of property and political rights to all loyal citizens, amnesty for civil and military officials, and the recognition of "existing" state governments.

Within a week Sherman's magnanimous truce had triggered a violent political storm and placed him in a very bad light with the new President. The Cabinet, led by Secretary of War Stanton, reacted with a shrill hysteria that many writers have since been unable to excuse or understand. "At this time,"

Sheldon wrote in 1891, "it is almost incomprehensible to us that Secretary Stanton, the man of iron will, and usually correct judgment, would have suspected, much less charged, General Sherman with treasonable intent in negotiating this treaty. But so it was!"

Indeed, Stanton had gone so far as to publish in New York newspapers the story of the Administration's repudiation of the truce, along with his suspicions of Sherman's motives. General Halleck, now commanding Union troops in Virginia, on April 26 issued public orders that all of his troops entering North Carolina would ignore Sherman's orders. Not until April 28, however, did Sherman get wind of these vicious remarks.

Such behavior makes more sense when viewed in the official climate of that time in Washington. The fact is that the key men of the Federal government were now living in constant fear of more assassinations. They also sensed that at this perilous time when an untried and insecure new President was beginning his tenure and a great war was concluding with several idolized generals potentially available for political chores, our traditional civilian supremacy was in direct jeopardy. Stanton and others, moreover, were nurturing dark suspicions that General Sherman was the Democrats' hope for 1868, that he might even emerge as "the coming man of the Copperheads." Indeed, Sherman had never disguised his contempt for civilian politicians, and had lately gone so far as to express public preferences for "monarchical government."[9]

Grant appeared at Raleigh on April 24 with the bad news for Sherman. The disappointed general was somewhat annoyed at the fate of his diplomacy, but he was doubly affronted when he learned four days later of the studied insults thrown at him in public by Halleck and Stanton. It is doubtful if he ever forgot them, and neither of those gentlemen was to live long enough to regain his cordiality. For the moment, however, Sherman still had his war to fight, and he promptly gave Johnston the necessary forty-eight-hour notice.

That was most certainly the one thing Joe Johnston didn't want! Many of his disheartened subordinates had concluded, as one soldier put it, "that the dam fulishness uv tryin to lick Shurmin had better be stoped." The Confederate commander immediately appealed for more talks. On Tuesday morning Force's 1st Division moved some eight miles northwestward from Raleigh along the railroad toward Durham "for the purpose of threaten old Jo Johnston to bring him to terms of Surrender," as Rockwood explained it in his diary. The next day the end came, with the formal surrender of Johnston's remaining force of 37,000 at Durham Station.[10]

# The Brotherhood of Battle

WHAT A DIFFERENCE a year had made! The celebrating Missourians at Raleigh only needed to think of April, 1864, when, as Sherman was to remind them, "we were gathered about the cliffs of Lookout Mountain and all the future was wrapped in doubt and uncertainty."[1]

Orders now were for Sherman's armies to move up to Washington, where President Johnson would honor the victorious soldiery with a Grand Review. "From thence our destination was uncertain," Sheldon recalled. "Some said we would go to Mexico to expel the French, while others thought we were bound for the Red River to compel the surrender of Kirby Smith's command." Henry Sawyer's buddies told each other that the Army might go to the Rio Grande or campaign against the plains Indians, but they agreed that either venture was a squalid sequel to the coming festivities in Washington. Most dared to hope that the next stop, after all, might be home.[2]

Three days after General Johnston surrendered, Sherman's host started northward. April 30 being muster day, the boys lay in camp along the Neuse to collect their pay. Probably the happiest men that payday were three whose promotions had but lately come in from Governor Fletcher's desk. Lieutenant Jones of Company A mustered as the regiment's newest captain, and with him two first sergeants rose to second lieutenancies—John A. Marine of A and George W. Norvell of C.

Thereafter, the tramp of Federal boots resounded day after day through the verdant landscape of upper North Carolina and southern Virginia. Across the Roanoke streamed the long blue lines, past Brentsville to Virginia's famed Dinwiddie Court House, and finally they came to rest on May 9 at Manchester, on the south side of the James, opposite Richmond. Sheldon remembered how the warm weather and hard marching "greatly fatigued" his brawny Missourians. "But," said he, "the prospects of soon going home held up their spirits and very few found their way into the ambulances."[3]

While here, the men made ready to enjoy to the fullest Sherman's tit for tat with Henry Halleck. Old Brains had lived too long in the kind of society where one could cut a rival's official throat while maintaining cordial personal relations with him. And so it was that Halleck went through the motions of inviting Sherman to be his overnight guest and to stage a review at Halleck's headquarters. Sherman just would not play the game. He curtly declined either to visit Halleck or to permit the review. He added one final insult by suggesting that Halleck hide out while Sherman's troops were in the vicinity!

"At any rate," Sheldon gloated, Halleck stood on his portico on May 12 while "we marched by . . . at a right shoulder shift, and without saluting in any manner. . . ."[4]

Once again death overtook the 18th Missouri on its way northward across the famed battlefields between Richmond and the Potomac. At Hanover Court House Sergeant John A. Drake, of Hatfield's Company B, was felled by sunstroke on May 13. Dr. Randolph worked with him all that night, but Drake died next morning. A native of Illinois, the sergeant had joined the company back at Laclede in November of 1861 and had subsequently suffered light wounds on the memorable July 22 before Atlanta. Surviving him were two motherless boys, in Wayne County, Iowa, who would be reared to manhood by their maternal grandparents.

The regiment, in its colonel's words, "passed through Fredericksburg on May 16th, and pressed rapidly on to Washington. . . . We camped near Mount Vernon one night, and many of the officers and men visited the famous old mansion, then considerably out of repair, though it had been, in a manner, neutral ground. . . ." On Friday, May 19, the Missourians bivouacked at Alexandria to await the coming week's extravaganza.[5]

The next day General Howard learned that Logan was to lead the Army of the Tennessee in the Grand Review and command it until its disbandment. Though Howard was even now preparing to take charge of the Freedmen's Bureau, he had hoped to stay with the Army long enough to enjoy the coming spectacle. But, said Sherman, Black Jack had a political career to make, and it would "be everything to Logan to have this opportunity." After a few minutes of protesting, Howard conceded the point. His consolation prize was to ride with Sherman as the latter's "deputy" at the head of the entire review.

The 18th Missouri and its companions bivouacked on the grounds of the Capitol on the night of May 23, following the departure of General Meade's troops from the District that afternoon. All onlookers at the first day's Review agreed that the Easterners had put on a snappy exhibition—shiny equipment, new uniforms, rhythmic step, and straight lines. Could Sherman's boys do as well?

They weren't going to try. Despite some issues of clothing back in North Carolina, the troops were still by and large a ragged lot. While they could hardly put on a fashion show, Sherman was certain the admiring crowds would never see "a finer display of legs and arms. . . ." As one British historian later said, Washingtonians were going to witness "no glittering pageant, but instead an exhibition of virility" by the "most practically trained, physically fittest, and most actively intelligent army the world had seen."

At nine o'clock on the brilliant morning of May 24, 1865, a signal gun was heard. Bands began to play as General Sherman's horse trotted out onto Pennsylvania Avenue, bearing its fearsome master through the circle where Grant's equestrian statue now stands. The street was lined with throngs of uniformed and civilian spectators, casting flowers before Sherman's horse and cheering constantly. "We were followed closely by General Logan and the head of the Fifteenth Corps," Sherman wrote. "When I reached the Treasury building, and looked back, the sight was simply magnificent. The column was compact, and the glittering muskets looked like a solid mass of steel, moving with the regularity of a pendulum."

In front of the White House, Sherman dismounted and entered the reviewing stand; there he subjected Stanton to the famous cold shoulder, met Andrew Johnson, and took up his post on the President's left. From then until about four o'clock he stood there, "while the army passed in the order of the Fifteenth, Seventeenth, Twentieth, and Fourteenth Corps. It was, in my judgment, the most magnificent army in existence—sixty-five thousand men, in splendid physique, who had just completed a march of nearly two thousand miles in a hostile country. . . ."

Of his Missourians, Sheldon always thought that they "had never marched better than they did that day, and the only regret in my mind was that all the old veterans, who had been with us during the dark days of the war, could not have been with us then, to enjoy this great ovation." To be sure, many of them had perished in battle or returned home. But on this gay Wednesday there were still in the 18th Missouri those who had seen the despair and the glory of four bloody years. Lance Beary, now a sergeant of Company B, was one of them. There were also Lieutenant Joe Stanley of C, Rockwood of D, Sergeant Grabosch of E, First Sergeant Cawood of G, First Sergeant Guffey of I, and many another whose memory went back to Chewalla, Shiloh, Weston, and the star-crossed Colonel Morgan.[6]

In midafternoon the 18th Missouri camped by the Piney Branch of Rock Creek, near 14th Street and the Silver Springs home of Montgomery Blair, older brother of the corps commander. Now came the inevitable climax. The parade was over and the cheers were dying away. What next? Sheldon learned that his command would be sent to Louisville, Kentucky, in all likelihood to be mustered-out of service. After all, the troops were getting ready to give the 35th New Jersey a send-off at the railroad station. If the Army was turning the Zoos out, it wouldn't keep the rest of Force's division in uniform, would it?

Sheldon's housekeeping chores were multiplying. Discipline was getting to be a major problem. Now that Confederate muskets were stacked, the boys saw no more point in spit-and-polish or sticking to camp, and things moved perilously close to getting out of hand. The young colonel cracked down hard, though, on officers as well as enlisted men. He even arrested Captain Jones briefly and gave Lieutenant Rockwood a tour of extra duty, besides arresting several enlisted men for unauthorized absences and "back-talk."

General Fuller took leave of the brigade while it was still on Piney Branch. Before he left, however, he graciously wrote Frank Blair a letter heartily recommending Sheldon for a regular commission at field rank in any of the combat arms.[7]

In early June, Force's division received orders to move to Louisville. Baltimore & Ohio passenger trains collected at the Washington Station, and the trip to Kentucky began on June 5. Within three days the division had concentrated at Parkersburg, West Virginia, where it took river steamers on the Ohio. "On our way down the river," Sheldon remembered, "we passed the homes of many of the members of the 27th and 39th Ohio, and some of them, in their anxiety to greet their families, jumped from the moving boat and swam ashore!" Not so fortunate was Private John W. McCarty of Lieutenant Manda's Company K, who sleepwalked off the *Ella Faber* into the swirling Ohio just a few miles out of Louisville. The regiment never saw the young Platte Countian again, and military authorities thereafter presumed him dead.[8]

Sheldon's troops went ashore at Louisville on June 10, but much to his disgust he had to lodge them in "a very undesirable camp, in a low marshy woods" some two or three miles southwest of town. Here they sat for nearly two weeks, before Sheldon was called up to command the brigade and thus had a little influence in choosing campsites. The 18th Missouri then packed up and moved from the swamp to "a fine position on the Turnpike" at the Prather farm.

While at the swamp the regiment played host to Governor Fletcher and Colonel Elwood Miller. Fletcher, having with him the Great Seal of Missouri, was ready to do all the business Sheldon wanted done. Twenty-six commissions showered down on the regiment during his working visit. Bill Edgar stepped into the lieutenant colonelcy vacated lately by Minter, notwithstanding the latter's direct appeal to Fletcher to give it to

Bill Hemstreet. Minter should have saved his stationery, for Elwood's uncle had a long memory.

But Ed Donnelly at last got his major's oak leaves, and that pleased Sheldon no end. Captaincies went to Hatfield, Stanley, Rockwood, Brantner, Mansfield, and Everest. Eight former second lieutenants now pinned on their gold bars: Marine, Riggen, Richardson, Norvell, Lowry, Manda, Abrigg, and Haynes. These promotions created vacancies for second lieutenant in all companies, and the Governor awarded commissions to ten sergeants: Samuel Frankfort (A), Robert Boyles (B), Vincent Bruce (C), William Scurlock (D), Charles Grabosch (E), Elias Perry (F), Lewis Fitzpatrick (G), Dan Carr (H), Ben Guffey (I), and John Milton Smith (K). Of these, Frankfort and Perry were prisoners at Shiloh, and nine were original members of the regiment. Smith, a young carpenter from Monroe County, Illinois, had enlisted in October of 1862.

Life in the swamp was very much a burden, but twenty-six officers and forty-four new sergeants and corporals always remembered the Governor's visit as a high old time.[9]

Colonel Sheldon's bookwork had become a serious problem in two ways: It caused a staggering load of office work and this in turn led to a delay in muster-out that created fresh discipline problems. Upon his arrival at Louisville, Sheldon had learned of the War Department's requirement that "no regiment should be mustered-out without turning over to the Government a full set of 'Company Books.' As ours had been lost at Shiloh, it became necessary to manufacture a new set to cover that time—a task of considerable magnitude."

As soon as Fletcher left camp, Colonel Edgar convened a special court-martial to attend to the accumulating cases. Private John W. Wallace of Company B drew a ten-dollar fine for jumping ship at Pomeroy, Ohio, "after being twice halted by the Sergeant of the Guard." Private John B. Priester of E lost a month's pay for abandoning fatigue duty to "return to his Qrs. and wilfully refuse to return to duty."

Somewhat more serious was a squabble that had erupted between Hemstreet, division provost marshal, and Captain Mansfield. Once the regiment had encamped in the swamp, Hemstreet started proceedings against Mansfield of Company

H, proceedings that resulted in his arrest on June 20. While commanding the divisional provost guards on the boat to Louisville, Mansfield had permitted prisoners "to escape on two occasions," Hemstreet charged. Moreover, the provost marshal was frothing over Mansfield's "repeated failures to prefer charges" against certain offenders. The case was tried in July, and although Mansfield was cleared of permitting the escapes he was adjudged guilty of laxity in preferring charges. For this, the court took a month's pay and lined him up for a chewing-out by an expert, General Force.

By this time, the division commander's temper was aroused anyhow. On June 21 a mob of idle soldiery had ransacked a purveying store on the Post. Force, outraged, set Hemstreet to ferreting out the ringleaders and their accomplices, and for about a week the provost marshal gave the matter most of his attention. Unfortunately, it proved impossible to build a decent case against anyone, and the upshot of the affair was Force's decision to levy an assessment of $700 on the entire division. The brunt of the charges fell on the 27th and 39th Ohio, but Force estimated the 18th Missouri's share in the skulduggery at $40, collectible at final muster.[10]

Captain Fallis, assisted by Boyles and Scurlock, constituted a special court-martial a week after the move to Prather's farm was completed, June 29. Within a week Fallis disposed of a dozen cases involving mostly overnight AWOL incidents in which small fines and "Extra Duties" were levied. Private James Hagerty of Company E drew a fine of $15 and "detention until mustered out" for allowing beer sales in barracks while he was on guard duty. It might not have gone so hard with Hagerty had he not used "unbecoming language" to the Officer of the Day when that dignitary discovered the infraction.

A Canadian-born lad in Company I gave the men a lot more to chuckle over late on the afternoon of July 6. Since the regiment was turning out for dress parade, Lieutenant Lowry was naturally anxious for his I Company boys to make a good showing. At the last moment, he sent Sergeant James A. Winger and a mop-up squad through the barracks to get the laggards out into line. One soldier was still at his bunk, oblivious to the hustle and bustle outdoors.

"Out of barracks and into the ranks!" Winger barked.

"Kiss my ass, Winger!" the delinquent roared. "And tell Lowry to do the same! I'll be damned if I'm going on parade one more time!" The startled Winger drew up short, and then he ordered Private Pat Hughes to haul the offender bodily out on to the parade-ground. Hughes immediately found himself staring at the business end of a sixteen-shot Henry repeater. Winger and Hughes later swore that the man had threatened to kill anyone who touched him.

The rifleman's luck ran out after a few anxious moments. Captain Fallis stalked into the room. Without a moment's hesitation, fearless Little Dick seized the weapon and wrenched it from the startled soldier's grasp. It took Force and Hemstreet less than five days to convict the hapless fellow on a half-dozen counts that took away his pay and discharged him from the service dishonorably. General Force, reviewing the case, lamented that "some punishment could not be found more adequate to the offence." He evidently wanted a harsher sentence, for he confirmed the court's verdict as it stood.[11]

Meanwhile, preparations for final muster were going ahead. On July 4 General Sherman came by for an emotion-tinged final visit to his "old outfit." He made a brief speech to each brigade. The survivors of Fuller's old Ohio Brigade, now under Sheldon, "formed a hollow square in a stubble field" to hear the General's parting words. That was the last glimpse that most of them would ever have of the fierce Ohioan whose legend they had helped to create in the "dews and damps" of Georgia and the Carolinas.

With the companies pretty well shaped up, Sheldon organized his headquarters for the impending last muster. Sergeant Henry Adams was lifted from Company C and made the last sergeant major of the regiment. Henry Wells went to the end as quartermaster sergeant. Lieutenant Riggen went back to Company B on June 19, and Lieutenant Norvell succeeded him as regimental quartermaster. Abijah Everest continued as adjutant, even though K Company's roll bore him as its captain.[12]

The company books completed, equipment returns signed, and the last promotions given, Muster-Out was finally set for

July 18. On that happy Tuesday, the inspections were carried out and the last payroll compiled. As young Colonel Charles S. Sheldon, lately raised to brevet brigadier general, surveyed the ranks of his veteran regiment, he could see that thirty-one of the prisoners of Shiloh were still with him, including Lieutenants Haynes and Perry, Sergeants Cawood and Darius Tarble, and Corporals John Wagle and William Garringer of G and D Companies. Sixteen men wounded at the Bull Run of the West were still in line, among them Captain Runnels of E, Captain Fallis and Lieutenant Richardson of I, Sergeant James T. Riley of C, and Corporal James Knox of G. Moreover, of the nearly 900 men that Colonel Morgan had collected back in 1861, there were yet 187 in the ranks. And 245 of the 700 men now mustering-out had faced the Rebels at Shiloh on that bloody Sunday morning three years before.

Since that memorable summer when the 18th Missouri had been only an ambitious gleam in Colonel Morgan's eyes, 1,556 men had at one time or another cast their lots with the regiment. A study of the cumulative roster at Louisville would have revealed that the sociological makeup of the outfit had changed remarkably little in four years of war. True, the percentage of foreign-born members had risen from ten to twenty-three during that time. But, on the other hand, the proportion of Ohio Valley natives (over 45 per cent in 1862) had remained static. The appreciable decline in the overall "native" character of the unit was somewhat counterbalanced by the slight rise, from 13 to 15 per cent, of native Missourians in the ranks.

More than a third of the men who joined the 18th Missouri had sooner or later either been wounded or captured or had died from diseases, accidents, or battle wounds. While 77 had died from battle causes and 8 had lost their lives in mishaps of various kinds, 192 had succumbed to diseases. 104 had suffered non-fatal wounds verifiable from surviving records, and 198 others had sampled Confederate prison accommodations ranging from the creek-bottom where Jim Coddington had been detained to the gloomy old "Libby Hell" that Charles Grabosch and Dan Shelton never forgot. During the nearly four years of the regiment's life, 210 men had been given disability discharges for causes varying from Jimmy Morgan's extreme youth to Alexander McCloud's advanced years. Another 103 men, amounting to over 6 per cent of the total, had either deserted or been dropped from the rolls for failure to rejoin their companies in good time.

With Sheldon and Everest holding their discharges and money, the men sailed for home that afternoon on the *Edinburgh*. Four days later, on Saturday morning, July 22, they docked in St. Louis, greeted by Mayor James S. Thomas and a demonstrative welcoming crowd. Many personal friends, including some former members of the regiment, were on hand to cheer the returning heroes as Frank Boehm's Silver Cornet Band provided the music. It had been one year to the day since that furious afternoon when the 18th Missouri helped Fuller's brigade to thwart Hood's counterattack from the woods southeast of Atlanta.

After forming up at the dock, Sheldon's men moved out at a rapid pace behind the band. Their route, which took them up the principal streets of downtown St. Louis, ran past the headquarters of the Department of the Missouri. Halting his troops there, Sheldon led them in three rousing cheers for General Dodge.

Responding to the cheers in the street, Dodge stepped out to address the men:

> Soldiers: You and I are not strangers. Two years' service upon battle-fields, I trust, has made us fast friends. You no doubt all remember well, as the anniversary rolls around, the well-fought battles in front of Atlanta, in which you took a prominent part. I thank you all for the hearty support you have always given me; and I hope you will now return to your homes and be as good citizens as you have been true and brave soldiers, and that there you will meet the hearty welcome of your friends.

This, said a local reporter, "called out three more cheers, heartier than the first. . . ." General Sprague then appeared, to the accompaniment of more cheers, and made a speech in the same tenor as Dodge's. After this the regiment marched on to the Mayor's residence, where His Honor favored them with a lengthy but patriotic harangue. The last stop before Benton

Barracks was Uhrig's Cave, where, a newsman noted, "a liberal supply of lager beer was distributed to the men, and many old friends crowded around to shake them by the hand."

In one last formation the following Monday morning, Brevet Brigadier General Sheldon gave out the money and discharges. Colonel Edgar, for his part, made a brief address to the men in which he sentimentally reminded them that many of their old comrades "lie buried from the confines of Missouri down to the sea, sacrificed on the altar of liberty and Union. Cherish them in your memories." Sheldon then bade his beloved Missourians a fond farewell, advising them to "let the dead past bury the dead."

They would not, nor would he. "We little thought," admitted Sheldon a generation later, "as we separated on that bright and beautiful morning, that many of us would ever meet again, and I am sure very few of them recognized the strength of the ties that four years of service had knit! We all now feel, however, that no ties, save those of home and family, are stronger than the brotherhood of battle."[13]

# The 18th Missouri
# After the War

Most of the veterans of the 18th Missouri returned to homes in northern Missouri, Platte County, or the greater St. Louis area after mustering-out. A few remained in uniform, but very few. Major Donnelly went into the Regular Army as an enlisted man and died in the service. Ken Breeman returned to the Army as a private under another name in 1868, and after a couple of hitches he dropped out, married in 1878, and died in an asylum in Iowa two years later. Peter Dolman raised a Home Guard company in Chariton County in the winter of 1864-1865 and commanded it until the end of the war. After the war John Abrigg headed the Brunswick State Guard, a militia unit, until 1878, when it was disbanded. The most successful military career was that of former Adjutant Conway, who had left the 18th Missouri in the spring of 1863. Retiring in 1870 as a first lieutenant, after eighteen years of service, the hardy Irishman lived to the ripe age of eighty-five. At the time of his death in West Philadelphia, Pennsylvania, in 1915, he was a major on the retired list.[1]

Since the Mississippi Valley area stood on the eve of its agricultural heyday, few readers need to be told that a majority of Sheldon's men went into farming in 1865. Most of them stayed in Missouri, and most of the Missourians stayed in Putnam County—ever afterward the "heartland" of 18th Missouri alumni activities. There Dan Shelton farmed at the east edge of Unionville, raising five youngsters in the course of a long and fruitful life that ended in 1907. Lance Beary and his brother-in-law, Peter Bucher, returned home from Company B with the Pollocks to farm around St. John, and both of them lived to the early years of the next century. When Henry Wells died at Lucerne in 1913, he had farmed nearly a half-century in the southwestern part of Putnam. Operating the Fair View Farm was J. B. Martin of Company D, who specialized in Shorthorn cattle and Shropshire sheep. The old bugler of Company D, Charles Rex, farmed near Unionville to support a family that in time grew to include sixteen children.[2]

Sullivan County farmers from the regiment included Lawrence Hoover, Henry Runnels, and William Carter Green. All three farmed in the northern part of the county, and they all died in Green City. The last of them to "muster-out" was Carter Green, who died on July 22, 1928, the sixty-fourth anniversary of Atlanta. A grandson said of Hoover that "He seemed to think things had to be done on the run." As the proud owner of one of the first mowing machines in the county, the energetic Hoover experimented somewhat unwisely by speeding his team up to a trot. Something broke, as luck would have it, and Hoover was soon petulantly explaining to a blacksmith that he couldn't see "vie it had to broke. I vas jest driving in a little shig of a trot." Living at high velocity, the chunky little German had become a prototype of the modern American.[3]

Captain John Lomax, finishing the war as Provost Marshal of North Alabama, returned to Linn County to farm north of Laclede. Colonel Pratt was also there, struggling to hold together the agricultural properties that he had purchased in 1860. It proved too much for his financial resources, however, and in the course of the 1870's he lost his estate and was left to die a poor man. At the time of his death in 1893, the onetime Brigadier General of the Missouri State Militia was a night-watchman for the Federal government in Washington. Ezra Havens, after serving as a captain in the Mississippi Marine Brigade and a sergeant in the 9th U.S. Volunteers, returned to farm for a time in the northern section of Linn County, near Browning. John R. McEfee tried farming in Kansas, but in the wretched later seventies he returned to Linn County to stay. A former corporal in Company C, Quincy Bruce, returned home with his brother, Lieutenant Vincent Bruce, to farm north of Laclede.[4]

The men were less numerous in other counties of Missouri. In Chariton County there was the first sergeant of Company H, Joseph Gross, who farmed east of Brunswick and was so successful with his orchards that he was widely regarded as "one of the best posted fruit men" in the county. He was nearly eighty-six when he died in 1929. Elias Perry died in 1926 at the age of eighty-nine. For six decades he had been a prominent and respected farmer in Carroll County, living just west of DeWitt. Farming in Grundy County were Henry Sawyer and his original company commander, William P. Sherman. Over in Schuyler County there lived Elias Johnson, the only man to survive the wounds suffered by Company D that dark October night in Snake Creek Gap. Former Lieutenant Sam Frankfort, residing on a farm near Novinger, in Adair County, lived to be ninety-five. Out in Platte County lived several others, including John R. Clements of Company G and Henry S. Cochran of K.[5]

In tune with the times, many of the men also moved out of the state to try their fortunes. Captain Wyckoff farmed many prosperous years in beautiful Appanoose County, Iowa, where he died in 1925. Captain Havens moved to northwestern Arkansas, dying at Fort Smith at the age of ninety-one, in 1918. Ike Shipley farmed in southeastern Kansas for nearly forty years prior to his death in 1932. Captain Rockwood, after persuading his father and two brothers to homestead with him in Kansas, on Indian Creek between New Albany and Fall River, died there some time in the early 1870's. All attempts to locate the grave or relatives who knew the circumstances of his death have proved fruitless. Sergeant Cawood buried his first wife shortly after his return home, and soon resolved to put the scenes of his bereavement behind him. With a second wife, who bore him four daughters, he moved to the vicinity of Miller, South Dakota; when death came to him in 1911, he was seventy-four years old. Company C's original first sergeant, Thomas McComb, died of cancer in June of 1876 at his farm home near Bonaparte, Iowa.[6]

Some found opportunities in the rising towns and cities of the West. Mikesell was a successful meat-packer at Quincy,

Illinois, and Sheldon eventually started his own packing-house at Caldwell, Ohio, after a number of years as a commission-merchant in St. Louis and in Muscatine, Iowa. James N. Wilson, late sergeant of Company A, opened a store in Laclede right after the war, and John Lomax did the same there at the turn of the seventies. Jeff Rummell set up his general store at Brookfield and remained a leading merchant there until death claimed him in 1901. D. W. Pollock had an interest in several stores in Putnam County, and Chaplain Garner had his own little neighborhood grocery in Springfield. Cudworth was a cashier at Brookfield until the 1880's, and Lawrence Hoover owned an interest in the Green City Bank at the time of his death in 1913. D. W. Pollock was a founder and was president for many years of the Unionville National Bank. Pollock's remarkable career, which included promotion of the Milwaukee Railroad through Putnam County and the piling up of a handsome fortune in cattle-buying and shipping, inspired a local journalist to acclaim him "a hustler from away back." At his death in 1910, he owned 2,765 acres in farm properties.[7]

Real estate ventures interested several of the men. For example, Madison Miller grew wealthy from real-estate dealing and contracting in the St. Louis area. Former Sergeant Major Schaap moved out of Platte County to engage in real-estate work at Atchison, Kansas. Because he had escaped from local Confederates trying to impress him into the army in 1861, Schaap felt reasonably certain that he would never be safe after dark in Platte County. D. A. Cudworth, on reaching St. Paul, Minnesota, in 1887, bought an interest in the company developing the St. Anthony Park addition to that city.

Erstwhile Quartermaster Sergeant Kuemmel went back to St. Louis as a watchmaker, and Robert Benecke became a manufacturer of photographic equipment there. First Sergeant Kurtz, who lost his arm before Atlanta, was a stationer at Weston and Kansas City until his death near the end of the century.[8]

Others followed the professions. Chaplain Garner continued for a time to serve churches in northern and western Missouri, and Merritt Young preached in southern Iowa. Colonel Edgar practiced law in St. Louis to his death in 1895, and Harry Lander was a Brookfield attorney until he died in

1903. Dan Carr went to Kansas to become a pioneer lawyer in Elk County. Louis Benecke was Brunswick's leading barrister for many years prior to his death in 1919, and he put his considerable talents to many worthwhile purposes, particularly in securing pensions for the many old comrades of the 18th and 49th Missouri Volunteers who lacked the ability to fight their own battles with the Pension Bureau. James A. Price became a leading dentist in northwestern Missouri, and rose to treasurer of the State Dental Association in the 1890's. Captain Bell practiced medicine in Wichita, Kansas, until his death in 1876. Lieutenant Stille, after resigning in 1863, resumed work as a physician in Unionville, and Dr. Houts went back to his civilian patients in St. Louis. Norman Hamlin and Richard Endicott, the latter of K Company, became doctors in California, while Lieutenant Douglas went on to eminence as a New York surgeon. Oliver Denslow, discharged in 1863, practiced medicine at various places in northern Missouri and eastern Kansas until his death in 1904 at Bonner Springs, Kansas. Dr. Randolph took up his old practice in Norwalk, Ohio.

The country doctor *par excellence*, however, was Ben Guffey. Establishing himself first in eastern Putnam County, he eventually moved to Novinger and struck it rich caring for the growing mining community in Adair County. "My father was a very jolly person and was well liked by everyone," a daughter told the present writer, "and I can remember his response to calls day or night." Wrote a journalist of him: "He practically kept his horse saddled and his saddle pockets filled, for in those days a physician carried a small drugstore with him on all his trips." When Ben died in 1924, hundreds flocked to LaPlata from distant places to "pay a last tribute of love to their doctor, friend, and counselor."[9]

The old soldiers found it frequently possible to combine their regular work with public service. Three made their way into the Missouri Senate at one time or another. When the war ended, Miller and Pratt were holding seats, with Miller privileged to board at the Governor's Mansion when the General Assembly was in session. While Pratt was serving quietly as Chairman of the Committee on the State University, Miller stirred up a hornets' nest by introducing "An act to make

346 | THE EIGHTEENTH MISSOURI

treason odious," which provided a heavy fine for anyone convicted of failing to address former Confederate officials by the
title of "Rebel." This vindictive measure died in the Judiciary
Committee, but not before "conservatives" from the Mississippi
to the Bronx had developed severe palpitations.

By the close of the wartime decade, both Miller and Pratt
had gone into political eclipses from which they were never to
emerge. In 1870 Pratt was beaten in the Radical convention in
an attempt at election to Congress, and his backers believed ever
afterward that had he been willing to bolt to the Liberal Republicans he surely would have gone to Washington. In January of
1875 he sought election to the Constitutional Convention. While
losing Linn, Chariton, and Sullivan counties, he carried faithful
old Putnam by a 2-1 majority. Putnam could not save the old
Radical warhorse this time, as it had in 1863, and with his final
rebuff he retired from the political stage. Miller never sought
elective office again after retiring from his term in the Senate.

In the 1870 elections, Louis Benecke won a seat in the
Senate. He stayed one term and dropped out in 1874 to attend
to his growing law practice and other public-spirited activities
closer to Brunswick. Using his own funds, Benecke built, staffed,
and prescribed the curriculum for the first school established
in Brunswick for freedmen's children. After the Federal Soldiers' Home went into operation at St. James, Governor Lon V.
Stephens in 1897 appointed Benecke to the Board of Trustees,
of which he became president for a four-year term. In 1909
Governor Herbert S. Hadley named him to a second term.[10]

The lower house of the General Assembly twice contained
veterans of the 18th Missouri. Peter Dolman was elected from
Chariton County in 1870 and served one term prior to moving
to Montana, where in 1889 he became a member of that new
state's first Senate. Later, in 1888, Linn County sent up Harry
Lander as its representative. The other legislator in the ranks
of the regiment was Captain Wyckoff, who served in the Iowa
House during the nineties.[11]

At the county level were many more survivors of the 18th
Missouri. Wagonmaster Pollock won the post of Presiding Judge
in Putnam County at the 1866 elections, and he held that office
through 1872. This county, thanks to the 18th Missouri, became

in the 1860's the most intransigently Republican section of the state. Until the middle of the following century, to be a Democrat was to be thought an oddity, to be a Democratic *office-holder* a distinct improbability. In the 1890's Charles Cassady, formerly of I Company, served as a judge, representing eastern Putnam. Captain Stanley was a two-term Sheriff of Sullivan County in the late sixties, while Charles Grabosch and John H. Morgan were deputies in Putnam at various times.

Out in Kansas two more of the men parlayed their war records into political preferments. In 1878 "Honest Dan" Carr, then a Howard lawyer, swept into office as County Attorney on an all-victorious Greenbacker slate. In the 1890's Archibald Abel, once of K Company, "served two terms in a very proficient manner" as Treasurer of Jackson County, north of Topeka.

Other county offices held by the men included court clerkships for John R. McEfee in Linn County and Bill Hemstreet in Brooklyn, New York. Joe Stille was the first Public Administrator of Putnam County, taking office in 1867, a year before his untimely death.[12]

Some held various posts at the city and township level. Mikesell served as Mayor of Quincy, Illinois, for three years in the early 1890's, following six years as a councilman. Benecke was Mayor of Brunswick before and after his years in the State Senate, and he was a longtime president of the school board there. Another mayor from the 18th Missouri was James A. Price. At the close of the war he was a colonel, having raised the 39th Missouri following his resignation down in Mississippi. After two unsuccessful races for sheriff, he won election as Mayor of Weston in 1869, holding the job intermittently until 1882. He had learned what Clements would discover in 1888: In Platte County the conservative and Secessionist voters were quite powerful and in no hurry to forgive prominent Unionists of the sixties, such as Clements, Price, or Schaap.[13]

At least five veterans of the 18th Missouri were city councilmen: Ault and Stille (Unionville), Mikesell (Quincy), Sheldon (Caldwell, Ohio), and Dolman (Butte, Montana). Among the postmasters were Bill Brantner (Kiddville and Greencastle), Price (Weston), and Milt Hudson (Hale). Major Williams was many years a Justice of the Peace at Laclede, as were Brantner at Trenton and Joe Anderson at Weston. George W. A. Preston, the same who had borne the colors of Company E to safety from the field of Shiloh, acted as a Justice of the Peace in Sullivan County until his death in 1898. Captain Wyckoff put in many years as chairman or member of a board of township supervisors near Cincinnati, Iowa. D. A. Cudworth was a member of the St. Paul Water Board until his death in 1924, at the age of 88 years.[14]

No less important was the work of railroad-promotion in postwar Missouri. D. W. Pollock's success in getting a branch of the Chicago, Milwaukee, St. Paul and Pacific built through Putnam County from Chillicothe, Missouri, to Ottumwa, Iowa, was one example. Louis Benecke used his powers of persuasion to see that the Wabash Line served Brunswick. Another type of rail-promotion, for which Madison Miller had a special aptitude, was that of fund commissioner for the Pacific Railroad, under construction between St. Louis and Kansas City. Shortly after the war, Governor Fletcher appointed his distinguished brother-in-law to reorganize and discharge the company's debt to the state.[15]

The 18th Missouri was represented to some degree in all of the major veterans' organizations. Miller, Sheldon, and Godfrey were for years members of the Society of the Army of the Tennessee, an organization of officers who had served in that army. Miller, in fact, was a vice-president of the Society in 1893. All three attended the 1873 reunion in Toledo, when the membership present "drank standing and in silence" the "Toast to the Memory of McPherson," facing the vacant chair reserved at the head of the banquet table for the fallen hero.[16]

Claiming the attention of a far greater number of the regiment's veterans was the Grand Army of the Republic. By the heyday of the G. A. R., in the 1890's, eight posts in Missouri had been named for nine men of the 18th Missouri. Captain Charles W. Mansfield having died and been buried beside his brother William in 1866, the old soldiers named their Wyreka Post for them both. Among its commanders were D. W. Pollock and John Howry. Elwood Miller died of cancer at his father's home on St. Louis' Lay Avenue in 1889. Soon there flourished in South St. Louis an Elwood Miller Post of the Grand Army, and the sorrowing General Miller appropriately commanded it himself until his own death in 1896. The men in eastern Sullivan established a post at Sticklerville and named it for Johnson Downen, whom the boys of E Company had buried at Chewalla. Veterans at Martinstown, in Putnam, founded a post named in honor of Sergeant Virgil Rogers of Company D, who had died at the Marietta hospital in the summer of 1864. Captain Rockwood's name was given to the post at Lemons, in southern Putnam; Charles Grabosch commanded it for one term and was for years its adjutant. The Thomas G. Wade Post at Unionville was named for one of the men lost in the Snake Creek Gap reconnaissance of October, 1864. Henry S. Wells and his comrades around Lucerne organized a George E. Wells Post for the lamented brother who had succumbed to disease at Chewalla in 1863. Carter Green, Henry Runnels, and others established a Jacob L. Clark Post at Green City, honoring the fallen leader of E Company, who is buried in St. Louis.[17]

Some of the "old boys" attained considerable prominence in the G. A. R. Benecke rose to command the Department of Missouri in 1894, and Dolman headed the Montana Department the following year. Sheldon was the first "Officer of the Day" of the Noble Post at Caldwell, and Cudworth held several positions in the Rawlins Post in the Twin Cities. A very special kind of glory came to Joe Anderson at the 1905 Encampment of the national G. A. R. in Denver. A place was reserved in the parade for survivors of Shiloh, and he proudly took his place among the men of that thinning band. He died the following winter at Weston.[18]

The Military Order of the Loyal Legion, an organization for Union officers which was founded in the wake of Lincoln's assassination, drew a small representation from the 18th Missouri. Particularly active in the Legion were Benecke, Hamlin, and Madison Miller. In addition, Cudworth on one occasion headed the Order's Minnesota Commandery. In his last years, according to a relative, the old soldier experienced "difficulty in getting around, sort of a palsy—but he was never so helpless that he could not get to the dinners and meetings of the Loyal Legion. How he loved those meetings and 'the boys'!"[19]

Many of the old veterans became confirmed "joiners," and

were frequently active in fraternal orders. The Masonic and Odd Fellows lodges claimed most of the men in this category. Especially active in Masonic affairs were John Lomax and William P. Sherman. The latter, for several years just prior to his death in 1873, was secretary of the lodge at Lindley. James A. Price held several state offices in both the Masons and the Odd Fellows. Lawrence Hoover and Johnathan Yates were Masons for many years, as was also the original bugler of Company H, Morris Schnapp. Prominent Odd Fellows were D. W. Pollock, Bill Brantner, Joe Anderson, Jake Ault, Henry Sawyer, and Milt Hudson.[20]

It would hardly surprise the modern reader to learn that the men as a rule expressed themselves politically through Republican activities. Even after Pratt's final defeat, he continued to nurture "very decided ideas of his own," as one writer said, "which he did not hesitate to express plainly and pointedly, and like all positive men he made both warm friends and bitter enemies." Louis Benecke, on the other hand, was never defeated. On several occasions he was a delegate from Missouri to Republican national conventions, including the two that nominated William McKinley.

The political nerve center of the 18th Missouri was Putnam County. There, in 1868, when local veterans organized to get behind the Radical Republican state ticket, men of the 18th were the head and body of the movement. Presiding over the caucus was Judge Pollock, with his son David providing his share of booming oratory. Lance Beary, who had married the Judge's daughter Isabella, was also on the scene to help. Judge Bill Neighbours, Charles Rex, John Centers, and Joseph Stille were also in Radical harness as precinct delegates.

William Garringer, late corporal of Company D, made another kind of political noise. To celebrate McKinley's first inauguration, Garringer rigged up a wooden cannon by boring out a log, around which he wrapped baling wire for reinforcement. He loaded his weapon with gunpowder, put it outside the fence around his yard in eastern Putnam, and lit the fuse. The contraption flew to pieces in a great explosion of smoke and flame. Several yards of the fence crumpled up in the holocaust, and neighbors came running from all directions, sure that the Garringer house was burning.[21]

"Old soldiers love as no other class of men can love," said Chaplain Garner in the evening of his life. "They are united by ties of danger and suffering that men in other relations of life know nothing about." And so it was only natural that when those young warriors of '61 became gray about the temples, they would turn more and more to each other's company. After all, the Civil War, once its disasters and anxieties were behind them, loomed up as America's great folk epic, and those who fought in it came to cherish increasingly their onetime closeness to the heartbeat of history. Joining with the others in commemorative rituals proved the most satisfying way to relive those years long past that had marked the emotional high tide of their lives.

With the approach of the 1890's the men of Putnam County began to yearn for an 18th Missouri Association. Many of them had attended Soldiers' Reunions in various parts of the state, such as that staged at Milan July 3-4-5, 1884. Bill Brantner had not only made one of the major addresses then, but had served as deputy commander of the naturally victorious "Union forces" participating in the sham battle of July 4. Why not, the men asked themselves, have an annual get-together just for the old 18th Missouri?

D. W. Pollock, successful and affluent, living in daily contact with dozens of the "old boys," rose to the occasion. He called together a steering committee in the spring of 1889 to formulate plans for a late-summer assemblage at Unionville. With Pollock as its perennial commander and chief benefactor, the 18th Missouri Infantry Association went into action, holding annual meetings for the next twenty years. On one such occasion the men brought out their trusty old Springfields to defend a ridge near the fair grounds in Unionville against "Rebel infantry." The 18th Missouri prevailed, as it always had. Attendance rose from about a hundred in the first years to a peak of 320 in 1897. Attendance and membership dropped steadily after that time, and when the meeting took place at Green City in 1900, only about thirty appeared, representing Companies A, B, C, D, E, G, and I. Captain Pollock's retirement in 1908, and his death two years later, struck the Association a mortal blow, and its white-whiskered survivors turned again to the G. A. R. to refreshen memories of the brilliant morning of their lives.

But the Association had been wonderfully satisfying while

it lasted. It was usually possible in the 1890's to get a keynote speaker like the redoubtable General Prentiss (postmaster at Bethany) or Colonel Miller to come and recall for the men those dark days of '62 when the future of the 18th Missouri was encompassed by clouds of uncertainty. Many of the old soldiers were too far away and getting too infirm for prolonged travel, however, and this was another factor making for an early decline of the Association. Writing from Brooklyn in 1892, Bill Hemstreet had told Pollock that "Away off here by myself, where no one knows my war history, I have become very comrade hungry, having seen only two members of the 18th since we were mustered out. . . ."

Captain Pollock did not have to work alone. Serving as his vice-presidents from year to year were such old stalwarts as Wyckoff, Benecke, Elias Perry, Roscoe Torrey, Carter Green, Howry, and McEfee. Sheldon accepted a vice-presidency in 1892, but he was never able to make it to the meetings. Lance Beary, Jeff Rummell, Bill Scurlock, and Henry Wells worked long and faithfully in lesser offices.[22]

The ranks had dwindled steadily after the guns fell silent. Former Lieutenant George Morgan died under mysterious circumstances at Helena, Arkansas, before the war was over. So Garner, who was close to the Morgan family, understood. There stands today in the little hilltop Confederate Cemetery a simple stone slab which reads cryptically: George Morgan, killed 1864. But no one remains to explain why this Yankee lieutenant, if the headstone be his, slumbers among the Confederate dead atop that lonely bluff.

In 1866 Colonel Morgan himself died at Natchez, Mississippi, and the present writer has been unable to find further explanation of the cause of this sudden end to his tragic career. His descendants have ignored appeals to shed more light on their distinguished forebear's life and death.[23]

Also among the first to "muster-out" was Andy Morgan, late of Company B, who died of traumatic encephalitis near St. John in the late spring of 1866. His doctor pronounced the head wound of July 22, 1864, as the predisposing cause. Morgan was not apparently related to the colonel's family.

The following decade removed more familiar faces. John

Lomax died early in 1877 at Laclede and was buried with full Masonic rites. Among those tendering condolences to the family was George E. Spencer, late colonel of the 1st Alabama and currently a carpetbag U.S. Senator from that state. "I have always regarded Capt. Lomax as one of the best of men," Senator Spencer wrote. On December 30, 1878, the tuberculosis which had sprung up in Joe Stanley's lungs during that winter in the Carolina swamps claimed his life. As he was laid to rest under the auspices of Milan's Masonic Lodge, a journalist lamented that Sullivan County had been "called upon to part with a citizen of such outstanding worth."

"Uncle Tom" Pollock, full of years and youthful vigor, fell from his pony in the spring of 1879 and never recovered. The following Saturday morning, May 31, Mrs. Pollock was helping him to a chair near a window where he could see a rosebush. "Mother," he said, "my old army hurt is troubling me again." Then he clutched her by the waist, gasped a time or two, and died in her arms.[24]

Death wore many masks in the final years of the old century. Tom Hatfield, once captain of Company G, died of a heart attack near Wyreka in July of 1886. Colonel Minter, for years a Federal revenue agent, eventually discharged a revolver into his temple, suffering from what the widow described as "temporary insanity caused by the [head] wound for which he was pensioned." This, his only escape from recurrent agony, took place one July day in 1888 at Deland, Florida. Death overtook Madison Miller in his eighty-sixth year, on February 27, 1896, in the form of a fatal apoplectic stroke in a bathroom of his St. Louis home. Miller was alone when the "last call" sounded, for his youthful second wife was downtown on G. A. R. business. His death was discovered when a teamster entered the house to get his signature on a receipt for some construction materials, only to find General Miller's faithful fox terrier standing guard over his master's body.[25]

In its issue of January 10, 1900, the *Unionville Republican* carried the glaring headline: A HERO GONE. Colonel Sheldon, known at last as General Sargeant out in 18th Missouri country, had died on January 2 in his Chicago home and been buried at Caldwell, Ohio. Since the turn of the nineties he had suffered from heart trouble and had drawn a disability pension. Death slipped up on him unexpectedly while he was sitting at lunch with his family.

However, the world paid scant notice to this departure of another great captain of the Civil War. One Chicago newspaper —and one only—noted his death, with a brief article. Another announced the issuance of the burial permit. Attempts of the present writer to locate surviving descendants by inquiry and by travel have been to no avail. So far beyond memory's horizon had he ridden by mid-century that even the probate court in his home town could offer no information on him, and the compilers of a well-known anthology of Civil War literature could think of no other way to identify this brevet brigadier save as "a Union soldier named Charles Sheldon Sargeant."[26]

Among others who did not live to see the First World War were Silas Haynes, Milt Hudson, D. W. Pollock, and Lance Beary. Haynes died near Cole Camp, Missouri, on October 17, 1902. Newspapers in the area had plenty of room for full-column treatment of the death of a notorious outlaw, but none in which to commemorate the passing of this loyal soldier to whom his country owed so much. Milt Hudson died more dramatically, collapsing with a heart attack while sweeping the sidewalk in front of his post office at Hale in August of 1905. Restless Dave Pollock, who had sold all his business interests in 1908 on the urgent advice of his doctor, found it impossible to tolerate idleness. He repurchased his old enterprises and went back to his feverish commercial activities. Then, in early 1910, a heart attack struck him down. On February 28, sorrowing friends and relatives saw him buried beside his parents "surrounded by the largest concourse . . . ever assembled in St. John." In April, 1914, Lance Beary followed his dynamic brother-in-law "across the river." Five surviving children and Isabella Pollock Beary were at the bedside when he died.[27]

The autumn of 1915 swept away two company commanders. First to go was Uncle Billy Brantner, a nephritis victim, who had gone to California in 1913 hoping that a change of climate might improve his health. He died at Long Beach in late October, and a daughter brought him home to a grave in the Odd Fellows Cemetery overlooking Trenton's west side. Uncle

Billy had lived long enough to see his son Sherman married to Joe Stanley's daughter Nora Kate. Not long after this funeral, eighty-four-year-old John Mikesell injured his hip in an accidental fall on a sidewalk in downtown Sioux City, Iowa. He died on November 30, and his daughters interred him in a local cemetery.[28]

A variety of circumstances attended the deaths of John Howry, John McEfee, Henry S. Cochran, and Bernhard Little. In early 1919 Howry died of apoplexy at St. John. Late that summer McEfee lost his life as the result of a fall from a second-story window of his Laclede home. He was buried at Milan beside his brother-in-law, Joe Stanley. Cochran, a former corporal of Company K, died at his Smithville home in January of 1924 from injuries inflicted by a maddened Polled Angus bull. Finally, Little, an eighty-two-year-old illiterate German-born laborer who had served more than two years in Company E and had been wounded in the siege of Atlanta, burned to death at Lacey, Washington, one night in 1927, in a fire presumably caused by tobacco ashes.[29]

Bill Hemstreet, brevetted lieutenant colonel by Andrew Johnson, died in Brooklyn on October 15, 1920. He was past 86. Journalists noted that the brilliant old soldier had twelve years before his death given Columbia University "the old carved mantel shelf before which Edgar Allan Poe wrote 'The Raven.' " He was survived by two sons and two daughters.[30]

Well before the turn of the century the "old boys" had become rather sentimental about each other. Because of the high martial drama which had dominated their youthful years, these veterans were probably our most unabashedly sentimental and emotional generation. Jahiel Conn, late first sergeant of Company G, described for the *Unionville Republican* readers how the first Memorial Day was celebrated at Wyreka on May 30, 1869. Pastor George E. Wells, father of Henry and the son who had died at Chewalla, "opened his address by referring to a large chart of A. Lincoln and fallen heroes, hanging on the wall beside him, and commenced eulogizing the departure of Putnam County's soldiers, and when suddenly referring to his own son, his own name lying buried in Tennessee, many were the eyes that wept—many were the tears that fell. . . ."

William Carl Pilatz, late private of Company H, went home to Brunswick and assumed the role of a one-man memorial society to provide the graves of Union soldiers with head-stones, and with proper decorations at appropriate times. To his children he invariably sang at bedtime "Tenting Tonight"—the only war song whose English words he knew. Wrote a daughter: "He always put his brass GAR buttons . . . on his blue coat and emblems on his hat every Decoration Day. My mother, being much younger than my father, assisted him for years in placing a flag and a bouquet of flowers on every Civil War veteran's grave—including the 'grey coats' as he called them." Moreover, said the daughter, "Most all the government stones in the three cemeteries here were set by my father and ordered by him. Many Civil War veterans would never have had a marker of any kind if it hadn't been for my father."[31]

The sentimentality of the old veterans took a different turn with ex-Quartermaster Jack Riggen. In the middle nineties he revisited Chewalla and found only one log remaining of what had been the most remarkable fortress in the District of Corinth. Riggen shipped the log to his home in What Cheer, Iowa, and he cut it up into souvenirs for distribution at reunions. The supply could not possibly meet the demand, however.

Living to see the election of Franklin D. Roosevelt were ex-Corporal George W. Corporon of Company D, Private Henry N. Braden of E, Lieutenant Sam Frankfort of A, Private Frank-lin Green of A, Teamster Henry Sawyer of C, and Lieutenant Charles Grabosch of E. All six were in their nineties by then, and the first to go was Corporon, who died at Centerville, Iowa, in March, 1933, at the age of ninety-two. Braden, also ninety-two, died in Sullivan County, near Greencastle, the following year. Frankfort, long an enthusiastic visitor with the "old boys of '61," died in 1934 at the age of ninety-five. In January of 1935 Frank Green was laid to rest at the Illinois Soldiers and Sailors Home. Sawyer, after a long life of robust health, died at ninety-five in January of 1936, and the family buried him in the cemetery where Uncle Billy Brantner had slumbered for twenty years and more.[32]

Lieutenant Grabosch celebrated his ninety-fifth birthday on February 10, 1936. None of the old boys came around to wish him well, for all of those blue-coated comrades with whom he had gone through the crucible of war were now waiting for him on the far bank of the river. Jahiel Conn had said just before his death in 1882: "I am prepared for the change, and it makes no difference to me when it comes." The towering, white-haired Grabosch must have felt the same way about it, for in 1934 he composed his own obituary. It only remained for his Maker to fill in the date—December 12, 1936—and beckon him to eternal rest on a shady hillside in Unionville.[33]

# Notes to Chapters

## CHAPTER I. MORGAN'S RANGERS

1. (1) Senate Document 412, 57th Cong., 1st Sess., "Missouri Troops in Service during the Civil War" (Washington, 1902), 12. (2) William H. Lyon, "Claiborne Fox Jackson and the Secession Crisis in Missouri," *Missouri Historical Review*, LVIII (July, 1964), 422-41. (3) A. R. Kirkpatrick, "Missouri in the Early Months of the Civil War," *Missouri Historical Review*, LV (April, 1961), 261-66.

2. (1) John McElroy, *The Struggle for Missouri* (Washington, D. C., 1909), 48-50. (2) William E. Parrish, *Turbulent Partnership* (Columbia, Missouri, 1963), 7-10. (3) John C. Moore, "Missouri," *Confederate Military History* (Clement A. Evans, ed.; Atlanta, Georgia, 1899), Vol. IX, 19. (4) Richard S. Brownlee, *Gray Ghosts of the Confederacy* (Baton Rouge, Louisiana, 1958), 31.

3. (1) *The War of the Rebellion: Official Records of the Union and Confederate Armies* (70 vols. in 128; Washington, D. C., 1880-1901) [hereafter, *O. R.*], Series III, Vol. I, 793-95. (2) Walter B. Stevens, *Missouri: The Center State* (Chicago, 1915), 274-75. (3) J. Thomas Scharf, *History of the St. Louis City and County* (Philadelphia, 1883), Vol. I, 483. (4) *Dictionary of American Biography* (New York, 1957) [hereafter, *D. A. B.*], Vol. I, 332-34.

4. (1) McElroy, 190-20. (2) Parrish, 32.

5. (1) McElroy, 133-36. (2) *O. R.*, Ser. I, Vol. III, 406.

6. (1) *Messages and Proclamations of the Governors of the State of Missouri* (Columbia, Missouri, 1922), Vol. III, 405-14. (2) Senate Document 412 (124). (3) John M. Schofield, *Forty-Six Years in the Army* (New York, 1897), 54-55.

7. (1) Census of 1860, Chariton County, Missouri (Yellow Creek Township). (2) *History of Adair, Sullivan, Putnam, and*

*Schuyler Counties* (Chicago, 1888), 483, 487. (3) *The Tribune* (Liberty, Mo.), August 23, 1861. (4) Col. W. A. Shelton, "Pioneer Talks with Putnam's Eminent Men," July 20, 1900, MS in possession of A. B. Shelton, Unionville, Mo. (5) *Unionville* (Mo.) *Republican*, January 18, 1893. (6) Letter, Col. W. James Morgan to Maj. Gen. Henry W. Halleck, February 15, 1862, in W. James Morgan Military Records, National Archives.

8.  (1) *Grundy County Gazette*, October 17, 1935. (2) Interview with Mrs. Rose Sawyer Russell (daughter of Henry Harrison Sawyer), Trenton, Mo., October 10, 1964.

9.  (1) "Statement of Isaac V. Pratt, Late Lieut. Col. 18th Mo. Vols. Infantry," April 6, 1887, in Isaac Pratt Pension Papers [hereafter, Pratt], National Archives. (2) *The United States Biographical Dictionary* (New York, 1878), 625-26. (3) Senate Document 412 (221). (4) O. R., Ser. II, Vol. I, 212. (5) *Unionville Republican*, January 18, 1893.

10. Department of the Missouri, Letters, Book 18, National Archives.

11. (1) Muster Rolls and Descriptive Rolls, 18th Mo. Vols., in custody of the Adjutant General of Missouri. (2) A. B. Shelton and others, *Souvenir History, Unionville Centennial* (Unionville, Mo., 1955), 6. (3) Interview with James L. Grabosch (son of Charles Grabosch), Unionville, June 16, 1964. (4) Muster-In Roll, Jacob Clark's Company, July 27, 1861, MS owned by A. B. Shelton.

12. (1) Muster-In Rolls, 18th Mo. Vols., in custody of the Adjutant General of Missouri. (2) Descriptive Rolls. (3) *Unionville Republican*, January 18, 1893. (4) Letter, Capt. Francis M. Bell to Gov. Hamilton R. Gamble, December 1, 1862, in Regimental Papers, Office of the Adjutant General of Missouri. (5) Record of Events, 18th Mo. Vols., Record Group 594, National Archives. (6) *The Brookfield* (Mo.) *Gazette*, December 12, 1903. (7) Harry Lander and Eugene W. Godfrey Military Record, National Archives. (8) Letter, Carl A. Landrum (Quincy, Ill.) to the author, November 1, 1966.

13. *Unionville Republican*, January 25 and February 1, 1893.

14. *Unionville Republican*, February 15, 1893.

15. (1) Department of the Mo., Letters, Books 18 and 19. (2) Darius A. Cudworth, "Memories of Fifty Years Ago," *Glimpses of the Nation's Struggle* (Minneapolis: Military Order of the Loyal Legion, 1909), 226-28.

16. (1) *The History of Linn County, Missouri* (Kansas City, Mo., 1882), 344-45. (2) *O. R.*, Ser. II, Vol. I, 223.

17. *Unionville Republican*, February 22 and March 29, 1893.

18. (1) *Unionville Republican*, March 1, 1893.

19. (1) Muster and Descriptive Rolls. (2) James D. Coddington, Ezra S. Havens, John Howry, and James W. Morgan Pension and Military Records. (3) *Annual Report of the Adjutant General of Missouri for the Year Ending December 31, 1865* (Jefferson City, 1866). (4) *The Sioux City* (Iowa) *Journal*, December 1, 1915.

20. (1) Muster and Descriptive Rolls. (2) Letter, Dr. Paul Lomax (grandson of John Lomax) to the author, October 26, 1964. (3) George MacAdam, "The Life of General Pershing," *The World's Work*, XXXVII (November, 1918), 51. (4) Donald Smythe, "The Early Years of John J. Pershing," *Missouri Historical Review*, LVIII (October, 1963), 2-6.

21. (1) Muster and Descriptive Rolls. (2) Interview with Thomas H. Pollock (grandson of Cpl. Thomas Pollock and son of Capt. David W. Pollock), Unionville, August 7, 1964. (3) Ora Pollock Miller, *History of Thomas and Isabella Pollock and Descendants* (Unionville, 1955). (4) Walter Williams, *History of Northeast Missouri* (Chicago, 1913), Vol. III, 1446.

22. (1) Senate Document 412 (226). (2) Muster and Descriptive Rolls. (3) Sylvester S. Collins and Jacob R. Ault Pension and Military Records.

23. (1) Muster and Descriptive Rolls. (2) Louis Benecke, *Historical Sketch of the "Sixties" in Chariton County* (Brunswick, Mo., 1909), 5. (3) Interview with R. W. Benecke (son of Louis Benecke), Brunswick, August 5, 1964. (4) Ella Lonn's *Foreigners in the Union Army and Navy* (Baton Rouge, 1951), errs in listing Company K as the foreign-born company of this regiment (p. 669).

24. (1) Muster and Descriptive Rolls. (2) Keith Lingenfelter (great-grandson of Thomas McComb), ed., "Notes from the Family of Thomas McComb," paper in possession of H. C. McComb (grandson), Prairie Village, Kansas.

25. (1) McElroy, 231-35. (2) O. R., Ser. i, Vol. iii, 3, 567. (3) Otto Eisenschiml and Ralph Newman, eds., *The American Iliad* (New York, 1947), 35.

26. (1) O. R., Ser. i, Vol. iii, 568. (2) O. R., Ser. i, Vol. viii, 434. (3) Senate Document 412 (125). (4) Maj. Gen. J. F. C. Fuller, *The Generalship of Ulysses S. Grant* (Bloomington, Indiana, 1960), 76.

27. (1) Schofield, 55-56. (2) 1 *Battles and Leaders* (New York, 1887), 314-34.

28. (1) O. R., Ser. ii, Vol. i, 238. (2) Frederick H. Dyer, *A Compendium of the War of the Rebellion* (New York, 1959), Vol. iii, 1330. (3) Muster Rolls. (4) Record of Events, 18th Mo. Vols.

29. (1) O. R., Ser. ii, Vol. i, 238. (2) W. M. Paxton, *Annals of Platte County* (Kansas City, Mo., 1897), 322. (3) Record of Events, 18th Mo. (4) Letter, David W. Pollock to William L. Pollock, December 12, 1861, from David Wilson Pollock Letters, made available to the author through the generosity of Thomas H. Pollock, Unionville, Missouri.

30. (1) Paxton, 321. (2) Chaplain John M. Garner, in his account of the 18th Missouri's sojourn in Platte County, passes over the burning of Platte City with complete silence. See *Unionville Republican*, March 8, 1893. (3) McElroy, doggedly anti-Confederate, blames "Price's men" for the conflagration (p. 290). (4) Cincinnati (Ohio) newsmen heard that the fires were set "by some rebels, but suppressed by troops under Col. Morgan." See Frank Moore, ed., *The Rebellion Record* (New York, 1862), Vol. iii, 112. (5) *History of Clay and Platte Counties* (St. Louis, 1885), 699.

31. (1) *History of Clay and Platte Counties*, 699-700. (2) Department of the Missouri Letter Books 552, 21, 103, National Archives. (3) Letter, D. W. to W. L. Pollock, January 18, 1862 (D. W. Pollock Letters).

32. (1) *Unionville Republican*, March 8 and 29, 1893. (2) Let-

ters, D. W. to W. L. Pollock, December 12, 1861; January 18,
1862. (3) *Annual Report of the Adjutant General of Wisconsin
for the Year Ending December 31, 1865* (Madison, 1866), 154.

33. (1) Descriptive Rolls. (2) Paxton, 324, 328, 348.

34. (1) *O. R.*, Ser. III, Vol. I, 796. (2) See also Regimental Papers,
in Adj. Gen. Office, Jefferson City. (4) Descriptive Rolls.

35. (1) Record of Events, 18th Mo. (2) Letter, Daniel Torrey to
Isabella Pollock, February 14, 1862, in D. W. Pollock Letters.
(3) Letter, David W. to W. L. Pollock, January 18, 1862.

36. (1) John H. Morgan Military and Pension Records. (2) Letter, W. James Morgan to Maj. Gen. George B. McClellan, February 5, 1862, in W. James Morgan Military Records.

37. (1) *O. R.*, Ser. I, Vol. III, 77. (2) *Appleton's Cyclopedia of
American Biography* (James Grant Wilson and John Fiske, eds.;
New York, 1888), Vol. IV, 328. (3) Charles S. Sargeant, *Per-
sonal Recollections of the Eighteenth Missouri Infantry in the
War for the Union* (*Addenda* by Madison Miller), no pagina-
tion. (4) Madison Miller Papers, Missouri Historical Society,
St. Louis. (5) *Journal of the House of Representatives of the
State of Missouri*, Twenty-First General Assembly, First Session,
January 17, 1861 (107).

38. (1) *Unionville Republican*, September 24, 1890. (2) Letters,
Capt. Madison Miller to Asst. Adj. Gen. of Mo., January 31,
1862, in Madison Miller Pension Papers. (3) Special Orders
[SO] 99, HQ, Dept. of the Missouri, January 31, 1862, in Miller
Pension Papers.

39. (1) Sargeant. (2) Letter, James Carrie to Fanny Carrie, Feb-
ruary 3, 1862, made available to the author by the generosity of
Mrs. Leolin Moore, Milan, Mo. (3) W. James Morgan Military
Records.

## CHAPTER II. THE FATHER OF WATERS

1. (1) *Unionville Republican*, March 15 and 29, 1893. (2) Letter,
James A. Price to Miller, February 17, 1862, in Miller Papers,
St. Louis.

2. (1) Record of Events, 18th Mo. (2) Letter, D. W. Pollock to
Mrs. Thomas Pollock, February 24, 1862. (3) Dept. of the
Mo., Letters, Book 467, National Archives. (4) Cudworth.

3. (1) Letters, D. W. Pollock to Mrs. Thomas Pollock, February 24 and March 9, 1862. (2) Letter, James Carrie to Fanny Carrie, March 7, 1862, made available to the author through the generosity of Mrs. Leolin Moore. (3) *Unionville Republican*, April 5, 1893.

4. (1) Muster Rolls. (2) Letter, Mrs. Grace F. Cudworth (daughter-in-law of D. A. Cudworth) to the author, February 17, 1966. (3) Darius Alonzo Cudworth Pension Record. (4) Letter, Cudworth to Asst. Adj. Gen. of Mo., May 28, 1862, in Regimental Papers. (5) *Unionville Republican*, March 22, 1893.

5. (1) *Annual Report*. (2) Letter, Capt. Francis M. Bell to Governor Gamble, December 1, 1862. (3) Department of Mo. Letters, Book 22. (4) Letter, D. W. Pollock to Miss Isabella Pollock, March 13, 1862. (5) Barbara Cheeney, Lloyd J. Cooper, Ezra S. Havens, William H. Minter, and Sylvester S. Collins Pension Records. (6) Letter, Mrs. Evelyn Sheets (Trenton, Mo.) to the author, September 4, 1964. (7) Muster and Descriptive Rolls. (8) Dyer, 1330.

6. *Unionville Republican*, April 5, 1893.

7. (1) *O. R.*, Ser. I, Vol. LII, Pt I, 222. (2) D. W. Pollock Letters, February 24 and March 9, *supra*. (3) James Carrie Letter, March 7, 1862. (4) Letter, Benjamin Guffey to Caroline Guffey, March [?], 1862, made available to the author through the generosity of Mrs. Wineyfred Guffey Ashlock (daughter of Benjamin Guffey) and Donald F. Hulin, Tacoma, Washington. (5) Letter, Lawrence to Eliza Hoover, March 2, 1862, kindly loaned the author by Vernia Hoover Childers (granddaughter of Lawrence Hoover), Green City, Mo.

8. See Fuller's *The Generalship of Ulysses S. Grant*, 65-68.

9. George Fort Milton, *Conflict* (New York, 1941), 164-65.

10. John Fiske, *The Mississippi Valley in the Civil War* (Boston, 1901), 52-65.

11. (1) John Codman Ropes, *The Story of the Civil War* (New York, 1898), Vol. II, 51-57. (2) Fuller, 95.

12. (1) Pratt. (2) *Unionville Republican*, April 19, 1893. (3) Daniel R. Hudson Military Record. (4) Miller *Addenda* to Sargeant. (5) Dept. of the Mo. Letters, Book 467. (6) Descriptive Rolls.

13. (1) Pratt. (2) *Unionville Republican*, April 19 and 26, 1893. (3) *O. R.*, Ser. I, Vol. x, 86. (4) Miller *Addenda*. (5) *Grundy County Gazette*, October 17, 1935.

14. (1) *Unionville Republican*, May 10, 1893. (2) Descriptive Rolls. (3) "Historical Background: Benjamin Musgrove," assembled by A. B. Shelton. (4) "The House of Musgrove," historical album owned by Miss Minnie Musgrove (granddaughter of Benjamin Musgrove), Omaha, Mo. (5) Case 528, Putnam County (Mo.) Probate Records.

15. (1) Letter, D. W. to W. L. Pollock, March 25, 1862. (2) *Annual Report*. (3) John J. Heisel and John Howry Pension Records. (4) Muster and Descriptive Rolls.

16. (1) *Unionville Republican*, May 10, 1893. (2) *O. R.*, Ser. I, Vol. VIII, 77-79. (3) I *Battles and Leaders*, 46-62.

17. (1) I *Battles and Leaders*, 502-503. (2) Manning F. Force, *From Fort Henry to Corinth* (New York, 1881), 103. (3) *O. R.*, Ser. I, Vol. x, Pt II, 67. (4) *Unionville Republican*, May 3, 1893.

18. (1) *D. A. B.*, Vol. VIII, 188. (2) John S. C. Abbott, *The History of the Civil War in America* (New York, 1863), Vol. I, 445. (3) I *Battles and Leaders*, 469-81, 490-91, 536.

19. (1) *Unionville Republican*, May 17, 1893. (2) Record of Events, 18th Mo.

20. (1) *O. R.*, Ser. I, Vol. LII, Pt I, 19. (2) I *Battles and Leaders*, 502-503. (3) Fiske, 72-75.

21. (1) Fuller, 89-98. (2) Ropes, I, 58-61. (3) Fiske, 69-71. (4) Brownlee, 77.


CHAPTER III.   THE CHAPEL IN THE WOODS

1. For a fuller discussion of the broad strategic picture in April, 1862, the reader is advised to consult Milton (170-71, 326-28), Ropes, II (62-75), Fuller (98-112), and Fiske (84-93).

2. (1) See Garner's accounts in *Unionville Republican*, May 24, May 31, June 7, and July 19, 1893. (2) Josef Ruff (12th Michigan), "Civil War Experiences of a German Immigrant. . . ," *Michigan History Magazine*, XXVII (1943), 294. (3) James D. Coddington, *Unionville Republican*, September 13, 1893. (4)

Report of Brig. Gen. Benjamin M. Prentiss in *O. R.*, Ser. I, Vol. x, Pt I, 277-79. (5) Force, 140-43.

3. (1) Coddington. (2) *Unionville Republican*, May 31, June 7, June 14, and July 19, 1893. (3) Miller *Addenda*. (4) Madison Miller, Shiloh Diary, in Miller Papers, St. Louis. (5) Pratt. (6) *O. R.*, Ser. I, Vol. x, Pt I, 248-54, 280-82. (7) Letter, Gebhart Kurtz to James A. Price, June 30, 1890, in possession of Miss Forestyne Loyles (great-granddaughter of James A. Price), Weston, Mo. (8) James A. Price Pension Record. (9) Leander Stillwell (ex-lieutenant, 61st Illinois), *The Story of a Common Soldier* (Erie, Kansas, 1920), 47. (10) *Annual Report of the Adjutant General of Wisconsin* (1865), 294. (11) Prentiss.

4. (1) *O. R.*, Ser. I, Vol. x, Pt I, 257-60. (2) William T. Sherman, *Memoirs* (New York, 1875), Vol. I, 237. (3) I *Battles and Leaders*, 500. (4) *Official Roster of the Soldiers of the State of Ohio in the War of the Rebellion, 1861-1865* (Akron, 1887), 675.

5. (1) *O. R.*, Vol. x, Pt I, 203-208, 231, 283-86. (2) George W. Adams, *Doctors in Blue* (New York, 1952), 81. (3) Stillwell, 47. (4) Coddington. (5) Miller Diary and *Addenda*. (6) *Unionville Republican*, June 14, 1893.

6. (1) *O. R.*, Vol. x, Pt I, 165-67, 280-82. (2) Prentiss Report.

7. (1) Mark M. Boatner, *The Civil War Dictionary* (New York, 1959), 754-55. (2) H. S. P. L. Jones, *Decision at Shiloh* (St. Joseph, Mo., 1961), 40. (3) Gen. P. G. T. Beauregard (*O. R.*, Vol. x, Pt I, 385-92) glosses over the Hornets' Nest incident, summarizing in less than 200 words the action at Shiloh before he took command. (5) Prentiss Report. (6) Miller *Addenda*.

8. (1) *O. R.*, Vol. x, Pt I, 152-54, 549. (2) U. S. Grant, "The Battle of Shiloh," *The Century Magazine*, xxix (February, 1885), 597.

9. (1) George W. Wyckoff, *Unionville Republican*, September 6, 1893. (2) See also *Unionville Republican*, September 24, 1890. (3) I *Battles and Leaders*, 506.

10. (1) *O. R.*, Vol. x, Pt I, 101, 149, 550. (2) Joseph M. Brown, *Unionville Republican*, May 30, 1894. (3) Abraham Van Meter, *Unionville Republican*, June 20, 1894.

11. (1) Cf. Coddington, Wyckoff. (2) Carl A. Landrum, *Quincy in the Civil War* (Quincy, Ill., 1966), 43-45.

12. (1) *O. R.*, Vol. x, Pt i, 19, 104, 279. (2) Muster and Descriptive Rolls.

13. (1) Daniel McD. McCook, "The Second Division at Shiloh," *Harper's New Monthly Magazine*, xxviii (May, 1864), 828-33. (2) Paxton, 444. (3) McElroy, 165. (4) Sherman, Vol. i, 230.

14. (1) *O. R.*, Vol. x, Pt i, 104, 280-82; Pt ii, 101. (2) Muster and Descriptive Rolls. (3) Force, 183.

15. Daniel Morgan Shelton, "Biography and Service Record of Daniel M. Shelton from 1861 to 1865," undated, MS in possession of A. B. Shelton (grandson), Unionville [hereafter, Shelton].

16. (1) Descriptive Rolls. (2) Interview with A. B. Shelton, Unionville, June 16, 1964.

17. (1) Letter, D. W. to W. L. Pollock, April 11, 1862. (2) *Unionville Republican*, August 29, 1894. (3) Brown. (4) Case 174, Putnam Co. (Mo.) Probate Records. (5) Lloyd J. Cooper Pension Papers. (6) The roster of dead on April 6 included Adjutant William A. Edgar (HQ), Lt. John B. Sharp (Co. F), First Sgt. John Downey (B), Sgt. George A. Hindman (B), Cpl. Leroy Guthrie (A), Cpl. Joseph A. Linscott (A), Cpl. Talman Smith (K), Cpl. Benjamin A. Wood (E), Pvt. Rolla Brantner (A), Pvt. William Capps (F), Pvt. James Carrie (E), Pvt. John I. Cochran (B), Pvt. Patrick Gernon (A), Pvt. James Johnson (E), Pvt. Isam Lunsford (E), Pvt. Simeon Maffit (B), Pvt. Joseph A. Menzer (H), Pvt. Noah Mullenax (B), Pvt. Joseph Muffley (K), and Pvt. James R. Simmons (B). Cf. Muster and Descriptive Rolls.

18. (1) Eugene W. Godfrey, Jacob L. Clark, Delight Dayton, Joseph Darwin, and Joseph von Arx Pension and Military Records. (2) Letter, Mrs. Delight Dayton to Adj. Gen. of Mo., June 27, 1864, in Regimental Papers. (3) *Quincy* (Ill.) *Daily Whig*, April 26, 1862. (4) Dying of wounds after April 6 were Capt. Eugene W. Godfrey (Co. F), Capt. Jacob L. Clark (E), Capt. William H. Cooper (Co. C), Lt. John R. Dayton (A), First Sgt. Joseph Darwin (F), Pvt. John W. Alderman (G),

Pvt. Andrew J. Alexander (D), Pvt. Joseph von Arx (H), Pvt. Daniel Aylor (C), Pvt. William Brei (H), Pvt. Nicholas Craig (I), Pvt. Bryant Flanigan (G), Pvt. Alexander E. Glenn (E), Pvt. Charles Gray (D), Pvt. William F. Jones (G), Pvt. John Kerr (E), Pvt. William Kräntzke (H), Pvt. Teeter Masoner (F), Pvt. Mathew Morris (B), Pvt. Ambrose Payne (F), Pvt. Alexander Roesch (H), Pvt. Gilbert M. L. Shelton (E), Pvt. Edward Simpson (I), Pvt. Hiram Summers (I), Pvt. Joseph Thompson (E), Pvt. Noah Waggoner (E). Cf. Muster and Descriptive Rolls.

19. (1) Thomas Cawood, *Unionville Republican,* March 23, 1876. (2) Joseph M. Brown, *Unionville Republican,* June 6, 1894. (3) Abraham Van Meter, *Unionville Republican,* July 11, 1894. (4) Miller *Addenda,* Diary. (5) Coddington. (6) See also Pratt, Wyckoff.

20. (1) Benecke, 10-11. (2) Letter, Robert W. Benecke to D. W. Pollock, August 16, 1897, reprinted in *Constitution of the 18th Missouri Infantry Association* (Unionville, 1897), 16. (3) *The History of Linn County* (1882), 615-16. (4) Dying of wounds while prisoners were Capt. William H. Cooper of Company C and Cpl. Lewis Byram of Company H. Those who died of diseases while in captivity were First Sgt. Caleb Wells (Co. I), Sgt. Jefferson J. Smith (B), Cpl. John Caseldine (F), Cpl. John Wineholts (I), Pvt. George W. Crawford (G), Pvt. John T. Davis (A), Pvt. Dennis Ellis (K), Pvt. Philip Hart (I), Pvt. Eligah Hughes (H), Pvt. Van Buren Johnson (D), Pvt. Alford Kirk (C), Pvt. Samuel Miller (H), Pvt. William Newman, Jr. (D), Pvt. William Reeves (A), Pvt. Silas Shields (C); cf. Muster and Descriptive Rolls.

21. *O. R.,* Ser. II, Vol. IV, 704-705, 733. (Nineteen of the complaining soldiers were from the 18th Missouri.)

22. *Unionville Republican,* October 1, 1890.

## CHAPTER IV. ON TO CORINTH

1. (1) *Unionville Republican,* August 9, 1893. (2) Letter, H. C. McComb, Prairie Village, Kansas, to the author, February 7, 1965.

2. Letter, Benjamin to Caroline Guffey, April 21, 1862, made avail-

able to the author through the courtesy of Mrs. Wineyfred Guffey Ashlock and Donald F. Hulin, Tacoma, Washington.

3.  (1)*Unionville Republican*, August 16, 1893. (2) Muster Rolls.

4.  (1) *Unionville Republican*, August 23 and 30, 1893. (2) Elisha Stockwell, *Private Elisha Stockwell, Jr. Sees the War* (Byron R. Abernethy, ed.; Norman, Oklahoma, 1958), 31.

5.  (1) Muster Rolls. (2) Shiloh National Military Park Commission, *The Battle of Shiloh* (Washington, D.C., 1909), 96.

6.  (1) Letter, Maj. Gen. Henry W. Halleck to Governor Gamble, July 7, 1862, in Regimental Papers. (2) James A. Price Pension Record.

7.  (1) Letter, Brig. Gen. J. B. S. Todd to Asst. Adj. Gen., Dept. of the Mississippi, July 5, 1862, in Regimental Papers. (2) Letter, Lt. Col. H. J. Bradshaw, Office of the Adj. Gen. of Michigan, to the author, January 25, 1965.

8.  *Unionville Republican*, July 5 and August 16-30, 1893.

9.  (1) Descriptive Rolls. (2) Dept. of the Mo., Asst. Adj. Gen. Office, Book 478, National Archives. (3) U.S. Quartermaster Dept., *Roll of Honor* (Washington, D.C., 1866), *passim*. (4) Dept. of the Mo., Letters, Book 106, National Archives.

10.  *O. R.*, Ser. I, Vol. x, Pt II, 185-88.

11.  William Hemstreet Military and Pension Records.

12.  (1) *Unionville Republican*, October 4, 1893. (2) Morning Reports, 18th Mo., National Archives. (3) *Record of Service of Michigan Volunteers in the Civil War* (Kalamazoo, n.d.), 107. (4) John McDermott Military Record.

13.  (1) Descriptive Rolls. (2) Letter, Lt. Col. John McDermott to Halleck, May 6, 1862, in Regimental Papers.

14.  (1) Muster Rolls and Returns. (2) Letters, D. W. to Miss Isabella Pollock, *circa* May 15, 1862, and to W. L. Pollock, May 30, 1862. (3) Ropes, I, 93-95.

15.  (1) Force, 191. (2) *Unionville Republican*, November 15, 1893.

16.  (1) Muster Rolls and Returns. (2) Shelton. (3) *Unionville Republican*, December 6, 1893. (4) Letters, D. W. to Miss

Isabella Pollock, June 8, June 13, and July 20, 1862; D. W. to W. L. Pollock, May 30 and July 29, 1862. (5) Letter, Cudworth to Capt. W. F. Clark, May 29, 1862, with subsequent indorsements to June 3, in Regimental Papers.

17. *Unionville Republican,* November 22 and 29, December 13, 1893.

18. (1) *Unionville Republican,* October 4, November 1-15, 1893. (2) *O. R.,* Vol. x, Pt 1, 653; Pt 11, 248. (4) Record of Events.

19. (1) Muster Rolls and Returns. (2) See Morning Reports and Captain Ault's correspondence in Regimental Papers. (3) Letter, Victor Lomax (Washington, D.C.) to Floyd and Alice Lomax Ream (Clinton, Mo.), October 28, 1964, in Lomax Papers, copies in author's custody. (4) Frederick Palmer, *John J. Pershing* (Harrisburg, Pa., 1948), 7. (5) Brownlee, 76-91.

20. James A. Price Pension Record.

21. (1) Letters, Thomas to Isabella Wilson Pollock, [August] 7, August 25, 1862, in Thomas Pollock Letters, made available to the author by the generosity of Thomas H. Pollock (grandson), Unionville, Mo. (2) Letter, D. W. to Miss Isabella Pollock, August 22, 1862. (3) Letter, D. W. to W. L. Pollock, August 22, 1862.

22. (1) Muster Rolls. (2) Letter, D. W. to Isabella Pollock, August 25, 1862. (3) Henry Valentine and Thomas Brooks Pension and Military Records.

23. (1) Dept. of the Mo., Letters, Book 23. (2) David Y. Thomas, *Arkansas in War and Reconstruction* (Little Rock, 1926), 383.

24. Garner's memory tricked him in this case, for the date of June, 1863, that he gives for Riley Howe's death cannot be substantiated either by the soldier's records or those of the regiment. See *Unionville Republican,* August 15, 1894 and compare with Descriptive Rolls.

25. (1) Basil H. Liddell Hart, *Sherman* (New York, 1958), 144-45. (2) Fiske, 143-45. (3) 11 *Battles and Leaders,* 738.

26. Essential details relating to Federal strategy during this period may be extracted from Fiske (145-55); Ropes, 11 (390-409); Liddell Hart (144-46); and Milton (178-91).

## CHAPTER V. CORINTH

1. (1) Muster and Descriptive Rolls. (2) *History of Adair, Sullivan, Putnam, and Schuyler Counties*, 768.

2. For detailed analyses of the strategic situation before and after the second Battle of Corinth, the reader should consult Fuller, 116; Fiske, 154-60; II *Battles and Leaders*, 741-53; Milton, 181; Bruce Catton, *Grant Moves South* (Boston, 1960), 309-17; and G. W. Dudley, *The Lost Account of the Battle of Corinth* (Monroe F. Cockrell, ed.; Jackson, Tennessee, 1955), *passim*.

3. Letter, D. W. to Miss Isabella Pollock, September 15, 1862.

4. *Unionville Republican*, December 20, 1893.

5. (1) Muster and Descriptive Rolls. (2) Letter, D. W. to Isabella Pollock, September 24, 1862.

6. (1) *O. R.*, Ser. I, Vol. XVII, Pt II, 237, 240, 249. (2) *Unionville Republican*, December 6, 1893.

7. (1) *Unionville Republican*, December 27, 1893. (2) Muster Rolls. (3) Norman S. Hamlin Pension and Military Records.

8. *Unionville Republican*, February 21, 1894.

9. (1) *Unionville Republican*, December 27, 1893. (2) John Hancock and W. H. Tucker, *The Fourteenth Wisconsin Infantry: Corinth and Shiloh* (Indianapolis, 1895), 26.

10. (1) *O. R.*, Vol. XVII, Pt I, 356. (2) Muster Rolls. (3) *Unionville Republican*, January 3, 1894.

11. Shelton.

12. *Unionville Republican*, February 24, 1892; January 10, 1894.

13. Letter, John Lomax to William M. Lomax, December 12, 1862, made available by the generosity of Mrs. Blanche Wilkins (granddaughter), Parsons, Kansas, and Mrs. Alice Lomax Ream (great-granddaughter of John Lomax), Clinton, Missouri.

14. (1) Letter, John to W. M. Lomax, December 12, 1862. (2) *Unionville Republican*, January 10, 1894. (3) *Harper's New Monthly Magazine*, XXVI (December, 1862), 130.

15. (1) *Unionville Republican*, January 17, 1894. (2) *Grundy County Gazette*, October 17, 1935.

16. (1) *Unionville Republican,* January 31, 1894. (2) Muster Rolls and Returns.

17. (1) *O. R.,* Vol. XVII, Pt 1, 356. (2) Letter, Thomas to Isabella Wilson Pollock, October 9, 1862, from Thomas Pollock Letters, made available to the author through the generosity of Thomas H. Pollock, Unionville, Mo. (3) *Unionville Republican,* February 21, 1894.

18. (1) Muster Rolls and Returns. (2) *O. R.,* Vol. XVII, Pt 1, 176. (3) Charles H. McCully Pension Record.

19. *O. R.,* Vol. XVII, Pt 1, 336, 340, 356.

20. (1) *O. R.,* Vol. XVII, Pt 1, 172. (2) *O. R.,* Vol. XVII, Pt II, 297-98. (3) Letter, Benjamin to Caroline Guffey, April 18, 1863.

## CHAPTER VI. CONVALESCENCE AT CHEWALLA

1. For the details of the strategic picture in 1862-1863 the reader would do well to consult: (1) Catton, *Grant Moves South,* 319, 395-96; (2) Fiske, 161-78, 182-241; (3) Henry M. Cist, *The Army of the Cumberland* (New York, 1882), *passim.*

2. *O. R.,* XVI, 641-42; 654-55.

3. (1) Sargeant. (2) Muster Rolls. (3) Letters, D. W. to Miss Isabella Pollock, November 1, November 19, and December 18, 1862 (from David Wilson Pollock Letters).

4. (1) Headquarters [HQ], Dept. and Army of the Tennessee, Endorsements, Vol. XI, National Archives. (2) Letters, D. W. to Isabella Pollock, November 1, November 14, November 19, 1862.

5. (1) *The Nonpareil* (Council Bluffs, Iowa), January 4, 1916. (2) Special Orders [SO] 19, HQ, Dept. and Army of the Tenn., November 15, 1862 (National Archives).

6. (1) Muster Rolls. (2) Parrish, *Turbulent Partnership,* 101. (3) *Annual Report.* (4) Orlando B. Douglas Pension Record.

7. (1) Letter, Capt. Francis M. Bell to Governor Gamble, December 1, 1862, in Regimental Papers. (2) Letter, Capt. Jacob R. Ault to Brig. Gen. Grenville M. Dodge, December 5, 1862, with subsequent indorsements, in Regimental Papers. (3) *Civil War Dictionary,* 243.

8. (1) Sargeant. (2) *Annual Report.* (3) Woodson S. Estes Pension Record. (4) Letter, Col. William D. Wood to Governor Gamble, November 10, 1862, in Gamble Papers, Mo. Hist. Soc. St. Louis. (5) HQ, Dept. and Army of the Tenn., Endorsements, Vol. IX.

9. (1) Sargeant. (2) Descriptive and Muster Rolls. (3) *Annual Report.* (4) See also Regimental Papers, Jefferson City.

10. Letters, D. W. to Miss Isabella Pollock, December 18, 1862, and January 15, 1863.

11. (1) Sargeant. (2) Charles S. Sargeant Pension and Military Records. (3) *History of Noble County, Ohio* (Chicago, 1887), 282. (4) Isaac V. Pratt Pension Record. (5) *Journal of the Senate of Missouri: First Session of the Twenty-Second General Assembly,* 4-5.

12. (1) Sargeant. (2) *Unionville Republican,* May 16, 1894. (3) Letter, D. W. to Miss Isabella Pollock, January 15, 1863.

13. (1) Sargeant. (2) Muster Rolls. (3) *Unionville Republican,* March 7, 14, and 21, 1894. (4) See Inspector General's Reports, HQ, Dept. and Army of the Tenn., 1863 (National Archives). (5) Letters, D. W. to W. L. Pollock, *ca.* October 20, 1862, and January 8, 1863.

14. (1) *Unionville Republican,* December 6, 1893. (2) Robert S. Henry, *"First with the Most" Forrest* (Indianapolis, 1944), 102-21.

15. (1) Sargeant. (2) Muster Rolls.

16. (1) Muster and Descriptive Rolls. (2) *History and Biography of Linn County, Missouri* (Chicago, 1912), 378-79. (3) Letter, John to W. M. Lomax, December 12, 1862. (4) *Unionville Republican,* March 14, 1894.

17. (1) Sargeant. (2) *Unionville Republican,* September 8, 1890.

18. (1) Shelton. (2) Muster Rolls. (3) William Hammel Military Record. (4) Letter, D. W. to W. L. Pollock, February 19, 1863. (5) *O. R.,* Ser. I, Vol. XXIV, Pt III, 256.

19. (1) Regimental Returns. (2) Muster Rolls. (3) Muster-Out Rolls, July 17, 1865. (4) Sargeant, in his Personal Recollections, disclaimed any bias against the discharged officers. Miller,

in his *Addenda* to Sargeant's work, passed up a chance similarly to purge himself of prejudice. (5) Cf. Letter, D. W. to Miss Isabella Pollock, February 2, 1863 (David Wilson Pollock Letters).

20. (1) Muster Rolls. (2) Letter, Ault to Miller, April 14, 1863, in Ault Military Record. (3) *Annual Report.* (4) Letter, Henry F. Simmons (St. Louis) to the Adj. Gen. of Mo., April 28, 1863, in Regimental Papers. (5) Jonas Durman and John P. Mikesell Pension Records. (6) Dodge subsequently enlisted in the 6th Missouri Infantry. His pension application made no mention of his commissioned service in the 18th Missouri (See Oliver H. Dodge Pension Record).

21. (1) Muster Rolls. (2) Sargeant. (3) Madison Miller Papers, St. Louis.

22. (1) Letter, D. W. to W. L. Pollock, February 8, 1863. (2) Letter, Benjamin Guffey to Caroline Guffey, April 18, 1863, made available to the author by the generosity of Mrs. Wineyfred Guffey Ashlock and Donald F. Hulin, Tacoma, Washington.

23. (1) Sargeant. (2) *O. R.*, Ser. 1, Vol. XXIV, Pt 1, 26-27, 340-41.

24. (1) Muster Rolls. (2) Letter, D. W. to W. L. Pollock, March 21, 1863.

25. *Unionville Republican,* August 29 and September 5, 1894.

26. (1) *Unionville Republican,* May 23, 1894. (2) Letter, Benjamin to Caroline Guffey, April 18, 1863.

27. Parrish, *Turbulent Partnership,* 121.

CHAPTER VII. THE SUMMER THE TIDE TURNED

1. (1) *Unionville Republican,* April 11, April 25, May 9, and May 16, 1894. (2) Muster Rolls. (3) Letter, Benjamin to Caroline Guffey, May 5, 1863, in possession of Mrs. Wineyfred Guffey Ashlock (daughter) and made available to the author through her generosity and the courtesy of Mr. Donald F. Hulin, Tacoma, Washington. (4) Sargeant. (5) Letters, D. W. to Miss Isabella Pollock, May 4, 1863, and to W. L. Pollock, May 14, 1863 (David Wilson Pollock Letters).

2. (1) Muster and Descriptive Rolls. (2) *Annual Report.* (3) Edwin J. Conway Military Record.

3. (1) Muster Rolls. (2) *Unionville Republican,* June 6 and August 8, 1894.

4. See letters made available to the author by the generosity of Alice Lomax Ream (great-granddaughter of John Lomax): (1) Anna Shank Lomax and Elizabeth A. Lomax to Capt. John Lomax, June 10, 1863, originals in the possession of Dr. Paul Lomax of Maplewood, New Jersey; (2) Mrs. Laura McVay to Alice Lomax Ream, October 29, 1964; (3) Mrs. Mary Elizabeth Carothers to Alice Lomax Ream, October 21, 1964; (4) Victor W. Lomax to Floyd and Alice Lomax Ream, October 28, 1964; and (5) Elizabeth A. to W. M. Lomax, June 13, 1863.

5. (1) *O. R.,* XXIV, Pt I, 481; Pt II, 26-27. (2) Sargeant.

6. (1) Sargeant. (2) *O. R.,* XXIV, Pt II, 473-84; Pt III, 417.

7. (1) *History of Thomas and Isabella Pollock and Descendants.* (2) Letters, Thomas to Isabella Wilson Pollock, June 1 and June 28, 1863 (Thomas Pollock Letters).

8. (1) *Unionville Republican,* August 15 and September 19, 1894. (2) Muster Rolls. (3) Cist, 156-57, 169.

9. (1) Sargeant. (2) *Unionville Republican,* September 8, September 24, and October 1, 1890; May 2, 1894. (3) Muster Rolls. (4) See XVI Corps Letter Book 32 (National Archives). (5) Letter, Thomas to Isabella Wilson Pollock, June 15, 1863 (Thomas Pollock Letters). (6) Letter, D. W. to W. L. Pollock, June 24, 1863 (David Wilson Pollock Letters).

10. (1) *Unionville Republican,* May 16, 1894. (2) Regimental Returns.

11. (1) Muster Rolls. (2) *O. R.,* XXIV, Pt II, 684.

12. Letter, Asst. Adj. Gen., Left Wing, XVI Corps, to Col. Madison Miller, August 31, 1863, in XVI Corps Letter Book 32 (National Archives).

13. (1) McElroy, *The Struggle for Missouri,* 40, 45-46. (2) *Civil War Dictionary,* 823. (3) *Home Letters of General Sherman* (M. A. DeWolfe Howe, ed.; New York, 1909), 278. (4) See Letter, Asst. Adj. Gen., HQ, Left Wing, XVI Corps, to Brig. Gen. Thomas W. Sweeny, September 15, 1863, in XVI Corps Letter Book 32.

14. See Letters, Madison Miller to Brig. Gen. John B. Gray, *ca.* August 15, 1863, and September 15, 1863, in Regimental Papers.

15. (1) Benjamin P. Thomas and Harold M. Hyman, *Stanton* (New York, 1962), 371-75. (2) Descriptive and Muster Rolls. (3) State of Missouri, Certificate of Medical Board, St. Louis, June 23, 1863, in Regimental Papers. (4) Shelton. (5) *Unionville Republican,* May 1, 1895.

16. (1) Descriptive and Muster Rolls. (2) *Unionville Republican,* March 21, April 4, and September 19, 1894.

17. (1) *Stanton,* 286-90. (2) Cist, 230. (3) *O. R.,* Ser. I, Vol. XXX, Pt I, 161-62. (4) Sherman, *Memoirs,* I, 350.

## CHAPTER VIII. MIDDLE TENNESSEE

1. For fuller treatment of general strategic questions, see Liddell Hart (212); Sherman, *Home Letters* (277-79) and *Memoirs,* I (357-59); Cist (234-64); Fiske (281-316); *O. R.,* XXX, Pt IV, 55; and U. S. Grant, *Personal Memoirs of U. S. Grant* (New York, 1886), Vol. II, 46ff.

2. (1) *Unionville Republican,* February 28 and October 31, 1894. (2) Muster Rolls. (3) D. Leib Ambrose, *History of the Seventh Regiment Illinois Volunteer Infantry* (Springfield, Illinois, 1868), 198-99.

3. (1) Eugene O'Sullivan and James D. Coddington Pension and Military Records. (2) Muster Rolls.

4. (1) Muster Rolls. (2) *O. R.,* Vol. XXX, Pt II, 730-95.

5. (1) See Letters, Lt. Col. Charles S. Sheldon *et al* to Col. Madison Miller, October 20, 1863, and Miller to Gamble, October 23, 1863; John Williams and Jackson Grimshaw to Orville Hickman Browning, October 1, 1863, with subsequent correspondence—all in Regimental Papers, Jefferson City. (2) *D. A. B.,* II, 175-76.

6. *O. R.,* XXX, Pt IV, 378.

7. *Unionville Republican,* November 7, 1894.

8. (1) Sargeant. (2) *O. R.,* Ser. I, Vol. XXXI, Pt I, 821.

9. (1) C. R. Barnes, *The Commonwealth of Missouri* (St. Louis, 1877), 446. (2) *Unionville Republican*, November 21, 1894. (3) *Journal of the House of Representatives of the State of Missouri: Adjourned Session of the Twenty-Second General Assembly*, 427. (4) *Journal of the Senate of Missouri: Adjourned Session of the Twenty-Second General Assembly*, 111. (5) *The Missouri Republican* (St. Louis), November 27, 1863.

10. (1) *Unionville Republican*, November 7, 1894. (2) Sargeant. (3) Muster Rolls. (4) Isaac F. Shipley Pension Record.

11. (1) *Unionville Republican*, November 7, 1894. (2) Muster Rolls.

12. (1) For the itinerary of the regiment, see *O. R.*, xxx, Pt III, 289. (2) *O. R.*, xxxi, Pt III, 82-83. (3) Benjamin F. Sweet, "Civil War Experiences," edited by Vivian Kirkpatrick McLarty, *The Missouri Historical Review*, XLIII (1948-49), 248.

13. (1) Sargeant. (2) *Unionville Republican*, November 14, 1894.

14. (1) Sargeant. (2) *O. R.*, xxxi, Pt III, 121. (3) Muster Rolls. (4) See Personal Biography of Maj. Gen. Grenville Mellen Dodge (Unpublished MS, Iowa Dept. of Archives and History, Des Moines), Vol. I, 128-29. (5) For a skeptic's view of G. M. Dodge's role in building the Union Pacific, see Wallace Farnham, "Grenville M. Dodge and the Union Pacific," *Journal of American History*, LI (March, 1965), 632-50.

15. (1) *Unionville Republican*, May 1 and 15, 1895. (2) Letter, Gen. G. M. Dodge to Col. Moses M. Bane, November 19, 1863, in XVI Corps Letter Book 32.

16. (1) *O. R.*, xxxi, Pt III, 224, 373, 413-14. (2) Shelton. (3) Sargeant. (4) Muster Rolls. (5) Ambrose, 211-17. (6) Letter, Miller to Bane, December 6, 1863, in Grenville Dodge Papers (Iowa Dept. of Archives and History), Vol. 5.

17. (1) *Unionville Republican*, May 8, 1895. (2) Sargeant.

18. (1) *Unionville Republican*, May 15, 1895. (2) Interview with James L. Grabosch (son of Charles Grabosch), Unionville, Mo., June 16, 1964. (3) Charles Grabosch Pension Records. (4) John Halmark Military Record.

19. Descriptive and Muster Rolls.

20. (1) *Unionville Republican,* May 22, 1895. (2) See also Letter, Sweeny to Bane, January 17, 1864, in Madison Miller Military Record.

21. (1) *O. R.,* Ser. I, Vol. xxxII, Pt II, 188. (2) Sargeant.

22. (1) Muster Rolls. (2) Sargeant.

23. (1) See Register of General Courts Martial, Cases NN 2865 and 1266 (National Archives). (2) Letter, Col. Henry R. Mizner to Dodge, February 5, 1864, in Grenville Dodge Papers, Vol. 6. (3) Personal Biography of Maj. Gen. Grenville Mellen Dodge, Vol. I, 161. (4) Descriptive Rolls.

### CHAPTER IX. "THREE CHEERS AND A TIGER!"

1. (1) Thomas and Hyman, *Stanton,* 298. (2) Ambrose, 217. (3) Circular Letter, HQ, Dept. of the Mo., December 21, 1863, in Library, Adj. Gen. of Mo.

2. (1) Sargeant. (2) Letter, Sheldon to Brig. Gen. John B. Gray, February 2, 1864, in Regimental Papers. (3) Muster Rolls. (4) See HQ, Dept. and Army of the Tenn., Letters Received, Vol. VII, National Archives.

3. (1) War Dept. SO 35 (January 23, 1864), Regimental Papers. (2) Parrish, *Turbulent Partnership,* 175, 179.

4. (1) See Letters, Capt. George F. Balch to Madison Miller, January 27, 1864, and Miller to Asst. Adj. Gen., Dept. of the Tenn., February 10, 1864, in Madison Miller Papers, St. Louis. (2) M. Elwood Miller Military Record. (3) Descriptive and Muster Rolls. (4) See Register of General Courts Martial, Case NN 1940, National Archives. (5) Letter, Col. George E. Spencer to Madison Miller, February 13, 1864, XVI Corps Letter Book 32. (6) Personal Biography of Maj. Gen. Grenville Mellen Dodge, Vol. I, 168-69.

5. (1) Shelton. (2) Sargeant. (3) Diary of Henry Harrison Sawyer, 1864-65, made available to the author by the generosity of Mrs. Rose Sawyer Russell (daughter), Trenton, Mo.

6. (1) Sargeant. (2) Sawyer Diary. (3) Letter, Sheldon to Gray, February 25, 1864, in Regimental Papers.

7. (1) Muster and Descriptive Rolls. (2) Rhoderick R. Rockwood Military Record.

8. (1) Sargeant. (2) *Unionville Republican,* June 5, 1895. (3) Sawyer Diary. (4) Letter, Sheldon to Gray, March 8, 1864, in Regimental Papers.

9. (1) *History of Adair, Sullivan, Putnam, and Schuyler Counties,* 498-501. (2) Paxton, 336, 349, 352, 371. (3) *O. R.,* xxxiv, Pt ii, 742; Pt iii, 96. (4) Letter, D. W. to W. L. Pollock, *ca.* April 10, 1863 (David Wilson Pollock Letters).

10. (1) Sargeant. (2) Muster Rolls. (3) Cf. R. Ernest Dupuy, *The Compact History of the United States Army* (New York, 1956), 126.

11. (1) *Unionville Republican,* June 12, 1895. (2) SO 104, HQ, Dept. of the Missouri, April 15, 1864, in Regimental Papers. (3) Letter, Price to D. W. Pollock, September 15, 1892, reprinted in *Constitution of the 18th Missouri Infantry Association: Proceedings of the Reunion of 1892* (Unionville, 1893), 17. (4) John M. Garner Military and Pension Records.

12. (1) Muster Rolls. (2) GO 67 (May 7, 1864) and 71 (May 13, 1864), HQ, Dept of the Missouri, in Library, Adj. Gen. of Mo.

13. (1) Muster and Descriptive Rolls. (2) *Unionville Republican,* May 22, 1895. (3) Sawyer Diary.

14. (1) Cf. Sawyer Diary and *Grundy County Gazette,* October 24, 1935. In an interview for the *Gazette,* the nonagenarian Sawyer understandably confused his memories of the 1862 and 1864 voyages down the Mississippi. (2) Sargeant. (3) Muster Rolls.

15. (1) Sargeant. (2) Sawyer Diary.

16. (1) Letter, Col. Thomas C. Fletcher to Hon. Henry T. Blow, April 15, 1864, in Case NN 1940, Register of General Courts Martial. (2) M. Elwood Miller Military Record. (3) Parrish, *Turbulent Partnership,* 185 ff. (4) Grenville Dodge Papers, Vol. 7.

17. (1) Sargeant. (2) Muster and Descriptive Rolls. (3) Sawyer Diary. (4) *O. R.,* Vol. xxxii, Pt iii, 564.

18. (1) Sargeant. (2) *O. R.,* Vol. xxxviii, Pt i, 117. (3) Thomas and Hyman, *Stanton,* 298.
19. Sargeant.

## CHAPTER X.  FROM RESACA TO KENNESAW

1. (1) Sargeant. (2) Sawyer. (3) Shelton. (4) Muster Rolls.

2. (1) Sargeant. (2) *O. R.*, XXXVIII, Pt I, 89-108. (3) Broader treatment of strategic matters touched upon in this chapter is found in Liddell Hart, *Sherman* (238-64); Fiske (325-26); Joseph H. Parks, *Leonidas Polk, C. S. A.* (Baton Rouge, 1962), 373-82; Jacob D. Cox, *Atlanta* (New York, 1892), 36-37; Stanley F. Horn, *The Army of Tennessee* (Indianapolis, 1941), 323, 334; Sherman, *Memoirs*, II (34-61, 391); Gilbert E. Govan and James W. Livingood, *A Different Valor* (Indianapolis, 1956), 269-302; David P. Conyngham, *Sherman's March through the South* (New York, 1865), 78; Freeman Cleaves, *Rock of Chickamauga* (Norman, Oklahoma, 1948), 214-24.

3. (1) *O. R.*, XXXVIII, Pt IV, 69, 70, 85. (2) Sargeant.

4. *O. R.*, XXXVIII, Pt IV, 71, 79, 86-87, 90-94.

5. (1) IV *Battles and Leaders*, 298. (2) Shelton. (3) Sawyer. (4) Lurton D. Ingersoll, *Iowa and the Rebellion* (Philadelphia, 1866), 720. (5) GO 32, HQ, 4th Div., XVI Corps (May 9, 1864), in XVII Corps Orders, Book 21, National Archives.

6. *O. R.*, XXXVIII, Pt III, 375-76; Pt IV, 104-105.

7. (1) *O. R.*, XXXVIII, Pt III, 376-77, 493, 501. (2) Muster and Descriptive Rolls. (3) Sargeant. (4) T. Franklin Green and Joseph D. Hamilton Pension Records. (5) Charles H. Smith, *History of Fuller's Ohio Brigade* [hereafter *Ohio Brigade*] (Cleveland, 1909), 146-48.

8. (1) Joseph E. Johnston, *Narrative of Military Operations* (New York, 1874), 316. (2) Johnston, "The Dalton-Atlanta Operations," *The Annals of the Army of Tennessee*, I (April, 1878), 2-3. (3) Sargeant. (4) *O. R.*, XXXVIII, Pt IV, 106. (5) See also Consolidated Morning Reports, 9th Illinois Vol. Inf., National Archives. (6) *Report of the Proceedings of the Society of the Army of the Tennessee at the Thirty-Sixth Meeting* [hereafter, *S.A.T.*], Council Bluffs, Iowa, November 8-9, 1906 (Cincinnati, 1907), 191.

9. (1) Sawyer. (2) Sargeant.

10. (1) *Annual Report* (1865). (2) Sawyer. (3) Muster Rolls. (4) *O. R.*, XXXVIII, Pt III, 377; Pt IV, 161, 196.

11. (1) Sargeant. (2) Sawyer.

12. (1) Descriptive and Muster Rolls. (2) Conrad Fischer Pension Record.

13. (1) Sargeant. (2) Sawyer. (3) *O. R.*, xxxviii, Pt iii, 379.

14. (1) Sawyer. (2) *Annual Report* (1865).

15. (1) *O. R.*, xxxviii, Pt iii, 379. (2) *O. R.*, xxxviii, Pt iv, 309-14. (3) Muster Rolls.

16. *O. R.*, xxxviii, Pt iv, 313-14, 380.

17. (1) Muster and Descriptive Rolls. (2) Sawyer. (3) *Annual Report* (1865).

18. (1) *O. R.*, xxxviii, Pt iii, 130. (2) Sargeant. (3) Morning Reports, 18th Mo. Vols., National Archives.

19. (1) *Annual Report* (1865). (2) *O. R.*, xxxviii, Pt iii, 380-81, 489; Pt iv, 381. (3) Personal Biography of Maj. Gen. Grenville Mellen Dodge, Vol. 102 (Folder).

20. (1) Descriptive Rolls. (2) Sawyer. (3) Parrish, *Turbulent Partnership*, 181-84. (4) Daniel and Priscilla Torrey Pension Records.

21. (1) *O. R.*, xxxviii, Pt iii, 381, 484. (2) *Annual Report* (1865). (3) Sargeant.

22. (1) Sargeant. (2) John Bell Hood, *Advance and Retreat* (Bloomington, Indiana, 1959), 318.

23. (1) Sargeant. (2) William H. Minter Pension Record. (3) Muster and Descriptive Rolls. (4) *Annual Report* (1865). (5) Regimental Orders [RO] 7 (June 26) and 9 (July 1, 1864), 18th Mo. Vols., National Archives.

24. War Record of Benjamin F. Sweet [hereafter, Sweet], Western Historical Manuscripts Collection, Columbia, Missouri.

25. (1) Descriptive and Muster Rolls. (2) *Unionville Republican.* May 1, 1895. (3) Elkanah W. Howard Pension Record. (4) *Confederate Military History*, Vol. vi, 315.

26. (1) Sawyer. (2) *Annual Report* (1865). (3) *O. R.*, xxxviii, Pt iii, 381; Pt iv, 554-55. (4) Member of the Rock City Guards, "Battle of Kennesaw Mountain," *Annals of the Army of Tennessee*, i (June, 1878), 109.

27. (1) *Home Letters of General Sherman*, 297-98. (2) Sawyer. (3) Muster Rolls.

28. (1) Whitelaw Reid, *Ohio in the War* (Cincinnati, 1868), 905-906. (2) *O. R.*, xxxviii, Pt iii, 384-85, 484.

29. (1) Sawyer. (2) Letter, Benjamin to Caroline Guffey, June 30, 1864, in possession of Wineyfred Guffey Ashlock and made available to the author through her generosity and that of Donald F. Hulin of Tacoma, Washington.

30. (1) Sargeant. (2) Letter, Sheldon to Gray, September 22, 1864, in Regimental Papers.

31. *Annual Report* (1865).

## CHAPTER XI. "ATLANTA IS OURS . . ."

1. (1) Muster and Descriptive Rolls. (2) *O. R.*, xxxviii, Pt iii, 485, 490, 498. (3) *Annual Report* (1865). (4) Frederick Partenheimer and John B. Priester Pension Records. (5) *Ohio Brigade*, 157-60.

2. Strategic matters treated in this chapter may be studied at greater length in Sherman, *Memoirs*, ii, 67-110; F. Y. Hedley, *Marching through Georgia* (Chicago, 1890), 140; Cleaves, 229-40; O. O. Howard, *Autobiography of Oliver Otis Howard* (New York, 1907), ii, 6-40; Grenville M. Dodge, *The Battle of Atlanta and Other Campaigns* . . . (Council Bluffs, Iowa, 1911), 39-58, 131; *Confederate Military History*, vi, 329, 350-51; Liddell Hart, *Sherman*, 285-87; Conyngham, 190-201; Hood, 207, 322; Horn, 353-56.

3. (1) Muster Rolls. (2) Sargeant. (3) Johnathan M. Yates Pension Record. (4) *Grundy County Gazette*, October 24, 1935.

4. (1) *Grundy County Gazette, ibid.* (2) Muster Rolls. (3) *O. R.*, xxxviii, Pt iii, 486. (4) Sargeant.

5. (1) *Annual Report* (1865). (2) Sargeant. (3) Shelton. (4) Sawyer. (5) Descriptive Rolls.

6. (1) *O. R.*, xxxviii, Pt i, 108. (2) *Civil War Dictionary*, 869.

7. *Annual Report* (1865).

8. (1) *O. R.*, xxxviii, Pt i, 486; Pt iii, 384-85, 475, 486, 490. (2)

*Annual Report* (1865). (3) Sargeant. (4) Grenville Dodge Papers, Vol. 7 (unbound letters).

9.  (1) Sargeant. (2) *O. R.*, xxxviii, Pt iii, 499, 503. (3) *Unionville Republican*, June 12, 1895. (4) D. A. Cudworth, "Memories of Fifty Years Ago," 235.

10.  (1) Sargeant. (2) War Record of Benjamin Sweet. (3) *O. R.*, xxxviii, Pt iii, 479. (4) Cudworth.

11.  (1) Sargeant. (2) Shelton. (3) *S. A. T.*, *Seventh Annual Meeting*, Toledo, Ohio, October 15-16, 1873 (Cincinnati, 1877), 166-67; . . . *Thirty-Sixth Annual Meeting*, Council Bluffs, Iowa, November 8-9, 1906 (Cincinnati, 1907), 191. (4) Wilbur G. Kurtz maintains that W. H. T. Walker was never in Fuller's sector. See his "The Death of Maj. Gen. W. H. T. Walker," in *Civil War History*, vi (1960), 174-79.

12.  (1) Sargeant. (2) *O. R.*, xxxviii, Pt iii, 495-96. (3) *Annual Report* (1865).

13.  (1) *O. R.*, xxxviii, Pt iii, 165; Pt i, 72. (2) Sargeant.

14.  (1) *O. R.*, xxxviii, Pt iii, 385, 516, 952-53. (2) Smith's *Ohio Brigade* (165-73) is unable to give the 18th Missouri the slightest recognition for its share in the battle of July 22 alongside the Ohioans.

15.  (1) Sargeant. (2) Letter, Sheldon to Gray, August 1, 1864, in Regimental Papers.

16.  (1) Descriptive and Muster Rolls. (2) *The Weston* (Mo.) *Chronicle*, February 16, 1906. (3) Sargeant. (4) *O. R.*, xxxviii, Pt iii, 373. (5) Simon and Mathew Kredel, Joseph Anderson, Henry Pagin, Andrew J. Morgan, and John A. Drake Pension Records.

17.  (1) Letter, Sheldon to Gray, August 1, 1864. (2) Muster and Descriptive Rolls. (3) Sawyer. (4) Benjamin F. Johns, Silas W. Haynes, and Daniel Dewitt Pension Records.

18.  (1) *O. R.*, xxxviii, Pt iii, 385; Pt v, 252-53. (2) ii *Battles and Leaders*, 326. (3) *S. A. T.*, *Twenty-Third Annual Meeting*, Chicago, October 7-8, 1891 (Cincinnati, 1893), 548; *Twenty-Ninth Annual Meeting*, Milwaukee, Wisconsin, October 27-28, 1897 (Cincinnati, 1898), 62. (4) See Case LL 2995, Register of General Courts Martial, Record Group 94, National Archives.

(5) XVI Corps Letter Book 32 and HQ, Dept. and Army of the Tenn., Endorsements, Vols. ix and xi—Supplement, National Archives. (6) Grenville Dodge Papers, Vol. 7.

19. (1) Sargeant. (2) See also James P. Jones, "The Battle of Atlanta and McPherson's Successor," *Civil War History,* vii (1961), which ignores the role of Fuller's 4th Division in the battle (393-405).

20. (1) Sargeant. (2) *S. A. T., Twenty-Sixth Annual Meeting,* Council Bluffs, Iowa, October 3-4, 1894 (Cincinnati, 1895), 134. (3) Sawyer. (4) *Annual Report* (1865).

21. (1) *Annual Report* (1865). (2) Sargeant. (3) *O. R.* xxxviii, Pt iii, 486.

22. (1) Sargeant. (2) Letter, Sheldon to Gray, August 1, 1864. (3) Sawyer. (4) *O. R.,* xxxviii, Pt iii, 60-61.

23. (1) Sargeant. (2) Letters, Sheldon to Gray, July 6 and August 1, 1864. (3) Muster and Descriptive Rolls. (4) Regimental Orders [RO] 10, HQ, 18th Mo. Vols., July 10, 1864, National Archives. (5) Reuben Pinion Pension Record. (6) See HQ, Dept. and Army of the Tenn., Letters Received, Vol. ix, and Endorsements, Vol. x, National Archives.

24. (1) Muster and Descriptive Rolls. (2) Gebhart Kurtz Pension Records. (3) Quartermaster Department, U.S. Army, *Honor Roll,* Vol. xxiii, *passim.*

25. (1) Sargeant. (2) Hodding Carter, *The Angry Scar* (New York, 1959), 112. (3) *The Atlantic Monthly,* ix (February, 1862), 10.

26. (1) *S. A. T., Thirty-Seventh Annual Meeting,* Vicksburg, Mississippi, November 7-8, 1907 (Cincinnati, 1908), 138-39. (2) Sargeant. (3) *O. R.,* xxxviii, Pt i, 108. (4) Personal Biography of Maj. Gen. Grenville Mellen Dodge, Vol. i, 264. (5) Barbara Cheeney and Daniel Hudson Pension Records. (6) Muster Rolls.

27. (1) *Annual Report* (1865). (2) Sawyer. (3) Sherman, 104.

28. (1) Diary of Capt. Rhoderick R. Rockwood, made available to the author through the courtesy of Mr. Forrest C. Rockwood, Kalispell, Montana. (2) *O. R.,* xxxviii, Pt iii, 535. (3) Muster Rolls.

29. (1) Rockwood Diary. (2) *Annual Report* (1865).

30. (1) Sargeant. (2) Rockwood. (3) *Annual Report* (1865). (4) Hood, 207.

31. (1) Sargeant. (2) Rockwood. (3) Sawyer. (4) RO 20, HQ, 18th Mo. Vols. (September 12, 1864). (5) See XVII Corps Letter Book 23, National Archives.

32. (1) Muster Rolls. (2) Thomas Pollock Pension Record. (3) Letter, Peter R. Dolman to D. W. Pollock, January 13, 1893, reprinted in *Constitution of the 18th Missouri Infantry Association: Proceedings of the Reunion of 1892* (Unionville, 1893).

33. *O. R.*, xxxix, Pt ii, 444, 477, 557.

34. (1) *O. R.*, xxxviii, Pt iii, 499. (2) Muster Rolls. (3) GO 22, HQ, Dept. and Army of the Tenn. (August 26, 1864), National Archives. (4) HQ, Dept. and Army of the Tenn., Letters Received, ix. (5) Scharf, i, 481.

35. (1) Parrish, *Turbulent Partnership*, 185-94. (2) Brownlee, *Gray Ghosts of the Confederacy*, 208-27.

### CHAPTER XII. TO THE ALABAMA LINE

1. General information on Hood's "march to the rear" may be consulted in Hood (253-63); Liddell Hart (317-26); Sherman (145-61); *Confederate Military History*, vi (357); *Annual Report* (1865); Cleaves (247); Howard, ii (65); George Ward Nichols, *The Story of the Great March* (New York, 1865), 286-87; Parrish, *Turbulent Partnership*, 185-94.

2. (1) Rockwood. (2) Sawyer. (3) Sargeant.

3. (1) Sargeant. (2) Rockwood and Sawyer Diaries. (3) Henry T. McDowell Pension Record. (4) Special Field Orders 142, HQ, Dept. and Army of the Tenn. (October 20, 1864), National Archives. (5) Muster Rolls.

4. (1) Sargeant. (2) *O. R.*, xxxix, Pt iii, 293-94.

5. (1) Descriptive and Muster Rolls. (2) *Roll of Honor*, Vols. xi, xxiii. (3) Letters, Billie E. Embree (grandnephew of Thomas G. Wade) to the author, August 26 and September 14, 1966. (4) Letter, Mrs. Nathan E. Wells to the author, August 22, 1966.

6. (1) Sargeant. (2) Rockwood.

7. (1) Sargeant. (2) Sawyer.

8. (1) Sargeant. (2) Rockwood.

9. (1) Sargeant. (2) *O. R.*, xxxix, Pt ii, pp. 419-20. (3) *S. A. T.*, *Thirty-Sixth Meeting*, 242. (4) *Dictionary of American Biography*, Vol. vii, 299-300. (5) Nichols, 286-87.

10. (1) *O. R.*, xxxix, Pt iii, 533. (2) Letters, Isaac V. Pratt to Governor Hall and Maj. Gen. W. S. Rosecrans, April 8, 1864, in Regimental Papers. (3) Sawyer. (4) Rockwood. (5) RO 47 (November 10, 1864). (6) Muster Rolls. (7) John W. Fuller Papers, Union Staff Officers File, National Archives. (8) George W. Wyckoff Military Record.

11. Howard N. Monnett, *Action before Westport* (Kansas City, Mo., 1964), 77-126.

12. Rockwood and Sawyer Diaries.

### CHAPTER XIII. MARCHING THROUGH GEORGIA

1. General sources consulted for this account of the March through Georgia are Cist (237); Parrish (196); Howard ii (87-92); Nichols (577-78); *Annual Report* (1865); John M. Gibson, *Those 163 Days* (New York, 1961), 16-91; iv *Battles and Leaders* (663-72); Sherman, ii (171-231, 380); Liddell Hart (329-38); Conyngham (238-89); *Confederate Military History*, vi (359-60).

2. *O. R.*, xliv, 65-66, 452, 460.

3. (1) *S. A. T.*, *Thirty-Sixth Annual Meeting*, 241. (2) *O. R.*, xliv, 459.

4. Sweet.

5. Gibson, 16.

6. (1) *O. R.*, xliv, 874. (2) The term "oasis of loyalty" was coined by Sherman's son, Father Thomas Ewing Sherman, in 1897. Cf. *S. A. T.*, *Twenty-Ninth Annual Meeting*, 66.

7. (1) *O. R.*, xliv, 32-33, 63-66, 147-51. (2) Muster Rolls. (3) George Ward Nichols, "Sherman's Great March," *Harper's New Monthly Magazine*, xxxi (October, 1865), 577.

8. (1) *Unionville Republican,* June 12, 1895. (2) Sargeant. (3) *S. A. T., Twenty-First Annual Meeting,* Toledo, September 5-6, 1888 (Cincinnati, 1893), 98.

9. Robert C. Black, *The Railroads of the Confederacy* (Chapel Hill, North Carolina, 1952), 261.

10. (1) Muster Rolls. (2) *O. R.,* XLIV, 32-33, 60, 147-48. (3) Diary of Elias Perry, Western Historical Manuscripts Collection.

11. (1) Muster Rolls. (2) *O. R.,* XLIV, 149-51. (3) Sargeant.

12. (1) Descriptive Rolls. (2) Letter, the Adjutant General, U. S. Army, to the Adjutant General of Missouri, March 28, 1917, in Regimental Papers.

13. (1) Sargeant. (2) Rockwood and Perry Diaries.

14. (1) *O. R.,* XLIV, 8, 207, 214. (2) Case 578, Probate Court Records, Putnam County, Mo.

15. (1) *O. R.,* XLIV, 61, 147-48. (2) Lloyd Lewis, *Sherman: Fighting Prophet* (New York, 1958), 442. (3) Sherman's estimate of "stragglers captured" was a little low. Cf. Muster Rolls. (4) Letter, the Reverend George W. Corporon to the author, May 3, 1966.

16. *O. R.,* XLIV, 104, 928.

17. *O. R.,* XLIV, 9, 649, 659, 669.

18. (1) Joseph M. Stanley Pension Records. (2) Muster Rolls.

19. Theodore F. Upson, *With Sherman to the Sea* (Bloomington, Indiana, 1958), 139.

20. *O. R.,* XLIV, 111, 701, 705-706.

21. Cf. Muster and Descriptive Rolls.

22. *O. R.,* XLIV, 147-51, 730-32.

23. *O. R.,* XLIV, 33.

24. Jefferson Davis, *The Rise and Fall of the Confederate Government* (New York, 1881), 573.

25. W. G. F. Shanks, "Recollections of General Sherman," *Harper's New Monthly Magazine,* XXX (April, 1865), 640-46.

26. (1) Sargeant. (2) Perry, Rockwood, and Sawyer Diaries. (3) RO 52 (December 23) and 53 (December 27, 1864).

27. (1) Sargeant. (2) Muster Rolls.

28. (1) Muster Rolls. (2) RO 50 (December 23, 1864). (3) War Department Special Orders 256 (November 12, 1881).

29. (1) Barbara Cheeney Pension Record. (2) Sargeant. (3) Kenton F. Breeman Military Record.

30. *O. R.*, Ser. III, Vol. I, 796.

31. Lewis, 442, 547.

CHAPTER XIV. "GRAB A ROOT, COLONEL!"

1. (1) Chief sources for the broader aspects of the winter campaign in South Carolina were Howard, II (95-137); Liddell Hart (360-62); Sherman, *Home Letters* (321, 326); Sherman, *Memoirs*, II (254-300); *Annual Report* (1865); Gibson (134); John G. Barrett, *Sherman's March through the Carolinas* (Chapel Hill, 1956), 48-107; Conyngham (301-28); Nichols, *The Great March* (154-60); Hedley (368-70); IV *Battles and Leaders* 687. (2) *S. A. T., Thirty-Fourth Annual Meeting*, Washington, D. C., October 15-16, 1903 (Cincinnati, 1906), 125.

2. (1) Sargeant. (2) Perry and Sawyer. (3) Muster Rolls. (4) Mrs. John A. Logan, *Reminiscences of a Soldier's Wife* (New York, 1913), 181. (5) *O. R.*, XLVII, Pt II, 27.

3. (1) Perry and Rockwood. (2) *O. R.*, XLVII, Pt I, 91.

4. (1) Muster Rolls. (2) *O. R.*, XLVII, Pt II, 1020.

5. (1) Letter, Sheldon to Col. Samuel P. Simpson, January 16, 1865, in Regimental Papers. (2) David Wilson Pollock Pension Record. (3) Muster Rolls. (4) RO 3 (January 10), 5 (January 15), 8 (January 19), and 9 (January 20, 1865).

6. (1) *Messages and Proclamations of the Governors of Missouri*, Vol. IV, 65, 186, 188, 191. (2) William Brantner Pension Record. (3) *O. R.*, XLVII, Pt II, 70; Pt III, 152.

7. (1) Sargeant. (2) Perry. (3) *O. R.*, XLVII, Pt I, 91.

8. (1) Sargeant. (2) RO 6 (January 17) and 12 (January 28, 1865).

9. RO 10 and 11 (January 27, 1865).

10. (1) Sargeant. (2) *Unionville Republican,* June 12, 1895.

11. (1) Sargeant. (2) Perry and Rockwood Diaries. (3) *O. R.,* XLVII, Pt I, 375, 386-89. (4) Walter Williams, *History of Northeast Missouri* (Chicago, 1913), Vol. III, 1519. (5) Bruce Catton, "Glory Road Began in the West," *Civil War History,* VI (1960), 229-37.

12. *O. R.,* XLVII, Pt I, 386-89, 400-401.

13. (1) Rockwood and Perry Diaries. (2) Sargeant.

14. (1) Rockwood and Perry Diaries. (2) Sargeant. (3) *O. R.,* XLVII, Pt I, 376-77, 386-89, 393-98. (4) Sweet. (5) Muster and Descriptive Rolls. (6) *Ohio Brigade,* 264-67.

15. (1) Muster Rolls. (2) *S. A. T., Thirty-Sixth Annual Meeting,* 243.

16. (1) Sweet. (2) *O. R.,* XLVII, Pt I, 377-78.

17. (1) Perry. (2) Sargeant. (3) *O. R.,* XLVII, Pt I, 399-402.

18. RO 13 (February 12, 1865).

19. Rockwood and Perry Diaries.

20. (1) Rockwood. (2) Sargeant. (3) *Unionville Republican,* June 12, 1895.

21. (1) Rockwood. (2) Sargeant. (3) *O. R.,* XLVII, Pt I, 92, 379.

22. (1) Muster Rolls. (2) Sargeant. (3) Rockwood and Perry.

23. (1) Sargeant. (2) Perry. (3) *O. R.,* XLVII, Pt I, 381.

24. (1) Perry and Rockwood Diaries. (2) *O. R.,* XLVII, Pt I, 381-82. (3) Sargeant.

25. Rockwood.

26. (1) Sargeant. (2) *O. R.,* XLVII, Pt I, 92-93, 382; Pt II, 690, 703, 718, 731, 740, 761. (3) Rockwood and Perry.

27. (1) Sargeant. (2) *O. R.,* XLVII, Pt II, 822.

### CHAPTER XV. THE LAST DITCH

1. General works consulted for this account of the Bentonville campaign were Jay Luvaas, "Johnston's Last Stand—Bentonville," *North Carolina Historical Review,* XXXIII (June, 1956), 332-58; *Annual Report* (1865); Sherman, *Memoirs,* II (303-

51); Sherman, *Home Letters* (334-44); Barrett (163-269); Hedley (406); Howard, II (146-50); Liddell Hart (384-97). See also (1) Perry. (2) Sargeant. (3) *O. R.*, XLVII, Pt I, 382-83; Pt II, 848, 865, 876, 889.

2. (1) Sargeant. (2) Perry. (3) *O. R.*, XLVII, Pt I, 383; Pt II, 901-903.

3. Perry.

4. (1) *O. R.*, XLVII, Pt I, 69-70, 383-84, 391, 395-97, 399, 403-404, 1097-98. (2) Sargeant. (3) Perry and Rockwood Diaries. (4) Muster and Descriptive Rolls. (5) Joseph M. Brown Pension Record. (6) Ambrose, *Seventh Illinois*, 301. (7) *Ohio Brigade*, 273-76.

5. (1) *O. R.*, XLIV, Pt II, 942. (2) Perry.

6. (1) Letters, Sheldon to Simpson, January 16 and March 28, 1865, in Regimental Papers. (2) *Unionville Republican*, June 12, 1895. (3) Perry and Rockwood Diaries. (4) RO 15, 16, 17, 18, 19, 20, 21, 23, and 24 (March 25-April 4, 1865). (5) Muster Rolls. (6) Henry W. Godfrey Pension and Military Records. (7) Minter Pension Record.

7. (1) *O. R.*, XLVII, Pt I, 93. (2) *D. A. B.*, III, 511-12. (3) Letter, Joseph A. Mower for William Hemstreet, March 27, 1865, in Regimental Papers.

8. *Grundy County Gazette*, October 24, 1935.

9. (1) Thomas and Hyman, *Stanton*, 402-18. (2) Sargeant.

10. (1) Rockwood. (2) Sargeant.


### CHAPTER XVI. THE BROTHERHOOD OF BATTLE

1. Sherman, *Memoirs*, II, 379.

2. (1) Sargeant. (2) *Grundy County Gazette*, October 24, 1935.

3. (1) Sargeant. (2) *O. R.*, XLVII, Pt I, 94. (3) Rockwood. (4) RO 36 (May 29, 1865).

4. (1) Thomas and Hyman, 414. (2) Sargeant.

5. (1) John A. Drake Military and Pension Records. (2) Sargeant. (3) Descriptive and Muster Rolls.

6. (1) Sargeant. (2) Sherman, *Memoirs* II, 376-77. (3) Howard, II, 210-12. (4) Liddell Hart, 401. (5) Descriptive Rolls.

7. (1) Letter, Brig. Gen. John W. Fuller to Maj. Gen. Francis P. Blair, Jr., May 25, 1865, in Record Group 98 (XVII Corps, Book 23), National Archives. (2) RO 35, 37, and 38 (May 29-June 2, 1865). (3) *O. R.*, XLVII, Pt III, 584.

8. (1) Sargeant. (2) Descriptive and Muster Rolls.

9. (1) RO 47 (June 17, 1865), 61 (June 28), 46 (June 16), 59 (June 26), and 60 (June 27). (2) Letter, Minter to Fletcher, May 1, 1865, in Regimental Papers. (3) *Annual Report* (1865). (4) Muster and Descriptive Rolls.

10. (1) RO 53 (June 20), 57 (June 23) and 48 (June 18, 1865). (2) XVII Corps General Orders, Book 21, National Archives. (3) Sargeant.

11. (1) RO 63 (June 29) and 68 (July 8, 1865). (2) XVII Corps General Orders, Book 21.

12. (1) Sweet. (2) RO 49 (June 19), 67 (July 6), 69 (July 11), 1865. (3) *O. R.*, XLIX, Pt II, 1047-48. (4) Smith (*Ohio Brigade*, 303-304) omits mention of Sherman's "last visit" to the brigade, vividly described by Sweet.

13. (1) Sargeant. (2) Descriptive and Muster Rolls. (3) *Tri-Weekly Missouri Democrat* (St. Louis), July 24 and 28, 1865.


## APPENDIX
### THE EIGHTEENTH MISSOURI AFTER THE WAR

1. (1) Sargeant. (2) Edwin J. Conway and Barbara Cheeney Pension Records. (3) *Report of the Adjutant General, State of Missouri, for the Years 1877 and 1878* (Jefferson City, 1879). (4) Senate Document 412 (232).

2. (1) *Plat Book of Putnam County, Missouri* (Philadelphia, 1897), no pagination. (2) *Unionville Republican*, March 7, 1906; May 13, 1914. (3) Henry S. Wells Pension Record.

3. (1) Interview with Vernia Hoover Childers (granddaughter of Lawrence Hoover), Green City, Mo., July 18, 1966. (2) *Green City* (Mo.) *Press*, July 18, 1913; May 2, 1918. (3) Letter,

Lawrence Hall (grandson of Lawrence Hoover) to Vernia Childers, April 11, 1966. (4) Letter, Mrs. Velma Watt (niece of Henry Runnels) to the author, April 18, 1966.

4. (1) *The History of Linn County, Missouri*, 615-16, 579. (2) *History and Biography of Linn County*, 378-79. (3) Letter, Mrs. Evelyn Sheets (Trenton, Mo.) to the author, October 10, 1964. (4) *Brookfield Gazette*, May 12, 1893; April 7, 1900. (5) Isaac V. Pratt Pension Record.

5. (1) Letter, Mr. and Mrs. Bert Gibson, DeWitt, Mo., to the author, July 4, 1966. (2) *DeWitt* (Mo.) *Herald*, April 15, 1926. (3) Probate Records, Carroll and Schuyler Counties. (4) *History of Grundy County* (Kansas City, Mo., 1881), 542. (5) James E. Ford, *A History of Grundy County* (Trenton, 1908), 721. (6) *The Weekly Graphic* (Kirksville, Mo.), September 28, 1934. (7) Paxton, 608, 881. (8) *The Democrat-Herald* (Smithville, Mo.), January 25, 1924.

6. (1) *Baxter Springs* (Kansas) *Citizen*, March 16, 1932. (2) *History of Wayne and Appanoose Counties, Iowa* (Chicago, 1886), 708-709. (3) Interview with Bert Wyckoff (grandson of G. W. Wyckoff), Unionville, Mo., August 7, 1964. (4) Letter, Mr. and Mrs. Forrest C. Rockwood, Kalispell, Mont., to the author, October 29, 1964. (5) Thomas Cawood and Ezra Havens Pension Records. (6) Lingenfelter, "Notes from the Family of Thomas McComb."

7. (1) *Unionville Republican*, December 8, 1889; March 2, 1910. (2) *St. Paul* (Minn.) *Pioneer Press*, November 27, 1924. (3) *History and Biography of Linn County, Missouri*, 378-79. (4) *The Sioux City* (Iowa) *Journal*, December 1, 1915. (5) *The Springfield* (Mo.) *Daily Leader*, September 30, 1904. (6) *History of Noble County, Ohio*, 282-84. (7) Interview with Vernia Childers, July 18, 1966. (8) *Brookfield* (Mo.) *Gazette*, March 8, 1919.

8. (1) Paxton, 348. (2) William Kuemmel Pension Record. (3) See *In Memoriam* File, Missouri Commandery, Military Order of the Loyal Legion, Missouri Historical Society. (4) *St. Louis Post-Dispatch*, February 28, 1896. (5) *The Atchison* (Kansas) *Daily Globe*, January 4, 1918.

9. (1) *LaPlata* (Mo.) *Home Press*, November 20, 1924. (2) Letter, Wineyfred Guffey Ashlock (daughter of Benjamin Guffey) to the author, September 1, 1964. (3) Interview with La-

fayette Shelton, Unionville, Mo., July 21, 1966. (4) James A.
Price, Orlando B. Douglas, and Richard Endicott Pension
Records. (5) Paxton, 324, 328, 470, 525, 572, 705, 955. (6)
*Unionville Republican,* October 8, 1868. (7) *San Francisco*
(Cal.) *Chronicle,* April 13, 1891. (8) Letters, William R.
Denslow and Mrs. Goldie Worth to the author, September 26
and August 24, 1964. (9) *The Times* (Independence, Kansas),
August 20, 1909. (10) Interview with R. W. Benecke (son of
Louis Benecke), Brunswick, Mo., August 5, 1964. (11) *History
of Linn County, Missouri,* 260-61.

10. (1) *Unionville Republican,* January 21 and February 11, 1875.
(2) *Historical, Pictorial, and Biographical Record of Chariton
County, Missouri,* 238-39. (3) See *First Biennial Report of the
Board of Trustees of the Federal Soldiers' Home* (Rolla, Mo.,
1899), 5; and *Eighth Report . . .* (Mexico, Mo., 1913), 11. (4)
Madison Miller Papers. (5) *Journal of the Senate of the State
of Missouri at the Regular Session of the Twenty-Third General
Assembly,* 51, 78; . . . *Twenty-Sixth General Assembly,* 4. (6)
Howard K. Beale, ed., *The Diary of Edward Bates, 1859-1866*
(Washington, D. C., 1933), 519.

11. (1) *Journal of the House of Representatives of the State of
Missouri at the Regular Session of the Thirty-Second General
Assembly,* 5. (2) *The Press-Journal* (Louisiana, Mo.), July 14,
1904. (3) J. T. Pratt, *Pen-Pictures of the Officers and Members
of the House of Representatives of the 26th General Assembly*
(n.p., 1872), 40-41. (4) Interview with Bert Wyckoff.

12. (1) *The Jackson County World* (Circleville, Kansas), May 19,
1905. (2) *Howard* (Kans.) *Courant-Ledger,* November 21,
1878. (3) *Official Manual of the State of Missouri for the Year
1899-1900* (Jefferson City, 1899), 224. (4) *Unionville Republican,* February 7, 1868; June 19, 1879. (5) *Milan* (Mo.) *Republican,* January 3, 1879. (6) *The New York Times,* October
16-17, 1920.

13. (1) Interview with Mrs. Irene Loyles (granddaughter of James
A. Price) and Miss Forestyne Loyles (great-granddaughter of
Price), Weston, Mo., July 3, 1965. (2) Paxton, 608, 881. (3)
Interview with R. W. Benecke. (4) Theodore Calvin Pease and
James G. Randall, eds., *The Diary of Orville Hickman Browning*
(Springfield, Illinois, 1933), Vol. III, 380.

14. (1) *History of Noble County, Ohio,* 303-304. (2) *History of
Wayne and Appanoose Counties,* 708-709. (3) George W. A.
Preston Pension Record. (4) S. K. Turner and S. A. Clark,

*Twentieth Century History of Carroll County, Missouri* (Indianapolis, 1911), 707-709. (5) *History of Adair, Sullivan, Putnam and Schuyler Counties*, 572. (6) *The Weston* (Mo.) *Chronicle*, February 16, 1906.

15. For an authoritative discussion of the financing of postwar railway construction, one should consult William E. Parrish's *Missouri under Radical Rule* (Columbia, Mo., 1965), 186-210.

16. See *S. A. T., Seventh Annual Meeting*, 166, 185, 189, 193; *Twenty-Fourth Annual Meeting*, 151, 191.

17. (1) *Unionville Republican*, April 30, 1890; February 10, 1892. (2) *The Republic* (St. Louis, Mo.), August 8, 1889. (3) Descriptive Rolls. (4) Madison Miller Papers.

18. (1) *St. Paul* (Minn.) *Pioneer Press*, November 27, 1924. (2) Interview with R. W. Benecke. (3) *Unionville Republican*, June 6, 1894. (4) Records of Noble Post 491, G.A.R., in Ohio Historical Society, Columbus.

19. Letter, Mrs. Gertrude Hersey Cudworth (daughter-in-law of D. A. Cudworth) to the author, November 25, 1965.

20. (1) *Unionville Republican*, March 8, 1877; September 18, 1929. (2) *The Republican-Times* (Trenton, Mo.), January 30, 1936. (3) *The Trenton Daily Republican*, October 27, 1915. (4) Turner and Clark, 708-709. (5) *The Republican-Record* (Carrollton, Mo.), May 20, 1920. (6) Letter, Mrs. Evelyn Sheets to the author, September 23, 1964. (7) Interview, author with Mrs. Vernia Childers. (8) Letter, Dr. Paul Lomax (grandson of John Lomax) to the author, October 26, 1964.

21. (1) *Unionville Republican*, April 23, 1868; April 23, 1890; March 10, 1897. (2) Williams, *History of Northeast Missouri*, III, 1446. (3) *Brookfield Gazette*, May 12, 1893. (4) Interview with Benecke.

22. (1) *Unionville Republican*, August 13, 1890; September 24, 1890; October 1, 1890; January 4, 1893; September 8 and 22, 1897; October 3, 1900; March 2, 1910. (2) *Milan Republican*, July 10, 1884. (3) *Constitution of the 18th Missouri Infantry Association: Proceedings of the Reunion of 1892*. (4) *Constitution of the 18th Missouri Infantry Association: Roster of Surviving Members . . .* (Unionville, 1897).

23. Sargeant.

24. (1) Andrew J. Morgan Pension Record. (2) Lomax Papers. (3) *Milan Republican*, January 3, 1879. (4) *Unionville Republican*, June 19, 1879.

25. (1) *Unionville Republican*, August 5, 1886. (2) William H. Minter Pension Record. (3) *St. Louis Post Dispatch*, February 28, 1896.

26. (1) Charles S. Sargeant Pension Record. (2) *The American Iliad,* 648. (3) Interview with Mrs. Violet Morgareidge (former Village Clerk, Caldwell, Ohio), June 8, 1864. (4) Interview with Mr. Clare Tipton, Caldwell, June 8, 1964. (5) Leslie Anders, "Missourians Who Marched through Georgia," *Missouri Historical Review,* LIX (January, 1965), 192-209. Sargeant's widow died in Chicago in 1939 and was buried beside her husband at Caldwell.

27. (1) See *The Cole Camp Courier, Sedalia Democrat*, and *Benton County Enterprise* (Warsaw) for October, 1902. (2) *Carrollton Daily Democrat*, August 10, 1905. (3) *History of Northeast Missouri*, III, 1519. (4) *Unionville Republican*, March 2, 1910; May 13, 1914.

28. (1) *The Sioux City* (Iowa) *Journal*, December 1, 1915. (2) *The Trenton Daily Republican*, October 27, 1915.

29. (1) Bernhard Little and John Howry Pension Records. (2) *The Democrat-Herald* (Smithville, Mo.), January 25, February 8, 1924. (3) *The Laclede* (Mo.) *Blade*, September 19, 1919.

30. *The New York Times*, October 16 and 17, 1920.

31. (1) *Unionville Republican*, June 17, 1869. (2) Letter, Wanda Pilatz Martin to the author, June 28, 1966. (3) Interview with Wanda Pilatz Martin and Freda Pilatz Waller (daughters of W. C. Pilatz), Brunswick, Mo., July 18, 1966.

32. (1) Letters, George W. Corporon (nephew of G. W. Corporon) to the author, May 3 and 16, 1966. (2) *History of Adair, Sullivan, Putnam and Schuyler Counties*, 767. (3) Franklin Green Pension Record. (4) Samuel Frankfort Pension Record. (5) *The Republican-Times* (Trenton, Mo.), January 30, 1936.

33. (1) Interview with James L. Grabosch (son of Lieutenant Grabosch), Unionville, Mo., June 16, 1964. (2) *Unionville Republican*, December 28, 1882.

# Index

397